"*The Long Deep Grudge* is the gripping tale of another Heartland—a Midwest filled with militant workers who took on one of the world's largest corporations and, for a time, won dignity, high wages, and power on the job. It is the story of the kind of radicalism that comes from fighting a corporate giant like International Harvester. Union stalwarts like Gilpin's father fought not to improve the company's productivity, but 'to claw back as much corporate wealth as possible.' Told with vigor and wry humor, *The Long Deep Grudge* has lessons for trade unionists, radicals, and anyone struggling for a better world in the here and now."

—Tobias Higbie, faculty chair of labor studies, University of California, Los Angeles

"Combining the expertise of a historian, detailed eye of a journalist, and flair of a novelist, Toni Gilpin breathes life into an important and fascinating story that, in lesser hands, could be as dull as dishwater. Gilpin aspires to tell no less a story than the epic battle between a corporate behemoth and the working-class radicals who—for decades—fought it tooth and nail. The plucky, interracial, leftist Farm Equipment Workers union that sought to wrest control of the shop floor from the owners and managers of International Harvester is the story of America."

—Peter Cole, author, *Wobblies on the Waterfront*

"Toni Gilpin brings us a vivid story of greed, revenge, and the search for justice. It's about the McCormick family, whose passionate anti-unionism helped to bring us the Haymarket tragedy, and the multiple generations of workers who refused to forget, and finally took them on. This is a riveting labor history drama that will stir your soul. Farm equipment workers in the 1930s rekindled the spirit of resistance, providing a model for thinking about how to get power, and how to act with a radical vision. They refused to concede the structuring of the workplace or the economy to corporations; they connected union rights with civil rights; and they learned how to create an effective strike. From Chicago to Louisville, Kentucky, they built an interracial coalition and defied the corporate attempt to defeat unionism through outsourcing of jobs. They fashioned a class war, and for a time it seemed they would prevail. We know the costs of the red-baiting that purged this union's legacy: today ten tiers of wages are considered normal, and the McCormick's strategy of divide-and-conquer is triumphant. So there is much to learn here about how solidarity was created in an earlier time."

—Rosemary Feurer, author, *Radical Unionism in the Midwest*

"*The Long Deep Grudge* takes labor history to the barricades, where a small union deeply committed to class struggle on the job squares off against a corporate giant determined to enforce managerial prerogatives. This epic tale is also an entirely human-scale drama that brings to life multiple generations of radical labor leaders, rank-and-file workers, captains of industry, and public officials dedicated to the defense of private wealth. Though they won quite a few battles, the story's chief protagonists—communist organizers who founded the Farm Equipment Workers and unionized International Harvester when even John L. Lewis thought it couldn't be done—ultimately lost the war, for reasons that go a long way to explain why the US labor movement is so much weaker now than it was in the FE's heyday. That labor liberals' capitulation to anti-communism ultimately weakened unions comes across loud and clear, as does the folly of dependence on labor-management cooperation as opposed to the FE's maxim that "a strong picket line is the best negotiator." More important, the FE's history teaches by example that a union can punch far above its weight when members stand ready to come out swinging, not only because they're angry at the boss but also for love of one another and an organization that truly belongs to them. For that alone, *The Long Deep Grudge* ought to be required reading for every labor activist in the United States."

—Priscilla Murolo, coauthor of *From the Folks Who Brought You the Weekend*

"We need unions like the Farm Equipment Workers, Toni Gilpin proves emphatically in her study of this left-led Midwest once-powerhouse. She shows the direct line between union leaders' rock-hard belief that 'management has no right to exist' and the way FE members organized to defend themselves, constantly, on the shop floor—with many thrilling tales of class struggle in the flesh. Without FE leaders' socialist politics, the union could well have gone the way of its rival, the United Auto Workers, on a short path to a belief in 'management's rights' and therefore an acceptance of speedup—and outsourcing, plant closings, and a bureaucratic grievance procedure instead of quickie strikes. No wonder the rank and file loved that union."

—Jane Slaughter, *Labor Notes*

"Toni Gilpin's *The Long Deep Grudge* is a remarkable accomplishment, which succeeds on multiple levels. The definitive history of an important but largely forgotten labor organization and its heroic struggles with an icon of industrial capitalism, this book is also a compelling and deeply moving reflection on the tragic history of radical industrial unionism in twentieth-century America. It is essential reading for anyone who truly wishes to understand the history of labor and class struggle in this country."

—Ahmed White, author, *The Last Great Strike*

"In *The Long Deep Grudge*, Toni Gilpin does more than simply excavate the story of a largely forgotten midwestern union with a small but vibrant heyday more than six decades ago. This highly readable history contains important insights for those concerned with revitalizing a more activist-oriented labor movement to overcome the stark economic inequalities surrounding us today. This saga of the Farm Equipment Workers' victories over major industrialists in 1940s Chicago and Louisville offers a vivid reminder that in a nation built on racial capitalism, the hard work of bridging long-standing racial divides and of promoting Black leadership is vital to successful organizing to improve working people's lives. Unions work best, Gilpin's work illustrates, when they inspire their members to push past the norms around them to advance a passionate shared vision for a fairer workplace. Highly recommended."

—Catherine Fosl, director, Anne Braden Institute for Social Justice Research

The Long Deep Grudge

A Story of Big Capital, Radical Labor,
and Class War in the American Heartland

Toni Gilpin

Haymarket Books
Chicago, IL

Published in 2020 by
Haymarket Books
P.O. Box 180165
Chicago, IL 60618
773-583-7884
www.haymarketbooks.org
info@haymarketbooks.org

ISBN: 978-1-64259-033-3

Distributed to the trade in the US through Consortium Book Sales and
Distribution (www.cbsd.com) and internationally through Ingram Publisher
Services International (www.ingramcontent.com).

This book was published with the generous support of Lannan Foundation
and Wallace Action Fund.

Special discounts are available for bulk purchases by organizations and
institutions. Please call 773-583-7884 or email info@haymarketbooks.org
for more information.

Cover and text design by Eric Kerl.

Library of Congress Cataloging-in-Publication data is available.

10 9 8 7 6 5 4 3 2 1

Printed in Canada

To Gary and our own rebel girls, Amy and Esther

Map of Select International Harvester Plants

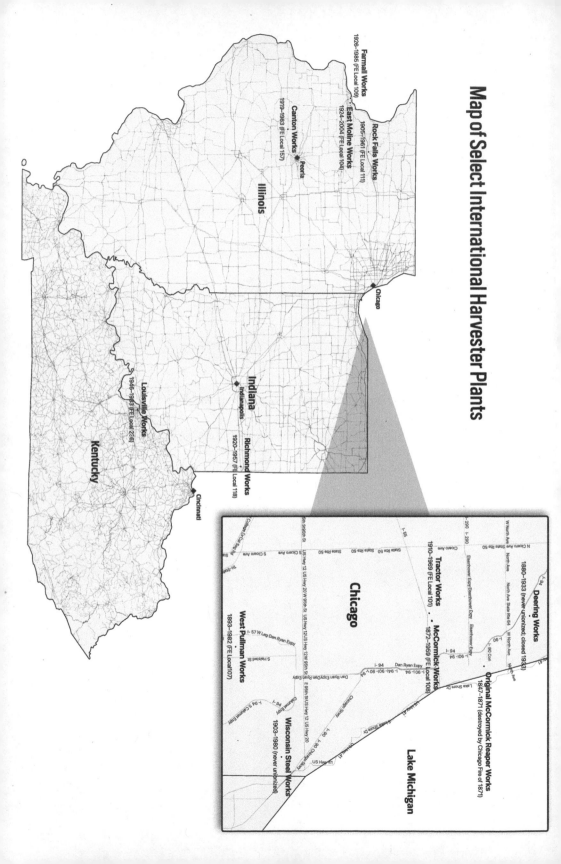

Farmall Works
1926–1985 (FE Local 109)

East Moline Works
1924–2004 (FE Local 104)

Rock Falls Works
1905–1961 (FE Local 111)

Canton Works
1919–1983 (FE Local 157)

Peoria

Illinois

Chicago

Indiana

Indianapolis

Richmond Works
1920–1957 (FE Local 118)

Louisville Works
1946–1983 (FE Local 236)

Kentucky

Cincinnati

Chicago

Deering Works
1880–1933 (never unionized; closed 1933)

Original McCormick Reaper Works
1847–1871 (destroyed by Chicago Fire of 1871)

Tractor Works
1910–1969 (FE Local 101)

McCormick Works
1872–1969 (FE Local 108)

West Pullman Works
1893–1982 (FE Local107)

Wisconsin Steel Works
1903–1980 (never unionized)

Lake Michigan

"City of the big shoulders" was how the white-haired poet put it. Maybe meaning that the shoulders had to get that wide because there were so many bone-deep grudges to settle. The big dark grudge cast by the four standing in white muslin robes, hands cuffed behind, at the gallows' head. For the hope of the eight-hour day.

The grudge between Grover Cleveland and John Peter Altgeld. The long deep grudges borne for McCormick the Reaper, for Pullman and Pullman's Gary. Grudges like heavy hangovers from men and women whose fathers were not yet born when the bomb was thrown, the court was rigged, and the deed was done.

And maybe it's a poet's town for the same reason that it's a working stiff's town, both poet and working stiff being boys out to get even for funny cards dealt by an overpaid houseman long years ago. . . .

Where undried blood on the pavement and undried blood on the field yet remembers Haymarket and Memorial Day.

—**Nelson Algren,** *Chicago: City on the Make,* 1951

Contents

Part Four: Reaping the Whirlwind

Abbreviations

AFL—American Federation of Labor

CIO—Committee (later, Congress) of Industrial Organizations

CP—Communist Party

ERP—Employee Representation Plan

FBI—Federal Bureau of Investigation

FE—United Farm Equipment Workers of America

FEWA—Farm Equipment Workers Association (precursor of the FE)

FEWOC—Farm Equipment Workers Organizing Committee (precursor of the FE)

HUAC—House Un-American Activities Committee

IH—International Harvester

IWW—Industrial Workers of the World

NAACP—National Association for the Advancement of Colored People

NDMB—National Defense Mediation Board

NLRB—National Labor Relations Board

SCC—Special Conference Committee

SMWIU—Steel and Metal Workers Industrial Union

SWOC—Steel Workers Organizing Committee

TUUL—Trade Union Unity League

UAW—United Auto Workers

UE—United Electrical Workers

WLB—National War Labor Board

FE dues buttons and 1944 convention badge. [Collection of Toni Gilpin]

Gleanings

FE leaders Grant Oakes (left), DeWitt Gilpin, and Jerry Fielde (right), at the 1940 convention of the Congress of Industrial Organizations (CIO). The CIO was founded in 1935 to organize workers, regardless of skill level, ethnicity, race, or gender, along industrial lines—that is, all steelworkers in one union, all farm equipment workers in another, etc. [Collection of Toni Gilpin]

FE national officials Jerry Fielde (standing, extreme right), DeWitt Gilpin (standing, left) and Milt Burns (seated center, leg crossed) confer with members of Local 101—the FE's first local—which represented workers at International Harvester's Tractor Works in Chicago. Local 101 official Jimmy Majors is seated, center, in plaid coat. [Collection of Toni Gilpin]

Harold Ward (shaking hands, in hat), an FE local official at McCormick Works, called "the key man" in the 1952 strike, was arrested for the murder of a strikebreaker in the midst of the walkout. [UE Archives, University of Pittsburgh Library System]

The 1952 strike proved to be a decisive showdown in the deep-rooted, bitter conflict between the FE and International Harvester. Picket line confrontations were frequent occurrences during the strike, as here at McCormick Works, where Chicago police are attempting to clear the way to allow strikebreakers into the plant. [Chicago History Museum, IHCi-177215]

Preface
Heavy Hangovers

In smoky Ottawa, Illinois, a local glass factory has laid off more than a fifth of its workforce, and a worried union functionary named DeWitt Gilpin braced United States Senator Charles Percy at a Lincoln's Birthday-week luncheon. "It just kind of seems the bottom has fallen out of the system," he told the senator dolefully, "and no one's doing anything about it. We're just drifting—downhill."

—*Newsweek*, February 24, 1974

That's my dad, the "union functionary" with the gloomy outlook. He'd been an organizer nearly all his life, and had started his union career in the late 1930s with the left-wing United Farm Equipment Workers of America (FE), a small union, now long defunct, that few people have ever heard of. Later he moved to the United Auto Workers; he'd been on the staff of the UAW for about twenty years when the *Newsweek* piece appeared. With a sizable membership and a fat treasury, the UAW in the mid-1970s was a formidable force, comfortable in the corridors of power and permanently entrenched, so it seemed, within the nation's system of industrial relations. Nonetheless, my father was uneasy: something was amiss that threatened hard times ahead for working people. He turned out to be right about that. Before the twentieth century was over the UAW, and the whole labor movement along with it, stopped drifting and instead began hurtling downhill, on the way to near-oblivion. As organized labor collapsed, so did the standard of living for the American working class. How did my dad see that coming? Certainly not because he possessed any special gift of prescience. His foreboding sprang instead from the distinct perspective he'd developed many years back, during the time he spent with that little leftist union: the FE.

But for me the UAW was the ubiquitous presence as I was growing up in the 1960s and '70s—the days when unions still had more active members than retirees and newspapers maintained labor beats. My father served on the staff for the UAW's Region 4, which at that time covered Illinois, Iowa, and Nebraska and had the largest membership of any region in the union. There were some auto plants within the area, but most UAW members in Region 4 assembled farm and earth-moving equipment, in sprawling factories located in places like East Moline and Dubuque and Peoria and Chicago. In my youth, the UAW logo—a wheel, its sprockets composed of thick stick figures with interlocked arms—was everywhere, embossed on the briefcases my dad carried to work, emblazoned on the jackets worn at the picnics and picket lines we would visit, enlarged to heroic proportion behind the speakers' platform at conventions and at the interminable banquets where processions of politicians, from the minor-leaguers on up to the power players, droned on professing their undying devotion to the labor movement in general and the UAW in particular.[1]

My father was legislative director for Region 4—the chief lobbyist, in other words—and his slim leather address book was crammed with the phone numbers of reporters and community leaders and elected officials from state legislatures to the halls of Congress. In those days, though, when the UAW still had considerable clout, those folks were just as likely to call him, hopeful for a campaign contribution or a commitment for election day troops or an inside story about how contract negotiations were going. One of the politicians who maintained close contact with my dad, it's worth noting, was Charles Percy, the Illinois senator who toured the Ottawa glass factory. Percy was a Republican, but worked hard to foster a good relationship with labor, and in fact the UAW endorsed him, rather than his Democratic challenger, in Percy's successful 1978 reelection campaign. Times have certainly changed.

I was proud of my dad and proud of the mighty UAW, steeped as I was in its official lore: the occupation of the factories in Flint; the moxie of all those riveting Rosies; the sea of signs, funded by the United Auto Workers, held aloft at the 1963 March on Washington. And I was always a little in awe of UAW members themselves—the broad-shouldered (and sometimes broad-bellied) men (in those days they were predominantly men) who built the tractors and cars that kept America moving forward. I was only dimly aware that before I was born my father had been in the leadership of that other union, the Farm Equipment Workers, which had been the first to organize titanic International Harvester (IH) and other firms in the agricultural implement industry; the FE, I understood, had been absorbed by the UAW in the mid-1950s. When he was with the FE he'd also been, at least for some portion of that time, a member of the Communist Party. My father was neither apologetic nor remorseful about his former association with the Party, but didn't regale his children with anecdotes from his "red" period, either—it was something it seemed he'd consigned to the past. (I was, however, from a young age instructed not to answer questions should any FBI agents ever present themselves at our home, which to this day makes me unduly suspicious when strangers, especially if they're wearing suits, knock on my door.) Nonetheless, before I had much grasp of the ins and outs of radical politics in American history, I recognized that the considerably left-of-center views my dad had burnished during his years with the Farm Equipment Workers tended to distinguish him from many of the other "union functionaries" he worked with in the UAW.

Though my father served as a dedicated member of the UAW staff for decades, I knew too, though he didn't expound on it much, that for him there was always something special about the FE, the union he had worked for so many years back. He believed that the UAW's agricultural implement contracts, which had originally been negotiated by the FE, were unquestionably superior to the UAW's agreements in the auto industry. He regarded the FE's thorny relationship with management and the union's exceptionally contentious rank and file as marks of distinction. There was a great story there, worthy of a novel, he thought. He'd been hoping to write one, after he retired from the UAW, a couple of years after he made the doleful comments recorded by *Newsweek*. But he died before he got the chance. He was quoted, though, in a posthumous piece in *The Nation*, reflecting one last time his sense that trouble was brewing. "Those outside labor have no sympathy for the movement anymore. Only the membership is loyal, because they realize the benefits they have accrued from it. Of course, labor is at fault too. We have failed to build bridges with minority groups, as the old C.I.O did." With a sigh, I imagine, or perhaps a grimace, he added, "Too much of labor is in cahoots with big business and big government."[2]

As it turned out, the year my father died—1979—was the last in the twentieth century that might have been called a good one for the UAW and the American labor movement. That year more Americans than ever before—some twenty-one million of them—were union members; more than 20 percent of the nation's workers were organized, the majority of them in the private sector. The UAW saw its ranks swell past a million and a half for the first time in history. Buoyed by the strength in these numbers, more than a million workers participated in some 235 walkouts nationwide. UAW members were among them, scoring "an overwhelming victory" after a record-breaking six-month strike against International Harvester. Unions were even big at the box office that year, as the popular film *Norma Rae* brought Sally Field an Academy Award for her role as a gutsy (and successful) rank-and-file organizer.[3]

Now, despite my own high opinion of my father, I wouldn't suggest that once he was gone, the labor movement was doomed, but nonetheless: after him the deluge. Big labor, it turned out, wasn't too big to fail. Late in 1979, as the Chrysler Corporation teetered near bankruptcy, the UAW consented to stiff wage and benefit cuts and the age of concessions bargaining was born. The give-back gamble proved to be a clear loser for labor; job losses continued unabated while union membership nosedived. Since 1979 the total number of Americans holding union cards has declined by one third. More signifi cantly, by 2018 the percentage of the workforce within the ranks of orga- nized labor had plunged to 10.5 percent. In a reversal of what was once true, unionization rates are now far higher for public- rather than private-sector employees, so if government workers are excluded from the calculation, the percentage of those organized is an even more discouraging 6 percent. As US manufacturing atrophied, industrial unions were especially hard hit: the UAW has lost over three-quarters of its membership since its 1979 peak and by 2018 represented fewer than four hundred thousand workers.[4]

With the ranks decimated, labor's most potent weapon—the strike— has been rarely deployed. During the thirty-three-year period between 1947 and 1979, there were, on average, 303 major strikes (meaning involving a thousand or more workers) each year; since 1980 the number of strikes has declined dramatically, with the falloff most precipitous in the twenty-first century. There were just five major strikes in 2009, the lowest number since records have been kept in the US; second place goes to 2017, when only seven took place. An encouraging increase in union activism, most notably among teachers, saw twenty major walkouts recorded in 2018, the highest number in more than ten years. That figure still pales in comparison, how- ever, to strike statistics in the mid-twentieth century.[5]

The collapse of the labor movement meant there has been little to stop the already rich from getting even richer by raking back more of what the working class has earned. Once again, 1979 marks a key demarcation point: Before that year, as the US economy grew, so too did workers' wages and benefits, as would be expected in any reasonably equitable society. Since then, however, as national economic productivity has continued its upward tra- jectory, only the fortunate few have reaped the benefits: incomes for those at the top increased exponentially, as have corporate profits, but the bot- tom 90 percent of all wage earners have seen their compensation stagnate or decline. The 2008 recession only exacerbated this gulf, and the subsequent "recovery" has done little to alter it. "Corporate profits have rarely swept up a bigger share of the nation's wealth, and workers have rarely shared a smaller one," the *New York Times* acknowledged in 2018: the most affluent 1 per- cent of American families now possess nearly half the country's wealth, a concentration of financial might not seen since the roaring 1920s.[6]

The consequences of such yawning economic inequality are registered daily in our decaying social fabric. But with the diminution of its ranks, organized labor's political influence has dwindled as well—in terms of both the campaign contributions and the voters it can deliver—undermining what had been the most significant counterbalance to plutocratic control over electoral politics. Once politicians sought out people like my father; now union officials can have trouble getting Democrats to return their phone calls, and certainly Republicans are no longer consulting them. This new reality has been broadly felt, because the labor movement had been a prime mover working to achieve—and defend—America's landmark civil rights legislation; social programs designed to assist children, seniors, and those in poverty; and government regulations protecting workers on the job and in their communities. As the labor movement has been redefined as just another "interest group," and an increasingly marginal one at that, it's not just union members who have suffered.[7]

So what happened—how did organized labor, and powerhouse organizations like the UAW, drop so far so fast? And was there something particular in my father's experience that led him to sense that this downfall was in the offing?

It turns out that there's much to be divined about these questions through an exploration of the history of the Farm Equipment Workers. Shortly after my father died, while I was still in college, I began to get curious about the FE. At this point labor's slide wasn't yet clearly manifest, so initially I just wanted to find out more about this union that had been largely overlooked, even by historians of the labor movement. On the face of it, the FE's obscurity seems fair enough: founded in 1938, it was in existence for less than twenty years, and its total membership, located primarily in the Midwest, never broke one hundred thousand. When it has been referred to in previous studies, it was usually just listed among those unions that had been deemed "communist-dominated" and cast out of the mainstream labor movement during the Cold War era. But the more I found out, the more I became convinced that the FE punched above its weight; there's good reason for both historians and those concerned with the current state of the labor movement to know more about it.

There really *is* a good story there, for one thing. It's intertwined with the rise and fall of American industry, the explosive growth of Chicago, the accumulation of a family fortune, and the ghosts of Haymarket. It pits the bantam FE against heavyweight International Harvester, once the country's fourth-largest corporation and second to none in its anti-union animus. The clash between the FE and IH was punctuated by picket line free-for-alls, Communist Party machinations and anti-communist hysteria, recurrent wildcat strikes, factory occupation, racial antagonisms and anti-segregation protests, and even—toward the end of it all—a sensational murder. Various terms could be used to describe the FE (and many were) but "dull" would not be one of them.

Embedded within all this drama, however, is a story with both deep rooted and present-day significance. It is a tale that underscores the formidable power of capital, illustrating as well the varieties of working-class resistance that evolved to challenge it. At International Harvester that struggle stretched back to the origins of America's Industrial Revolution. In the nineteenth century skilled workers, who through their essential knowledge and cooperative code exercised considerable control over the terms of their labor, were confronted by an employer ready and willing to supplant them by any means necessary. By the early twentieth century IH, having wiped clean from its factories all traces of artisanal autonomy, became a chief proselytizer for the once-contested—but soon broadly accepted—proposition that sweeping managerial prerogatives were requisite to "progress." When a new form of workers' organization surged across the United States in the 1930s, Harvester held out longer against the rising tide of industrial unionism than any other major corporation. It took an unrelentingly combative union—the FE—to break through at IH. It was immediately apparent, and in the ensuing years became more so, that the FE's singularly radical leadership, influenced by an association with the Communist Party, embraced an altogether different vision of progress than what had long been promulgated by the captains of industry.

But this is also a story about the pivotal conflict within modern American unionism, the rift that would define the labor movement's current character. From early on the FE engaged in a bitter feud, jurisdictional on its face but philosophical at its heart, with the much larger, and avowedly noncommunist, UAW. The possibility of mutually beneficial, cooperatively achieved economic growth, championed in the years following World War II by UAW President Walter Reuther and echoed by labor's establishment, met its most vociferous challenge from the stubbornly class-conscious FE leadership. At issue were two antithetical definitions of how unions could best deliver for their members and for working people generally, in both the short and the long term. Historian David Brody has suggested that the labor movement should operate by this maxim: "First, power. Then, maybe, cooperation." The FE leadership was never satisfied that the union had secured enough power; consequently, little cooperation was offered up.[8]

Spoiler alert: it was Reuther's vision and the UAW that, by the mid-1950s, carried the day, and thereafter the assumptions he had relied upon became so broadly accepted that it became difficult to discern the ideological infrastructure governing trade union practice. Labor became tethered to the premise of an ever-expanding American economy; when the economy faltered, union leaders were left without a framework to clearly assess who was doing what to whom, and they lacked the vocabulary to articulate a challenge to the crisis that might, at least, have allowed workers to channel their fear and anger. Instead, those feelings have festered into cynicism and despair and the demoralizing sense of personal, rather than systemic, failure. Unions seemingly did all they could possibly do within the constraints of American capitalism, ratifying what might be characterized as the labor addendum to Margaret Thatcher's dictum "There Is No Alternative." Within its brief lifespan, however, the FE endeavored to counter that notion, strenuously insisting that there was, in fact, a contrasting conception of the proper role for unions in America.

As I began to poke into the FE's history some years ago, I recognized with some chagrin that I was obliged to reconsider what I had long taken for granted growing up within the UAW community. Many of the UAW's great victories, so the FE maintained, were built on sand. The political and economic analysis my father had once contributed to as part of the FE's leadership no doubt accounted for his growing unease in the 1970s: the labor movement's weak foundation, he had believed, was giving way. When organized labor appeared securely planted, in the 1950s and 1960s, it seemed perhaps understandable that the FE's dissident critique had been consigned to obscurity. But as time has gone by, what the FE leadership thought about wealth—where it comes from and how labor can get more of it—is relevant to the critical contemporary debate regarding the evolution of capitalism, the nature of work, and the trajectory of inequality in twenty-first-century America.[9]

At this moment, with the labor establishment largely moribund, activists are back at the drawing board, grappling for strategies that can be effective in the twenty-first century. There are, however, examples from the nation's past that offer alternative visions, not just of how unions can fight to win, but just what they should be fighting for. The FE provides one such case in point. It is a good story—and a valuable one, for those who hope to see the working class begin marching uphill toward victory again.

Introduction
Undried Blood on the Pavement

A Black man, murdered in the pre-dawn darkness on a South Side street: in 1952 Chicago, the rule was that such an event didn't matter much, not downtown anyhow. Reporters wouldn't be dispatched to cover it, the police would take their time investigating it, and in corporate suites the death would have passed without notice.[1]

But this particular killing got plenty of attention. The victim was fifty-two-year-old William Foster, an employee in the malleable iron foundry at the sprawling McCormick Works complex, the cradle of corporate behemoth International Harvester. He'd been a few blocks from his home, heading to work early on a mild October morning (the factory was nearly five miles away, so he always began his commute before sunup) when he met up with someone who struck him on the head and fractured his skull. Foster died a short time later, without identifying who had attacked him. He left behind a wife and two children. No witnesses came forward, at least not right away.

The police, the press, and executives at International Harvester, however, were immediately certain where the guilty party could be found. Captain George Barnes, head of the Chicago Police Department's notorious labor detail, had no doubts about the motive for the assault. This was "obviously a labor slugging," he promptly declared, because the Farm Equipment Workers union was in the midst of a bitter strike against International Harvester, and Foster had chosen to cross the FE's picket lines. Within hours of Foster's death, International Harvester offered a $10,000 reward for the arrest of his assailant. "This company will make every effort to safeguard every employee who comes to work. This crime must not go unpunished," said Harvester president John McCaffrey in a statement publicized across the country. The *Chicago Herald-American* rushed an editorial into print, less than a day after Foster died. "[A] labor dispute gives no one license to impose his own will, by assault and murder, on those who disagree with him. We hope these murderers—or this murderer, if there is only one—will learn this lesson in the electric chair." Then the *Chicago Tribune* weighed in. "There is good reason to believe that the Foster murder was communist inspired. The union at the particular Harvester plant where he was employed . . . is the Farm Equipment Workers union, which was kicked out of the CIO because it is controlled by Communists."[2]

In what may have been a first, Chicago law enforcement announced that finding the killer of an African American man was its number one priority. Police Commissioner Timothy O'Connor said that his department would direct every resource "to find and arrest Foster's slayer, and to furnish adequate protection to non-striking Harvester employees," and he ordered his officers to round up everyone who might be connected to the crime. The suspects, though, had one thing in common: they were all union members. Some thirty FE officials, Captain Barnes announced, would be hauled in for questioning by homicide detectives.[3]

Harold Ward—thirty years old, married, the father of two young boys—was someone the police were taking a hard look at. Ward was also employed at the McCormick plant, though he hadn't been on the job lately. As financial secretary of FE Local 108, he'd been spending his time bolstering rank-and-file support for the union's walkout. Ward "is the most important Negro leader of our strike—the key man," said Matt Halas, the Polish American president of Local 108. In fact, Ward had stepped into a leadership role with the FE from the moment he first walked into the McCormick plant, back in 1944. That spelled trouble as far as Harvester was concerned. By 1952 Ward's militant advocacy on behalf of aggrieved workers had resulted in numerous reprimands and disciplinary suspensions by IH management.[4]

Six feet tall, handsome, and solidly built, Ward sported a trim mustache and favored fedora hats when he was off work. But it wasn't Ward's fashion sense that had already drawn notice from the authorities. "Ward has always been a thorn in the side of Chicago's strikebreaking Police Labor Detail," the union claimed. "He is always one of the first persons on a picket line to be arrested, regardless of how peaceful his picketing activities are. The police know from experience that he is one of the most militant and able strike leaders in Chicago." His politics, too, had been duly noted. "Ward has a long list of communist associations," the *Chicago Tribune* pronounced. Police "observers," said the *Tribune,* "heard Ward laud the soviets and praise their country." Both in and outside the plant, it was evident, Ward was not easily intimidated or cowed by controversy. And he was well familiar with what Chicago police stations looked like from the inside.[5]

But was he also a killer? Local law enforcement said he was. "Union Leader Charged with Strike Murder," the front pages declared when Ward was arrested, a week after Foster's death. Perhaps it wasn't surprising that they'd come after Ward: he was already out on bail for an altercation from the previous month. Another McCormick employee who'd crossed the FE's picket lines claimed that Ward had confronted him while he was on his way to work and beaten him with a baseball bat.[6]

Ward's earlier assault charge had kept FE officials fervently engaged in the effort to keep him out of jail; now they needed to save him from the electric chair. But Ward's troubles weren't the only ones facing the FE. Its strike against International Harvester, which involved nearly thirty thousand workers at factories in several states, had been going on for over seven weeks when Ward was arrested, with no end in sight. Strike-related scuffles were daily occurrences, and local FE leaders were routinely hauled off the picket lines and hurled into police wagons. And the rancor between the company and the union, already at fever pitch, was intensifying by the hour.

Not that the FE was unfamiliar with, or averse to, taking on IH: quite the contrary. Since its formation in the late 1930s the union had instigated, with gusto, hundreds of walkouts, from chain-wide shutdowns on down to departmental work stoppages. But this one was different. Harvester's executives had made their intentions clear: they were going to be rid of the FE once and for all. The union's leaders, said IH president McCaffrey, are "irresponsible radicals, who have no respect for their contracts . . ." When the 1952 negotiations began, Harvester management proceeded to demonstrate *its* respect for the contract by gutting it completely, and told FE leaders to take it or leave it. They would keep their plants open if the union walked out, company officials vowed, and once the strike began they embarked on a concerted campaign to draw workers across the FE's picket lines.[7]

And while its 1952 stance may have been acutely aggressive, such bare-knuckle bargaining was standard operating procedure for Harvester management. John McCaffrey was only the latest in a succession of Harvester executives animated by a singular strain of anti-unionism that seemed to course through their veins. Most of the men who'd run the century-old company, after all, had been united by blood as well as sentiment: they were members of the McCormick family, descendants of Cyrus McCormick, inventor of the mechanical reaper. McCaffrey, who'd moved into the Harvester presidency in 1946, was one of the few non-McCormicks to hold that post, and was overseen through much of his tenure by Fowler McCormick, the chair of Harvester's board of directors. The McCormicks had promulgated a culture of confrontation with their employees since the nineteenth century, and strikebreaking was an especially ingrained habit. Cyrus II was at the helm in 1886, when anarchists and the push for the eight-hour day were both gaining traction in Chicago; several workers were killed when police officers waded into a throng of strikers outside McCormick Works. Outrage over this brutality prompted a demonstration the next evening, at Haymarket Square, where a bomb was hurled toward an advancing line of policemen. The fallout from that explosion

resulted in a decimated workers' organization at the McCormick plant and
death sentences for several anarchists, whose radical movement expired along
with them. Cyrus McCormick II had learned a lesson he never forgot, which
he ensured would be permanently featured in the company's playbook: when
labor flexed its muscle, a knock-out blow was often the most effective response.
But McCormick was also savvy enough to recognize that he was engaged in
a long-term struggle for the hearts and minds of his workforce, and so by the
latter part of his career he adopted more sophisticated and often pioneering
methods to stymie union organizing. Lawyers and industrial relations consultants, more so than vigilantes, came to dominate the company's defensive line.

In the nineteenth century, the McCormicks hadn't liked anarchists, and
in the twentieth century Harvester management didn't like the FE leadership—there was too much common ground there. The company's undifferen-
tiated anti-unionism had by this point narrowed to a very specific antipathy.
"We don't have trouble with *labor*. We just have trouble with FE," the company pronounced. And in 1952 Harvester did its best to educate the public
about what accounted for the FE's uniquely obstreperous behavior. "It is our
belief, and has been for many years," said Harvester advertisements run in
newspapers during the strike, "that the most influential leaders [of the FE]
are either Communists or Communist sympathizers and fellow travelers." In
the ad's background floated a shadowy hammer and sickle—the symbol of
the international communist movement.[8]

But what was then the stereotypical exemplar of American radicalism—
that is, a big-city (usually, New York City) denizen with suspect citizenship
who espoused, in accented English, imported ideologies—wasn't replicated
much within the FE. Harold Ward didn't fit that image (though, as an assertive African American man, he possessed other characteristics that earned
him troublemaker status) and neither did the FE's national leadership.

Grant Oakes, the FE's longtime president, was born in upstate New
York, graduated from high school, and then studied electrical engineering
for three years at a technical college, and so he had more years of formal
education than any other member of the union's top leadership. He arrived
in Chicago in 1928, got a job as a mechanic at International Harvester's
Tractor Works plant, and soon became involved with clandestine organizing efforts there. Husky and tall, with thick salt-and-pepper hair neatly
combed back from his forehead, Oakes maintained a stolid and dignified
demeanor, along with a taste for fine tailoring, which seemed to befit his
engineering background. He could well have passed for a corporate executive. "Grant was so different looking," recalled Sonya Burns, the wife of

another FE official. "Now he came out of the plant, yet he didn't have that macho kind of thing. . . . There was a quietness about him, a gentility about him that I think the workers appreciated." Oakes was thirty-eight when the FE received its official CIO charter in 1942, making him the union's elder statesman.[9]

While Oakes was the union's titular head, Gerald "Jerry" Fielde was often described, with justification, as the FE's driving force. "When you were in Jerry's presence, you knew you were in the presence of a leader," according to Al Verri, a Harvester worker who became an FE staff member after World War II. "He had a fine analytical mind, he'd take great pains to explain things to you, and he could liven up a crowd. That's what made him so popular with the rank and file: everybody would say, 'Wait until you hear Jerry Fielde!'" Fielde was a Chicago native. Though he lacked Oakes's formal schooling he too was a skilled worker (as were so many other early advocates of the CIO); during the Depression he found employment as a machinist at McCormick Works and was soon active with the underground union drive. When the FE came into being Fielde became its secretary-treasurer and served also as the union's chief negotiator with International Harvester. Six years younger than Oakes and nearly a head shorter, Fielde's brash temperament stood in counterpoise to the FE president's reserve. That Oakes and Fielde had come out of the two plants that in many ways constituted the emotional heart of the FE, and had been integral to the union's early organizing campaign, rarely failed to resonate among the membership even as the years passed. While fiery Fielde, in part due to his key role in contract negotiations, was more often in the spotlight, Oakes's steadiness and personal integrity—which was rarely questioned, even by the union's harshest critics—were undoubtedly vital to the FE's cohesion over the years.[10]

The other two men—DeWitt Gilpin and Milt Burns—who contributed the most to the FE's character only occasionally held highly visible posts in the union. Both were short, wiry, and possessed of similarly intense dispositions. Neither of them ever worked in a Harvester plant; between the two of them, in fact, it would have been difficult to chalk up a year of factory experience. They were both writers and organizers by trade.

Gilpin was born in 1912 in the small town of Excelsior Springs, Missouri. In the early years of the Depression he got a job as a relief worker in Kansas City, but he didn't last long there: his efforts to organize the unemployed got him fired. So he headed north, hitchhiking and riding boxcars to make his way to Detroit and then Chicago. By the late 1930s Gilpin was writing frequently for the *Daily Worker*, the Communist Party newspaper, and its Chicago-based offshoot, the *Midwest Daily Record*, and by 1941 he transitioned from covering the FE's organizing drive at International Harvester to taking a leadership role with the union. Milt Burns was born in New York City, but in his youth his family moved to Chicago. In his early twenties he too found a place at the *Midwest Daily Record*, where for a time he turned out a politically attuned sports column. Sometime in 1940 Burns joined the FE staff and after World War II became the union's director of organization.[11]

These four men—Oakes, Fielde, Gilpin, and Burns—had much in common which drew them together but which sometimes distinguished them from the leadership of other unions, even left-led ones. They were white and all had working-class roots, and while Burns and Gilpin were reputed to be the FE's "intellectuals," only Oakes, with his vocational training, managed any formal education beyond high school. They were, as well, native-born Americans, so theirs was an indigenous radicalism. Oakes, Fielde, and Gilpin came from families that had been in the United States for generations; Burns, who had a Jewish heritage but was decidedly nonreligious, was the sole member of the quartet who could be identified as "ethnic" in any sense. With the exception of Oakes, they all spent most or all of their early years in the Midwest. Fielde and Burns were city born and bred, but Gilpin and Oakes shared nonurban upbringings. In his youth Gilpin resided in more rural parts of mid-America and worked on farms from time to time. Oakes, the son of a railroad worker, hailed from Westfield, New York, an iconic small town complete with a gazebo in the park. By the mid-1940s the FE's three younger leaders held one other status in common: all were combat veterans of World War II—Fielde served in the Merchant Marine, Burns in the Marines, and Gilpin in the Army.[12]

Similar experiences, though, were not the most important ties that served to bind the FE's top leadership: more essential was the particular interpretation of left-wing unionism they all embraced. "I think ideologically they saw things the same way," Al Verri said of them, "and as a result they usually came to the same conclusions." This collective consciousness came to define the union, and was shared—in whole or in part—by many of the FE's rank-and-file leaders as well. At one point Milt Burns summed it up this way: "The philosophy of our union," he declared, "was that management had no right to exist." Worker-run factories may have been the distant vision, but on a daily basis this translated to confrontation, rather than cooperation, from the bargaining table on down to the shop floor: just what got Harold Ward into hot water at International Harvester. And, like Ward, the chief officials of the FE had long been scrutinized for their "communist associations."[13]

These characteristics were on full display during the 1952 strike. "A strong picket line is the best negotiator," read a Local 108 flyer, a sentiment endorsed, and acted upon, at all levels within the union. When thirteen men were arrested in late September in front of McCormick Works, because, so said Captain Barnes, they were endeavoring "to overturn an automobile carrying nonstrikers to their jobs," the papers noted that those detained included "top leaders" of the "left-wing" FE—Milt Burns and DeWitt Gilpin. The leadership's politics, along with its pugnacity, became further fodder for the headlines. The House Un-American Activities Committee (HUAC) came to town shortly after the strike began, on a mission to expose communism within labor's ranks in Chicago. Oakes, Fielde, and Gilpin were called to testify but declined to answer the committee's questions; "UNION CHIEFS DEFY U.S. QUIZ; Refuse to Say Whether They Are Commies," blared the banner on the front page of the *Chicago Tribune*.[14]

By the end of 1952, Harold Ward was fighting for his life, and the survival of the union he was committed to was in question as well. The charges against Ward, the FE said, were emblematic of "a new Haymarket frame-up." In fact, FE leaders were quite cognizant that they were taking on the same forces that had been arrayed against the anarchists: the press, the police, the courts, local and federal officials, a hostile labor establishment, and—most resolute of all—a powerful company, controlled by the McCormick family, determined to eradicate a radical organization that had won the allegiance of its workforce. As the strike dragged into November, the FE leadership was scrambling to ensure that things would work out less catastrophically for their union—and for Harold Ward—than they had for the anarchists back in 1886. They looked to rely on what had first allowed them to break through at International Harvester and what had sustained them ever since: support from the FE's rank and file. But would that be enough this time?[15]

To understand this strike, however, and the significance of its conclusion, the story needs to begin well before FE members began massing on the picket lines in 1952. The deep grudge between the FE and IH was rooted in a long-standing struggle over how work would be done in each of the company's plants, what each job was worth, and who would benefit from what was produced. That contest had been ongoing, in one form or another, since the McCormicks first opened up shop. Explaining this concerted culture of conflict, then, necessitates a close look inside the factory where the International Harvester empire got its start: McCormick Works. It was in this labyrinthine brick manufactory, back in the 1880s, that a very young Cyrus McCormick II became immersed in his family's business, familiarizing himself with the shop's myriad assortment of complex and temperamental machines—and taking the measure of the men who operated them.

McCormick Works, the sole factory of the McCormick Harvesting Machine Company, Chicago, 1885. It was the largest farm equipment factory in the world. [Wisconsin Historical Society, WHS-68083]

Part One

Weeding Out the Bad Element

Cyrus McCormick II, eldest son of the "Reaper King," in 1880, when he was twenty years old. Cyrus II became president of the McCormick Harvesting Machine Company in 1884 and then served for several decades as the head of International Harvester after its founding in 1902. [Chicago History Museum, IHCI-31326]

This 1881 illustration depicts McCormick Works, the products produced there, and workers in some of the plant's many departments, including the machine shop (upper left) and the foundry (bottom right). [*Scientific American*, internet archive, scientific-american-1881-05-14]

A clash on May 3, 1886, between workers and police outside McCormick Works left several workers dead and triggered the protest rally at McCormick Works the following evening. [Chicago History Museum, IHCi-03659]

August Spies, thirty years old, after his arrest in 1886 for his part in the Haymarket "riot." He was executed the following year. [Chicago History Museum IHCi-30017]

The famous "REVENGE" circular, written by Chicago anarchist and labor leader August Spies (though someone else added on the "REVENGE" header) following the confrontation "at McCormicks." [University of Illinois Digital Collection]

Harold McCormick, Cyrus II's younger brother, and his first wife Edith Rockefeller, in 1895. This matrimonial merger proved critical to the formation of International Harvester and the McCormick family's ability to maintain control over the corporation. [Wisconsin Historical Society, WHS-8374]

A 1915 scene inside McCormick Works, now part of the International Harvester empire. Note the foreman on the extreme right. [Wisconsin Historical Society, WHS-7958]

Few women were ever employed in McCormick Works, but many were in the adjacent Twine Mill, where some aspects of the production of binder twine were deemed "women's work." This photo is from 1912. [Wisconsin Historical Society, WHS-9108]

In 1928, workers pour out of McCormick Works as their shift ends. At its height nearly eight thousand people were employed at the plant. [Wisconsin Historical Society, WHS-9370]

1.
The Reaper Kingdom

I t was the sunlit springtime of 1879 at Princeton College and the magnolias were in bloom, but as Cyrus McCormick II traversed the campus he was absorbed by thoughts of his hazy and foul-smelling hometown. He had just received a letter from William Hanna, a devoted member of the office staff of the McCormick Harvesting Machine Company in Chicago. The senior Cyrus, widely known as "the Reaper King," still presided over the manufacturing concern he'd founded, but he was more than seventy years old and by this point exercised no oversight over its day-to-day operations. The factory, Hanna warned in his letter, "practically has no head"; employees "are allowed far too much freedom, and feel quite independent." Hanna urged the industrial heir to interrupt his studies and return to the family firm. "The place is ripe for you," Hanna wrote. "I rejoice that this business . . . is about to take new life and fresh impetus in the person of one who bears the full name and character of him who founded it so long ago."[1]

Cyrus McCormick II was just nineteen years old. He was darkly handsome, tall and strapping, and very, very rich. Many young men in those circumstances would prefer to dally longer in college—graduation was a few months away—and then engage in some serious carousing before shouldering adult burdens. Young Cyrus was clearly daunted by just how much he was being asked to do. "It was, I confess," he later reflected, "a somewhat staggering responsibility, for our business practically covered the world. We were at home in every wheat field on the globe. We had agencies in many lands and had to keep in touch with agricultural, business, and financial conditions all over." This was a role, though, he had been groomed for since birth. His parents, both ardent Old School Presbyterians—as befit the McCormicks' Scotch-Irish heritage—resolved to instill in their children the cardinal Calvinist principles of self-discipline, duty, and toil. Cyrus and his siblings were required to note how long they spent getting dressed and brushing their teeth, so they might become more efficient stewards of their time and not keep others waiting at the breakfast table. But as the oldest, Cyrus II was singled out for particular attention, and by his early teens he was already immersed in the family enterprise. "My father taught me that I must work, and must work out my own salvation," Cyrus said; in practical terms this meant "that I must apply my whole energy to learning every phase of the business."[2]

The business he was called on to understand did not simply manufacture products: it also made history. Cyrus McCormick I's mechanical reaper, introduced in 1831, substituted horse for human power and cut and threshed grain in one efficient process; by effecting an exponential increase in agricultural output it made modern farming, not to mention the growth of the United States, possible.[3] Determining that the vast territory out west was where his reaper's potential would be best realized, McCormick left his native Virginia in 1847 and headed for a frontier outpost with no sewers or paved streets, where livestock still ambled freely through town: Chicago.[4] He set up shop in a building smack in the heart of the city, on the north branch of the Chicago River. Within a year he'd sold eight hundred reapers; by 1860 he'd built a new three-story brick factory—said to be the largest in the world—where some 250 workers turned out more than four thousand machines annually. Chicago by this point was an emergent industrial powerhouse and had become the fourth-largest metropolis in the United States. "Tool maker, stacker of wheat," so Carl Sandburg would one day define the city, and McCormick's company involved both, producing the implements that transformed the Great Plains into the nation's breadbasket and fixed Chicago at the center of the commodification of grain.

Cyrus McCormick also expanded his enterprise through his aggressive business acumen, introducing practices that later became commonplace, like fixed prices, installment payments, traveling sales agents, and widespread advertising. He outmaneuvered, out-innovated, or bought out his competitors and energetically marketed his brand overseas; by the 1870s McCormick reapers were in use as far away as Russia and New Zealand. McCormick also built a giant portfolio, diversifying his wealth and investing heavily in property, which included the family mansion, an ersatz Louvre that sprawled over a full city block. He became Chicago's biggest landlord and one of nineteenth-century America's few multimillionaires.[5]

With all his energy directed toward his business, Cyrus I was nearly fifty when he married twenty-three-year-old Nettie Fowler. It was in all respects a fruitful partnership. From the outset Nettie evidenced a keen business sense and an iron will, and she was utterly determined that her eldest son would take his rightful place within the family enterprise. Indeed, she ensured that the business survived so that he might inherit it. When the great fire of 1871 decimated Chicago, sixty-two-year-old Cyrus I inspected the smoldering ruin that had been his sole manufacturing establishment and considered calling it quits. Nettie would have none of that. "Rebuild at once," she insisted. "She had in mind," one biographer said, "the future of another Cyrus

H. McCormick, by this time twelve years of age."[6] So Cyrus I bought a far bigger parcel of land, this time on the city's Southwest Side, and constructed a colossal plant capable of producing fifteen thousand reapers a year.

From an early age Cyrus McCormick II demonstrated the character traits his parents had hoped to instill in him. Intense and serious, he was devoted to his mother and idolized his father, at no point evidencing even a trace of rebelliousness. When Cyrus II was a teenager, it appeared possible that he might be dispatched to Paris on company business by himself, a prospect that horrified Nettie: she envisioned her boy "like a lamb among wolves [in] that most dangerous and gilded pathway to destruction!" Father and son ultimately went to France together—but young Cyrus reassured his mother nonetheless. "Please don't worry about me," he said. "I shall always be conservative."[7]

Thus, when William Hanna's anxious entreaty reached Princeton, young Cyrus never considered refusing it. He was no reluctant prince. He missed the graduation festivities (but was recognized as a member of the Princeton class of 1879 nonetheless) and hastened back to Chicago. It had fallen to nineteen-year-old Cyrus II to rescue the McCormick Harvesting Machine Company and perpetuate his father's legacy.[8]

Young Cyrus would now be spending most of his time at the factory commonly called the McCormick Works. To get there from the family's North Side estate, he would point his carriage toward the intersection of Blue Island and Western avenues, heading far past Chicago's downtown bustle, out to where the streets faded into farmland. His destination was impossible to miss: he would see first, from some distance away, the towering smokestacks and their inky plumes that draped a perpetual shroud of soot over everything in the vicinity. And then the Works itself would come into view, ascending multiple stories and spreading out over acres of prairie grass. There was nothing else of any size anywhere near it. Jutting abruptly up from a flat plain, it looked a bit like an industrial Versailles, albeit one composed of red brick and devoid of decorative detail. And rather than tranquil gardens, the factory was surrounded by a noisy tangle of transportation: a constant flow of carts and wagons, railroad tracks that fed trains directly into the plant's warehouses, schooners on the adjacent branch of the Chicago River bringing in raw materials from distant ports.

Once through the iron gates and into McCormick Works the din did not subside. In the twenty-acre factory yard, teams of draft horses and mules—the company maintained a stable full of them—snorted as they strained against the weight of freight cars loaded down with supplies and finished goods. By this point the works was producing reapers, mowers, and binders, all composed of numerous parts crafted from metal and wood. A cacophony emanated from the blacksmith shop, where parts were tempered and banged into shape. Enormous grindstones, driven by steam-powered overhead belts, whirred continually in the knife department, where the edges of sickle bars were sharpened and serrated. Saws and planing equipment buzzed in the vast series of rooms devoted to woodworking, and a constant clatter arose as towering piles of lumber were replenished. And once in the packing department a drumbeat reverberated as crates in a multiplicity of sizes were hammered shut so that the finished machines—which were shipped in pieces with final assembly completed on-site by McCormick dealers—could be whisked off to farmers in time for the next harvest.[9]

As he traversed the gaslit factory Cyrus would pick up other sounds, too, from the workers who wielded the tools and ran the machines and, through their skill and muscle, transformed metal and wood into McCormick products. Mostly they had to shout to be heard. Their voices were as varied as the equipment they operated: Irish inflections were common, and then there many with thick German accents, some of whom knew no English at all. When others conversed, their intonations revealed that they had been born in Sweden or Norway. Cyrus would have detected some Polish and Czech being spoken as well, though these languages would be more frequently heard in later decades. All the workers, though, were white men: in the nineteenth century there were relatively few African Americans in Chicago, and as yet no women were present in the factory.

This multiethnic workforce was dominated by skilled craftsmen: blacksmiths, carpenters, machinists, and even painters, who utilized brushes—no spray guns or dips—to coat McCormick implements with their trademark red finish. These workers were capable of performing a variety of tasks and generally did so during the course of their ten-hour day. Common laborers were also employed at the plant—some of them boys as young as twelve years old—but their primary function was to assist the skilled workmen, fetching them supplies or cleaning up what they discarded. Workers moved independently throughout their departments, as they switched machines, hunted down tools, or took an occasional break, while raw material and finished goods spilled over in jumbled piles on the factory floor. There was a system to be discerned within all this hubbub, but to young Cyrus McCormick, with his propensity for order and discipline, it looked like chaos.[10]

McCormick Works in 1879, in other words, bore almost no resemblance to a modern factory. There were no assembly lines and little of the production process had been standardized. Consequently, just what work was to be done and how fast it would be accomplished was not dictated by technology but was determined largely as a matter of daily negotiation between management and labor. Most employees received bonus pay for each properly finished part they produced—piecework, in other words—which, in theory at least, provided incentive for them to work quickly and competently. But foremen—salaried employees, who were likely native-born Americans— were tasked with driving up output, and they wielded the ultimate weapon: they could discharge workers for any reason. These frontline managers were often the most loathed individuals in the plant.[11]

The skilled craftsmen at McCormick Works, however, could not be easily intimidated: they were indispensable to production, and they knew it. Nowhere was this more true than in the cavernous foundry, where a large percentage of the parts incorporated in McCormick products were fabricated, and so its steady operation was crucial for proper workflow. In the foundry, a smoldering world unto itself, the heat was nearly unimaginable and the air hung heavy with a toxic haze that settled deep in the lungs. In this infernal arena iron molders, who created the patterns from sand and wood that received molten metal, reigned supreme. To do their jobs well they needed to be swift, strong, and smart: molds improperly constructed, for instance, could explode, propelling flaming shrapnel across the shop. Becoming an iron molder required a long apprenticeship, and teamwork and trust were essential on the job.[12]

Like many craftsmen in this era, the molders shared a "disciplined ethical code" that governed their interactions with their employers. Because skilled workers knew far more about the processes they were engaged in than their bosses did, they were often able to regulate how much they would turn out, maintaining strict quotas that kept the pace of production within tolerable levels and ensured safer conditions. And, certainly, they would refuse to labor alongside those not recognized as members of their trade. These rules were enforced by the workers themselves—transgressors were ostracized—and underscored the value of cooperation, rather than competition. Skilled workers in the nineteenth century were "unmistakably and consciously group-made men who sought to pull themselves up by their collective bootstraps." Their ethos imbued them with faith in the dignity of their labor and a recognition of their worth. They were thus loath to suffer disrespect directed at them by their bosses, whether those insults took the form of directives barked out by foremen or wage cuts imposed by top management.[13]

Within McCormick Works, the iron molders had wielded their strength effectively, for they were the highest paid workers in the plant. And their collective clout was exercised in a manner increasingly relied upon by craft workers in the nineteenth century: through a trade union. These early labor organizations were occupation-specific—printers in one union, carpenters another—and composed only of skilled workers. The molders had first organized at McCormick in the early 1860s, affiliating with the National Union of Iron Molders. Thereafter, the McCormick molders caused no end of trouble for their supervisors. "Our molders are now going on their fourth strike for an advance of wages since last fall! . . . We are powerless," one company official wrote in 1864. "The union is controlling our shop," lamented another. They represented only about 10 percent of the plant's workforce, and were the only organized group in McCormick Works, but the molders' militancy had a trickledown effect, since the wage hikes they secured were generally followed shortly thereafter by increases for employees throughout the plant. While at Princeton Cyrus had received word of the excess of "freedom" exhibited by employees within his family's enterprise. The iron molders surely topped the list of those who needed to be reined in.[14]

His college days became a distant memory as Cyrus focused obsessively on McCormick Works, arriving early in the morning and often remaining past midnight, "studying the processes of manufacturing, and seeking to discover how better machines could be made at a smaller cost of labor, time and materials." The young man found an ally in Lewis Wilkinson, a veteran of New England industry who in 1880 became superintendent at McCormick Works. Wilkinson was a proponent of what was called the American System of Manufactures: specialized, single-purpose machine tools and standardized devices that would turn out uniform, interchangeable parts. With such equipment the knowledge held by autonomous craftsmen could be usurped from them and transferred into the machines. Such technological innovation, therefore, was purposed to redistribute power on the shop floor, providing employers with the means to assert control over the production process by shattering the traditional prerogatives exercised by skilled workers. No wonder, then, that by the late nineteenth century industrialists were putting the American System into widespread use.[15]

Thus, Lewis Wilkinson and his eager assistant Cyrus II set out to transform the McCormick plant. They began in the machine shop, engaging the most able toolmakers to create prototypes for the many parts integral to McCormick implements; machines were then devised that could produce identical pieces matching those models. As the experienced machinists painstakingly perfected the patterns used to develop the single-purpose equipment, they simultaneously designed themselves—along with many carpenters and blacksmiths—out of work. Each machine cost "thousands of dollars to build," but anticipated payoffs inspired the company's sizable investment: this new equipment would be operated by cheaper semiskilled or unskilled labor. Other consequential changes were taking place in the quieter and cleaner company offices. In 1880 McCormick accountants began, for the first time, to separate labor out as an expense distinct from that of materials when evaluating the manufacturing cost per machine, and thus they could ascertain just how big a bite their workers—most of them still of the skilled persuasion—took out of the company's profits. At this point, before they'd begun extensive acquisition of timber fields, coal mines, and steel mills, the McCormicks had limited ability to affect the prices of the raw materials necessary for their products. Labor costs, however, they could do something about.[16]

Lewis Wilkinson left after a year at McCormick Works, but young Cyrus had already learned what he needed to know. He had once promised his mother that he would "always be conservative," but he was wrong about that. When he assumed the superintendent's position at McCormick Works in 1881, Cyrus set out, in unmistakably radical fashion, to remake the way work was done within it. Cyrus McCormick I had pioneered a transformative product and launched a company; Cyrus II would revolutionize its manufacturing procedures and build an industrial empire. Father and son were bonded by their belief in the glory of the McCormick enterprise, and they shared another staunch conviction: that within their family firm no outsiders should dictate company policy—even if those "outsiders" were their own long-term employees. Cyrus II determined to assert managerial control so the McCormicks would no longer be "powerless" within their own shop. He would usher in what he dubbed a "new regime" to accomplish that—and when he was through, little of the traditional labor processes within McCormick Works would be conserved.

His innovations quickly began to bear fruit. Production shot up: in 1884 the plant's output was more than double what it had been in 1879, the year young Cyrus joined the firm's management. During this period of economic recovery and the cultivation of the Great Plains, the McCormicks could sell everything they produced, and so as their market expanded they reaped the financial rewards. But just as critical to their accumulating wealth was "the new and persistent emphasis of the company upon greater economy and efficiency of operation by all of its departments" achieved under Cyrus II's "new regime." They were not only selling more, their margins were higher: between 1881 and 1882, for instance, the labor cost per machine dropped 20 percent and profits jumped a whopping 40 percent. This was true even though overall employment doubled during the early 1880s, from about six hundred workers to over twelve hundred. Skilled labor, however, constituted an ever smaller percentage of the growing workforce; cheaper labor meant more in the company's coffers. Young Cyrus's initial success only stiffened his resolve to reduce his dependence on those pricey craftsmen.[17]

Despite what he'd accomplished by this early juncture, however, Cyrus II was everywhere still "spoken of as the son of the 'great reaper man,'" a designation which continued to weigh heavily on him. "It makes me feel keenly the tremendous responsibility of the position in which you have put me," he told his father in 1882, "and to fill it creditably and according to your wishes is my constant aim and care." Soon enough, though, he would have to fulfill his father's wishes without consulting with him directly. Cyrus McCormick I died in 1884, at the age of seventy-five, leaving a tremendous fortune to his family.[18] And the presidency of the McCormick Harvesting Machine Company passed to twenty-five-year-old Cyrus II.[19]

Now in full command of the McCormick enterprise, Cyrus forged ahead with his mission to recalibrate, in management's favor, the balance of power within the sprawling factory. He had not yet breached, however, skilled labor's citadel: the foundry. That would be his next target. His assault on the craftsmen's dominion there would trigger an epic struggle, earning the McCormicks the abiding enmity of trade unionists the world over. It took place in the midst of swelling national unrest, with Chicago at the epicenter of a dynamic (and dynamite-prone) radical workers' movement. In this outbreak of genuine class warfare—the unvarnished, violent variety—the new company president would engage a slew of enemies, but two men would emerge as his particular antagonists: one, a veteran union organizer, would challenge McCormick from inside his own plant; the other, a charismatic young anarchist, would lead the charge from the outside. When the battle was over, one side had scored a decisive victory—while for some of the defeated, absolutely all had been lost.

2.
Birds of the Coming Storm

yrus McCormick stepped into the presidency of his family's firm convinced of the need for sweeping change. He wasn't alone in those thoughts. Chicago in the 1880s pulsed with discussions of the issues McCormick was confronting: the purpose of work, the merits of mechanization, the fundamentals of value and profit. These exchanges took place not only in company offices but in saloons and across kitchen tables and at open-air meetings. They might have been in English, but they could well have been in German or Czech, Norwegian or Polish, or the conversations may have slipped fluidly from one language to another. And these topics were taken up by the city's many newspapers—not just in the establishment press, like the *Chicago Tribune* and the *Daily News*—but also in widely read publications with names like the *Journal of United Labor* and the *Arbeiter-Zeitung*. A new economic order was taking shape during this Gilded Age: about that there was little argument. Should this redesign conform to the blueprint Cyrus McCormick and his fellow industrialists had drawn up? That was the crux of the controversy.

Chicago in the nineteenth century: the town where "everything goes and goes like thunder." The city's booming growth awed even its most avid boosters, as nothing—not even that most famous of fires—seemed to slow it down. In the single decade of the 1880s the population doubled, topping one million: expansion that rapid was a nearly unheard-of demographic feat. During this period, nearly 80 percent of all Chicagoans were foreign-born or were the children of immigrants; a large percentage were German or Irish, though an increasing number were from eastern and southern Europe. Ensconced in the American heartland, Chicago could seem, and sound, like a foreign country.[1]

But as immigrants poured into this teeming city they soon realized this was no new world paradise they'd found. They came looking for work, of course. They might seek it at McCormick Works or at the packinghouses, the steel mills, the lumber yards, or at the multitude of other factories and construction sites in the city. What positions they could find were often nasty, brutish, and of short-term duration. Wages were low, hours were long, workplaces were unsafe, job security unheard of. Living conditions for these new arrivals were abysmal; in the city's slum districts several families might crowd into a single room within an unventilated, barely heated flat that lacked indoor plumbing. The carcasses of dead horses and dogs festered alongside piles of refuse left uncollected on sodden, unpaved streets. It was a world geographically proximate but nonetheless far removed from the one Cyrus McCormick inhabited. His North Side mansion featured an opulent private theater that could easily accommodate three hundred people; that single room alone would have dwarfed the living space available in an entire tenement building.

Not all of Chicago's working class, however, endured circumstances quite that dismal. Those who had come to the city earlier, and especially those who were skilled, possessed the bargaining power that enabled them to better provide for themselves and their families. Within McCormick Works this was true for the iron molders, most of them Irishmen. They had no doubt registered with anxiety the changes that the new company president had initiated in other parts of the plant; the molders would not readily accommodate "improved" techniques that would undercut their welfare on the job and might relegate them to the ranks of the desperate poor that thronged Chicago's streets. A showdown was brewing.

The employees at the plant already distrusted young Cyrus McCormick; shortly after he assumed the company presidency they had reason to despise him. In December 1884, evidently immune to the Christmas spirit, Cyrus announced major wage reductions for the entire workforce. The nation was in the throes of yet another economic depression, and Chicago was especially hard hit, though there was no gloom in the McCormick Company office, where record profits had just been recorded. McCormick imposed the pay cuts not because he had to, but because he believed he could: with tens of thousands unemployed—many "in a state of destitution that is appalling"— there were plenty of jobseekers willing to take whatever was being offered.[2]

As they had for decades at McCormick Works, the molders took the lead in this dispute. Veteran enough to hold their fire, they waited until the spring production rush before insisting that the pay cuts be rescinded. When their demand was ignored, the members of the molders' union— about ninety men—walked out of the plant in late March 1885. For the moment, the remaining twelve hundred employees at the plant continued to report to their jobs. This was of little consequence to the molders; because they were linchpins in the production process they expected, as had long been the case, that management would be obliged to negotiate with them regardless of what the rest of the workforce did.[3]

Not this time. President McCormick was not in a bargaining mood; instead, he intended to exploit Chicago's widespread misery to school his workforce about just who was in control of the shop. The company put out the call for replacements for the molders, and hastily erected temporary barracks inside the plant gates to house them. A fleet of horse-drawn buses was assembled to ferry managers and strikebreakers in and out of the factory, and a host of private armed guards from the Pinkerton Detective Agency were enlisted to protect them.

But it was Cyrus McCormick, it turned out, who still had some learning to do. Despite the recession, skilled molders were still in demand and finding substitutes for them proved difficult. Whatever inducements the company extended to potential strikebreakers, moreover, had to be evaluated against the very real threats to life and limb offered up by the molders' union. The molders were tough men whose labor involved great risk; with a vested interest in their jobs they felt no moral compunction against intimidating interlopers who coveted their positions at McCormick Works. "We intend to hold our own and do not propose to let scabs take our places," one of the molders told the *Tribune*, using the time-honored epithet aimed at those who cross picket lines. Just after the strike began two prospective employees found out precisely what that meant: they were badly beaten in a saloon near the plant, and so wound up in the hospital instead of inside the plant.[4]

Yet the roughhewn molders soon discovered that their Ivy-League adversary possessed more grit than they might have presumed. When the strike began, rather than wait out the conflict safely ensconced in his mansion, Cyrus McCormick, all alone, guided his carriage to the plant entrance. The molders congregated there "gasped at his temerity," but otherwise made no move to interfere with him. "He waved a good morning, spoke to his horse, and drove through the press to the gate at McCormick Works. . . . He gave an order to the guard within, the gate swung open with a rattle of loosening chains, and he entered." A few moments later he returned with a message for the crowd. "Come on in, boys, if you want to work. The gate is open."[5]

Despite McCormick's invitation, most potential strikebreakers had second thoughts once they faced warning glares from pickets patrolling the plant gates. But there were other approaches to the McCormick factory, and on a dark evening a few weeks into the strike, twenty-five molders were ferried down the Chicago River aboard the company's tugboat and secreted onto the plant grounds. These were men purported to be "ex-convicts and other hard characters," and while they were no doubt not especially talented molders, they managed to get production going in the foundry. And work continued in the rest of the plant, since the overwhelming majority of the employees were not party to the strike and so reported in as usual. It seemed evident that the union molders, acting on their own, could no longer command the respect they had long been afforded. Cyrus McCormick, at any rate, was making his disrespect for them clearer by the day.[6]

But if the old form of craft organization could not force management's hand, new forms of solidarity might. And within the molders' local at McCormick Works one man, in particular, was especially adept at deploying more broad-based strategies. Irish-born Myles McPadden was a veteran iron worker but was, in 1885, a relative newcomer at the McCormick plant. Before he took a job there he'd been busy plying his other trade as an organizer, first in the 1870s as national secretary of the Iron Molders, and then in the leadership of the Knights of Labor, the largest workers' organization of the period. The Knights envisioned a "cooperative commonwealth" of worker-controlled establishments that would overcome capitalist exploitation. In marked contrast to the craft-exclusive trade unions of the time (including, of course, the molders' union), the Knights embraced artisans and common laborers alike, including women and African Americans. They emphasized political engagement as the primary method to advance workers' interests, advocating legislation to establish an eight-hour day at a time when most employees routinely labored sixty hours a week or more. McPadden had an easy way with workers—skilled or unskilled, Irish or otherwise—and was a veritable organizing "juggernaut" who'd added thousands to the Knights' membership rolls throughout the country. He utilized the same line of attack wherever he set up camp: in order to "demonstrate the power of collective action," he endeavored to enlist the entire workforce at one particular establishment, zeroing in on "the city's most hated employer." Perhaps that's why he'd secured a position in the McCormick foundry.[7]

And so, with their independent effort faltering, the molders adopted McPadden's inclusive approach. As McCormick employees headed toward the factory early on an April morning, they were invited to a mass meeting held on the open land adjoining the plant. Speeches in multiple languages rang out over the prairie grass, and when the talk was through, "the men as a body decided not to go to work until wages were restored to their old figure." The Irish molders were no longer fighting for themselves alone: now, several weeks into the strike, the battle was joined by workers throughout the plant, two-thirds of them German. In the face of this show of strength, Cyrus McCormick remained obdurate; when a strikers' committee attempted to meet with him he refused to see them, insisting he would never grant them "recognition as a body" or accede to any wage increases.[8]

McCormick Works was now in a state of siege. More than a thousand striking workers thronged the streets around the plant, making clear their intent "to see that no new men were admitted to the works." Inside the gates, as the *Tribune* detailed, "A full supply of provisions has been laid in" for the strikebreakers, and the factory had been transformed into a fortress, where "guns and revolvers are scattered about in profusion."[9]

With both sides armed and agitated, confrontations were inevitable. Just after the general walkout began, strikers intercepted a bus as it left the plant, grabbing the horses' reins and forcing the panicked animals to halt. Surrounded by several hundred men, the dozen Pinkerton guards aboard opened fire, spraying nearby buildings with gunshots and severely wounding a worker in the crowd. As might be expected, "this had the effect of enraging the strikers to a greater degree," and so a few hours later strikers bombarded the same bus—now headed into the plant—with a hail of bricks and bullets. This time the "badly frightened" Pinkertons abandoned the vehicle and fled. The triumphant workers were all the more elated to discover, stashed in the bus, twenty Winchester rifles and two boxes of cartridges. They carried these off—and unhitched the horses—before they pulled the bus out to the nearby prairie, set it ablaze, and reduced it to a pile of smoldering ash.[10]

He had lost control of the situation, and so he'd lost the strike: Cyrus McCormick could see that now. The solidarity embraced by the entire workforce meant that production had ceased, and the strikers had received promises of aid from shopkeepers and a host of other unions in the city, ensuring they could endure a longer walkout. McCormick was obliged to settle, and to meet with the strikers' committee, which was nearly as objectionable. He agreed to rescind the pay cuts and to dismiss all the strikebreakers as well.[11]

The strikers had won big, through "the power of collective action" promoted by Myles McPadden. As skilled craftsmen were increasingly supplanted, it would be this new source of strength that workers at the McCormick factory would come to rely on. But—their success in 1885 notwithstanding—embracing their collective power would happen only gradually and imperfectly, and would be impeded all along the way, in every possible fashion, by Cyrus McCormick, who had come to recognize just what a united workforce could achieve. The three-week walkout, timed by the strikers to coincide with the height of production, was the principal reason the company saw its profits drop by more than 50 percent in 1885. But in the wake of the debacle McCormick was disciplined enough to engage in a thorough assessment of his failure, and there was one action above all else he resolved to take.

"I do not think we will be troubled by the same thing again," he predicted, "if we take proper steps to weed out the bad element among the men."[12]

There was no question where that "bad element" was concentrated. By the end of the summer of 1885, McCormick had installed automatic molding equipment throughout the foundry. The new machines necessitated the employment of a large number of common laborers whose total compensation far outstripped what the skilled molders as a body had once commanded, undermining the oft-repeated mantra that the onrush of new technology is both inevitable and propelled by obvious cost-saving advantages. There was just one purpose driving the mechanization of the McCormick foundry: to eliminate the molders' union. Cyrus McCormick would do his weeding using a very expensive bulldozer. He ensured, though, that one particular troublemaker was plucked out early. Well before the new machines were introduced, he had Myles McPadden fired.[13]

But McPadden would not merely fade away once he had been dismissed from McCormick Works; nor was he the only Chicagoan intent on changing conditions for the workers there. "Mr. McCormick has a nest of dangerous, vicious men in his employ," read a Pinkerton assessment, "and he will have lots of trouble to get rid of them." The problem, the report warned, was that his workforce had been infiltrated by "socialists." So it was, it seemed, for much of Chicago in the mid-1880s. Within the teeming city, union ranks began to grow and revolutionary rhetoric became common parlance. In part this was due to the continual influx of newcomers from Europe, some of whom brought with them radical new ideologies grounded in the proposition that it was labor, not capital, that generated all wealth. These imported tenets intermingled with homegrown principles of liberty and equality, and this heady mix fueled the growth of a politically conscious labor movement.[14]

Or movements, more properly, for in Chicago—"the capital of American radicalism"—there were those pushing beyond the craft consciousness exemplified by the molders' union and even the expanded sense of solidarity promoted by the Knights of Labor. Anarchism—devoted to the "destruction of existing class rule, by all means"—flourished, particularly within the German community. In fact, anarchists in the city developed their own theory of revolutionary unionism—dubbed the "Chicago Idea"—that held that class-conscious unions would be the lever used, not to extract short-term gains, but to erect a new social order to be run by and for working people. And to wage their struggle against a repressive state, anarchist leaders increasingly voiced support for violent tactics and expressed "a sentimental interest"—at the least—in the use of dynamite.[15]

The strike at McCormick Works deepened the resonance of the radical cause. For the anarchists, young Cyrus McCormick's conduct during the confrontation elevated him to the status of class enemy number one—that was saying something in the Gilded Age—and the trappings of his wealth, like his lavishly appointed mansion, became a frequent target of scorn in the anarchist press. And the strike provided the perfect example of how capitalists could be defeated. Workers united across demarcations of skill and ethnicity had humbled a patrician industrialist, and routed the detested Pinkertons in the process, which seemed like a giant leap toward the realization of the Chicago Idea.[16]

The chief promulgator of that concept would soon step to the fore as Cyrus McCormick's most fearsome opponent. "Barbarians, savages, illiterate, ignorant Anarchists from Central Europe, men who cannot comprehend the spirit of our free American institutions—of these I am one."[17] So August Spies introduced himself in his autobiography, and some aspects were correct: German-born Spies arrived in Chicago in 1873, when he was eighteen years old. He began moving toward radicalism when he witnessed the violent suppression of striking railroad workers in 1877. His views hardened as corruption stymied socialist efforts to secure reform through the electoral process. By the early 1880s Spies and Texas native Albert Parsons had become the leading lights of Chicago's radical workers' movement.[18]

But otherwise Spies's self-description could only be taken ironically. He'd been raised in comfortable circumstances in Germany, and it was only the early death of his father, a government official, that propelled him to emigrate. Once in Chicago he became a skilled upholsterer. Fluent in German, English, and French, he read broadly in all three languages. He edited the Chicago *Arbeiter-Zeitung*, and under his management circulation of the socialist paper soared. A passionate speaker and master wordsmith, Spies could intermingle scathing invective, historical illustration, and literary inspiration within a single paragraph. Lean and intensely charismatic, with blue eyes, a neat mustache, and thick auburn hair, Spies appreciated well-tailored suits and had a reputation, in the parlance of the day, as a "ladies' man." Even his upper-class detractors were obliged to acknowledge that there was almost nothing of the barbarian about him. Nothing, that is, except for his decidedly impolite political beliefs.

In fact, if August Spies and Cyrus McCormick ever sat down together (there is no evidence that they did) they might have managed a few minutes of pleasant conversation based on their mutual interests. They were young men only a few years apart in age. They possessed an affinity for the rugged outdoors; Spies had hoped to become a forestry agent—his father's occupation—had he stayed in Germany. McCormick, on the rare occasions when he took a vacation, retreated to a remote spot in northern Michigan, for "camping in the woods is the best thing I know of." They were classically educated and shared a high regard for one author in particular: McCormick described reading the transcendentalist Ralph Waldo Emerson as akin to savoring "a nut full of sweet meat," while Spies wrote admiringly of "the anarchist Emerson." McCormick and Spies possessed similar character traits too: both were supremely self-possessed, unflinching, and relentless. What they were each driven to accomplish, however, generated an unbridgeable chasm between them, and while the basis of their enmity was ideological, it would take on personal overtones as well. In terms of what mattered most, they knew full well they had nothing in common.[19]

Spies and his anarchist colleagues were determined to organize throughout Chicago; Myles McPadden, however, was focused exclusively on the thirteen hundred workers in his former workplace. By retrofitting the factory, Cyrus McCormick had achieved his purpose: by mid-1885 there were no union members in the foundry or anywhere else in McCormick Works. McPadden rose to the challenge, and by early 1886 had succeeded in organizing three-quarters of the entire factory, enlisting workers into the Knights of Labor and/or the anarchist-backed Central Labor Union. And by then there were even a few union members in the foundry as well. The automatic molding machines were proving so problematic that McCormick had been obliged to hire fifteen skilled molders to produce the more intricate castings. Most of them were members of the molders' union; five, however, were non-union.[20]

McPadden was exceptionally good at his job, but he wasn't solely responsible for the upsurge within McCormick Works. Something was in the air: in 1886 hundreds of thousands of workers across the country signaled they were unwilling to endure their dismal circumstances any longer. They walked off their jobs, as strikes became commonplace, and into labor organizations, sending membership figures for unions soaring. This national movement—with Chicago at its epicenter—was propelled by one specific demand: an eight-hour day. The anarchists initially had mixed feelings about such a "reformist" effort, believing at least that agitation should insist on pay levels remaining the same if the workday was shortened. But as the call caught fire, Spies and his comrades joined with Knights of Labor organizers and craft unionists to promote a nationwide general strike, set for May 1, 1886, in support of the eight-hour day. Their combined push resulted in "the largest, most broadly-based coalition of workers ever assembled—however briefly—on this continent."[21]

But at McCormick Works union members would make some demands of their own ahead of that deadline. In February 1886 a workers' committee in the plant requested a hefty wage increase. They insisted on something else as well: that "the scabs in the foundry"—the non-union molders—be discharged, and in their place, "preference should be given the old hands."[22]

How Cyrus McCormick reacted indicated he'd done considerable re-thinking about how to best rein in unruly employees. His response also un-derscored what really mattered to him: he would grant immediate financial concessions if they would buy greater management control. So this time around McCormick promptly acceded to a wage increase, but adamantly re-fused the workers' other demand. "The right to hire any man," he insisted, "was something I would not surrender." Remarkably, despite the pay increase they'd been offered, McCormick employees, meeting as a body, vowed to walk out if the non-union workers in the foundry were not dismissed. Even more remarkably, before the workers had the chance to begin their strike, Cyrus McCormick ceased production and locked them out. All this over five men who had been working at the factory for only four weeks. But this was a matter of profound principle, one that at the end of the nineteenth cen-tury was still being contested. If it was management's exclusive prerogative to decide who would be hired and fired—and thus craftsmen could be freely replaced with non-union labor—skilled workers would be fully stripped of the collective power they had exerted for decades. McCormick had already utilized mechanization to challenge the power that craftsmen had exerted in his shop. Now, by shattering his workforce's emergent sense of solidarity, he looked to finish the job.[23]

He kept the plant closed for two weeks. Then, on a cold and damp March morning, smoke began to loft up from the chimneys, signaling that the fac-tory was back in business. Three hundred pickets gathered outside, and Cyrus McCormick, as usual, was on hand when the gates opened; "We will start up and keep running if we have only ten men," he pledged. He got more than ten, though not as many as he needed: a few hundred workers reported in. But the violence that had been widely anticipated failed to materialize. This time, Mc-Cormick favored the Chicago police over hired guns, and four hundred uni-formed officers were on hand to ensure safe passage for strikebreakers, supple-mented by seventy-five police detectives who mingled in plainclothes among the pickets. On the plant grounds, the company provided the policemen with hot meals, and Cyrus McCormick strolled among them, filling their coffee cups himself. Despite this display of company resolve bolstered by civic force, Myles McPadden, addressing eight hundred McCormick strikers later that day, remained insistent that the non-union men must go. "Go to work on this condition," he warned, "and every man of you who has so far stood firm or who dares to belong to a union will soon either find himself discharged, or his wages cut down."[24]

McCormick was convinced that McPadden could not, this time, hold the strikers together: with the wage increase in place he was betting that the ongoing dispute would be seen as strictly a molders' concern. But for many weeks too few employees were in the shop and production was hampered severely; the company would report even lower profits in 1886 than it did in 1885. McCormick nonetheless was steadfast in his refusal to negotiate. "I don't want to see any committees or propositions whatsoever," he told a reporter. "They might as well send me a menu card of a Christmas dinner and sign 'Committee' on the bottom as send me any proposition. I shall only treat with these men as individuals."[25]

Some of those individuals remained firmly committed to their principle— that of workers' collective power—and they did not return to their jobs at McCormick Works. But as the weeks dragged on more employees began straggling back. The strike never formally ended, but as spring breezes began to ripple through the tall grass around the plant, it was clearly petering out. Cyrus McCormick no doubt breathed a little easier as he drove his carriage into the factory. His gamble seemed to have paid off.[26]

But he wasn't able to relax completely, not while labor activists of all stripes were organizing for the eight-hour general strike. When the first of May dawned, "the eyes of the country were upon Chicago," August Spies wrote. "Here, everybody knew, the decisive battle would be fought." On that sunny Saturday, at least thirty thousand Chicagoans enlisted in the fight and left their jobs, and this mass action compelled many of the city's employers to quickly concede to the shorter work day. Included within the strikers' ranks were half the employees at McCormick Works—so some of those working in the plant as strikebreakers now joined (or rejoined) picket lines around the plant. With his push to get production back to normal in serious jeopardy, on Monday, May 3, Cyrus McCormick also granted his workers an eight-hour day, but he would extend it only to employees who were back on their jobs by the next morning. Those who chose to stay away would no longer be welcome at the plant. McCormick's concession could be seen as a significant victory for the eight-hour forces—except that it required abandoning the principle that had driven workers there to strike many months before.[27]

On that Monday afternoon August Spies was within sight of McCormick Works, hastening down the cinder-strewn pathway known as the Black Road. He had come to address striking workers at the lumber yards located across the prairie from the McCormick plant. Exhausted from a flurry of speechmaking and writing, he had only reluctantly agreed to attend the meeting, which was underway when he arrived. But at least Spies was gratified by the sizable audience of some six to ten thousand people. Most of them were lumber workers, but there were likely McCormick Works employees there too, a mingling of those who had joined the general strike just a couple days earlier, with others who'd been locked out since February. Spies climbed up on a freight car and proceeded, in German, to exhort the lumber workers to "realize their strength" to secure the eight-hour day. He didn't mention McCormick Works.

But someone did. When the afternoon bell sounded, voices toward the rear of the crowd cried out that strikebreakers were leaving the McCormick factory, and about 150 people broke away and charged toward the plant. Who was among them—specifically, how many McCormick strikers might have been in their ranks—is unknown. But they nonetheless behaved as though they had a serious grudge against Cyrus McCormick, as the group set upon the employees leaving the plant, pummeling them and driving them back inside the factory. Then they focused their wrath on the Works itself. "Get out you damned scabs, you miserable traitors!" they shouted; a barrage of stones and bricks shattered the plant's windows and the small guardhouse that stood near the gates was demolished. Initially there were only two policemen present, who were also attacked, but within minutes several police wagons hurtled onto the scene, and about two hundred officers weighed into the fray, clubbing workers and firing their revolvers into the crowd. Some workers were also armed and responded in kind; they either aimed poorly or carried unreliable weapons, as no policemen were shot. But a number of workers were wounded and bloodied, though precisely how many was never determined. At least one was killed.[28]

All this began while Spies was in the midst of his speech, but once the gunfire broke out he sprinted toward the melee. He was "horrified," not only by the carnage inflicted by the police "murderers," but also by the response from other workers when he urged them to join the battle around the plant. "With an exasperating indifference they put their hands in their pockets and marched home, babbling as if the whole affair did not concern them in the least," he said. These red-hot sentiments melded into what would become his most famous written work. "REVENGE! WORKINGMEN, TO ARMS!" proclaimed the headline affixed to the circular Spies drafted that evening. "Your masters sent out their bloodhounds—the police; they killed six of your brothers at McCormick's this afternoon," the flyer proclaimed, in both English and German. "If you are men . . . then you will rise in your might," it exhorted, "and destroy the hideous monster that seeks to destroy you."[29]

While he indicted the bosses and the police, the establishment press held Spies fully responsible for the "barbarian attack" upon McCormick Works. So did Cyrus McCormick. "August Spies made a speech to a few thousand anarchists," he said, in news accounts the next morning, May 4. "He put himself at the head of a crowd, which then made an attack upon our works."[30]

Within a few hours Spies would get his chance to respond. The anarchists had called a protest meeting that evening to be held just west of the downtown area, at the square—really just a widened street in the grocers' district—popularly known as Haymarket. It was misting and dark when Spies arrived and about a thousand people milled about, nothing like the massive crowd he had addressed the day before. But he was obliged to begin, as he was the evening's first speaker, and the audience was growing more listless in the drizzle. He clambered up onto a grocer's wagon. "All over the land we behold vast armies of producers, no longer begging, but demanding that eight hours shall henceforth constitute a normal working day. And what say the extortionists to this?" he said, this time in English. "Look at the slaves of McCormick! When they tried to remonstrate with their master he simply called upon 'the protectors of these free and glorious institutions'—the police—to silence them." To Cyrus McCormick's effort to blame him for the "massacre" the previous day, he retorted: "McCormick is an infamous liar." A few people cried out, "Hang him!" No, no, Spies said, quieting the calls for vengeance. But it was the false bravado, not the concept of violence, that he rejected: "Make no idle threats," he told the crowd. "There will be a time, and we are rapidly approaching it, when such men as McCormick will be hanged. There will be a time when monsters who destroy the lives and happiness of the citizens (for their own aggrandizement) will be dealt with like wild beasts. But," he maintained, "that time has not yet come."[31]

This would be the last speech Spies would make as a free man. At the tail end of the meeting, as the weather worsened and most of the audience had drifted way, a few hours shy of midnight in the gaslit gloom, a column of police, enough to fill the entire street, abruptly advanced with guns drawn and ordered the remaining audience to disperse. At first there was confusion, and for a moment a short silence. Then a plume of orange light sailed overhead toward the police lines. And then a blast, loud enough to be heard many blocks away: a bomb. Then gunfire, as the police broke ranks and fired indiscriminately on the panicked, scattering crowd. Seven policemen were killed—some felled by the bomb, some by their fellow officers in the chaotic barrage of bullets—and at least four workers were shot dead. It was all over in a matter of minutes. But the explosion reverberated across Chicago, throughout the country, and around the world. Its impact can still be felt.

August Spies was among those who fled for his life once the "wild carnage" began, but though he dodged the bullets that night the events at the Haymarket sealed his fate. No witnesses could identify who threw the bomb—to this day no one knows who did—but among those with power and influence there was immediate certainty about who the culprits were. "Anarchy's Red Hand" had been exposed by the "hellish deed" at Haymarket, so the local and national press declared, and stories about the martyred policemen (the dead workers drew little notice) stoked national hysteria that dynamite-toting terrorists had begun a full-scale assault on the forces of law and order. The result was a crackdown on labor activists of all stripes, though those with foreign accents and/or radical proclivities were subject to particular persecution. In Chicago, the retribution was swift. Within days Spies was arrested and soon thereafter charged with murder, along with Albert Parsons and six other anarchists. Their trial would begin on June 21. Only Spies and one of the other defendants had been at the Haymarket when the violence erupted, and both had been plainly visible on the wagon that served as the speakers' stand. None of the eight men were accused of actually throwing the bomb, but there was no doubt, said the *Tribune,* that they were part of a "murderous communistic conspiracy." Their words—not their deeds—were to stand in judgment.[32]

Words were Spies's stock-in-trade, but he did not use them to plead for clemency when his life was on the line. He spoke, as he always had, of workers and revolution. "The state where one class dominates over and lives upon the labor of another class, and calls this *order*—yes, I believe that this barbaric form of social organization, with its legalized plunder and murder, is doomed to die," he told the court. The trial could not change what he saw as inevitable. "If you think that by hanging us, you can stamp out the labor movement . . . if this is your opinion, then hang us! Here you will tread upon a spark, but there and there, and behind you and in front of you, and everywhere, flames blaze up! It is a subterranean fire. You cannot put it out. The ground is on fire upon which you stand."[33]

Such defiance from the anarchists made it easier for those endeavoring to ensure that they were found guilty. Cyrus McCormick was chief among them. On the day after the bombing, he joined a committee made up of prominent Chicago businessmen—including Marshall Field, George Pullman, and Phillip Armour—to pay a call on Mayor Carter Harrison. With their approval, the mayor issued a proclamation decrying "the body of lawless men who, under the pretense of aiding the laboring man, are really endeavoring to destroy all law," and he pronounced that henceforth, "gatherings of people in crowds or processions on the streets are dangerous and cannot be permitted." McCormick's committee would meet daily while the Haymarket trial was underway, and covertly raised more than $100,000 "to help stamp out anarchy and sedition." Much of the money was funneled to the prosecution during the Haymarket trial. If Cyrus McCormick had anything to say about it, Spies and his fellow defendants would be quieted for good.[34]

"Nooses FOR THE REDS," said the *Tribune*, when the guilty verdict was returned in late August. There would be appeals, and not all of the original defendants would ultimately be sent to the gallows. But on November 11, 1887, August Spies, Albert Parsons, and two others were. Spies managed one last promise to Cyrus McCormick and the other capitalists who believed they had triumphed. "The time will come," he pledged, as the noose was slipped over his head, "when our silence will be more powerful than the voices you strangle today." His neck was not broken when the floorboards opened beneath him; instead, he strangled to death over a period of several minutes, "writhing horribly" the entire time.[35]

"We are birds of the coming storm—the prophets of the revolution," August Spies had said of the anarchists. A storm had broken that night at Haymarket Square, but the revolution did not come. Emboldened employers across the country stepped up their use of lockouts, blacklists, and vigilantes to break unions of all sorts. The radical movement the anarchists built in Chicago was eviscerated, and nationally the Knights of Labor faded to obscurity. The avowedly conservative American Federation of Labor (AFL), a consortium of craft organizations espousing "pure and simple unionism," was founded in late 1886, but struggled for traction. What followed was a long period of little organized labor activity, especially as far as industrial workers in Chicago were concerned and particularly at McCormick Works. And the eight-hour day, which so many workers had made a reality through their mass actions the previous May, became once again merely an aspiration. In Haymarket's wake, business owners promptly reneged on their concessions of shorter hours; by the end of 1886 the eight-hour day applied to only a few thousand employees in the entire state of Illinois. Among those to revoke his agreement was Cyrus McCormick. Shortly after the guilty verdicts had been pronounced for the anarchists, ten-hour shifts were resumed at McCormick Works.[36]

The factory remained devoid of union presence for decades. But the imprint left by both August Spies and Myles McPadden—who drifted away from union work and ultimately opened a saloon in Chicago—would not be entirely erased. Haymarket quickly became a symbol of radical resistance, with the martyrdom of the Chicago anarchists indelibly linked to the workers' holiday celebrated (internationally, at least) on May Day. When union advocates returned to McCormick Works in the twentieth century, they were, like McPadden, consummate and relentless organizers, determined to unify all the workers in the plant. And like Spies—whose memory they would conspicuously invoke—they viewed the chasm between labor and capital as unbridgeable; through their radical union they would pursue their own version of the anarchists' Chicago Idea.

That would be a long time coming, however. Cyrus McCormick—just twenty-seven years old at the end of 1886—had fulfilled his mission to "weed out" the troublemakers in his plant; his mechanization plans would now proceed unchallenged. But by the end of the nineteenth century other impediments stood in the way of maximizing his company's power and profitability. He would attend to those next.

3.
The Difficult Birth of a Behemoth

I t was the wedding of the century—or certainly the biggest one to close out the nineteenth, anyhow. John D. Rockefeller, the richest man alive (in fact, the wealthiest American who's ever lived) would see his daughter Edith marry Harold McCormick, the second son of Reaper King Cyrus I, just a few days before Thanksgiving in 1895. One thousand of the best sort eagerly awaited the ceremony, to be held on Fifth Avenue in Manhattan at what was widely known as "Rockefeller's Church." The interior needed to be reconfigured to accommodate the oversized guest list and to ensure that everyone could catch at least a glimpse of the bride, whose ivory satin gown with its voluminous train would be accented by a lace veil "of rare value" held in place by a "superb diamond tiara" that was Harold's gift to her. The many bridesmaids would be clad in blush-colored dotted silk and carry "dainty sable muffs" that Edith had given them. A small army of carpenters had labored furiously to construct an immense circular stage with curved stairways that would allow the bridal party to ascend above the spectators seated in the pews, while another battalion of florists wove sheaves of pink blossoms and palm fronds into a gigantic arch at its center. It was to be an occasion marked by "extreme good taste" and one "unique in the history of New York weddings."[1]

Except it never took place.

The marriage did—but in what surely came as a crushing disappointment to all those elite invitees, the lavish service was scuttled at the last minute. Harold McCormick had contracted a sudden case of pneumonia and his doctors vetoed any undue exertion. Rather than postpone the ceremony, Edith Rockefeller opted to hold it in her bridegroom's quarters at the Buckingham Hotel. "Instead of the splendor of a church wedding," sighed the society columnists, "the wealthiest bride of the season and one of America's greatest heiresses will be married in the shadow of the sickroom." It was nonetheless a pretty sizeable sickroom, for more than fifty people fit comfortably into the suite as the two twenty-three-year-olds exchanged vows and joined their families, and their families' fortunes, together. That the proceedings were scaled back wouldn't have troubled Cyrus McCormick, who was of course present to witness his younger brother's nuptials. At thirty-six, Cyrus had married several years earlier, but he'd chosen a less splashy partner—a woman from well-to-do, but not wealthy, circumstances—and their wedding had been a relatively modest affair. The marital extravaganza conceived by Edith Rockefeller wouldn't have much appealed to staid Cyrus McCormick, but he could at least take comfort in the knowledge that the bride's family wouldn't ask for help in paying for it.[2]

The union of the McCormick and Rockefeller dynasties occurred at an especially auspicious moment, in the midst of what has been dubbed "the nation's first great merger movement," though that designation referred to combinations of the corporate rather than the conjugal variety. From 1890 through the first few years of the twentieth century, American capitalists were seized by merger mania, as hundreds of smaller operations were melded into colossal industrial enterprises. During this period monoliths like General Electric, United Fruit Company, DuPont, and U.S. Rubber were redefining just how big big business could get. Towering above them all was U.S. Steel, established in 1901, the world's first billion-dollar corporation. Of course, some immensely powerful monopolies had been founded a few decades earlier, like John D. Rockefeller's Standard Oil, which exercised near complete control over the petroleum industry. These consolidations were facilitated by increasingly powerful financial institutions, most especially the House of Morgan, which had, for instance, underwritten—and profited handsomely from—the formation of U.S. Steel.[3]

But, up to his brother's wedding and for a time thereafter, Cyrus McCormick resisted the merger momentum, preferring instead to expand operations within his family firm. In the years following the Haymarket affair, the massive McCormick Works complex grew even larger, swallowing up more acres of prairie as buildings were added and the workforce burgeoned to over six thousand. Newer farm equipment manufacturers, however, were challenging the McCormicks' dominance of the industry, principal among them the Deering Manufacturing Company, also based in Chicago. Cyrus remained reluctant to consider a consolidation with other firms, not because he held any principled objections to monopolies, but because he harbored serious reservations about negotiating—or even being in the same room—with his chief rival Charles Deering. They were only a few years apart in age and ran in the same social circles, but the two industrialists detested each other. The McCormicks regarded the Deerings as unworthy upstarts who had merely stumbled into their success in the noble enterprise of agricultural improvement. The two firms slashed prices as they struggled for supremacy, which was good news for farmers but bad for the manufacturers' profit margins; a merger that would end the cutthroat competition seemed the obvious answer. In the 1890s the two families made some half-hearted attempts to broker such an agreement, but amid bitter feelings the talks foundered each time.[4]

By the early twentieth century, however, the benefits attendant to a U.S. Steel–type monopoly in the farm equipment industry became too enticing for Cyrus McCormick to ignore. And by this point he knew just whom to turn to for advice and more than a little material support: John D. Rocke feller, who had grown quite fond of his new son-in-law Harold McCormick. Rockefeller offered to invest his own funds to bring about the consolidation, and suggested that George Perkins, J. P. Morgan's right-hand man at the Morgan Bank, handle the delicate negotiations necessary to effect it. Cyrus McCormick agreed, but remained resolute that his family would dominate whatever new industrial entity might be cobbled together.[5]

George Perkins was well aware that he would need all the diplomatic prowess he could muster to bring this deal to fruition. The McCormicks and the Deerings were summoned to the Morgan Bank in New York City, but Perkins kept the feuding families sequestered in separate rooms, while he shuttled proposals back and forth across the hall. "As much like an incident in comic opera as an affair of business," one observer noted. But without maintaining such distance, "the old hurtful rivalries would break out afresh and the project might snap off like a broken dream."[6]

But this time the lucrative dream became reality. On July 28, 1902, the McCormicks and the Deerings sat together, briefly, at the same table to sign the papers and the International Harvester Company—its name chosen to underscore the firm's global presence—was born. Upon formation, the new corporation controlled 85 percent of the harvesting machine business in the United States. The McCormicks contributed their sprawling Chicago manufactory to the enterprise along with twine and saw mills, hundreds of thousands of acres devoted to timber and hemp production, an extensive network of sales offices, and the Illinois Northern Railway. For their part the Deerings added their Chicago factory and their new steel mill on the city's far South Side, along with coal and iron mines ranging from Minnesota to Kentucky. Two smaller farm equipment companies were also absorbed by the merger, and their factories became part of the IH empire. Perkins selected Cyrus McCormick to serve as Harvester's president and made Charles Deering chairman of the corporate board; Harold McCormick and another Deering heir were named vice-presidents.[7]

Yet this delicate balance of power didn't ease tensions between the McCormicks and the Deerings, and for the first two years of its existence, International Harvester functioned like an unruly confederation of warring fiefdoms. The Deerings threatened to sue to recover "their property," while the McCormicks at one point became convinced that the Deerings were planning to storm and occupy McCormick Works. Production slumped and the big profit increases that seemed certain to follow the creation of a farm equipment monopoly failed to materialize. The Deerings, finally, decided they'd had enough, though their surrender left them materially unscathed. By 1904 they'd largely withdrawn from Harvester management and cashed in their stock, allowing Charles Deering and his brother James to build sumptuous neighboring estates in Florida, amass world-renowned art collections, and donate a library to Northwestern University. The end of the inter-family feud was consummated in 1914, when Marion Deering, the daughter of Charles Deering, married Cyrus McCormick's cousin Chauncey.[8]

Cyrus McCormick had ousted the Deerings from the IH executive suite, but he was determined to secure financial supremacy as well. To do that he turned again to his familiar, and invaluable, ace in the hole. As the Deerings shed their stock the Rockefellers bought it (or lent the McCormicks money so that they could acquire it), and thus in a few short years the McCormick-Rockefeller alliance succeeded in securing majority interest in International Harvester. IH was a corporation—and after 1908, technically a publicly held one—but by the second decade of the twentieth century it was one firmly controlled, as Cyrus McCormick had determined it would be, by his family; through his perseverance he had ensured that "a virtually uninterrupted succession of McCormick descendants" would rule the company for the next eighty years.[9]

The significance of Rockefeller money in this contest, however, cannot be overstated: because of it the McCormicks were able to operate Harvester entirely as they saw fit. This critical access to capital came about thanks to the romance young Harold McCormick had struck up with Edith Rockefeller. "The company's exceptional financial resources," noted a 1913 federal government report, "including its connections with J.P. Morgan & Company and John D. Rockefeller, constitute one of its chief sources of power."[10]

With its managerial conflicts resolved, International Harvester would fully realize that power. The company launched new product lines, expanded overseas, and gobbled up rival enterprises so rapidly that "by 1907 there remained no semblance of competition." Sales doubled and profits leaped eightfold in the five years between 1905 and 1910. By this point Harvester's assets were so extensive that it stood as the fourth-largest corporation in the United States. Its products—seven hundred thousand harvesting machines a year—were turned out by thirty thousand workers employed at sixteen factories spread across North America. Harvester retained its own steel mill (which, though located on Chicago's South Side, became known as Wisconsin Steel) and kept its furnaces running with fuel supplied from the company's twenty-three thousand acres of Appalachian coal fields; the miners who dug it out lived in Benham, Kentucky, built and wholly owned by International Harvester. Then there were the timber and ore properties and the railroads as well, along with plantations in Central America and Cuba devoted to the production of binder twine. The company's holdings were so vast that no one—not even Cyrus McCormick—had seen them all.[11]

He had learned what he needed to know about farm equipment, and the workers who manufactured it, from the time he spent on the shop floor at the factory that bore the family name. When conflicts erupted, he himself stood at the gates of McCormick Works to prevent organized labor from gaining a foothold in his plant. But that had all changed now: given International Harvester's immense scope, Cyrus McCormick could no longer maintain firsthand knowledge about the workforce or personally intervene at the scene of each crisis. Corporate capitalism, he came to recognize, necessitated new forms of organization, and his company pioneered techniques for managing labor that within a few decades became standard practice within American businesses. Some things, though, remained unchanged. Harvester's labor policies were defined by the bedrock principle that Cyrus McCormick had enunciated in the nineteenth century: no "outsiders"—certainly including unions—would be allowed a voice in the family's business. And for the first decades of Harvester's existence, one other thing remained constant as well: when labor troubles arose, they were centered at McCormick Works.

4.
Fair and Square Fifty-Fifty

In the early spring of 1916 Cyrus McCormick sat at his desk reviewing reports sent to him by his lower-level managers. One short sentence he read may well have caused McCormick to sit up a little straighter in his chair.

"Some I.W.W. men have been holding meetings," the memo said, "and a few of our men have signed up."[1]

For a number of years following the formation of International Harvester all remained quiet on the labor front. As Europe became engulfed in the Great War, however, circumstances at home became more unsettled. The conflict propelled many of the foreign-born to return to their home countries, and immigration to the United States was cut off. As labor shortages intensified, workers began talking about unions again; the craft affiliates of the American Federation of Labor were enlisting members, while alternative organizations harkened back to August Spies's Chicago Idea. Much to Cyrus McCormick's chagrin, his hometown was, as always, in the thick of the ferment. The Industrial Workers of the World (IWW) had been founded in 1905 in Chicago, and those IWW men that caught his attention were determined to unite all workers in a single revolutionary organization. The Wobblies, as they were called, castigated capitalism and embraced shop-floor disruption and sabotage to hasten its downfall. It all sounded drearily familiar to Cyrus McCormick. He'd vanquished the anarchists decades before but now radical agitators were once again nosing around his plants.

And there were now more of those factories to pay attention to, though half of Harvester's industrial workforce remained concentrated in Chicago. McCormick Works remained the colossus in the enterprise and had grown even larger since IH was founded, with more than eight thousand workers engaged in increasingly mechanized tasks. As automatic binders came into use, the McCormick Twine Mill, opened in 1901 adjacent to the main plant, had ballooned in size, becoming the largest operation of its kind in the world—"a monstrous Bedlam of noise and fuzz"—where employees twisted enough twine in a day to encircle the globe. Handling these fibers was deemed suitable for women, and several hundred of them now labored at the mill. And by this point there were two foundries, where nearly sixty million castings a year were produced: the original facility and a newer one devoted to malleable iron production that stood some distance from the main plant. Some of the iron workers were Irishmen still, and there was a small but growing number of African American men employed in the foundries, but most in this era were Polish or from other eastern European countries.[2]

The world unto itself that was McCormick Works captured the attention of the muckraker Upton Sinclair, whose 1906 novel *The Jungle* exposed the wretched conditions in Chicago's packinghouses. But Sinclair's protagonist Jurgis Rudkus briefly escapes "the filth and repulsiveness that prevailed at the stockyards" when he secures a temporary position at the McCormick plant. He soon discovers that one thing above all else defines the employees' experience there: piecework. By this point few traces remained of the craftsmen's practices that provided workers a measure of safety and a modicum of respite. Jurgis observes a friend laboring in the foundry, where workers were paid only for "perfect castings," meaning nearly half their work was "going for naught."

> You might see him, along with dozens of others, toiling like one possessed by a whole community of demons; his arms working like the driving rods of an engine, his long, black hair flying wild, his eyes starting out, the sweat rolling in rivers down his face... All day long this man would toil thus, his whole being centered upon the purpose of making twenty-three instead of twenty-two and a half cents an hour ...[3]

Harvester's piecework system was the reality for workers at its other plants as well. With nearly six thousand employees, the Deering Works, located on Chicago's North Side, was almost as big as the McCormick factory. On the far Southwest Side was the smaller West Pullman Works, and further south lay the Wisconsin Steel Mill, where several thousand were employed. And just across the street from McCormick Works, thirteen hundred people labored at Harvester's newest plant, opened in 1910 and devoted to producing the latest piece of equipment that promised to revolutionize agriculture yet again: Tractor Works.

Yet despite the frenzy imposed by piecework, pay rates and working conditions were better at IH than at many other businesses. And invasive agitators in the shops continued to be uprooted. So while the warning he'd received about the IWW may have given him pause, Cyrus McCormick was not overly concerned about union trouble. He was about to find out how wrong he was. In late April 1916, IH management abruptly cut wages in the McCormick Twine Mill; in response the entire workforce—twelve hundred men and two hundred women—walked out in protest. They were immediately joined by twelve hundred iron molders, and within a few days workers from other departments were reinforcing the picket lines; moreover, the strike was spreading. By May 2, at least eleven thousand workers from the McCormick and Deering plants had joined the walkout, and Tractor Works was virtually shut down. Speaking through a nascent committee, the strikers insisted that the twine shop pay cut be rescinded; more broadly they called for "recognition of their newly formed union," "better conditions for the workers in the shops," and the abolition of the piecework system, which would become an issue, in one form or another, in every subsequent labor conflict at International Harvester.[4]

Blindsided by his first multiplant walkout, Cyrus McCormick recognized that in the wartime economy his leverage was limited. But one item remained nonnegotiable: there would be no union recognition of any kind. To avoid that, McCormick, as he'd proved willing to do before, offered a relatively generous concession on wages. Workers slowly filtered back to all the plants, though troublemakers were again weeded out, with special attention, as always, paid to foundry workers, most of whom had become union members. They would need to be replaced, Cyrus McCormick reported to Harvester's directors, which "will cause us more or less expense," but it would be worth it. "One of the advantages of building a new foundry organization will be that we will not have to have such a large percentage of Poles," who, he said, "are very excitable and are easily led astray."[5]

The 1916 walkout, as it turned out, marked a turning point for International Harvester. Cyrus McCormick managed to keep his plants union-free during the strike, but he could take comfort in little else; the disruption had proved costly and generated bad press castigating the Harvester "monopoly." Some top managers argued that the massive enterprise was well overdue an overhaul of shop-floor practice, which had been little altered since the nineteenth century. Within IH plants, foremen still wielded formidable authority: they retained the power to hire and fire, and could readjust piecework prices for individual workers, often rendering meaningless the wage rates announced by top management. There was no company-wide structure for hearing employee complaints, so grievances festered until they exploded in events like the 1916 walkout.[6]

Cyrus McCormick, now in his late fifties, had reached an age when he might have been resistant to sweeping change. But as he mulled over his most recent set-to with labor he too concluded that a new approach was in order, so long as it would serve his long-standing paramount principle. "What can we do now in the way of improving our relations with our own workers," McCormick asked in a memo to IH executives after the strike, "so that there will be less chance of any successful attack on us next May by the labor unions from outside—either the IWW or the Federation of Labor?"[7]

One unusual concept appealed to him. It would be a good idea, McCormick concluded, "to have one man in the Company whose sole duty would be to think over and keep in touch with the relations of the workmen to the Company." International Harvester thus became one of the very first firms to establish such a position, and to find the right person for it, McCormick would turn to a familiar source. Arthur H. Young had been the point man handling labor trouble at the Rockefeller-owned Colorado Fuel and Iron Company, and in 1918 John D. Rockefeller dispatched Young to Chicago to head Harvester's new Department of Industrial Relations.[8]

Young would implement a host of pioneering managerial practices at Harvester, and the leading capitalists in America were at that moment paying close attention. By the time World War I concluded, at the end of 1918, the United States was a recognized global industrial powerhouse, with giant enterprises like Harvester securing near-complete hegemony over their markets that they would exert for decades. Absent pesky competitors, executives in these firms began to focus with microscopic intensity on the behavior of individual workers, seeking to tweak more profit out of each employee. The emerging field of industrial relations was purposed to achieve that end.[9]

Central to this reconfiguration were the techniques for the "scientific" management of labor that came into widespread use during World War I, as Frederick Winslow Taylor, armed with just a stopwatch and a clipboard— his emphasis was not technological innovation but the organization of work—ushered in the era of modern factory production. By breaking down complex jobs into component steps, Taylor's system further facilitated the replacement of skilled, and even semiskilled, labor by machine tenders who would be trained to perform one simple (and strictly timed) operation. The movement toward interchangeable parts and assembly line production also accelerated during the war and provided management with greater control over precisely how, and how fast, work was done.

But as Cyrus McCormick discovered back in the nineteenth century, when management unilaterally redesigns the production process things don't always unfold as smoothly as planned. Workers, whatever their level of expertise, proved less than enthusiastic about tedious tasks incessantly repeated at breakneck speed. Quit rates in early twentieth-century factories were astonishingly high, sometimes greater than 300 percent annually; turnover of such magnitude sowed chaos and undermined productivity. Moreover, reducing the use of skilled labor might not provide the anti-union panacea management hoped for, for as the machine tenders multiplied, new entities, like the IWW, promised to organize them. Even the craft-based AFL began to make noise about unionizing, in its own fashion, the burgeoning ranks of the unskilled.[10]

Most ominous was the specter that was inducing nightmares for capitalists the world over, as the toppling of the Czar and the communist assumption of power in Russia in 1917 demonstrated the lengths to which a really disgruntled working class might go. "The Russian wants not only a share in the management but the entire management," exclaimed an alarmed Cyrus McCormick, and he knew directly of what he spoke: International Harvester had a plant outside Moscow that was seized by the Bolsheviks, a multimillion-dollar loss for the company. The shockwaves from the Russian Revolution reverberated among the proletariat far from Red Square. "Sixty-five percent of the strikes which have taken place in Central Europe since the war are of purely syndicalist origin," McCormick said, while "the ever-widening clamor for nationalization of industry" was heard in England. Uncharacteristically assertive American workers were suddenly issuing "demand after demand catalogued under the term of 'better conditions.'" In 1919 the Communist Party of America was founded, naturally in Chicago; it was surely exasperating for Cyrus McCormick that radicals maintained such a lingering fondness for his hometown.[11]

So as the captains of industry looked toward the 1920s they faced on their immediate horizon two interconnected challenges: ensuring uninterrupted production from their growing and increasingly alienated workforces, while staving off the threat represented by outside unionism, or those even more menacing radical movements. They would not confront these problems in isolation. The Special Conference Committee (SCC) was created in April 1919 to bring together the industrial relations directors at the nation's biggest firms to confer regularly about personnel policies, wages and benefits, and methods for handling worker unrest. Arthur Young, from International Harvester, was one of the SCC's founding and especially influential members. Other participating companies included DuPont, General Electric, General Motors, Goodyear, and Standard Oil. Though it is fairly obvious from the roll call, the members of this select group commanded a staggering amount of wealth and power. By the late 1930s, these corporations employed nearly one and a half million people and claimed total assets well in excess of thirteen billion dollars.[12]

The SCC, which continued to operate into at least the early 1940s, insisted that it did not dictate policy, but the gravitas of its member corporations guaranteed that its actions would have an impact on public policy and be reflected in the procedures of less powerful companies. And since the field of industrial relations itself had only recently come into existence, the decisions made by the small group of executives who comprised the Special Conference Committee would have a profound and abiding impact on business practice in the United States.[13]

Guided by the SCC, management's program for the 1920s and beyond eschewed ham-handed opposition to organized labor, at least on the record. Instead, business leaders proclaimed a dawning era of industrial cooperation that would render unions obsolete. Under the general umbrella of "welfare capitalism," Harvester and other corporate giants experimented with a host of initiatives—pensions, stock options, in-plant cafeterias—to demonstrate that management benevolence, not outside agitators, would provide workers with what they desired. (That these programs were often available only to "loyal" employees or revoked summarily did not blunt their public relations value.)[14] Cyrus McCormick's oldest son—Cyrus III—who was by this point rising in the ranks of IH management, became one of the principal spokesmen for this approach. "Capital and labor have this new way of working out their problems," Cyrus III said in 1920. "We find that here is this new channel for getting at something that we have been seeking for a long time, and now, even in these troublesome days . . . perhaps the sunrise is just a little bit clearer."[15]

The "new channel" the McCormicks were so enthused about was the Employee Representation Plan. ERPs—derisively dubbed "company unions"— were management creations said to provide employees with a voice in the affairs of the enterprises they worked for. They would come into widespread use in America during the Great Depression, as business owners scrambled to keep their workers from being swept along by the rising tide of organizing activity. But the corporations that belonged to the Special Conference Committee, IH included, had acted well before that. The executives at these elite firms had recognized that employee representation promised to promote the slogan of the era—"the business of America is business"—where it mattered most: in the workplace, at the locus of conflict between labor and management. As Harvester officials devised their own system through which capital and labor would "work out their problems," they asserted a broad purview for capital while narrowly confining labor's prerogatives, an articulation of "management rights" that shapes industrial relations to this day. The corporate conception of the proper allocation of power—which is to say, workers got none of it—would remain the rule at IH until the union came calling in the late 1930s.[16]

Arthur Young, in close consultation with Cyrus McCormick II, spent nearly a year perfecting a plan uniquely suited to International Harvester.[17]

Each of the company's twenty factories was to have a works council made up of both management and worker representatives. Employee representatives would be elected by the workers at each plant, though the plan sharply delimited just whom they could choose to speak on their behalf: minimum age and length-of-service stipulations narrowed the field, while the requirement that employee representatives be American citizens excluded at least half the workforce at McCormick Works; the same was true at Tractor Works and Wisconsin Steel.[18]

Nonetheless Harvester's "Industrial Council Plan," would, so the company said, bring "the workers and the management of each individual plant onto a fair and square fifty-fifty basis," and the concept was unveiled with great fanfare in early March 1919. Workers at IH had been kept in the dark until then, when they received a letter promising that employee representation would "make for the greater contentment and well-being of us all." The new arrangement would be subject to approval by the employees in each plant in management-supervised elections to be held just two days later. Surely it was made clear to Harvester workers how their bosses wanted them to vote, and at any rate they had little time to mull over the proposal or discuss it amongst themselves.[19]

Given all that, what is remarkable is not that the plan was approved at most of Harvester's plants but that it was rejected in three of them. Predictably McCormick Works led the recalcitrant trio; the McCormick Twine Mill (which voted as a separate facility) and neighboring Tractor Works also voted down the proposal. A second election later in March led to the plan's adoption at Tractor Works and the Twine Mill, but the wayward workers at the McCormick plant again said no thanks to employee representation.[20]

As it turned out, the imposition of its Council Plan, everywhere but at McCormick Works, proved particularly fortuitous for Harvester management, for Chicago was about to enter its Red Summer—an apt appellation for more reasons than one. The end of World War I brought with it inflation and layoffs; communists, Wobblies, and pure and simple trade unionists tapped into mounting economic distress. The massive strike wave of 1919—which involved over four million workers nationwide, nearly one-quarter of the nation's private workforce—washed over the city and pulled thousands of Chicagoans off their jobs. Bloody race riots left dozens dead; in the city's steel mills and packinghouses, employers exploited racial antagonisms by enlisting African Americans as strikebreakers. Harvester was not untouched by the turbulence: on July 15, nearly all the employees at McCormick Works and the Twine Mill walked out, and the next day, with large picket lines present, the company suspended operations at Deering and Tractor Works. Eleven thousand employees were idled and production in the four plants halted entirely. As per usual, company officials claimed to have no idea what prompted the walkout; the workers "suddenly quit their jobs without complaint, request, or demand of a general nature." But the strikers did issue demands, and familiar ones: union recognition, a shorter workday, and—once again—the complete elimination of piecework.[21]

At the outset of the 1919 walkout, Arthur Young was concerned that "the machine which we had so carefully built up might be taken over and put under the control of radical forces." But instead Young deftly utilized his "machine"— the Industrial Council Plan—to bring Harvester's recalcitrant workforce to heel. Company officials refused to engage with the striking workers, since, so they claimed, they were bound "to carry on negotiations . . . only through the Works Councils." Harvester's contention that genuine bargaining was conducted with the councils strained credulity, to put it mildly, but Arthur Young made good use of this false front. This time no concessions to the striking workers were offered before Harvester began re-opening its idle factories on August 4. Those seeking to return were first interrogated by a works council committee; anyone whose name appeared on management's list of "intimidators" would not be rehired. For those who made it past that first cut, expressions of support for the strike or for unionism in general also constituted grounds for dismissal, and employees were obliged to profess allegiance to the works council if they wanted their jobs back. Harvester was once again weeding out the bad element within the workforce—with the pernicious added twist that "loyal" workers were assigned that dirty task.[22]

But at the McCormick factory, which had stubbornly refused to accept employee representation, such sophisticated techniques were unavailable. There Harvester officials fell back on old habits. As had been the case in the past, the police department proved cooperative; the labor press claimed that McCormick pickets were regularly arrested while strikebreaking employees were afforded extensive protection. Finally, in late summer, striking McCormick workers received a postcard bearing a short ultimatum from the company, indicating that the plant would be re-opened in a few days: "If you want to go to your old job, it will be necessary for you to report promptly." Employees would not be allowed back without a card, so their selective delivery "permitted the bosses to weed out the men they did not deem desirable," said the Chicago Federation of Labor, which was obviously familiar with the way things were done at Harvester. The IH walkout collapsed, the common outcome for strikes across the country in 1919; once again it had become apparent that so long as workers' solidarity remained incomplete, they would be bested by resolute and powerful employers.

The "weeding out" process applied in 1919 remade the McCormick workforce, at least in one key respect. The next time the Industrial Council Plan was submitted for a vote at McCormick Works, in 1921, employees there approved it. Works councils were now firmly rooted at all IH plants.[23]

Its pioneering employee representation plan, Harvester management had proclaimed with great flourish, signified a commitment to cooperative decision-making that would promote the "well-being of us all." Yet some workers proved determined to test the sincerity of that pledge.

5.

With the Men It Is Actual Experience

There's not much known about John Becker. All that is certain is that for a fleeting period he stood up to one of the most powerful corporations in the world.

Here's what can be gleaned from the record—the record being the McCormick Works Council minutes: In the summer of 1922 Becker was elected an employee representative on the McCormick council. Per the eligibility requirements he would have been employed at McCormick Works for at least a year and was an American citizen. McCormick employees had long come from various neighborhoods, some far from the plant, so where he may have lived is unknown. If he'd ever been a union member cannot be determined. But one thing is clear: John Becker believed McCormick workers deserved more than they were getting from International Harvester, and was willing to say so.[1]

The McCormick Works Council had been operational for over a year when Becker took his post, and with the 1919 turbulence receding from memory, everything seemed to be unfolding according to management's plan. At the council's initial meetings, the nineteen worker representatives met with an equal number of management officials to consider, for instance, how to keep lunchroom milk colder; they also sat through a talk from a company vice-president about his recent trip to Europe. Not that the council was all talk and no action. In October 1921, Arthur Young (who served as chairman of each works council) gave a lengthy presentation stressing the financial strain Harvester was experiencing. The employee representatives obligingly voted to accept a hefty wage reduction for themselves and their fellow workers. Nor was this all: the council members then visited with every McCormick worker to explain why the pay cut was necessary.[2]

John Becker had a different notion of how an employee representative should behave. He had no sooner taken his position on the council when he called for a 20 percent pay increase, and was joined in this demand by three other newly elected representatives. Becker had clearly done his homework—and probably some organizing—prior to the meeting. Annual food and rent costs in Chicago, as he detailed, meant that on Harvester's wages workers would come up at least $10 short, "with nothing for coal and shoes, clothing or anything else."

With Becker's demand the normally banal council proceedings livened up. Arthur Young "took exception to Mr. Becker's statement," and produced a chart purporting to illustrate that Harvester's wages more than covered living costs. But by this point other employee representatives proved ready to quarrel with management. Chester Laubly read a newspaper article noting rising food prices in the city; Fred Schroeder contended that his paycheck was inadequate to provide for his small family, adding that "the men around the shop claim the same thing—can't make ends meet." Schroeder didn't think much of Arthur Young's calculations. "The chart was figures," he protested, "while with the men it is actual experience."

Undaunted, Arthur Young plunged into a lengthy statistical discourse, apparently to prove that his figures better reflected reality than the workers' "actual experience" did. Shifting tactics, Young then insisted that an examination of Harvester's annual report would prove that in any event the company simply could not afford a wage increase. Maybe, Laubly suggested, Harvester keeps two sets of books—"one of actual conditions and the other for public inspection," an accusation that drew indignant denials from management officials. But the company's claims of fiscal distress would not deter John Becker. His "constituents," Becker proclaimed, "had requested they be granted a 20 percent increase in wages," and so he would "fight for this increase and would stick to it." A fundamental issue of credibility was at stake. "The men in the shop want to know what good the council is for the employee," Becker said flatly. "The functions thus far performed didn't amount to much."

A piqued Arthur Young reminded Becker that the councils served a purpose far more "essential" than "the granting of increases in wages." By smoothing over conflict, the councils helped ensure unhindered production, thus providing "continuous employment to the working force." Young then announced that "current conditions" made any pay hike "impossible."

Now it was Becker who was irritated. He noted that under the council rules Young did not have the final say and insisted that the wage increase be submitted to a vote. The employee representatives present lined up in favor, while management officials registered unanimous disapproval. The council's rules stipulated that tie votes be referred to Harvester's president for review, and the plan did provide the possibility of outside arbitration—at the president's discretion—in such a situation. But no arbitrator was invoked, and at a special meeting a week later, employee representatives got the answer Young had promised: the wage increase was denied. The employee representatives then passed a resolution indicating they found the president's response to their request "unacceptable," but there was nothing further they could do. By the rules of the Industrial Council Plan, the decision was final.[3]

There was nothing joint about Harvester's decision-making process, as John Becker had just discovered. Despite the "fifty-fifty" rhetoric that accompanied the introduction of employee representation, wage levels continued to be unilaterally set by Harvester management; the presence of the works councils merely changed how those fiats were communicated to employees. Even the one pay increase that was granted during the 1920s was simply announced by the plant's superintendent at the McCormick Works Council's February 1923 meeting.[4]

The councils failed as well to provide a mechanism for redress of individual grievances. Workers who felt unfairly treated were required to proceed "through the regular channels," which meant engaging the foreman, and then the plant superintendent, before employee representatives could intervene. Given that supervisory phalanx, it should come as no surprise that throughout its existence the McCormick Works Council never considered any grievance disputes. Piecework—the most common source of aggravation within Harvester's plants—was discussed only in a manner designed to serve management's ends, as council members were routinely subjected to presentations extolling enhanced efficiency and increased productivity. When an employee representative once suggested that it might not be in a worker's best interest to help make a job more "efficient" without a corresponding wage increase, he was assured that "such employees eventually received recognition by the Company." Council members were then expected to communicate what they'd been told—i.e. that producing more without getting paid for it was somehow a good thing—to their coworkers.[5]

But dogged John Becker kept pushing to make the works council something more than merely a management platform. He made it his business to nudge Arthur Young about Harvester's shortcomings, pointing out, for instance, that one of Chicago's big packinghouses had granted its employees vacations with pay, something IH had not done (and did not then choose to do, either). Moreover, he was the only employee representative ever to become vice-chairman of the works council. Plant superintendent James Grant had been elected to that position without opposition at the council's first meeting, but Becker decided to run against him in January 1923. The vote went through two ballots, and in the final tally Becker prevailed, as he actually won over one of the managers present. Becker's victory was a hollow one, however, for at the first meeting that Arthur Young could not attend, he sent a note indicating that Grant was to serve in his place. Becker angrily responded that if Young was permitted to do that, the vice-chair's position was meaningless, and he insisted the office should be abolished. The council, however, chose not to do that, and Grant presided over the meeting.[6]

Not too long after this incident, John Becker left the McCormick Works Council. His term expired in July 1923, and he did not reappear at the council's next sessions. The council minutes make it impossible to determine whether worker representatives had chosen not to run again, were defeated for reelection, or were no longer working in the plant when they vanished from the roster. The council members who had voiced support for John Becker's original demand for a pay increase were also all gone by 1925. Harvester had many ways to uproot employee representatives, ranging from transfers to outright discharge from the plant, and thus the councils provided Harvester with a new means to identify and then weed out those "bad elements" in the workforce. By attracting the few defiant employees who remained in the plant after 1919, and then stifling their dissent, the McCormick Works Council effectively undercut resistance and undermined organizing efforts that might have been initiated there. As John Becker and his contentious comrades faded from the historical record, the sparks of resistance at McCormick Works, for a long stretch, appeared extinguished as well.[7]

Duly cleansed of any representatives with confrontational inclinations, from the mid-1920s on the McCormick Works Council became a model of docile company unionism. Pay increases were no longer debated; in fact, wages weren't even mentioned. Safety was often discussed, for McCormick Works was one of Harvester's most accident-prone plants. But instead of, perhaps, urging the company to install less hazardous machinery, employee representatives instead focused on admonishing their fellow workers. A foundry worker who received a stomach contusion, for example, "was warned that the next time he was caught being careless he would be discharged." Council members were also subject to regular lectures about the "realities" of capitalism. As Cyrus McCormick II told the American Management Association in 1925, employee representation facilitated the transmission of what he called "economic laws and facts" directly to the workforce, as council members had "the vicious cycle of supply and demand" explained to them. It then became "a pleasure," he said, "to see how these workers, sitting on the councils . . . carried what they had learned out to their constituents and fellow workers in the shops."[8]

The carefully cultivated Industrial Council Plan, therefore, functioned just as Cyrus McCormick had envisioned, fending off attacks "by the labor unions from outside," diffusing shop-floor discontent, and providing a pipeline for management indoctrination. All that contributed to a bountiful harvest for IH management, as the company became, without question, "the greatest single agricultural enterprise in the world." Though American farmers faced economic difficulties during the 1920s, Harvester's dominance of the agricultural implement industry "drove the company to a new pinnacle of success by 1929," noted one business analyst. Through the decade profits at IH "were hitting spectacular highs," *Fortune* magazine noted approvingly. And, not incidentally, though at the time council representative Chester Laubly wouldn't have known just how right he was, Harvester did in fact keep two sets of books during this period. The company maintained a multimillion-dollar reserve fund "hidden away" from each year's earnings, a fact Harvester finally acknowledged in 1929. At the time there was nothing illegal about this secret kitty, but it did prevent the public—and Harvester employees—from recognizing just how wealthy the corporation was. Those "economic laws and facts" that IH management expected its workers to accept were not, as it turned out, quite so factual after all.[9]

Harvester's "spectacular" success was to be expected in the roaring, soaring decade fixed in the popular imagination by the glittering parties held at Jay Gatsby's mansion. But just like the story, jazz age prosperity was, for most, just fiction. Despite the upward surge in both America's gross national product and manufacturing output during the 1920s, wage hikes did not follow accordingly. Though material circumstances for working people were certainly improving—broader availability of public utilities like electricity and indoor plumbing made life easier, while credit and installment buying made consumer goods like automobiles, radios, and washing machines more attainable—the decade's impressive economic growth was mostly making the rich spectacularly richer.[10]

International Harvester provides a case in point: only one company-wide wage increase—the one announced to the McCormick Works Council in 1923—was granted during the decade. After that, despite Harvester's prodigious year-after-year profitability, there were no pay hikes at all. Common laborers made no gains whatsoever after the 1923 increase, and most pieceworkers actually saw their wages decline from that point onward. [11]

Since the 1920s were golden at International Harvester—for those at the top—they were gilded years for the McCormicks, still the principal beneficiaries of the company's success. In 1918, the first year that *Forbes* magazine compiled its annual list of the wealthiest Americans, Cyrus McCormick was among the top twenty, with a personal net worth of $60 million. That figure increased substantially in the next decade. Both the company's booming profits and the escalating value of its stock rewarded the family; Cyrus and Harold, in particular, owned a disproportionately large share of Harvester stock that far exceeded the holdings of any other individuals or entities.[12]

But on other fronts for the McCormick family these years proved somewhat less than lustrous. A changing of the guard, or at least a rearrangement of the chairs, had occurred within the corporate offices: in 1918 Harold McCormick stepped into place as Harvester's president. Cyrus remained closely involved with IH, becoming chairman of the corporation's board; it was from this position, for instance, that he exercised oversight over the creation of the Industrial Council Plan. But he was weary after running the company for thirty-five years. He hoped to remove himself from Harvester's day-to-day affairs, perhaps to return to the quiet pleasures gleaned from reading Emerson by a campfire in the Michigan woods, secure in the knowledge that his younger brother would guide the corporation through the next period in its history.

That idea didn't pan out. Bon vivant Harold—fond of bejeweled cufflinks and nights on the town—"preferred the full life," it was said. For a while he dutifully did what was expected of him, graduating from Princeton, doing time in the lower echelons of the company, and marrying really, really well. Due to his intimate Rockefeller connection, Harold played a key supporting role when the International Harvester merger was effected, and had been a corporate vice-president from that point on. But Harold could never muster his brother's singular focus on the family enterprise. It didn't seem like very much fun.[13]

But neither, after several years, was his marriage. Harold and Edith Rockefeller had five children—including one son who would go on to run International Harvester—but Edith was not one for quiet domesticity. Determined to become Chicago's leading socialite, she constructed a cavernous castle on Lake Shore Drive and acquired items like a sixteen-hundred-piece silver-edged table service from Napoleon's court and a million-dollar diamond tiara for her dog. Her excesses horrified her famously parsimonious father—they grew increasingly estranged—and even easygoing Harold was taken aback. Perhaps his sudden illness just before his wedding had been a sign. At any rate the marriage soured, and, in 1921, Edith Rockefeller and Harold McCormick went their separate ways.[14]

A high-profile divorce was titillating enough in those days, but Harold would soon provide the scandalmongers much more fodder. The press went into a frenzy when word leaked that fifty-one-year-old Harold had undergone a "gland transplant"—much in vogue at the time for older men seeking to regain their vigor. Reporters speculated about the origin of McCormick's donated "glands" (testicles, in reality): goats or monkeys were the usual source, but rumors were rife at the time that poor men were surrendering those vital bits of their anatomy in exchange for cash. Hence this reworked Longfellow stanza circulated widely throughout Chicago:

Under the spreading chestnut tree
The village smithy stands
The smith a gloomy man is he;
McCormick has his glands.[15]

Why Harold had subjected himself to such an ordeal soon became clear, for in August 1922 he married a much younger ravishing beauty, the Polish-born aspiring opera diva Ganna Walska, who just a month earlier had been granted a divorce from her third (and also enormously wealthy) husband. Of dubious talent (as a singer, at any rate), Walska was charitably described as a "temperamental" vocalist (during one performance "she veered so persistently off-key that the audience pelted her with rotten vegetables"), but Harold was besotted and did all he could to promote her career, utilizing his influence with Chicago's Civic Opera to ensure she be given leading roles there. For film buffs this may sound vaguely familiar: McCormick's obsessive relationship with Walska would be reimagined by Orson Wells in *Citizen Kane*.[16]

Just as Charles Foster Kane's dalliance with a singer cost him his shot at the governor's mansion, Harold McCormick would pay a price for his infatuation with Walska. This marriage didn't last either, leaving Harold saddled with a hefty divorce settlement.[17] There were consequences within the company as well. The salacious publicity surrounding Harold's private affairs proved too unseemly for the International Harvester board, and most particularly for his far more straightlaced and always business-conscious older brother. Cyrus insisted in 1922 that Harold step down as president; Harold, who hadn't really wanted to run the company in the first place, willingly obliged. But while this maneuver removed Harold from the high-profile presidency, he remained within Harvester's very tight and family-based inner circle. When the IH board of directors accepted Harold's resignation, they also created a brand new "executive committee," comprised of five members of the board, "which will have full charge of the company." The chairman of this entity was none other than Harold McCormick, and naturally his brother Cyrus (still chairman of the full board of directors) was one of the four other members. There were, for the moment, no suitable McCormicks available for the presidency, so IH vice-president Alexander Legge was appointed to the position. A former cowboy with only a few years of formal schooling, Legge traced his roots with Harvester back to 1891 and possessed unquestioned loyalty to the McCormick family. But the next generation of McCormick men were being groomed for leadership: Harold's son Fowler, along with Cyrus III, had joined Harvester's management in the 1920s.[18]

If he read the newspapers, John Becker would have been aware of the McCormicks' wealthy excesses, and perhaps they fueled some of his indignation on the McCormick Works Council. On the other hand, it's possible that Becker, along with his coworkers, thought the off-the-job antics of their bosses had little to do with them. But whether it was readily apparent or not, what was happening inside Harvester's factories fed directly into the McCormicks' material comforts. Because the McCormicks served as directors of the corporation and were its largest stockholders, it was both in their interests and in their purview to ensure that the employees of International Harvester got less, so that they could keep more. Driving labor costs down helped underwrite the gems and the estates and the divorces. The Industrial Council Plan, despite its fair-and-square trappings, proved to be a particularly effective vehicle to accomplish that end.

At least it did for nearly two decades. Harvester's works councils, however, were constructed on a contradiction that ultimately ensured their disintegration. The councils, Cyrus McCormick promised, would promote the common interests of capital and labor. But Harvester executives maintained their absolute authority over wages and shop-floor practices, and employee representatives became mere message-bearers for management. As that reality grew increasingly evident, the works councils were destined to falter.

"I shall only treat with these men as individuals."

So Cyrus McCormick had proclaimed back in 1886, and ever since he had crafted managerial policy to prevent the workers he employed from speaking or acting collectively. The works councils, whatever they promised on paper, did nothing to undermine that principle. But the movement to oust them and replace them with an organization that might serve as a genuine voice for Harvester workers did not, this time, begin at McCormick Works. For the next part of the story we need to move across the street.

The FE's first contract at International Harvester is celebrated in this 1938 cartoon from the *Midwest Daily Record*. [Collection of Toni Gilpin]

Part Two

The FE Lays Down Roots

An aerial view from the 1930s, looking east, depicts relatively new Tractor Works in the foreground, with venerable McCormick Works behind it, near the intersection of Blue Island and Western Avenues on Chicago's Near West Side. The canals in the photo have been filled in and by the late 1970s all the factory buildings had been demolished. [Collection of Toni Gilpin]

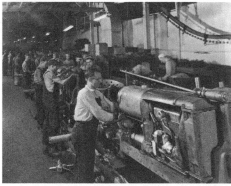

On the Tractor Works assembly line in 1938. [Wisconsin Historical Society, WHS-12234]

Early FE leader and Communist Party organizer Joe Weber (left) and CIO organizer Merlyn Pitzele, after they were arrested during the 1937 Fansteel sit-down strike in North Chicago. The two men soon took divergent paths: Pitzele become labor editor of *Business Week* and a Republican Party advisor. [Collection of Toni Gilpin]

Fowler McCormick, son of Harold McCormick and Edith Rockefeller, stepped into the presidency of International Harvester just before the 1941 strike began. [Wisconsin Historical Society, WHS-34872]

After the second Great Migration began in 1940, African Americans, like these Tractor Works employees, became present in ever-greater numbers at International Harvester's Chicago plants. [Wisconsin Historical Society, WHS-7254]

FE members at Tractor Works on strike in 1941. [Collection of Toni Gilpin]

Chicago police arrest an FE member near McCormick Works during the 1941 strike. [Wisconsin Historical Society, WHS-81708]

Prevented by injunctions from picketing near McCormick Works in 1941, FE members parade through the surrounding neighborhood instead, on Oakley Avenue at 25th Street. Note the police officer filming the crowd near the bottom right. [Collection of Toni Gilpin]

FE members, outside McCormick Works, celebrate victory after the 1941 strike. [Collection of Toni Gilpin]

Assembling equipment for the US Army in Tractor Works in 1941. [Collection of Toni Gilpin]

DeWitt Gilpin (right), on an Army furlough, visits with Jerry Fielde at the 1942 FE convention. Gilpin's movements at the convention were closely tracked by military intelligence agents. [Collection of Toni Gilpin]

In 1946, some thirty thousand FE members went on strike against International Harvester, joining the massive postwar strike wave. [Collection of Toni Gilpin]

6.
The ABCs of Industrial Unionism

They had no money of their own and no Rockefeller relations. No Ivy League networks, or contacts at elite law firms, or friends on newspaper editorial boards. No capital and no clout. Even those who were sympathetic didn't much like their odds: "The hardest job I know of," said labor leader John L. Lewis, when asked about the prospect of organizing at IH. But there are forms of power besides those rooted in wealth. At Tractor Works a determined group came to understand that, and they obliged company officials to hear their demands and negotiate with the workforce as a collective entity. They brought a union—the Farm Equipment Workers—to International Harvester, and they kept it there.

They were able to succeed where John Becker, and before him Myles McPadden and August Spies, could not.

It is not that they were more talented organizers than those who came before. To a large extent, what happened at Harvester in the 1930s reflected a much-changed climate that saw an upsurge in activism and resultant victories for organized labor across the country. While the explosion of Depression-era militancy seemed spontaneous, in many cases it represented an eruption of deep-rooted struggle. Certainly this was the case at Harvester, where a small group of union supporters conducted a clandestine campaign over many years. All of them, quite conscious of what had befallen labor activists in the past, were animated by a profound mistrust of Harvester management; some, as well, were driven by their desire to challenge not only the company but capitalism itself. Organizing IH necessitated a concerted push from both the inside and the outside, laced with a dose of ideological fervor similar to that embraced by August Spies and his anarchist comrades. For John L. Lewis was right: International Harvester, its character defined by Cyrus McCormick's guiding principles, was the toughest industrial giant of them all. General Motors, U.S. Steel, General Electric, Goodyear, and even the fanatically anti-union Ford Motor Company consented to collective bargaining agreements before International Harvester would. And when union organizers finally prevailed at IH, what looked like a sudden breakthrough reflected a legacy of resistance that stretched back nearly a century.

While in the nineteenth century craft unionism had been deeply rooted at the McCormick plant, industrial unionism—the labor movement's adaptation to twentieth-century forms of production—would emerge first at Tractor Works. There were some obvious reasons for this shift in the center of gravity.

Tractor Works stood in the shadow of the McCormick complex, across Western Avenue and just beyond a maze of railroad tracks. But despite the proximity the two plants were quite different. McCormick Works turned out hundreds of disparate implements that would be propelled by an independent source of power; none of them had engines of their own. Given the variety of intricate equipment produced there, large-scale assembly-line production, even once it became widespread throughout American industry, was never practical within the McCormick plant.[1]

Tractor Works, on the other hand, was International Harvester's first modern, one-story manufacturing facility, built from the ground up and opened in 1910. It was exclusively devoted to a single machine befitting the new age of automotive technology: a gasoline-driven tractor, destined to render obsolete the draft horses and mules that had for centuries partnered with farmers in the fields. Within a decade the goal at Tractor Works became "efficient production in quantities"; thus, "every known labor-saving device" was installed and the latest techniques of scientific management were applied so that "every operation, every inspection, every movement consumes the least time and the least cost." By 1928 the McCormicks had vanquished other competitors—including Henry Ford—and produced most of the tractors sold in America.[2]

Tractor Works, in fact, was then Harvester's closest approximation to a Ford-style factory; though not as titanic as Ford's River Rouge complex (which had a workforce of nearly one hundred thousand) it would grow to be plenty big, employing nearly seven thousand at its height. But there remained at least one crucial distinction: workers at Ford received an hourly wage, while most employees at Tractor Works, in keeping with Harvester's long-standing practice, were paid on a piecework basis. As distinct from the McCormick plant, however, group piecework was often the rule at Tractor Works, meaning that earnings were pooled; a single rate readjustment could affect many workers simultaneously, or low production by some workers in a group would offset the higher output of others. Thus, at Tractor Works piecework complaints were often commonly experienced rather than individually endured. These shared grievances would provide a critical impetus for organizing.

"All of the available evidence convincingly demonstrates that the cradle of the present Farm Equipment Workers Union is Tractor Works": so said a 1952 internal report commissioned by Harvester management assessing the genesis of radical unionism in its factories. That "cradle" was initially constructed by members of the Tractor Works Council. "Bitter experience," said the IH report, led several tractor employee representatives to conclude that their works council "was too weak to deal with the Works Management on an equal footing." Many workers at McCormick and no doubt at other Harvester plants believed that as well, but Tractor Works representatives, rather than being deflated by this realization, were galvanized by it. In the late 1920s, Tractor representatives raised a variety of piecework complaints in a Council meeting, but the plant superintendent refused to discuss them. Shortly thereafter the inevitable weeding process took place, as one of the more outspoken representatives was fired. That was one insult too many. As a result of this incident, "an understanding was reached among the works council members that the works council would have to go."[3]

And with that decisive break with management, the movement that would bring genuine industrial democracy to International Harvester was born.

But to understand just what was happening we need to step outside the plant gates and take a good look around, for as all this was brewing inside Tractor Works there were changes afoot in the broader landscape that would alter the sense of the possible for workers everywhere in America. The organizing drive at Tractor Works would gather momentum as the glitter of the 1920s gave way to the grit of the Great Depression. By 1932, one quarter of the American workforce was jobless, but heavily industrialized Chicago was hit even harder, with half the city ill-housed, ill-clad, ill-nourished, and out of work. Those were the official numbers, anyhow, and were merely rough guesses. That things had fallen apart seemed evident everywhere: in the hollow countenances of legions of men shamed by their enforced idleness; the bowed heads of women crowding into relief offices; the bewildered stares from evicted children sitting curbside amidst their belongings. State and local governments were swiftly tapped out, and charities and churches proved incapable of feeding the multitudes who lined up for bread. As desperation mounted one of the town's luminaries, not previously renowned for his generosity—but seriously in need of favorable publicity—stepped into the breach; on Thanksgiving Day 1930, with temperatures plunging below zero, Al Capone's soup kitchen on south State Street provided steaming bowls of stew for five thousand hungry Chicagoans. Not that everyone was suffering: that there were still some whose plates were full—like the McCormick family—did not go unnoticed. "The fields were fruitful," John Steinbeck wrote, "and starving men moved on the roads."[4]

In response to this human catastrophe—and the unconscionable disparities—many working people chose to do more than simply join the lengthening breadlines. After years of quiescence, labor activity exploded during the Depression; hunger marchers demanding relief crowded into city squares, while tumultuous strikes, some confined to one workplace, others engulfing entire cities, became regular occurrences. This collective unrest propelled profound political reformation, first with Franklin Roosevelt's election in 1932 and then through New Deal legislation, some of which provided unprecedented protection for the labor movement. In 1933, the National Industrial Recovery Act guaranteed the right to organize; later, in 1935, the Wagner Act codified unfair labor practices, established the National Labor Relations Board (NLRB) to monitor union elections and compelled employers to bargain with a union endorsed by a majority of the workforce. Union organizers were quick to leverage their newfound—if tenuous—alliance with the federal government. "If I were a factory worker, I would join a union," President Roosevelt declared in 1936, horrifying corporate executives, all the more so as those words began appearing on union leaflets distributed at factory gates.[5]

Workers were snatching up those flyers and signing union membership cards by the thousands, but the leadership of the American Federation of Labor was confounded by all the commotion and disinclined to modify the craft-oriented structure that had defined the AFL since its nineteenth-century founding. But that form of organization—iron molders in one union, carpenters in another—had become increasingly ill-suited for the largely unskilled population in the giant factories where steel, automobiles, and farm equipment were produced, and segmenting those enormous workforces into separate bargaining units would only dilute union strength. Hidebound and often racist AFL officials were also reluctant to welcome "foreigners" or African Americans to their ranks, which ruled out a sizable percentage of the workers clamoring for union representation. One AFL leader, however—John L. Lewis of the United Mine Workers—was a big man with a big vision to organize workers along industrial lines, and, in 1935, he launched the Committee (later Congress) of Industrial Organizations: the CIO. Soon thereafter members of the nascent United Auto Workers–CIO opted for an increasingly popular tactic—the sit-down strike—and scored big victories at General Motors and Chrysler; U.S. Steel officials chose to avoid that sort of disruption and agreed to negotiate with another CIO affiliate, the Steel Workers Organizing Committee (SWOC). Drives in textiles, rubber, meatpacking, electrical equipment and other sectors also resulted in union recognition, and by the late 1930s the CIO claimed nearly four million members.

Though he helped transfigure the American labor movement, John L. Lewis was hardly a revolutionary; he'd been a Republican before the

Depression and he'd go back to being one, in 1940, when FDR made him mad enough. But there were plenty of radicals involved in the CIO. During the Depression, when capitalism appeared to be on the verge (or perhaps past the point) of collapse, the American Communist Party (CP) experienced its period of broadest support and influence, and activists with CP connections—who were of course ideologically committed to mobilizing the working class—proved integral to the union upsurge of the 1930s. They never represented more than a minority within the labor movement, but party members were seasoned, highly effective organizers and the emerging industrial unions became reliant on their skill and dedication. Communists were engaged at the local level in many CIO affiliates but would also take top leadership positions in some unions. The Farm Equipment Workers, when it came into existence, would be one of them.[6]

During the 1930s the sweeping and interrelated changes that occurred in these three arenas—the federal government, the labor movement, and the radical left—reset the power dynamics between American workers and their employers. For union advocates, however, nothing came easily. Back inside the plant gates at International Harvester, the campaign to acquaint company officials with these new realities became the CIO's most protracted struggle.

And within IH the works councils remained solidly entrenched, despite the escalating contempt employees at Tractor Works felt for the one there. When, in 1933, Harvester slashed piecework rates throughout the plant, the worker representatives on the council voiced the widespread discontent to the plant superintendent. Surely they were not shocked by the answer they got: the new pay rates were nonnegotiable.

The representatives convened the next day, away from the plant, to mull over their next move. They agreed they would no longer speak up at council meetings—"to do so was to risk being railroaded out of the shop"—but they also decided not to relinquish their posts. They began gathering for regular poker sessions, during which they plotted "secret organizational activities." The clandestine campaign to subvert the works council was underway—and this was an especially high-stakes game.

The mechanism they constructed to carry out their mission mirrored better-known underground efforts like those of the French Resistance or the Irish Republican Army. Participants in those movements, of course, were risking their lives; Tractor Works Council representatives weren't putting quite that much on the line but their livelihoods were certainly in jeopardy, at a time when jobs of any kind were scarce, and family members were likely dependent on them. And if they were fired from Harvester for union activity they could expect to be blacklisted, making it that much more difficult to find employment elsewhere. So they formed an organization structured to be as impenetrable as possible: the "ABC" union. The "A" group, the nascent union's top leadership, was limited to the five most combative employee representatives on the council, who were known only to each other. The "B" group included all but one of the remaining council members, along with other in-plant leaders. The "C" category encompassed rank-and-file recruits, who would be made aware of other "C" group members in their part of the plant alone, and would have only one "B" group contact. Limiting information in this manner reduced the damage to the network that could be done by management informants. "Like 'underground' movements everywhere, the early union 'conspirators' at Tractor operated by code and group, each man a link in the chain but without knowledge of exactly where the chain led," said an FE publication, reflecting back on this organizing effort. "Out of the talks in the cabbage patches, out of the words spoken over lousy coffee in the cheap restaurants on the West Side, out of the fearful speeches of man and wife in the night with the kids asleep finally came the plan to take over the [works council] and make it a real union." [7]

Steadily, but always in the shadows, the ABC union activists reached out to workers throughout Tractor Works. One such employee was Hank Graber, who got a job at the plant in 1935. He was a sheet metal fabricator tasked with hammering fender corners into place and was, of course, on piecework. "It happened quite often," Graber recalled, "that I'd go home and I'd be black and blue from the waist up, from the hand up to the shoulder, from the vibration of forming these things, trying to make forty cents a piece, by hand." The punishing work prompted Graber to join the ABC effort as soon as he was approached about it; he kicked in his ten cents a month dues payment, and then began recruiting others. It was, as he recounts, "a slow process."

> We would never sign anybody up in the shop. If there was anybody who looked to me like he was pretty good material for the union, I would say, well Sam, or Joe, how about a beer on the way home? Just about everyone would say, sure, why not? And then we'd stop at the tavern, have a drink, and then of course we would talk union. And sign up new members.

"The whole shop never met in any one place," Graber says, for it was not a wise idea for all the ABC's supporters to congregate. Those from his area of the plant met at a bar a few blocks from Tractor Works. "You'd go in the tavern, and look up and down the bar to make sure there wasn't a company stool pigeon there, and then you ordered a beer and walked to the washroom.

By the washroom there was a door going down to the basement, and that's where we'd hold our meetings."[8]

Organizing under such circumstances took guts and a certain hard-headedness, and it helped that some ABC activists were steeled veterans of other protracted struggles. Charlie Lawson was a prime example. Born in Arkansas in 1893, Lawson became a miner when he was just thirteen years old, and roamed across half a dozen states in search of employment. Like his father before him, Lawson joined the United Mine Workers, and became the local president at one of the mines where he worked. There are few who understand the value of solidarity more than miners do, and there are none who are tougher. Lawson learned that as a child:

> As a boy of only five years old, I watched my parents and the many, many other families struggle to feed and clothe us kids. I can see a picture in my memory of being evicted from our homes, to go any place, just so we would be off company property.
>
> A picture of the Union men trying to find such a place, as the company owned most all the land.
>
> A picture of a little tent colony, my mother standing under a huge tree, trying to cook for us kids, hoping that it would not rain, for if it did we would not eat.
>
> A picture of a stockade built around the town with company guards all around.
>
> Yes, this and many more pictures are there to stay, put there by a strike in 1898. Young, you say, to remember. Yes, but go through it once, and I don't think anyone will forget.

Lawson eventually made his way to Chicago; in 1926 he took a job at Tractor Works and soon joined the clandestine campaign at Harvester. Through his long union experience he helped other workers recognize the ABC effort's value. "Organization is one of the greatest things that a working man can have," he told them. "It cannot be measured in dollars and cents."[9]

Both Lawson and Graber managed to keep their jobs while carrying out their ABC duties, but others were not so lucky. "Man after man was fired," the FE related, "and stumbled home to tell the wife that the fight, for them at least, had failed." Yet they persisted, for those who took up the ABC's cause had reached that tipping point when their sense of injustice eclipsed their fears. "Why did they keep it up?" the FE's publication asked. "Because while Harold McCormick was building a plush opera house for a lady he was going to marry, the heat and the speed-up in the Tractor hammer shop was so bad that men cracked up and dived into the water barrel." This juxtaposition between what workers endured and what the McCormicks enjoyed served as motivation for ABC activists and provided them with the talking points they needed to draw in new members.[10]

So the ABC activists within Tractor Works plodded ahead with the tedious but indispensable tasks involved in organizing, gradually expanding their network one conversation at a time. But one man keenly interested in this effort was not on the company's payroll. He shared that familiar antipathy for the McCormicks, but did not confine his hostility to one family alone: he broadened it to include the entire capitalist system. Under his tutelage, others who emerged as union leaders at International Harvester would come to share that perspective.

7.
Red Breakthrough

S ince this is the point at which the Communist Party begins to play an important part in this story, it seems necessary to consider just what it meant that the FE came to be labeled a "communist-dominated" union from almost the instant it was founded.

It is easier, though, to start with what it didn't mean. FE leaflets were not emblazoned with a hammer and sickle; union meetings were devoid of discourses on Leninist precepts; star-spangled American flags, rather than solid red ones, were unfurled at FE gatherings. When the FE's constitution was drafted, its prosaic goals failed to mention seizure of the means of production. Genuine card-carrying communists never constituted more than a small fraction of the union's membership, and throughout the FE's existence none of its leaders would admit to, much less proudly profess, a connection to the Communist Party. And while they engaged in some recruitment early on, after the 1930s those FE leaders who were also communists made no wholesale push to entice the rank and file to join the Party.[1]

The "red" reputation of the FE, then, along with the dozen-and-a-half other unions that would be similarly labeled, rested primarily on the political positions taken by the leaderships of those organizations from the late 1930s onward. In other words, if the editorials in a union's newspaper seemed in sync with those in the *Daily Worker*—the American Communist Party's official organ—that provided confirmation, for anti-communist crusaders anyhow, of direct control by the Soviet Union. But on issues of domestic and foreign policy, as will later become clear, there was not always unanimity within the FE leadership, and likewise there were openly stated, sometimes vehement, differences of opinion on such matters between FE officials and those in the other unions said to be in the CP's orbit. So any party "domination" of either the FE or the left labor movement more broadly was highly variable and imperfectly imposed at best.[2]

Yet while it was not commanded by the Communist Party, the FE at all levels was profoundly influenced by it. A reasonably held fear of repression kept FE officials—like nearly all "red" unionists—from publicly acknowledging their party ties, however ethically or strategically debatable such equivocation might have been.[3] But in fact the key leaders of the FE were members of, or sympathetic to, the Party when the union was founded, and that remained the case for years afterwards. Their CP involvement provided them with a grounding in Marxist analysis, a dedication to racial solidarity, and a belief in perpetual class conflict that would shape their political worldview and define all aspects of their engagement with International Harvester. Like their anarchist counterparts in the 1880s who preceded them, these twentieth-century radicals were zealous and unflagging, and their affiliation with a larger movement similarly sustained them and instilled discipline through what proved to be a drawn out, and frequently discouraging, campaign. But all that came at a price, as the FE leadership's efforts to comport with the often illogical twists and turns of Communist Party policy—much of it determined in Moscow—gave credence to the assertions that the union was in thrall to the Soviet Union.[4]

In many respects Communist Party activists were like followers of the Catholic Church: adherents of a hierarchical organization in which directives from on high are expected to be followed without question. But just like Catholics, Communist Party members—and especially those in the FE—were not absolutely devout; they embraced some doctrines with enthusiasm, while others were accepted only grudgingly, and some were rejected outright, though not necessarily publicly. Such selective application of dogma, however, was not indicative of any lessening of faith in the Communist Party specifically or the communist cause generally (Catholics who go their own way on birth control, for instance, can still consider themselves steadfastly Catholic). Until, that is, individual FE leaders began to break decisively with the Party—but that comes much later in the story.[5]

Suffice to say for now that the Communist Party's influence on the FE was complicated—sometimes good, sometimes bad, and often downright ugly—but it was always deeply relevant, and as the Communist Party shaped the union so too it affected the response from International Harvester. For the grudge match between this powerful company and this radical union hinged on something more fundamental than how much workers should get paid: it came to be a struggle for control over the very nature of work itself.

Cyrus McCormick II had boiled down the essence of the Russian Revolution succinctly: the Soviet government asserted control over "the entire management," and Harvester's losses in Russia only underscored the calamitous consequences, for capitalists anyhow, of such a one-sided approach. Shortly after its formation in 1919 the American Communist Party expressly acknowledged it would take direction from the Soviet-led Communist International. American Communists thus joined a revolutionary movement unlike any before it, for this one was abetted by the patronage of a sovereign foreign government: no wonder McCormick and his fellow businessmen were so uneasy. Through the first decade of its existence, however, the American CP was wracked by factional infighting—much of it tied to the leadership struggle in the USSR—and by the end of the 1920s there were fewer than eight thousand party members nationwide, most of them foreign-born and residents of east coast cities. The prosperity of the 1920s, however unevenly experienced, seemed to have thwarted any insurrectionist impulses among American workers, especially in the heartland. Industrialists in the United States grew confident that there would be no storming of the barricades here.[6]

And then the stock market collapsed, and they weren't so sure anymore.

During the Great Depression many who witnessed, or lived, the abject misery visited on the masses were drawn to the transformative promise of the Communist Party, and by the end of the 1930s the Party was recruiting thirty thousand new members a year, most of them, by that point, native-born Americans. Missourian DeWitt Gilpin was one of them. He was in his late teens when the Depression began; as his family often went hungry, he experienced "the shock, the confusion, the hurt that many kids felt about their fathers not being able to provide for them." But even more he was affected by witnessing his father—a skilled carpenter—degraded by an incessant struggle to secure any sort of work, "when the nation needed houses and his craftsmanship could have been used."[7]

Like Cyrus McCormick II, Gilpin was the firstborn in a large family, and both men remained acutely conscious of how much their fathers' aspirations—in one case thwarted, in the other richly realized—had shaped their own paths through life. But while the Gold Coast heir could travel his course in style, the carpenter's son rode less comfortably. By the time he was twenty, Gilpin had left home—one less mouth to feed would mean a bit more for his younger siblings—and was walking, hitchhiking, or riding the rails from town to town. He became impressed by the CP-affiliated Unemployed Councils, which instigated many of the marches, eviction protests, and labor actions that marked the early Depression years. The first strike Gilpin ever witnessed was among miners in southern Missouri, organized by Unemployed Council members. "I watched the meeting of the miners broken up by the local police and vigilantes," Gilpin recalled. "Like most strikes of the period, it made more of a political than an economic point. There was a lot of publicity in the St. Louis *Post-Dispatch* and other papers [that] pointed up the miserable conditions of the miners." He was convinced that the pressure applied by the Unemployed Councils "laid the basis for much of the New Deal legislation." But another lesson that stuck with him was the councils' willingness to improvise: "They sort of threw away the rule book and just organized people to get something to eat." The councils, he believed, "attracted people who subsequently became labor organizers, particularly in the CIO."[8]

But while the cataclysmic Depression radicalized some, like Gilpin, others had adopted their class consciousness well before the crash. Indeed, the key Communist Party organizer at International Harvester—in fact, the central player in the FE's early history—was making his pitch to workers in Chicago before Gilpin ever set foot there. Joe Weber was never employed at an IH plant, though he had lived for many years within walking distance of the McCormick and Tractor Works complex, aware of the bitter events that had transpired there decades before. "I grew up with the tradition of Haymarket," he said. But he was not a native Chicagoan: born in 1904, Weber emigrated with his family from Yugoslavia as a boy, and retained a trace of a Slavic accent throughout his life. In his teens he apprenticed as a machinist, and left Chicago shortly thereafter, picking up jobs around the country. While on the road, he discovered his true calling: organizing for the Communist Party. His parents took a dim view of his activities, and so they were relieved when at some point during this period he dropped his family name—Ruich—and became Joe Weber instead. He honed his skills in Russia, spending a good portion of 1929 in Moscow, probably at the International Lenin School, where a select group of party activists from around the world studied Marxism in theory and practice (there Weber "majored in strike strategy and revolutionary tactics," proclaimed the *Chicago Tribune*, but sadly failed to indicate what other majors—marine biology? business administration?—he might have chosen instead).[9]

Upon his return to the United States, Weber migrated for a while around tough territory for radical activists, striding directly into situations that those less committed would have skirted. A journalist described a ride he took in early 1932 with Weber, on his way to address a miners' union rally in Harlan County, Kentucky, where simply speaking up could be tantamount to a death sentence:

> As we entered Harlan we were met by a couple of miners, who told us that the mass meeting had been surrounded by sheriff's deputies— John Henry Blair's deputies; that machine guns were posted back of a newly built barricade of rocks overlooking the mass meeting, and these machine guns were trained on the speakers' stand, and that the deputies had gone up to the crowd and told them that as soon as Weber got there they would turn the machine guns loose on him and shoot him to pieces.
>
> Weber insisted on going through and making an attempt to speak anyway, and as we came through the Harlan streets we could

see the crowd being dispersed by the deputies. So, since the crowd was dispersed, Weber turned around and I went with him back to Pineville.[10]

Weber escaped injury that day, but shortly thereafter wasn't so fortunate. On a moonless night, Harlan County deputies clubbed Weber into insensibility and then dumped him in a ditch off a lonely tree-lined back road; he lay there unconscious for three days before other union supporters found him. After he recovered he left Kentucky, but his sojourn in the state would not have improved his opinion of capitalism, or, more specifically, of the McCormick family. The beating administered to Weber took place just outside Benham, Kentucky, the town entirely owned by International Harvester; its nearby mine produced coal for IH factories. Joe Weber may have lost that round, but the McCormicks would be hearing from him again, next time a little closer to home.[11]

The pay was lousy and the working conditions were hazardous but Weber loved his work nonetheless. A later photograph of him, following another of his many arrests (in this case, following a violent and consequential sit-down strike at the Fansteel Corporation in North Chicago) depicts a tall man with a middleweight's physique, unruly blond hair falling over his forehead, his large hands gripping the prison bars of his jail cell. His head is slightly cocked and he is grinning broadly, as though he is exactly where he wants to be.[12]

Even those who didn't care for Weber's politics were obliged to acknowledge his leadership abilities. One anti-communist union official described Weber as "quite an orator," the type who, "even if you didn't know him . . . he could convince you." He was, in short, "a very persuasive guy." In his Depression-era novel *Citizens*, the former *Chicago Daily News* reporter Meyer Levin included a character who is a thinly disguised alter ego for Joe Weber. That "Frank Sobol" is a radical is of little consequence to one of the workers in the book; his organizing talent is all that matters. "I don't care if Frank is a Communist or a Zulu," the worker says. "I don't give a hoot in hell . . . if he killed his grandmother, dammit he's a good union man and he can sign them up faster than any six of us . . ." By the end of 1932 Weber would be employing those powers of persuasion back in his hometown, as he returned to Chicago as an official with the Communist Party–directed Trade Union Unity League (TUUL). Created as the Depression began (and before the CIO was formed), the TUUL endeavored to build "dual" revolutionary industrial unions, to compete with the AFL's craft-based and decidedly nonrevolutionary ones: another iteration of the Chicago Idea. Weber focused on recruiting workers for the TUUL-affiliated Steel and Metal Workers' International Union (SM-WIU)—and, when possible, to get them to join the Communist Party itself—and as part of his mission he set his sights on the plants that dominated his old neighborhood: McCormick and Tractor Works.[13]

Yet even the most spellbinding communicator would have his work cut out for him at International Harvester, especially one who aimed not only to build union support but to promote enthusiasm for the Communist Party as well. There were, at best, perhaps four CP members in all of Tractor Works in the early 1930s. But the ABC effort was underway and Weber wasted little time connecting with the workers involved with it and acquainting them with the party-affiliated SMWIU. Though there was no vote of formal affiliation, "we were able to merge the activities of the company union and the [SMWIU]," Weber said. By early 1934 the SMWIU, according to the *Party Organizer* (a CP publication), was "carrying on a united front policy [with the ABC union]. As a result of this work we have been able to get about fifteen workers into our union so far, and the leadership of the A.B.C. has also joined our union." The leaders of the ABC organization, it bears repeating, were all works council representatives, so it seems apparent that an extraordinary transformation, albeit under the radar, had taken place. The Tractor Works Council—designed by International Harvester's management to serve its interests—had become, in practice, a Communist Party–affiliated labor organization.[14]

And this served Weber's other purpose, which was to enlist people into the Communist Party itself. "Every active member of the union," Harvester's internal report claims, was approached about party membership. Several of the people Weber recruited out of Tractor Works in these early years became central to the organizing drive and remained within union leadership thereafter, including Italian American Anthony Cavorso and African American Pleass Kellogg. And one of Weber's other key contacts—a level-headed engineer who began working for Harvester in 1928—got elected as a works council representative and soon became one of the principal ABC leaders behind the unionization effort in the plant. His name was Grant Oakes.[15]

By 1934 there were enough CP members within Tractor Works to warrant holding their own meetings, where they discussed shop issues that could be pressed through the ABC union. Whether these party klatches were nefarious or legitimate depended on your point of view. At ABC meetings, said Harvester's internal report, the demands developed by party members "were advanced as the 'spontaneous' and urgent desires of the districts represented by the delegates in question," and thus CP supporters were "by their unity controlling the program of the Union." Or, to put a different spin on it, they were engaged in the painstaking process of organizing. "No grievance of the workers, no matter how petty it may seem to us, is too small for our Party to give the closest attention to it," claimed a *Party Organizer* report about Tractor Works. "We of course discuss concrete conditions in the shop—just exactly what is happening in this and that department . . . we discuss how we can develop struggles in the departments around these developments."

And these efforts were proving effective. "The foremen no longer bully the workers nor swear at them as they used to before we became active," the *Party Organizer* insisted. "How did we do that? We organized a simultaneous agitation in all departments against the foremen's slave-driving bullying tactics. . . . Immediately, the workers notice that the foremen go easier on them." This could be written off as mere party puffery, but Harvester officials were increasingly aware that something they didn't like was going on within Tractor Works and were obliged to respond to the pressure. In early 1934 a special meeting, held away from the plant, brought together several top company officials with Tractor's employee representatives—a.k.a. ABC unionists, at least some of whom were also CP members. A week later, as "a result of ABC union activity," Harvester's report conceded, the widely detested Works superintendent was ousted from his job. That victory provided "impetus to the organization drive," which was probably putting it mildly.[16]

Harvester officials soon received further evidence—if they needed any—that they'd lost control of the works council at Tractor Works. In mid-1934, when the US Senate was in the midst of hearings that would, a year later, result in the Wagner Act, IH brought employee representatives from McCormick Works and Wisconsin Steel to Washington to vouch for the legitimacy of Harvester's works councils. Their counterparts from Tractor Works, however, refused to go. In his testimony before the committee, Harvester vice-president William Elliott insisted that his employees were thoroughly satisfied with the Industrial Council Plan. But when pressed he had to admit that at Tractor Works, "some converts are being made by this vigorous and, to some extent, inaccurate campaign which is being made to convert them to other forms of organization."[17]

Indeed, by this point, the ABC activists had gained enough converts to provide their "other form of organization" with a real name. Around the same time, the Communist Party's top leadership shifted gears and by 1935 openly embraced the Popular Front, meaning that the CP's sectarian agenda was jettisoned in favor of cooperative interaction with other progressive groups and fulsome support for the New Deal. So the SMWIU became defunct, which no doubt made things a bit clearer for the activists within

Tractor Works. Union advocates—communist or not—were now focused on building one organization at International Harvester: the Farm Equipment Workers Association (FEWA).

With a legitimate name FEWA began to function like a bona fide union. When, at a Tractor Works Council meeting in 1936, the representatives demanded a ten-cent wage increase, they refused this time to take no for an answer, and brought means of persuasion besides their debating prowess to bear: "About 1,500 workers of the first shift stood around the office waiting for the results of our meeting," one of the FEWA members later related in a letter. "You ought to see the white and trembling faces on some of [the] officials, boy it sure was great to see that big crowd milling around." He added, "It looks like our secrecy is about all gone to the dogs," a reasonable assumption. The show of strength led the company to offer a five-cent increase. The employee representatives chose not to respond immediately, indicating that they'd bring management's proposal to a meeting to be held the next night at a nearby union hall. At that gathering thirty-five hundred Tractor Works employees— more than half the workforce, all of them members of the once-underground union—packed the building; they voted to accept the five-cent increase as FEWA leaders pledged to continue pressing for the remaining nickel. A few months later, in fact, the company granted the additional five cents.[18]

Business as usual was no longer being practiced at Tractor Works.

"This incident clearly reveals the fact that the union membership had grown to the point where the overwhelming majority of the employees belonged to the union," Harvester's internal report stressed, "and the union was in a position to make its weight felt even though it was not recognized by the company." That would be FEWA's next step—the push for formal recognition from International Harvester. And that prospect appeared more promising, for a potent new organization had emerged to lend encouragement to Harvester workers: the CIO. Not that the CIO was yet able to provide much material support, as Tractor Works activist Hank Graber recalls:

> I think it was in 1936 we sent a delegation to see John L. Lewis, who was visiting in Chicago at the time, and staying at the Blackstone Hotel. We sent a delegation there to get help in organizing International Harvester. "Well," he said, "I tell you fellows. I have so many things cooking; I need organizers, and I just don't have enough to go around. Another thing—you fellows are bucking up against the worst anti-union lousy outfit I can think of. It's going to be the hardest job I know of to win an election at Harvester. But," he said, "I tell you what. I can give you a couple hundred bucks and God help you."

Well, we took the couple of hundred dollars and went out and did the organizing, but without the help of God, of course.[19]

If FEWA couldn't count on God's intervention at least it now had the imprimatur of John L. Lewis—for many American workers in this era, that was nearly as good—along with something else that mattered a great deal: the services of Joe Weber. Lewis, regardless of what the bosses sputtered, was no communist; he was "radical only in the sense that conservatism cannot organize the masses." But he was shrewd above all else. So to appeal to those masses Lewis pulled in the Communist Party's best and brightest, and Weber was one of them. He was tapped to become one of the principal leaders of the Steel Workers Organizing Committee (SWOC)—the precursor of the United Steelworkers of America—in the Chicago area. Weber focused much of his attention on the notorious "Little Steel" companies that lay along an industrial crescent on the lower edge of Lake Michigan from south Chicago into Indiana. But with Lewis's blessing Weber was also urged to continue his efforts to assist the unionization drive at International Harvester. He was more than happy to oblige.[20]

So long as FEWA remained confined to Tractor Works, the company simply could not be compelled to concede very much, and would certainly refuse to extend formal recognition to the union. Weber knew that, and FEWA advocates, since at least 1934, had been in touch with union sympathizers at other IH plants in Illinois and in other states. And, of course, FEWA had been making overtures to neighboring McCormick Works, still Harvester's bastion that any organizing campaign would need to breach. These contacts were stepped up when FEWA officially joined the CIO in early 1937, and to help extend the union beachhead Weber appointed a new staff member out of strategically vital McCormick Works—machinist and former employee representative Jerry Fielde—and named him codirector of the Harvester campaign.[21]

But if for the moment Harvester officials refused to acknowledge the desires of their employees at Tractor Works, there was a more powerful entity they could not so cavalierly disregard, however much they tried: the federal government. Having nurtured its works councils for nearly two decades, Harvester feverishly endeavored to preserve them (hence that company-sponsored foray to Washington in hopes that loyal employee representatives could sway Senator Wagner's committee) in the face of a rising public tide favoring genuine workplace democracy. That egalitarian sentiment was embodied in the National Labor Relations Board, a creature of the 1935 Wagner Act. In one of its very first rulings, the NLRB delivered, in November 1936, a scathing indictment of Harvester's Industrial Council Plan, declaring it "entirely the creature of the management." The works councils were ordered to be disbanded. That ruling didn't sit well with IH officials, who pretended they hadn't heard it while big business groups challenged the constitutionality of the Wagner Act (and hence the authority of the NLRB). Their foot-dragging continued into the spring of 1937, when the Supreme Court's *Jones-Laughlin* decision upheld the Wagner Act and for good measure reiterated that employee representation schemes, like Harvester's, were inherently subject to company domination and thus unlawful.[22]

It's worth noting that at the same time Harvester officials were doing all they could to subvert the Wagner Act, the company was benefiting from other components of the New Deal. The collapse of American agriculture, manifested by the grim westward trek of disoriented families driven from the land, had proved calamitous for farm equipment manufacturing in the early 1930s; during those initial lean years, Harvester suffered profit losses and layoffs were extensive. But federal intervention taken by FDR's administration to assist the nation's farmers propped up IH as well. Harvester's net profits recovered, employees were recalled to work, and by 1937 sales were surpassing pre-Depression records.[23]

The *Jones-Laughlin* ruling should have been it, finally, for the works councils, and following the decision Harvester did in fact officially terminate them. But like zombies the councils were not easily finished off. Overnight, literally, "independent" unions—called "Mutuals" or "Employee Associations"—sprang up at IH plants, led by employee representatives who had remained loyal to the company. Harvester promptly granted them exclusive bargaining rights.[24]

But the same old company union machine, merely sporting a new coat of paint, was going to be a tough sell at Tractor Works. By early 1938 FEWA had morphed into the Farm Equipment Workers Organizing Committee— underscoring its connection to the CIO—with Joe Weber as its director (and in 1942 its name was altered slightly again, as FEWOC became the full-fledged Farm Equipment and Metal Workers Union; for simplicity's sake it will be "FE" from here on). Weber called on labor's new ally in Washington to settle the matter of just who should represent employees at Tractor Works; an NLRB-supervised election, set for February 24, 1938, would pit the FE against the former company union, now called the "Employees' Mutual Association." An FE victory would mean "*Strife Hunger Communism Strikes*," warned a Mutual flyer distributed before the vote.[25]

Tractor Works employees had heard that before—from management. They were ready for something else. More than five thousand workers voted in the NLRB election and more than two-thirds of them indicated that they wanted the FE to represent them. This government-sanctioned exercise in democracy could not be ignored or superseded: with the official designation of FE Local 101 at Tractor Works, genuine union representation was now a reality at International Harvester. FE organizers had managed to pull off what John L. Lewis thought might be an impossible job—they'd won an election at "the worst anti-union lousy outfit" he could think of.[26]

A month later Harvester officials sat down with Joe Weber and other FE members to lend their signatures to an agreement, which granted little at this point beyond sole bargaining rights at Tractor Works to the FE. Yet it represented a monumental achievement. For the first time since Cyrus McCormick set out to break the molders' union back in the mid-nineteenth century, when he vowed that he would "only treat with these men as individuals," International Harvester was now forced to negotiate with an organization that represented the collective voice of the workforce, even if for the moment just in one plant. And those at the helm of the FE bore an uncomfortable resemblance to the radical agitators who fifty years earlier had been sent to the gallows. Joe Weber was well aware of the historical irony—or poetic justice—in evidence when, as he put it, "a known communist, or [someone] identified as a communist was able to sign the first contract with International Harvester since the struggles of 1886."[27]

The direct line from Haymarket to the FE was also underscored in the April 1938 issue of the Communist Party–sponsored *Midwest Daily Record*, by its labor reporter, DeWitt Gilpin:

> Today in International Harvester you can walk up to any supervisor on the lunch hour and say:
> "Those Haymarket Martyrs, in my opinion, Super, had the right idea—unionism, solidarity."
> And you won't get fired or thrown into jail . . .
> Today is a day for heroes, our heroes. Spies, Parsons, and their comrades . . . their martyrdom had ground into the minds of workers the worth of a union, for the McCormicks . . . have proved they imprison and murder to end one.

August Spies in particular would become a macabre mascot of sorts for the fledgling union. A month after the Tractor Works contract had been signed, FE supporters planned a May Day march to Haymarket Square. They would carry a banner bearing Spies's last utterance—*"There will come a time when our silence is more powerful than the voices you are strangling today"*—and Spies himself would be with them, at least as personified by the union member portraying him, standing atop a float with a black hood over his head and noose around his neck. "I wish Cyrus could read them!" said one longtime Tractor Works employee at the march, referring to the words on the FE banner.[28]

But the person for whom the 1938 resurrection of Spies was most pointedly aimed was no longer around to receive the message. Two years earlier, when he was seventy-seven years old, Cyrus McCormick II had been felled by a heart attack. He had remained on Harvester's board until a few months before his death, and might have wished for time to enjoy his retirement, but at least he got many more years than his nemesis August Spies had been allotted. Spies had sacrificed his life for a cause while McCormick had poured his into his company, their biographies forever fused by the deadly projectile that blew apart in that gloomy Chicago square in 1886. But they were connected, as well, through their lingering presence at International Harvester. McCormick's influence, of course, was obvious: the production methods he introduced, and the antipathy to unions he promulgated, would govern policy at Harvester as long as the company existed. Those ongoing practices, though, in large part evolved out of McCormick's efforts to protect management prerogatives from the challenge presented by the anarchists and their radical Chicago Idea. That threat had been extinguished along with Spies; that's at least what Cyrus McCormick labored assiduously to ensure.[29]

Yet, as Spies had promised, the subterranean embers had been rekindled, and in 1938 the fire threatened to spread. Joe Weber had recruited a network of local leaders who shared his radical proclivities and his determination to hoist the CIO's flag over Harvester's other plants. They came directly from the ranks and were "relevant, immediate, and fearless"—the leadership traits that matter most to a resentful and restless workforce.[30]

Pivotal though he was, however, Weber would not remain in the FE's leadership for long. The farm equipment industry was not his only target; as a SWOC director he had been immersed in the drive to organize the steel mills of south Chicago. The executives at the Little Steel companies eschewed more genteel forms of union avoidance, favoring instead the tried and true tactics of thuggery and terror. Tom Girdler, head of Republic Steel, stockpiled a massive private arsenal along with a vigilante force of four hundred men. But as it turned out Girdler didn't have to waste his own ammunition, for on Memorial Day in 1937, as striking steelworkers, families, and supporters assembled in a field near the Republic mill, Chicago police officers, intent on doing serious damage, careened into the crowd. In the frenzy to escape, people tumbled over each other, but some were not fast enough; "The police surrounded the fallen mass of men and women," said a US Senate report detailing what would come to be known in labor circles as the Memorial Day Massacre, "clubbing them as they attempted to rise." Many of the workers were beaten senseless, skulls split wide open and eyeballs dislodged from their sockets, while at least forty suffered bullet wounds. Ten strikers were killed by the police, seven shot down from behind while the others were hit in the side; all of them felled as they vainly tried to flee. Even once the gunfire faded the cruelty continued, as the police blockaded automobiles that had been hastily converted into ambulances and yanked out the injured passengers so they might be placed under arrest. One of those strikers had been shot in the thigh; in the process of tossing him into a patrol wagon the officers pulled loose a crude tourniquet, fashioned from someone's belt, that had stanched the flow from his severed artery. He died not long thereafter, his blood pouring out onto the floor of the wagon and saturating the clothing of the other battered workers who lay beside him.[31]

Joe Weber was not present at the melee, but he had been one of the main speakers at a rally held a short time before the violence began. In keeping with the way these things usually work, the local press held the union responsible for the tragedy; the *Chicago Tribune*'s banner headline proclaimed, "Two HELD AS RIOT LEADERS," and Joe Weber was one of those two SWOC "agitators" singled out. As he was interrogated for several days in the police station, Weber's thoughts may have drifted to another workers' gathering in Chicago, a half-century earlier, that also ended in bloodshed. What had been the case for the Haymarket anarchists was also true for him: his words, not his deeds, were his offense, for Weber was, according to the *Tribune*, "chairman of the meeting at which the strikers were so inflamed that they attacked the police . . ."[32]

Despite the *Tribune*'s braying accusations Weber would be spared the anarchists' grim fate, for at Republic Steel it was stubbornly apparent—not least because there was newsreel footage of the clash—that the Chicago police had been not the victims but the instigators of the savagery unleashed that Memorial Day. Weber was released, and for a time was able to continue his organizing activities. Yet the notoriety he garnered due to the "massacre" meant Weber's troubles were far from over, because he had something else in common with many in that earlier contingent of Chicago radicals: the "alien" status conferred on those born outside the United States. Following passage of the Smith Act in 1940, which allowed for the deportation of noncitizens who maintained memberships in "subversive" organizations like the Communist Party, FBI and immigration agents began to evidence particular interest in Joe Weber. Their attention was abetted by the *Tribune*, which regularly labeled Weber a "communist labor dictator" and a "conspirator in the Memorial day riots." Weber, soon battling the threat of both imprisonment and deportation, was forced to retreat from union activities.[33]

This contest proved exhausting and expensive for Weber as well as the organization he helped found, since the FE spearheaded his defense. It would not be the last time the FE would be obliged to divert its meager resources on behalf of a union leader hounded by the authorities. Ultimately, in 1950, Weber was fined and sentenced to serve a year in jail, but allowed to remain in the United States. His union career, though, was over; he returned to work as a machinist and moved to California in the late 1950s. Being beaten nearly to death in Harlan County hadn't stopped Joe Weber, but government harassment did: the man who could "sign them up faster" than nearly anyone else could organize no longer.[34]

Yet Joe Weber exerted outsized influence on the FE. His sustained focus on International Harvester, beginning in the early 1930s, helped establish an organizing nucleus that could expand when conditions for unionization grew more favorable. He cultivated capable and committed Harvester workers who would rise to assume critical leadership roles within the FE. And in many of them he instilled (or at least fortified) a class-conscious radicalism, manifested by their association with the Communist Party, that laid the framework for the organization they would construct.[35]

To build a union, however, FE leaders needed more than the foothold they'd established in 1938 at Tractor Works. They could conjure up August Spies all they wanted, but International Harvester was also keeping the soul of Cyrus McCormick alive and kicking back, hard. As the Depression decade drew to a close, it was unclear whose spirit would prevail. Many of the leading corporations in the country—including all of Harvester's preeminent partners on the Special Conference Committee—had grudgingly accommodated industrial unionism. Not so at IH, where Harvester management—soon to have a new McCormick running the show—would use every last method at its disposal to forestall the union's advance. The FE, headed now by Grant Oakes and Jerry Fielde, brought on extra personnel to help coordinate the fight. One of these new additions arrived from Detroit, where he'd already garnered legendary status for his left-wing views and his anti-management militancy. At the FE he fit right in.

The battle waged for company-wide recognition, however, would drag on for several more years; before it was resolved a much larger war, fought overseas, was underway.

8.
New Feet under the Table

s the giddiness over their 1938 electoral triumph at Tractor Works sub-
sided, FE supporters looked to the fortress across the street, the fluores-
cent letters on its giant tower beaming "McCormick" across Chicagoland
as darkness fell. No matter how many factories, mines, and mills International Harvester's burgeoning empire might encompass, McCormick Works
remained its citadel and until it was organized no union at IH could be fully
legitimate. But following their lopsided victory in the adjacent facility there
was reason for confidence. "The CIO intends to bring the same conditions to
McCormick that we have established in Tractor Works," said Jerry Fielde, just
after the FE signed its first contract with IH. They would be "pressing for a
speedy election in the plant to secure real bargaining rights."[1]

Of course, "speedy" is a relative term. In this case, it meant more than
three years.

The delay was Harvester's doing. To stave off unionization Tom Girdler at Republic Steel spent his money on guns; executives at International
Harvester opted for high-priced legal help, which proved to be a better investment. First the company set out to defend the "independent" unions, in
place at McCormick Works and thirteen other plants, that sprang into existence when the works councils were declared unlawful. Nobody was fooled:
Harvester "dominated and interfered with" the independents, said the National Labor Relations Board, which ordered them disbanded immediately.[2]

That ruling was inevitable, but Harvester's attorneys had managed to
forestall it until February 1941. And yet even with the independents out of
the way the FE still would not have an open field. Following the NLRB's
decision, the American Federation of Labor, which had not been engaged in
organizing activities at Harvester, abruptly claimed jurisdiction over several
Harvester plants. FE leaders charged that Harvester was behind this move,
that the same old works councils "had been taken in by the AFL and given a
union label to hide their company union moves behind." The sudden arrival
of the AFL on the scene certainly complicated the FE's recognition drive,
as it allowed Harvester officials to throw up their hands and claim it was
unclear which union, if any, its employees preferred.[3]

By this point FE Local 101 at Tractor Works represented the largest
CIO local in Chicago, but that fact provided cold comfort. Harvester's

stalling techniques had successfully checked the union's momentum; in fact, CIO advances in general stagnated toward the end of the 1930s as an economic downturn resulted in widespread layoffs. The New Deal order itself seemed to be deteriorating in the face of widespread conservative and corporate resistance, with the situation at IH providing a case in point. Before 1941, the FE had managed to win an NLRB election at just one additional IH plant, in Richmond, Indiana. To jump-start the union drive—indeed, to keep it from petering out altogether—securing recognition at McCormick Works was essential. Yet FE leaders remained uncertain about the depth of their support there, so calling for an election at the massive plant seemed awfully risky at this moment, now that the AFL—which would receive the company's tacit backing, as the much lesser of two evils—would be on the ballot. But how else might the FE wangle a win at McCormick Works?[4]

This was the conundrum facing the FE's leadership, reconstituted now that Joe Weber had largely left the scene. Grant Oakes had become the union's president while Jerry Fielde stepped into position as secretary-treasurer. Fielde was an organizing dynamo, spreading the FE gospel at agricultural implement plants throughout the Midwest, and in particular at the sizable Caterpillar tractor plant in Peoria, Illinois. To keep up the press in Chicago, by 1941 the FE had taken on new personnel. DeWitt Gilpin stopped writing about the FE to write for it, as he became the union's educational and publicity director. Milt Burns would come on board as a field representative. Burns and Gilpin had worked together previously at the *Midwest Daily Record*, and they had something else in common: both were protégés and close friends of Joe Weber. Burns had gotten to know him in Chicago and Gilpin first met Weber when they'd crossed paths in Detroit some years before.

And the FE's leadership team would for a short period in 1941 be bolstered by someone with experience transforming a determined minority into a commanding majority. Bob Travis was one of the principal architects of the 1936 United Auto Workers sit-down strike against General Motors in Flint, Michigan. Hailing from Toledo, Ohio, Travis never got past eighth grade, but possessed the strategic intuition he would have been unlikely to pick up in any school, except possibly at a military one. He was also mentored by Communist Party member Wyndham Mortimer, a former coal miner and Ohio autoworker who'd become a top official of the nascent UAW. It was Mortimer who assigned Travis, then just thirty years old, the Herculean task of organizing GM, which by the early 1930s had eclipsed Ford as the world's predominant auto manufacturer and employed nearly seventy thousand at its colossal multiplant complex in Flint.

Travis understood class warfare literally: Arrayed on one side stands "a well oiled, well disciplined outfit" armed with "all the hideous advantages of modern warfare—airplanes, poison gas, machine guns, long range guns, and hand grenades, and last but not least, their secret service." Facing the forces of capital "we see scattered battalions, unskilled . . . in this modern warfare, armed with bows and arrows, spears and swords," he said. "These men are doomed to defeat," Travis argued, "unless they concentrate their armies to enter upon the field equipped to fight fire with fire . . ."[5]

So Travis developed his formula for Flint. Using a template lifted from previous workers' actions in nearby places like Detroit and Akron and in spots more distant like Poland and France, disseminated via the Communist Party, he determined that autoworkers should occupy, rather than picket, several critical facilities in the General Motors complex. When the police endeavored to oust the sit-downers from one plant, he led the counterattack, bombarding the officers with the ready supply of metal auto parts to force their retreat. And Travis successfully subverted GM's extensive spy network, confiding to some workers, whom he knew to be company informants, of a secret plan to take over another plant in the complex. As police and company guards were hastily dispatched to the decoy, a small group of workers seized their real target—Chevrolet #4, the largest and, until that moment, most heavily secured plant in the General Motors empire. The takeover was decisive: within a week, GM's management capitulated, granting the UAW bargaining rights to end the forty-four-day strike. Travis had fought fire with fire, and won.[6]

Despite this epic achievement, factionalism and the increasing dominance of anti-communists within the UAW meant that by 1941 Bob Travis, with his CP connections, was on the outs with the union he'd helped establish. But he was welcomed by the FE leadership in Chicago. His job description at first was a bit fuzzy. "He's going to work for the FE, but where?" said Clarence Stoecker, a rank-and-file activist at McCormick Works, recalling the initial conversations.

> And Bob solved the problem. He said, what's the toughest plant you've got? And they all laughed at him . . . and they said, well, we've got one that's impossible—McCormick Works. And Bob was adamant about it. He says, McCormick's the worst one, the toughest one? Then give me McCormick.[7]

As FE leaders pondered their next move, restless Harvester workers provided them with some new options. In late January 1941, 350 workers at the small Harvester plant in Rock Falls, Illinois—where the FE had strong support but had not been formally recognized—walked off their jobs. Within a few weeks the sixty-five hundred FE members at Tractor Works and fourteen hundred at the IH plant in Richmond, Indiana, followed suit. Harvester managers suddenly had a multiplant strike on their hands—and the FE now had a tactical opening at McCormick Works. If it could be shut down as well, then FE leaders could demand recognition at McCormick as a condition for calling the strike off. In advance of any action at the plant, however, they demonstrated the union's deep support—and its long memory—with a rally in front of Tractor Works that drew a crowd of more than one thousand Harvester workers on a chilly February afternoon. On the speakers' platform was an elegant but elderly special guest, bundled up against the snow flurries lacing the air: Lucy Parsons, anarchist leader and widow of the Haymarket martyr Albert Parsons. In what was her last public appearance (she died the following year) Lucy Parsons reiterated to the crowd the same simple message she and her radical comrades had delivered to McCormick Works employees more than fifty years earlier: organize. In solidarity there is strength.[8]

Yet whether all seven thousand of the workers at the McCormick plant were convinced of that remained an open question. So Bob Travis again devised a daring military-style operation reliant on a small corps of union supporters. As he developed the scheme, Travis consulted with just a handful of trusted FE members, because International Harvester, like GM, still utilized an extensive network of company informants. The larger group of McCormick workers with union sympathies suspected something was brewing, but weren't sure just what it was or when it would take place.

They got their answer at precisely 12:30 p.m. on February 28, when eight FE members, located at strategic positions within McCormick Works, walked over to the main switches in their departments and shut them off. The plant was on strike, they proclaimed, and directed their fellow employees to go home. The FE contingent, which grew to several hundred, then rapidly traversed the factory, spreading the strike announcement and shutting down machinery as they went. Both the union's message, and its messengers, were hard to ignore. "It was all organized where these big burly men, you know, 220 to 240 pounds—nothing under two hundred pounds or under six feet—we had about a dozen of those [men] out in front," Clarence Stoecker recalled. "Very impressive to the people in the department." They certainly made an impression on the plant's foremen, some of whom tried, but were prevented from, restarting equipment. "The foreman and I had a real set-to," said Stoecker, who jumped the gun before the union's flying squadron arrived. "I'd turn off the power and he'd go start it up. I'd turn it off again and he'd come running down the aisle and start it up again." By his own admission Stoecker was not a big burly man so he was relieved when union reinforcements reached his department. "When they came through there—it was me five-foot-seven, about 130 pounds—and I'm up in the front with those guys—oh, I felt like a big guy but I sure looked like a small potato there."

It all unfolded as Travis had planned, as most McCormick employees either promptly walked out or joined the union's procession through the plant. Only when the FE forces reached the foundry—which retained a level of AFL loyalty, carried over from the nineteenth century—was the battle joined, quite literally. A group of workers pitched pokers, shovels, and assorted other heavy implements—the tools of their trade—at the invading FE members, who heaved them right back, along with any available bricks they could lay their hands on. The Chicago police finally charged in and ousted both sides of the fracas, but that suited the FE's purposes: McCormick Works had emptied out. "Oh gosh, I didn't know there were that many people working in the place," Stoecker remembers realizing when he finally left the plant. "It was just a tremendous thing to see them all out there in the yard. And it was jovial—everyone was in a festive mood." As the company's subsequent court complaint read, FE supporters "parading and marching in a loud, unruly, boisterous and violent manner, succeeded in pulling all the employees off their jobs." Using Bob Travis's blueprint, the union had demonstrated to both Harvester management and the McCormick workforce just who—at that very moment, at least—held the balance of power within the shop.[9]

In case there was any lack of clarity about what had occurred, FE supporters established a sizable picket line around McCormick Works, reinforced with union members from nearby Tractor Works, which was still shut tight by the strike. Harvester officials decried the FE's "deliberate use of violence and coercion," and with newfound respect for the NLRB, declared that "this is not only a strike against the company but against the whole body of the Wagner Act and labor board procedure." The company announced that it would keep McCormick Works closed for the time being. Four IH plants and more than fifteen thousand Harvester employees were now idle; the strike kitchens that kept the picketers at Tractor and McCormick Works fed were doling out ten thousand donuts and forty barrels of coffee every week. The FE made two simple demands: a pay hike at the four struck plants and union recognition at McCormick Works and Rock Falls.[10]

The Harvester strikers, as it turned out, were in the vanguard of what would be a year of heightened activism for American workers. In response to fascism's unchecked advances abroad, President Roosevelt pledged to make the United States the arsenal of democracy, and in 1941 manufacturers began posting "help wanted" signs for the first time in years. As the economy picked up so too did labor's prospects, and the CIO went on offense again. Auto, aircraft, and steelworkers engaged in protracted, often violent organizing battles, at long last winning union recognition at Ford and at Republic and the other Little Steel enterprises. John L. Lewis was, as always, defiant; he ignored commands from the White House and aspersions about his patriotism to direct tens of thousands of miners in walkouts that scored pay increases and enhanced security for the United Mine Workers. All told, over four thousand work stoppages took place in 1941, involving two and a half million workers, the largest strike wave since 1919.

But in early 1941, the only dispute that mattered to International Harvester's management was the one that had shut down four of its plants. And now there was a new McCormick at the company's helm, one with the most patrician pedigree yet. Born in 1898, Fowler McCormick, son of Harold McCormick and Edith Rockefeller, his "roots in reapers and refineries," was "a delicate Prince of Wales in two economic dynasties." He was also heir to the "certain not undistinguished goofiness" that made the McCormicks (other than Cyrus II, at least) fodder for the tabloids from one generation to the next. Since he grew up in one of the most sumptuously appointed mansions Chicago has ever seen, it would be a stretch to call Fowler's childhood "difficult," but it is fair to say that he received scant attention from either of his distracted and frequently absent parents—he could see his mother, it was said, by appointment only. His relationship with another Rockefeller, however, was considerably warmer: as John D.'s oldest grandson Fowler was doted on by the oil tycoon, and throughout his childhood they spent long periods of time together.[11]

Like his father and uncle Cyrus before him, Fowler attended Princeton University, and in 1921 newspapers reported that the college senior was engaged to nineteen-year-old Anne Stillman, the sister of his roommate Bud. Such a match seemed eminently suitable. The patriarch of the Stillman family was James A. Stillman, a New York financier who'd inherited a lot of money and made even more of it for himself on Wall Street; Stillman headed National City Bank (now Citibank) and so was already chummy with Cyrus McCormick II, a long-standing City Bank board member, and consistent with elite tribalism two of Stillman's sisters had married into the Rockefeller clan. But in fact Fowler was more interested in a different and not-so-appropriate Stillman: high-spirited, auburn-haired Fifi Stillman, the wife of James A. and mother of Fowler's purported fiancée, Anne, and his close friend Bud. This may be eyebrow-raising (and confusing) enough but the story rapidly became even more so. In early 1921 James Stillman sued Fifi for divorce, insisting that the couple's youngest son, Guy—Bud's and Anne's brother, in other words—was not his, but had been fathered by a fishing guide with whom Fifi had dallied while at the family's summer retreat in Quebec. An affronted Fifi denied the scandalous accusation and countersued, charging that her husband had carried on affairs with several women, including a New York City chorus girl who was raising two of James's illegitimate children.

The drawn-out divorce proceedings—"one of the longest, most expensive, and most notorious litigations of the kind"—provided front-page titillation for many years, and in the meantime Fowler did not marry Anne Stillman, but instead was frequently seen with her mother. "We are just friends," Fifi, who was twenty years older than Fowler, told the always-interested press. "Fowler and my son are the finest pals in the world." This dubious explanation gained only a modicum of plausibility when James Stillman's divorce suit was thrown out of court in 1926 and he and Fifi then announced a rapprochement; James presented his wife with a necklace worth half a million dollars and whisked her off for a three-month "second honeymoon" in Europe.

But it was Fowler McCormick's destiny to become stepfather to his college roommate and finest pal. "FIFI STILLMAN IS BRIDE AGAIN," read a June 1931 banner headline in the *Chicago Tribune*; the story overshadowed even Al Capone's surrender to the federal government. In what proved a shock to no one, James and Fifi Stillman's reconciliation had foundered, but they had managed to secure a hush-hush divorce. Just hours after the final decrees were signed, Fifi married Fowler McCormick on John D. Rockefeller's Hudson Valley estate. Bud Stillman served as best man. It has all the earmarks of a Depression-era screwball comedy, but nonetheless this was a real-life love story, and one with legs: Fifi and Fowler would remain married until her death, at eighty-nine, in 1969.[12]

And it was Fifi who pressed an uncertain Fowler McCormick, while they were in the "just friends" stage, to devote himself to his family's business. By the late 1920s Alexander Legge, then Harvester's president, was also urging Fowler to assume his rightful place within the kingdom, especially because by this point his cousin, Cyrus McCormick III—who'd gotten off to a promising start—had drifted away from IH to become instead a major landowner and art collector in New Mexico. Fowler served his apprenticeship in various lower-level positions before becoming, in 1941, International Harvester's president. He stepped into that position just as the confrontation with the FE was reaching its crescendo, but by heritage and training he was already imbued with the corporation's governing ethos.

Fowler seemed to be following that playbook to the letter, as he flatly refused the FE's demand for recognition at McCormick Works and Rock Falls, and insisted there would be no wage increases at any of the four striking plants, either. Just as his uncle Cyrus II had in the previous century, Fowler decided that the best way to end a strike was to bust right through it. McCormick Works, the company announced, would re-open on March 24.

Few with long memories in Chicago missed the parallels between 1941 and 1886: a combative union again mustered pickets outside McCormick Works, while the company prepared to usher strikebreakers through the lines. Fresher incidents left little question that the city's police remained capable of brutal excess to protect corporate interests. But just in case anyone overlooked the obvious, Bob Travis made sure to connect the dots. "We don't want a repetition of Haymarket or the Memorial Day Massacre," Travis insisted. "If there is any violence in this strike, the responsibility for it must be placed on the company and any police who decide to take orders from the company." And he issued this warning: "We are going to win this fight right out there on the picket lines, and if any group of strikebreaking company stooges think that they are going to crash those lines, all we say is let them try it!" Labor trouble was percolating across the country by this point in 1941, and as the factory's re-opening approached, tensions in Chicago neared the boiling point. CIO leaders implored President Roosevelt to intervene—he did not—while Mayor Edward Kelly and Illinois Governor Dwight Green both pleaded with Fowler McCormick to consider a delay. He would not.[13]

Fowler's resolve was fortified by assistance provided by various long-standing company allies. The *Chicago Tribune* proclaimed itself the "World's Greatest Newspaper"; it was at any rate the city's most widely circulated one and was run by Fowler's cousin Robert R. McCormick, possibly the world's greatest, or certainly most strident, reactionary. Though the cousins came from sides of the family that generally detested each other, Fowler knew that the influential *Tribune* would provide unabashedly unobjective coverage of the Harvester dispute. Since "Colonel" McCormick—his preferred title—had declared President Roosevelt a communist, a left-wing union would hardly fare better. So the *Tribune* posted headlines like this one a few days before McCormick's re-opening: "HARVESTER TIE-UP DIRECTED BY RED . . . DEWITT GILPIN COMMUNIST, CHAIRMAN CHARGES." The story aired proclamations from House Un-American Activities Committee Chairman Martin Dies—who said, "As long as these CIO unions retain known communists in important posts as those of education director . . . these unions constitute a menace we dare not ignore"—but didn't bother with any rebuttal from FE officials.[14]

Harvester got help from the courts, too: the company was granted an injunction prohibiting the FE from posting more than ten pickets anywhere near McCormick Works. And as had been the case in 1886, the Chicago police would serve and protect the company's interests: nearly fourteen hundred officers would be on hand for McCormick's re-opening. "If any man wants to go to work he will be given that opportunity by the police department," said chief John Prendergast. "Nobody is going to stop any man from earning a living to support his family." But there was really only one family, the FE insisted, that this massive deployment was intended to safeguard. "Pickpockets and thugs [are] free to prowl all over the city as half of the entire police force—the largest gathering in Chicago's history—'protect[s]' the McCormick family's empire."[15]

So, as had been the case in conflicts with the company before, union supporters at International Harvester had only each other to rely on. On the eve of the McCormick Works re-opening, Grant Oakes wanted it known, if there were to be trouble the next day, precisely who was responsible. He fired off a telegram to President Roosevelt, Governor Green, Mayor Kelly, and "the twelve members of the McCormick family" that—either purposely or subconsciously—echoed August Spies's famous REVENGE circular:

> THOUSANDS OF HARVESTER WORKERS HAVE SWEATED AND TOILED
> MANY YEARS IN THESE PLANTS TO PILE UP PROFITS FOR THE MC-
> CORMICK FAMILY. IF THESE WORKERS LINE THE MORGUE TOMOR-
> ROW, WITH THEIR BLOOD ON CHICAGO STREETS, RESPONSIBILITY
> FOR ANY SUCH MASS MURDER SHALL LIE SOLELY AND HEAVILY ON
> THE HEADS OF THIS GREEDY FAMILY WHICH WILL DO ANYTHING TO
> GAIN ITS ENORMOUS PROFITS.[16]

But there would be no blood spilled at McCormick Works when it opened for business on March 24. The picket restrictions and the formidable police presence ensured safe passage for those workers who chose to enter the plant. Employees partial to the AFL were among them, for the AFL leadership, still asserting jurisdiction over McCormick Works, had disavowed the strike. FE supporters attempted to march toward the plant the following day, but the police wielded their truncheons on the strikers to remind them that such demonstrations were not permitted. The FE leadership was surely disappointed, but probably not thoroughly surprised, that by the end of the week more than half the McCormick workforce had reported to the plant. The re-opening of Harvester's Richmond, Indiana, plant five days later triggered a violent clash between strikers, police, and "concerned" citizens—called vigilantes by the FE—but there too the company claimed that employees were returning to work.[17]

Once again, in a tumultuous period of labor agitation, it seemed that a resolute McCormick would win a war of attrition against a militant union. And if Bob Travis's gambit at McCormick Works fizzled, it might well sound the death knell for industrial unionism at International Harvester. But this time around there was a new player in the picture, one with enough clout to alter the outcome: the federal government. Whatever might be happening at Harvester's other plants, the FE's strength at Tractor Works was keeping it shut tight, a circumstance causing consternation in Washington. IH was already producing equipment for the US Army, which was growing anxious for the tractors it had been promised. With Nazi forces rolling across Europe in 1941 and the likelihood of US intervention in the conflict escalating, the military buildup took on increased urgency; the federal government thus created a series of agencies, generally composed of representatives from business, labor, and "the public," to adjudicate industrial conflict and minimize interruptions to defense production. The first, the National Defense Mediation Board (NDMB), was created in March 1941 and its initial case would be the walkout at International Harvester. Invoking executive authority, the NDMB ordered that the strike be terminated immediately and summoned Harvester and FE officials to Washington for a March 31 meeting to discuss terms of a settlement.[18]

Federal intervention does not always bode well for labor, but in this case the NDMB's action allowed the FE leadership to maneuver out of a tight spot: the union could call off its strike without appearing to have lost it. The rank and file first had to be convinced, however, and at Tractor Works at least, though the strike there had been ongoing for nearly two months, many FE members expressed the desire to engage in "all-out picketing," rather than end the walkout. Grant Oakes pressed the NDMB to provide a guarantee that there would be no discrimination against FE supporters if they returned to work: the union was well aware of Harvester's past practices on this score. With that assurance, at a membership meeting in late March, fifteen hundred workers from McCormick and Tractor Works voted to end the strike, though they insisted on parading around the Harvester plants first. Richmond and Rock Falls followed suit the next day.[19]

The FE delegation, composed of Grant Oakes, DeWitt Gilpin, and several local leaders, set out for Washington, hoping that the new government board would grant them the victory that the walkout had failed to deliver.

The union's proposal amplified its earlier demands: union recognition along with a raise in Harvester's minimum wage. They also called for the abolition of the piecework system, or short of that, at least a framework that would inject some semblance of democracy into it. "The union has to conduct defensive warfare against chiseling on piece work rates all the time," FE officials told the NDMB. "A system must be devised where wages in Harvester become a matter of collective bargaining." It was thus also imperative, so the FE insisted, that stewards—those workers in the plants who also serve as elected local union representatives—be paid for the time they were obliged to spend pursuing workers' grievances.[20]

Fowler McCormick, however, refused to engage with the union's demands. Instead, he simply maintained that the confused situation would be best resolved through NLRB elections that would allow employees a choice between the FE or the AFL. Harvester executives, however, did take time to underscore the political predilections of the FE leadership; Joe Weber, they said, "was an out and out Communist . . . that's what we had to deal with at Tractor Works . . . after Webber [sic] leaves in comes Travis, but he is just as bad."[21]

The NDMB's ruling, issued on April 3, 1941, thus pleased IH officials and left the FE leadership fuming. The board decreed only that NLRB elections should be soon held at various plants—McCormick and Rock Falls, along with the West Pullman plant in Chicago, IH facilities in Rock Island and East Moline, Illinois, and its factory in Milwaukee, Wisconsin. The NDMB said nothing, however, regarding the union's demands. The recent strike thus appeared as if it may have been fruitless, which threatened to undercut the FE's standing where it had already secured representation, to say nothing of its reputation at the unorganized plants.[22]

Fowler McCormick and Harvester management felt comfortable heading into the June 18 elections. The outlook seemed bleak for the FE. AFL officials stood ready to reap the benefits of well-cultivated anti-CIO sentiment.

The results were thus cause for alarm in the IH boardroom and elation at FE headquarters. Three out of the six contested plants—West Pullman, East Moline, and Rock Falls—voted for the FE, and a close tally at McCormick necessitated a runoff election. The Farmall plant in Rock Island, Illinois, and the Milwaukee Works chose AFL representation. In late July, nearly 90 percent of the McCormick workforce turned out for the final election at the plant; the FE chalked up 2,806 votes while the AFL got 2,565. The cornerstones of the Harvester empire, McCormick and Tractor Works, now belonged to the FE, along with four other plants in the chain; all told nearly twenty thousand IH workers were represented by the union.[23]

꩜

What went right for the FE? Against the odds—and International Harvester—how and why did the union win?

Certainly labor's breakthroughs elsewhere worked in the FE's favor. In April 1941, while the NDMB was deliberating about Harvester's situation, the UAW struck the Ford Motor Company and won recognition less than a week later. Within Illinois, and particularly in Chicago, IH employees crossed paths with steelworkers, packinghouse workers, and electrical workers who already belonged to the CIO. Harvester workers came late to industrial unionism, but they could not have been unaffected by the movement they witnessed around them.

But there were more specific and deeply rooted reasons underlying the FE's victory. Grant Oakes and Jerry Fielde, through their long tenure at McCormick and Tractor Works, and their participation on the works councils, understood that Harvester employees had, for decades, been schooled in a system of industrial relations designed to keep them docile and afraid. These workers needed to be convinced that the union would make a qualitative difference in their lives, but that would not be enough: they then also had to believe that they could challenge their powerful employer—and win. Getting IH workers to embrace both those concepts necessitated a long, concerted push. With tutoring provided early on by CP organizer Joe Weber, the nascent FE leadership had developed the long-view strategy and the patience required to make progress, incremental though it may have been.

As the FE's initial cadre looked to expand their drive, they enlisted others who best understood what they were up against: Harvester workers. After Tractor Works voted for the FE in 1938, union supporters met to discuss how to proceed at other factories. The FE, they determined, should "place its reliance in the organizing campaign on volunteer organizers from within the plants, rather than on salaried organizers." This may have been a necessity as much as a virtue: at that point the CIO, as John L. Lewis had made clear, didn't have deep pockets. But nonetheless the FE embraced and was reinforced by its rank-and-file structure; its "volunteer organizers" were supremely attuned to Harvester's workforce, since they remained part of it. FE activists emphasized the need for foreign language speakers at events, union announcements on ethnic radio stations, and literature printed not only in English but in Polish and Czech as well. By the spring of 1939, the front page of the FE's newspaper carried reports about separate mass meetings held for Polish and Italian employees of McCormick Works.[24]

The FE also aggressively solicited support from Black workers and pursued policies to enhance their opportunities within Harvester's plants. These positions were no doubt a reflection of the FE's association with the Communist Party, which, as one historian notes, had declared "the struggle for equal rights and full citizenship for African Americans essential to the victory of proletarian revolution in the United States." In the late 1930s a fulsome insistence on "full citizenship for African Americans" was a radical concept, well outside the political mainstream, but it was one that characterized the FE from the outset. In the midst of the organizing push at Tractor Works, African American employees there received a letter from the FE "telling of plans to end discrimination against them and give them equal opportunity with the white workers for promotion to better jobs." Just weeks before the 1938 NLRB election at the Tractor plant, white and Black workers attended an expressly integrated dance sponsored by the FE—not a typical occurrence at the time in racially divided Chicago. And once the FE secured representation at Tractor Works it made good on its promise to advocate for skilled jobs for Black workers—again, not standard practice, even within the CIO—extracting an agreement from IH management "to apply a policy of promoting Negroes in the machine shop." Such agitation had, by 1940, drawn favorable mention in the *Chicago Defender*, the city's influential African American newspaper.[25]

So, when the FE went up against International Harvester—and the AFL—the following year, the FE had already garnered a reputation that mattered within the Black community. "Even before [the FE] shut down the tractor works," wrote *Defender* columnist George McCray just after the 1941 strike began, "the company, on insistence of the union, had agreed to promote Negroes to positions in the plant they had never held before." Just before the final election at McCormick Works, McCray reminded his readers that the FE there "led the fight for promotion of Negroes to more skilled jobs." The FE itself made an issue of the company's employment practices throughout the strike, chipping away at the loyalty Black employees may have felt to IH management, or its surrogate, the AFL. "Negroes have the hardest and lowest-paid jobs at Harvester, working either in the labor gang or the foundry," said the FE's newspaper. "They are the first to be fired or shifted to lower-paid jobs."[26]

Moreover, African Americans were highly visible leaders within the fledgling FE, though it had then—and would retain throughout its history—a majority-white membership. Pleass Kellogg, one of the FE's early activists at Tractor Works, had become a member of the FE's executive board, and throughout the 1941 showdown with IH he was a featured speaker at union rallies and a spokesman quoted in news accounts. Other Black local leaders spoke at FE events, served prominently on strike strategy committees and as picket captains, and appeared in the pages of the union newspaper. Of the roughly eleven thousand then employed at Tractor and McCormick Works, about two thousand were African American, so they weren't hard to find and were not an inconsequential constituency. But no Black Harvester workers were listed on the program of an AFL pre-election rally. Of course, as the *Defender* regularly reported in its coverage of "Jim Crow Unions," Blacks had long been unwelcome in most AFL affiliates. In contrast, the presence of Black leadership underscored that the FE was genuinely reflective of the entire Harvester workforce.[27]

Thus the demands the FE advanced in 1941 were crafted with the knowledge of what mattered most to Harvester workers. Since nearly all African Americans at IH were at the lowest end of the pay scale, increasing the minimum wage would especially benefit them, the *Defender* reported. And for those employees paid by the piece—the majority of Harvester's workforce—the union promised to challenge the capricious harassment exercised by shop-floor supervisors. "I know because I am a Harvester worker," Grant Oakes said in a radio address on the eve of the 1941 McCormick walkout, that compensation at IH rested not on "the ability to turn out a fair day's work" but required remaining "in the good graces of company stooges." On the same broadcast, rank-and-file activist Richard Kelly emphasized how the FE's presence changed that: "No foreman approaches any employee at Tractor Works"; workers there need no longer fear "an act of discrimination that may place [them] on the street," Kelly insisted. FE supporters had declared early on in their organizing drive that "no grievance of the workers is too small," and in 1941 the union reiterated that belief. It was evidently a compelling argument.[28]

By this point Harvester employees had plenty of experience with organizations that purported to represent them but then failed utterly to act as their advocates. Bob Travis had said that the AFL was simply "the old company union with a new pair of britches," and as the AFL violated picket lines and issued no demands during the 1941 walkout his point seemed well taken. The FE, however, had demonstrated that it would not hesitate to go toe-to-toe with management. If Harvester workers had any lingering doubts on that score, Bob Travis's lightning strike at McCormick Works had obliterated them. Though it did not keep the plant shut for long, Travis's maneuver nonetheless was critical to the FE's success. One indisputable point had been made, even to those employees who returned to work: this organization was unlike any of the others they had known.[29]

There was one other thread running through the FE's 1941 rhetoric, interwoven from immediate injustices and past sins still unatoned for: a fierce loathing of Fowler McCormick and his kin. "Having made millions from the labor of the strikers last year," said the FE newspaper during the strike, "none of the McCormicks have tightened their belts"; instead "they congratulate themselves on the fact that the Harvester company tripled its profits in 1940 without raising wages." These denunciations proved a useful organizing device for the FE, putting a face (or faces) on Harvester's greed and exploitation. But the FE's leaders genuinely despised the McCormicks, and their red-hot hostility contrasted with the AFL, their far more compliant competitor. "Let the twelve members of the McCormick family who live in luxury off the swollen profits of the corporation they inherited fume and fret," Grant Oakes declared. "I owe them nothing . . . my people are the employees of Harvester."[30]

And at the end of the summer of 1941, some twenty thousand of those people were represented by the United Farm Equipment Workers of America.

They now had a union covering several IH plants, but they still didn't have a contract, and Fowler McCormick continued to do his utmost to live up to the FE's depiction of him. Collective bargaining sessions dragged on over five months as IH management, again, refused to make any concessions whatsoever. But, finally, shifting national priorities overcame the McCormicks' venerable obstinacy. Shortly after the United States formally entered WWII in December 1941, Harvester's unsettled situation came to the attention of the National War Labor Board (WLB)—it had superseded the NDMB—which after several months issued its decision in the case. This time around the FE was not disappointed. The WLB recommended a general wage increase; a grievance procedure mandating that the company pay stewards for all time they spent handling shop-floor disputes; and the important "maintenance of membership" clause, which obliged employees to become union members, granting the FE a significant measure of security. FE leaders immediately accepted the decision, while Harvester officials balked. But by this point Americans were fighting overseas, and the government leaned heavily on IH management to capitulate.[31]

So, at last, on May 10, 1942—nearly one hundred years after the McCormick Company began producing reapers in Chicago—Fowler McCormick became the first member of his family to sign a union contract covering several of the company's plants. As he gazed across the table while the FE's leaders in turn lent their signatures to the agreement, Fowler no doubt glumly recognized in them just the sort of "bad element" his uncle Cyrus had labored so fervently—and successfully—to keep well away from his workforce.

Back in 1919, Arthur Young, waxing philosophical about the Industrial Council Plan he'd created for International Harvester, said there would now be "new feet under the table—the feet of the workers—at which the working policies of the companies are decided." FE leaders had exposed that scheme as a sham, and proceeded to demonstrate that they would not conduct themselves like invited guests at Harvester's party. Securing the contract in 1942 was just the beginning; they were thenceforth prepared to contend with IH management—and the McCormicks—over every aspect of the company's "working polices."[32]

Experience taught them that if they wanted anything more than crumbs from Harvester's table, they'd need to put up a fight.

9.
The People's War

When disgruntled Harvester executives met with considerably more satisfied FE officials to finalize their 1942 agreement, one key player wasn't in the room. In fact, he wasn't even in Chicago. DeWitt Gilpin—my father—had by then bowed out of that particular fight to join another one, as he had a few months earlier enlisted in the US Army. News about the "victory in Harvester" reached Gilpin while he was at Camp Robinson, Arkansas. His new occupation consisted largely of "skirmishing and bayonet drill under a blazing sun," he wrote in a letter home. "But they need hard soldiers for a hard job, so we all take it, reserving our right as soldiers to beef about everything."

Though the US escaped the devastation that shattered Europe and Asia, World War II nonetheless disrupted American society at every echelon, reshaping personal destinies and redefining national priorities. Certainly this was true within the CIO, which had been in existence for only a few short years when war was declared, and unions were forced to regroup as many founding members departed for the military. As far as the FE's history goes, it might be tempting to breeze by WWII as an atypical period, during which a temporarily reconstituted leadership became bogged down in wartime bureaucracy, and recommence the narrative after the conflict overseas had come to an end. But to do that would miss something critical about both the FE leaders who joined the service and those who stayed behind. My father viewed his military experience as an extension of the organizing he'd already been engaged in. "What an army they will make," he wrote in one of his letters about the soldiers at Camp Robinson, "when this becomes, in all aspects, a really people's war." Back on the home front the FE leadership capitalized on the exigent circumstance of wartime to seize more power for Harvester workers and expand the boundaries of industrial democracy. For FE officials, in other words, the battle against fascists and the struggle with IH executives were inherently interrelated. They were part of the same "people's war," carried out on two fronts, oceans apart.

My father was, of course, only one among the legions of civilians hastily transformed into soldiers during World War II. There is a conventional image of those American troops, crafted, in large part, through the movies made back then (like *The Story of G.I. Joe*) and since (like *Saving Private*

Ryan): reluctant warriors, impertinent to superiors but resolute under fire, animated not by a cause but by camaraderie, their patriotism instinctive rather than ideological. Yet while the Hollywood portrait may have been a fair depiction of the typical American soldier, it failed in many respects to represent political radicals, like my father, who also donned uniforms. That DeWitt Gilpin was not exactly the average G.I. was duly noted, as he was singled out early for special attention by top brass in the army. Unlike the closing scene in the film *Casablanca,* however, this World War II story by no means marked the beginning of a beautiful friendship.

But before he enlisted there was a period in which Gilpin was every bit as reluctant to fight as Hollywood suggested he should be. In the fall of 1939 the Nazi government entered into a nonaggression treaty with the Soviet Union. The Nazi-Soviet pact induced the American Communist Party to instantaneously abandon its previous stance strenuously encouraging US aid to combat fascism in favor of vociferous opposition to any involvement whatsoever in the "imperialist" war. To say that this dramatic and largely incoherent policy lurch caused consternation for many party members was putting it mildly—"I felt like I had been hit by a bolt of lightning," said one—but organizations with strong CP ties, like the Farm Equipment Workers, endeavored at least publicly to adapt. So the Young Communist League's *Review,* in a February 1941 story on the FE's strike against Harvester, quoted "young DeWitt Gilpin" castigating FDR's provision of military assistance to Britain "as a policy leading directly to the participation of American boys in the slaughter abroad." But the FE's quarrel with Roosevelt was overshadowed, as all disputes always were, by its feud with International Harvester, and so critiques of foreign policy were folded into condemnations of the company. "It's hard to fool the workers of Harvester with smooth talk of 'national defense,'" said the *Review.* "They know that the company has a plant in Germany now producing tractors and materials of war for the Nazi regime at the same time it makes millions of dollars of profits producing here for the American and British governments." And stepped-up defense production opened up another avenue of attack for FE organizers, which may have been especially persuasive to one group of workers in particular. Tom Giles, one of the Tractor Works picket captains, identified as "Negro shop steward and active union man," insisted that "International Harvester, which is working on defense orders right now, will not allow Negroes to work on any equipment. I say that's unfair to the Constitution of the United States."[1]

Maintaining a detachment from the escalating "slaughter abroad"—on the part of the CP, the FE, my father, or the country generally—simply could not last. After the Nazis invaded the Soviet Union in June 1941 the Communist Party reverted to vehement anti-fascism and urged the United States to commit troops as well as aid to the war effort. That would happen a few months later, not due to the Party's insistence, needless to say, but because of what the Japanese did at Pearl Harbor in December 1941. DeWitt Gilpin was one of those American boys who promptly signed up, enlisting in the army in February 1942. But for him "boy" was a bit of a misnomer. While the Young Communist League had considered Gilpin part of its demographic, at twenty-nine he was several years older than the average soldier and already married, and so his enlistment was no reflection of the impetuousness of youth. Moreover, it was not a decision he made on his own—he no doubt discussed it with his wife, but he had also consulted with Grant Oakes and Jerry Fielde. "It would be fitting" they agreed, "for one or more of them to join the armed forces so that the membership of the union would be impressed with the fact that the war is a matter pertaining to all the people and, further, that the membership of the union would not be called upon to endure any greater hardship in prosecuting the war than those endured by their National Officers." Accordingly, Gilpin was the first within the FE's top leadership to sign up: Fielde was more vital to the union, and Oakes—then in his late thirties—would have been too old. Any reluctance about the war on Gilpin's part had been exorcised; now he was eager to join the front lines. Like thousands of other party members who enlisted, Gilpin's motivations transcended nationalism: he was driven not only to defend his country but also to obliterate fascism and preserve the Soviet socialist state. He expressed "a strong desire for combat service." He would get it.[2]

But first he had to complete basic training. That period in Gilpin's life is especially well documented, though not because he kept a diary or wrote any sort of memoir about his experience. He was, rather, being closely watched. Shortly after he enlisted Gilpin was placed under surveillance by the government and was monitored throughout his army career. Despite his keen desire to serve—and irrespective of the wartime alliance between the US and the USSR—he was suspected of "disaffection" because of his Communist Party ties and his leadership position with the FE. His military intelligence file, which runs into the hundreds of pages, was extensive enough to include not only his arrest records and citations from the *Daily Worker* but also the grades he received in kindergarten. An exhaustive background check included interviews with neighbors from his childhood residences in Kansas, one of whom offered that the "subject's father was a drunkard with very radical political ideas." A former high school teacher deemed Gilpin "a non-conformist" who should thus be regarded as "a dangerous man to have around."

At the various training camps he was sent to, informants in his barracks kept track of to whom he wrote letters, how he spent his free time, and that Gilpin "makes it a point to read the newspapers as often as possible." These reports were often disappointing for anyone hoping to find fiery Marxist exhortations. "I led Gilpin into a conversation regarding what would be the results of the war in the United States," one fellow soldier at Fort Benning noted in 1943. "He said that he thought there would be no revolutionary changes but that perhaps labor would have more to say." Another indicated "In trying to make a conversation with him regarding the war, the only statement I could force him to make was that, quote 'It would take longer than a year to take Germany,' unquote." Of course, it is quite possible that these statements were innocuous precisely because Gilpin knew to whom he was talking. He never saw his intelligence files—they were obtained after his death—and in my youth I heard little from my father about his military experience. But I remember that he did once recall, a bit wryly, that everywhere he'd been posted there were at least two guys whose only duties seemed to consist of following him around and endeavoring to engage him in political debate.

If Gilpin's communications with some of his fellow soldiers seemed vague he nonetheless had a clear sense of what he had signed up to do. Early on his letters register the usual grousing about army drills; from Fort Benning, in Georgia's sweltering summer heat, he wrote, "All day long we shoot guns, clean guns, dig fortifications, undig 'em, fall down, get up, march and then march some more." But he reassured his mother that "I have adjusted myself to life here and like it because to me it has more of a purpose than just to kill or be killed." That larger purpose, he continued, was a future "in which no small group of fascist capitalists can uproot the lives and hopes of the world just because they need to exploit everything and everybody to keep their rotten system from falling apart." He hoped, he said just after he entered basic training in 1942, "to be sent where the fighting is going on—somewhere around Smolensk," and thereafter repeatedly expressed a desire to get overseas "for that long awaited second front."[3]

Such enthusiasm caught the attention of his superiors, not all of whom deemed Gilpin's radical proclivities cause for concern. "Gilpin's record as a solider has no blemish of any sort. This is the main criterion on which advancement within military ranks should be based," said one of his commanding officers, adding that Gilpin "was officer material" who "deserved a commission." Several months after he earned his sergeant stripes in mid-1942, he was sent to officer candidate school at the Army Air Base in Dyersburg, Tennessee. Higher-ups in the War Department, however, intervened. The Fourth Service Command Headquarters declared Gilpin to be "potentially subversive" over the objections of Major C. W. Tazewell, the post's senior intelligence officer. Tazewell saw "nothing objectionable with Subject's activities or character," and offered further that "though Subject is an established Communist, the Russians are our allies, and there is nothing wrong with that." Whatever the ecumenical major may have believed, as far as the top brass in the army was concerned there *was* something wrong with that. Gilpin was released from officer candidate school and remained a sergeant for the remainder of his military career.

My father became part of the American invasion that swept through Normandy after D-Day. He was awarded a Bronze Star for his part in the fierce combat that liberated the town of Saint-Lô, and remained in the fighting with Patton's Third Army as it drove north. "France, like all places where soldiers go, is raining and muddy," he wrote home. "But small things happen to you that mean a lot—like the way the face of a spindle-legged, half-starved French kid lights up when you give her a piece of chocolate." The landscape he traversed seemed familiar in some ways but not in others. "Our region reminds me of northern Missouri, except the fields are much smaller. And Missouri farmers don't wear wooden shoes and pantaloons. And Missouri farmers don't have a hedge row every 200 yards, and we wish to hell these guys didn't either." As his unit drew closer to Belgium his letters grew more terse. "It's very rough here, honey," he wrote to his sister from just outside "the road junction city of Bastogne" in early 1945. "Lots of snow and very cold, with the doughboys having to fight frozen feet and hands as well as the Krauts." In the midst of the Battle of the Bulge, he was removed from the front and assigned to write for *Yank* magazine, the official military publication, and spent the remainder of the war reporting from Paris and Berlin.[4]

It seems fair to say that concerns about Gilpin's disaffection were—for the duration of the war, at least—overblown. But the considerable resources the government invested in keeping tabs on him, in a period when, in fact, the Russians *were* our allies, indicates that well before the Cold War the CIO's left-wing trade unionists were viewed as threats to national security. Even when surveillance revealed nothing incriminating, the communist label alone prompted government agencies to curtail the activities and narrow the options open to American radicals, in ways the individuals being watched may not always have recognized. This would of course become all the more true once the brief wartime dalliance between the United States and the Soviets disintegrated.

But the intrusion that proved a bane to party members can serve as a boon to historians, as these intelligence files provide some insight into what it meant, in practice, to be a left-leaning soldier. Thanks to the helpful reconnaissance of an informant, we know that my father refused to work on the base newspaper in Dyersburg unless the printing was transferred to a union shop (it was). Several reports noted that Gilpin "is very interested in the race problems in the South," and was critical of the way white Southerners "treat the Negro population." He also spent time visiting with the 99th Squadron, "a colored outfit, and discussed with them the race problem of the United States."

And because of his politics my father, as he had suspected, had company wherever he went, even when he was on leave. In September 1942, Gilpin received a furlough to attend the FE's first annual convention, held at the Jefferson Hotel in Peoria, Illinois. The agent assigned by military intelligence to tail him there took copious notes of a sort suggesting he aspired to a sideline writing screenplays for detective films. Posing as a newspaper reporter covering the convention, the agent followed Gilpin from his arrival at the Peoria train station until his departure five days later, noting whom he got into hotel elevators with, how often he went into the coffee shop, and how he carried himself ("very deliberate in all of his actions"). He provided thick descriptions of the various people Gilpin interacted with: one had "extra-long arms" while another possessed "dark, greasy skin [and] a large Jewish nose," and another had "prominent dark sunken spaces below the eyes." Almost all of them were said to walk either "with a swagger" or "with stooped shoulders" or in one instance, both, which is somewhat hard to picture. The agent also did his best to eavesdrop on Gilpin's discussions with his companions, but unfortunately, since they frequently "conversed in tones too low to distinguish" in booths at the hotel bar—the appropriately noir-ish Rocket Room—he failed to glean much of interest. He did report on Gilpin's address to the convention, but that seemed disappointingly innocuous: though Gilpin saluted the "tank factory workers of Stalingrad," he also praised "the CIO workers who were doing the job on the home front to produce tanks and other equipment" and urged them to keep at it.

Whether the agent's reporter ruse fooled anyone is questionable; he notes that at one point Gilpin approached him at the hotel bar, asked him what paper he represented, and then engaged him in conversation briefly about the newspaper guild. Since the agent's report didn't supply his responses to those queries it is difficult to gauge how authentic he sounded. But he did indicate that on the second night of the convention Gilpin seemed "suspicious" and "looked at all the occupants of the hotel lobby when leaving," and that he and his companions "looked to their rear often when walking to the C.I.O. party," presumably back at the agent, who would have been following them so that he could later record all the unease he was generating.

While the agent skulked around the corridors of the Jefferson Hotel, however, he failed to record something genuinely noteworthy: he undoubtedly encountered African Americans heading into the coffee shop, mingling in the conference spaces,.and retiring to guest rooms there. At that time no Peoria hotels admitted Blacks, either as overnight guests or as patrons in the restaurants and bars. At the FE's insistence, Black delegates to the convention were allowed to stay at the Jefferson, and thus, according to the union's newspaper, "for the first time in the history of Peoria succeeded in eliminating the former Jim-Crow practice of refusing admittance to the hotel to Negroes." The FE thus put into practice the non-discriminatory rhetoric being voiced at its convention, where the delegates, as the *Chicago Defender* noted, adopted resolutions calling for the integration of the armed services and professional baseball, the aggressive investigation of lynching, and the condemnation of the Ku Klux Klan and other white supremacist organizations as "the chief agents of domestic fascism." The convention also agreed to elect "one white and one Negro vice-president from the FE's Lake District"—its largest unit, the one that included the union's Chicago plants—a practice which would continue from then on.[5]

So while the FE engaged in the subversion of segregationist practice, this was not the sort of activity that piqued the interest of zealous intelligence operatives during World War II. But subversion of the sort they were looking for from communist sympathizers was hard to find, since CP members proved to be especially ardent win-the-war advocates. A few days after the attack on Pearl Harbor, officials of the AFL and CIO announced that walkouts of any kind would be off limits for the duration of the war, and communist-influenced union leaders voiced fervent support for this no-strike pledge. Gilpin's full-speed-ahead exhortation to the 1942 FE convention, for instance, was not his only such communication to the union membership. "I regard the Union's record of having maintained uninterrupted production since Pearl Harbor as a great tribute to our Commander-in-Chief and the armed services he commands," Gilpin wrote in early 1943, in one of several letters printed in the FE newspaper while he was in uniform."[6]

But Gilpin's worldview infused these messages to the membership in ways that went beyond the pep talks about full production. For one thing, the no-strike pledge didn't mitigate the vitriol aimed at International Harvester management, whom Gilpin accused of near-treasonous behavior. "A large section of big business, including IHC," he wrote, "still insists on going all out to win the war on its own terms—a policy that gives comfort to Hitler and a heartache to the boys who fought to their last Springfield at Corregidor." Nor did the fight against fascism mean the imperative to organize should be put on hold. Gilpin's letters to the FE paper encouraged "handclasps between the soldiers of the field and the soldiers of the shop," and to do that he urged the labor movement to establish "union soldier centers" that "could take their place alongside those operated by the USO and the various church organizations." Unions could thus communicate to soldiers that they "are supported by something more than their own love of family and country—they fight as you once fought aggression on the picket lines, surrounded by the solidarity of working men and women." No doubt Gilpin believed such solidarity would help transform the conflict into the "people's war" he hoped it would become.[7]

Of course, such "union soldier centers" never got off the ground, though it's intriguing to consider how veterans' organizations and the causes they are associated with might have been altered if they had. During World War II there were a lot of union workers in uniform, judging just from the FE's example: by mid-1942 there were already more than two hundred FE members from McCormick Works alone in the armed forces. By the end of the war there would be thousands more from the union's locals, and from the FE's top leadership both Milt Burns and Jerry Fielde would also see action, Burns in the Marines and Fielde in the Merchant Marine. It's probably fair to presume that as soldiers they (and their families) were sympathetic to Gilpin's call for unstinting production of the weapons of war. That was certainly the union's official position: throughout WWII, week after week, the *FE News* professed total commitment to the no-strike pledge.[8]

But in reality, all was not entirely harmonious on the home front. As the rhetoric regarding equality of sacrifice began to wear thin, workers chafed under wage restrictions imposed by the War Labor Board and grew impatient with the no-strike pledge. Within the FE, where members had been schooled to distrust management and rely on immediate pressure to resolve their grievances, it proved especially tricky to maintain the press for full production without alienating the rank and file, especially because most of them were only recent converts to the union in the first place.

Thus, while Gilpin and a number of former FE leaders were otherwise engaged overseas, Grant Oakes and the officials who remained at their posts were fighting a rearguard action in the "people's war," or at least in the Harvester workers' war. It was one they did not intend to lose.

10.

The Nefarious System

International Harvester's factories were far removed from the combat zones, but inside them the war's reverberations registered nonetheless. And that was true even before the FE intervened.

Not that Harvester—unlike the auto or aircraft industries—underwent a complete overhaul as a result of the massive wartime mobilization. People could forego luxury cars for the duration but they still had to eat, and American farmers were called on not only to sustain the nation's expanding military but also to help feed strapped England and its armed forces as well. So while defense contracts provided significant (and lucrative) business for Harvester, the company continued to produce agricultural machinery as well. Tractor Works turned out perky cherry-red tractors for the fields along with crawler-type olive-drab ones for the front lines; part of McCormick Works was retrofitted to produce torpedoes but farm equipment still accounted for 60 percent of the output there in 1943. Employment levels at IH rose throughout the war years—by 1945 the company employed nearly fifty-five thousand workers at its eighteen manufacturing facilities in the United States—though not nearly in as spectacular a fashion as was the case in defense centers like Detroit and Los Angeles.

Still, as more workers left for the service, Harvester was obliged to cast a wider net for employees. Women became more visible within IH; by 1944 they made up about 20 percent of the workforce in those plants the FE represented. That figure paled in comparison with the aircraft industry, though, where in some factories during WWII women constituted more than half the blue-collar workforce. At particular IH plants women had an even smaller presence: at McCormick Works they made up less than 10 percent of the workforce. So if you went looking for Rosie the Riveter—the kerchiefed gal with the rolled-up sleeves and the can-do spirit—you would have been somewhat hard-pressed to find her at International Harvester.[1]

If the workforce did not become substantially more female during World War II it was still significantly reconstituted, as African American employment at IH—of men, mostly—increased dramatically. This transition occurred almost exclusively at the company's Chicago plants; workforces at its small-town midwestern locations remained predominantly or exclusively white. At Tractor Works, for example, Black employment rose from 6.5 percent of the plant's workforce in 1940 to nearly 18 percent by 1945; by that year at McCormick Works more than one-quarter of the employees were Black, up from one-tenth when the war began. And at the nearby Twine Mill, where the work was arduous and mostly unskilled, Black employment more than tripled, so that the workforce was nearly 65 percent African American (and 60 percent female) by 1945. But unlike the employment of women in the defense industries, which was in general a transitory phenomenon (though that displacement was not entirely voluntary, as far as many of the women themselves were concerned), Black workers (both male and female) at Harvester stuck around once World War II ended. Some of them would step into critical leadership posts within the FE.[2]

But while the war was still going on this fresh influx of employees— many of them new not just to IH but to unionism too—increased the stresses on the FE leadership. Patriotism, furthermore, would not eclipse all shop-floor discontent, nor could the no-strike pledge contain mounting frustration. As the conflict overseas dragged on, employees found themselves working grueling swing shifts on twenty-four-hour, seven-days-a-week schedules, their wages capped by the War Labor Board. Meanwhile corporate executives seemed to be riding the war out in comfort: International Harvester, for instance, broke sales records every year. Unauthorized walkouts escalated at defense plants across the country, and IH proved no exception. Tractor Works employee Hank Graber, one of the union's earliest and most loyal supporters, did not hesitate to express his disagreement with the FE leadership's insistence on uninterrupted production. "I objected to the no-strike pledge in union meetings all the time," he said. "In the First World War, there were millionaires made. In the Second World War, there were billionaires made. The working class had to give their lives and their labor, and all the businessmen were doing was raking in the money. Was this equality of sacrifice?" Clearly plenty of others shared Graber's viewpoint, as IH recorded 36 walkouts in 1943, 75 in 1944, and in 1945, 164 walkouts that, in total, involved more than 40,000 employees. Like wartime stoppages in other industries, most of those at Harvester were brief and involved a small number of workers at a time. But the IH strikes were characterized by a familiar motif: the vast majority of them were sparked by confrontations over piecework.[3]

Thus whatever FE officials—whether they were across town or across an ocean—may have proclaimed publicly about the no-strike pledge, they could not afford to blithely override such restiveness within the ranks. Such a course would have been suicidal for the recently formed union, and not the natural choice for a leadership so attuned to the realities of life in the shops and animated by such fundamental mistrust of management. So the FE endeavored to meld the fight against fascism with its struggle against IH, exploiting to the hilt the federal government's expanded wartime authority in order to assert greater control over the company's vexatious piecework system.[4]

By now it should come as no surprise to hear that piecework was the predominant issue underlying shop-floor discontent at Harvester during World War II, since complaints related to pay practices were sounded during nearly every labor dispute in the company's long history. In the 1940s nearly three-quarters of Harvester's production employees were categorized as "pieceworkers," but this was a misnomer of sorts, as by this point the company's compensation system had evolved well beyond the relatively simple pay-per-unit-produced formulas utilized in the nineteenth century. In the 1920s, as efficiency emerged as the ethos of the era, IH overhauled its factories to bring "the work to the man rather than the man to the work," and simultaneously introduced an incentive payment scheme that would result in "maximum production, low costs and good wages." Time and motion studies—the brainchild of Frederick Winslow Taylor—were integral to this process, subjecting the many thousands of tasks in an IH factory to "scientific" analysis establishing how long each one should take and how much it was worth. But Harvester's rejigged wage system was every bit as much about control as it was about compensation. It was also designed to disguise just how much money the corporation was making off of each employee, for the unique occupational rating system perfected by Harvester management was purposely and mind-bogglingly complex.[5]

Here's what this meant in practice. At IH those jobs (such as in maintenance or repair) that could not be evaluated by output were "day work" positions paid on a straight per-hour basis. Most production employees, however, were on piecework, and thus received a baseline hourly wage plus additional compensation for the units of acceptable quality they turned out exceeding the minimum set for their job. The guaranteed hourly wages for pieceworkers were low (so not enough on their own to constitute decent compensation) and moreover employees were expected to meet at least their minimum output levels (otherwise they would likely be demoted or fired). Here, thus, was the "incentive" in Harvester's system, as workers drove themselves to exceed production quotas. Pay rates for pieceworkers (both their hourly minimums and their bonus rates) varied widely, depending on the general difficulty of the task and the skill required to perform it, and pieceworkers usually performed a variety of operations on any given day, each with its own pay rate. So two lathe operators, working side by side and performing seemingly the same work, might find a big difference if they compared their paychecks. And for some employees—assemblers, for instance—earnings were determined on a group piecework basis, requiring another form of computation.

Within each plant new tasks, and new rates for them, were introduced continually: the average was five hundred every week, and by the 1940s at Tractor Works there were some *thirty thousand* piecework prices that might be in effect at any given moment. But only management knew exactly how many—Harvester treated the hefty "Black Book," which catalogued its hundreds of occupations and wage ranges along with the key codes required to match them up, as highly classified information. Outside observers found all this profoundly baffling. A frustrated Department of Labor panel, indicating that Harvester officials "could not make the logic of this wage structure clear in extensive hearings before this Board," concluded that "it is hardly possible that the logic of this wage system could be clear to the individual worker in the Company's plants."[6]

So why would Harvester create and then zealously protect such a byzantine system? In the midst of such complexity, this much is simple: it was enormously profitable. IH management remained firmly convinced that its incentive system contained costs while it spurred "substantially more production" than a straight wages-per-hour arrangement would. Auto manufacturing, characterized more so than the farm equipment industry by assembly lines and single-product production, had by the end of the Depression largely eliminated piecework in favor of hourly wage rates. As a result, Harvester asserted, "production dropped at least 30%." And Harvester relied on its own examples closer to home. When it experimented with a straight day rate throughout Tractor Works, the plant's output was slashed in half. On this point, there was rare accord between IH and the FE. "Because the Company operate[s] on a piecework basis of pay," the FE said, "it is safe to assume that the production resulting therefrom was 25 percent greater than had straight day-rate prevailed."[7]

But that acknowledgment hardly constituted an endorsement from the FE. IH management insisted that its piecework rates were calculated utilizing "scientific" methods and were therefore intrinsically "correct." To Harvester workers, however, they seemed based on little beyond what the company could get away with. "Chiseling time studies must be stopped!" declared the newsletter put out by the FE local at McCormick Works in 1942, where employees knew that "the harder they work, and the more work they produce, the time study men work just as hard robbing them of their honest earnings." Jobs were assessed under perfect conditions, the union charged, thus making rates "tight" and bonus pay difficult to achieve. And there could be no rationality when the rules kept changing or fair play when management kept moving the goalposts:

> You work along, devising short cuts, a little more efficiency and make some more money. You can't relax too long. Any day now the time study man may come along and tell you the job is being changed. What's the change? Maybe nothing more than a minor speed or feed adjustment; a negligible tool change; or even moving the machine. What's the purpose? An excuse for re-timing the job to take advantage of all your well-earned experience and show that the time should be cut—in other words, cut the price.[8]

At Harvester, each job, every day, became a potential source of conflict and negotiation, certainly not a formula for harmonious industrial relations. Yet there was managerial method to this madness. The complexity of Harvester's "secret wage rate policy"—as the FE dubbed it—meant workers could never be certain just how much they were genuinely owed. The regular recalibration of tasks allowed the company to realize more production for the same or less pay, which the Marxist FE leadership recognized as a system fine-tuned to eke out as much surplus value from each and every worker as possible. Harvester's emphasis on "incentives" perpetuated the sense that earnings were based on individual initiative rather than what workers could command as a wage-earning collective. "Control through division" was how it felt to Ridley Bell, the FE local president at West Pullman. "This guy against that guy, with both guys sweating their shirts out to make a price." The acceleration of work allowed management to discard "inefficient" employees: "All over the plant men are being told to make out or else they will be fired," said a story out of Harvester's East Moline plant in 1939. "This move by the company is merely to cover the rotten way that they have treated some of their men who have been with the company for years, and who have been canned because they couldn't make out on a new job in a day or two." And it provided a mechanism to "weed out" those not sufficiently subservient: "The piecework system, with its thousands of rates and continual timing of jobs, offered an opportunity for time study men and foremen to harass CIO members with bad prices and bad jobs," said the FE while in the midst of its 1941 organizing campaign.[9]

"Harvester workers are the only ones I have ever seen who at a contract ratification meeting will get up and scream, 'To hell with the contract terms, did you get my grievance settled?'" Such was the primacy of piecework at International Harvester, which ensured that once unionism finally took hold at IH, it needed to be especially "relevant, immediate, and fearless." This imperative would not be diminished by America's entry into the overseas conflict, and so once World War II was underway FE leaders seized on newly available mechanisms that enabled them to challenge the core concepts integral to Harvester's compensation system. Through this home front skirmish in the "people's war," the FE encroached on management's turf, securing gains that going forward would undergird the union's strength.[10]

"I don't know who the true devil was in originating that system and keeping it so complex, but I do know figuring it out was one of the first tasks I set myself when I got involved in the Harvester situation." Aaron Murray Cantor was barely twenty-four years old when he went to work for the FE, and looked even younger, as he was slight—scrawny, it would be fair to say—with a thick head of curly black hair that added a little height to his short frame. Nonetheless he was endowed with the brash self-confidence particular to those born and raised in Brooklyn. There was no doubt that Cantor was smart: while working at a factory he put himself through the City College of New York, emerging with an economics degree in 1940. A bout of polio as a child left him ineligible for military service once WWII began, and so he accepted a post with the nascent War Labor Board in Kansas City. It was a given that his sympathies would lie with labor, as his father was a union carpenter and his mother had survived the notorious Triangle Shirtwaist fire. Grant Oakes, who met Cantor at a WLB hearing, recognized a good thing when he saw one and offered Cantor a job on the spot, creating a position for him, too, then and there: research director for the FE. And so Cantor moved to Chicago to become one of the FE's principal strategists during the World War II era. He zeroed in on Harvester's intricate wage structure, utilizing everything he had learned to earn his economics degree—and then some—to decipher it. Cantor vowed that "establish[ing] control over a very tricky and nefarious incentive wage system" would be priority number one for the union.[11]

In this regard Cantor's experience at the War Labor Board came in handy. The WLB, after all, provided Harvester workers something they had never had before: a chance to air their grievances before an entity other than IH management, with judgments to be enforced by the federal government. And to the extreme displeasure of Harvester officials, the FE took full advantage of this opportunity. "The locals have been instructed to flood the management with as many grievances as possible regardless of merit" and thus the FE was "making a farce of the principle of collective bargaining," so charged George Hodge, Harvester's head of industrial relations. That the company's industrial relations department had been originally purposed to prevent genuine collective bargaining from ever taking place was an irony Hodge left unremarked upon. For their part, FE leaders insisted that Harvester was "cutting prices on hundreds of jobs" in an "arbitrary and capricious" manner. Clearly the "we're all in this together" spirit of camaraderie was not trickling down into Harvester's plants. But by "bombarding" IH with a high volume of complaints the FE's objective was clear enough: to bypass the company in order to command the direct attention of the War Labor Board.[12]

Harvester officials wanted to avoid having cases heard by the WLB for one simple reason: they were losing there, often and consequentially. Technically, during the war, wage increases were to be granted only when inequalities within or between one company's plants could be demonstrated, but Harvester's complex piecework system made the union's job easy in that respect. And once the FE scored more money for even a handful of employees, that could be whipsawed into raises for other workers in the same plant or at another factory, a practice that Harvester management grumbled about regularly. But pay hikes here and there could be absorbed: the real source of anxiety, as far as the company was concerned, lay in the larger purpose behind the FE's use of the WLB. "Our incentive system of wage payment," said IH management, "is under constant attack." The adjustments the FE was achieving will "seriously distort" the company's rate structure, George Hodge protested, adding for good measure that the WLB's rulings "indicate incompetency, irresponsibility, and anti-company prejudice." Should the FE continue to chalk up such victories, "the incentive of the Company's piece-work system would be destroyed. Costs would increase and production would greatly decrease."[13]

This might just have been the usual panicky reaction from a company that had long resisted interference from "outsiders" of any kind, and plenty of corporate executives, not just those at Harvester, resented the labor board's oversight on general principle. But in their fears about the FE's designs IH officials were not entirely off the mark. The union was, in fact, utilizing the WLB to achieve what had theretofore been impossible: the assertion of (at least some) workers' control over the company's "tricky and nefarious wage system." A few important examples demonstrate just how the FE accomplished that.

In early 1943, the FE brought before the board a laundry list of demands on behalf of nearly twenty-two thousand Harvester employees in eight plants: McCormick Works, Tractor Works, and the McCormick Twine Mill among them. The case dragged on through the war years, with the major sticking points—which proved to be very sticky—related to piecework. The

FE sought significant revisions to Harvester's allowance guidelines, and also insisted that any alterations to piecework prices be subject to negotiation.[14]

The seemingly arcane allowance issue requires some explanation. With incentive pay schemes a worker who slacks off and produces less gets paid less: seems simple enough, and on paper, perhaps "fair." But what if the employee slows down because of a balky machine? Or hasn't been supplied with enough raw material and has to go track more down? For these and similar instances, allowances (based usually on average earnings) are granted to compensate workers who are unable to meet production quotas due to circumstances beyond their control. That's the theory, anyhow, but though IH had an allowance policy it was an especially parsimonious one. Harvester's system was designed to afford premium wages only to workers who were actually producing, and at maximum capacity, and so those who could not "make their rate" on a given day for whatever reason, usually received just their low hourly wage. Pieceworkers, therefore, obliged to labor at full tilt to earn their pay under normal conditions, absorbed all the loss when output slackened, even if the slowdown resulted from mechanical breakdowns or managerial interference (or incompetence). This was a matter of no small consequence: employees who were bumped down from premium piecework rates to an hourly wage lost a lot of money. For example, a pieceworker in Group 18 (there were many such categories, all with different wage scales) at McCormick Works in 1944 who made the rate would earn $1.64 an hour (and more if output was greater than the minimum required). But the hourly rate for that pay group was only $1.04. Determinations about allowances were entirely a company prerogative, underscoring again that this "scientific" system remained subject to a good dose of caprice. "If you can dig it out of them," one local FE official said in 1945 about Harvester's allowances, "you get it; if you can't, you don't."[15]

And so WLB case 111-2193-D became anything but a mere technical dispute. In its arguments to the WLB the FE maintained that pieceworkers, in almost all instances when their productivity was hampered, should receive nothing less than their average earnings. Harvester officials insisted they should not be obliged to reward pieceworkers with nearly top dollar for anything less than fully efficient labor. The majority of the Board's members found the union more persuasive, ruling in August 1944 that pieceworkers facing adverse circumstances should, in nearly all cases, receive their average earnings. And the WLB also stipulated that the union had to be notified—and, significantly, its approval sought—before new or altered piecework prices were put into effect.[16]

Harvester management was appalled by this ruling, as was the outvoted industry member on the WLB panel, who railed against it in his dissenting opinion. These altered allowance provisions "guarantee the maximum incentive earnings in periods of no production," which he proclaimed to be a formula for disaster. He foresaw workers wandering off for who-knows-how-long when they ran out of stock, or purposely disabling equipment, all the while being well paid for doing so. IH officials were just as apoplectic about the notification provision. Harvester "vehemently protest[ed]" the notion that piecework prices, which "are computed from factual time-study," should be subject to any form of negotiation.[17]

At Harvester's helm, Fowler McCormick responded predictably to such objectionable interference. First there was the foot-dragging—the decision was appealed—and when that failed, the company simply thumbed its nose at the WLB, developing an interpretation of the Board's order that provided less generous allowances than before the case was decided, resulting in lower wages for pieceworkers. The new policy was put into place in June 1945, initially just at one facility: McCormick Works.

Then, as might also have been expected, the five thousand FE members at the plant promptly walked out. Or actually, Harvester officials reported, first the workers "loafed on the job for more than four hours," and then, after being signaled by "the explosion of two aerial bombs" in a vacant lot adjacent to McCormick Works, they exited the factory. The WLB immediately telegrammed Grant Oakes to remind him that "this strike is in gross violation of labor's no strike pledge to which your union is a party," but the McCormick plant remained shut down nonetheless. This came as no surprise to the local FBI, which noted that though the FE's "official attitude" was "allegedly 'neutral,'" the union's top leadership "unofficially encouraged the strike." The workers finally returned after four days, but only after the union had secured a commitment from the WLB to "clarify" the allowance rules. More pressure was brought to bear on both the board and the company in mid-July, when the FE executed a coordinated ten-minute work stoppage at several other Harvester plants; simultaneously a throng of McCormick workers picketed outside the Chicago office of the WLB to indicate that "they would not tolerate wage cuts or more delay in deciding their case."[18]

When the WLB at last issued its final order on allowance rules, Harvester officials probably wished they had accepted the initial decision and kept quiet. In its October 1945 "clarification" the board rebuked the company, declaring that "our intention was to liberalize the allowance system," not "modify the existing rules or practices in any fashion that would have as its effect a reduction in wages." To underscore that point, the board expanded beyond its original ruling the circumstances under which the highest allowances would prevail. Again, Harvester management was incensed, charging that the board was mandating that the company pay "a premium or incentive rate of pay for little or, in the case of waiting time, no effort on the part of employees." IH petitioned to have the decision set aside, but that would come to naught: the War Labor Board was dissolved at the end of 1945.[19]

And this was far from the only instance during the war in which the FE utilized government boards to rewrite the rules within Harvester's plants. In November 1944, around the time DeWitt Gilpin was slogging toward Belgium with Patton's Third Army, a contingent of FE members at the IH factory in East Moline, Illinois, aggravated by stepped-up production levels, did some marching of their own, straight out of the plant. When the workers, all of them employed on the assembly line, returned three days later, they did so on their own terms, turning out far fewer harvester-thresher combines than those dictated by management's quotas. The plant superintendent then fired forty-six of the dallying assemblers, but workers in other departments refused to fill in for them. Wriggling around the strictures of the no-strike pledge, FE leaders, both local and national, indicated that "as a Union, they would take no action, but as individuals, they would not encourage employees to take the [assembly] jobs, but on the contrary would discourage them." Instead, the FE demanded that the discharged workers be rehired (with back pay) and the obligatory number of combines be reduced. Harvester offered to allow the assemblers back—and with a wage increase—if they would agree to the company's production schedule, but the union insisted that it was the punishing pace, not the pay, that was the crux of this dispute. And so the once-relentless assembly line stood motionless and uncommonly silent, and stayed that way for more than two months.[20]

The WLB stepped in to adjudicate the matter. After considerable back-and-forth Harvester buckled, agreeing in January 1945 to reduce the required quota and rehire the fired workers, and a later ruling held that the discharged assemblers were entitled to full wages for all those idle weeks they enjoyed away from the plant.[21]

Aaron Cantor played the central role in the union's sweeping victory in the East Moline case. He had either quickly absorbed the FE's ethos or was hired by Grant Oakes because he was already in full possession of the combative qualities deemed requisite for the job. "I do remember one action, and then I was sitting across the table from Fowler McCormick," Cantor recalled,

... and I was convinced at the time that the fellows in the shop were ready to walk and that it would not be an irresponsible act because I was fairly confident that success was at our beck and call if we took the right action. . . . After making phone calls to various key local people, I came back to the table, and pointed a finger at Fowler Mc-Cormick, and said Fowler, your plants are going to be down in 20 minutes if this is not solved. And it was solved.[22]

His engagement with the FE was relatively brief—Cantor remained on the staff for a few years after the war, but then left for law school and spent the latter part of his career at a Manhattan firm, in a handsome office at Rockefeller Center. But he recalled his time with the FE as particularly significant, personally and otherwise. "As I've looked back from time to time over the years, I think it was the most thrilling part of my life," he said. "A twenty-five or twenty-six-year-old, sitting across the table from Fowler McCormick, trading proposals with him, giving him deadlines for meeting demands. You had tactical exercises, intellectual exercises, all within the overriding context of what to me were very valued social objectives. What more could a young fellow want?" These "valued social objectives" proved to be very valuable indeed for Harvester workers, who were pocketing a lot more money by the time World War II drew to a close. That was true generally for many Americans during the course of the war, as average weekly earnings in manufacturing increased 65 percent from the end of 1941 through 1944. But the FE's rank and file at Harvester made out even better, for employees at the eight plants involved in the WLB's allowance case saw their wages rise by more than 80 percent. Incomes for FE members had increased "in every category," Harvester management said, "and from every possible approach." This was not an achievement Harvester officials proclaimed with pride. They had done everything they could to prevent it.[23]

But Aaron Cantor and the FE leadership sought something for Harvester workers beyond just that significant bump in their paychecks; their objectives in the "people's war" were of broader scope. They were determined to establish, Cantor indicated, "democratic control over the powers of management relating to the tenure and conditions of work, particularly the disciplinary powers of management." Much as the iron molders once had done, the FE leadership was challenging Harvester's exclusive right to establish the pace of production and the manner in which work would be carried out, prerogatives that in the twentieth century had come to be widely regarded as management's alone. Through their aggressive utilization of the WLB, and a reliance on extrajudicial tactics—even with the no-strike pledge in effect—FE leaders demonstrated just how serious they were about "democratic control" in the plants. Their achievements marked a shift in the balance of power between the company and the union. As World War II began to wind down, Harvester management was envisioning "those hoped for green pastures of the restoration of company unionism," so Grant Oakes insisted. But with the FE now on much more solid ground a return to the status quo ante was no longer a possibility. Oakes issued this warning directly to Harvester officials: "Either [IH] can cooperate for orderly relations and steady employment of their workers, or they can prepare for a head-on clash . . . in either event, gentlemen, we stand ready to meet you."[24]

The inevitable choice was the head-on clash.

11.
Postwar Warfare

t's a venerable union maxim: "No Contract, No Work." In early 1946, as the FE waged its second major strike against International Harvester, it would be often repeated. "Harvester people know that without a contract, countless grievances involving pay rates, piecework, allowances, and every other day-to-day factor in earning power would arise in every plant," said the *FE News*. The FE-IH contract, first secured in 1941, was then a slim booklet only a few dozen pages long. It was, however, heavy with history, which the FE leadership took pains to emphasize in 1946. Employees at the McCormicks' enterprise were thus again reading about August Spies and Albert Parsons. "Sixty fighting years have passed since McCormick workers in Chicago gave May Day to the world. Dead heroes then—a union contract now—but it took sixty years to get it."[1]

It's not entirely certain that Spies and Parsons would have wished to be invoked in defense of the union's contract, given the dubious regard the anarchists held for signed agreements between capital and labor. But they would have applauded the martial rhetoric employed by Jerry Fielde, who with the war's end had returned to his leadership post with the FE. "All the blueprints for this great fight against McCormick greed have been made," Fielde said on the eve of the 1946 strike. "So far as money is concerned, the scales are loaded against us. So far as everything else goes—we have all the power," he continued. "McCormick and the bankers can't make a doorknob, much less a tractor or a plowshare, without workers. Union solidarity at the plant gates will beat them. Hold every line!"[2]

As had been the case for the FE's first strike against Harvester, the 1946 walkout was set to begin in the dead of winter. Back in 1941, however, the strike had closed four factories; this time the FE represented Harvester employees at ten facilities in three states. For this second showdown there would be no need for surprise assaults; when the FE leadership called the strike, on January 21, 1946, some thirty thousand Harvester workers promptly shut their plants down. Temperatures hovered around zero in Chicago, but thousands rallied outside McCormick Works, and at every factory solid picket lines patrolled the gates. And the struck plants now included the sizable Farmall facility in Rock Island, since in 1944 the four thousand workers there had voted to switch their allegiance from the AFL to the FE.[3]

Something else was different this time around: many of those on strike had only recently returned to Harvester's employ after stints in the armed forces. A few days into the walkout, about 150 FE members chose to perform their picket duty in front of the International Harvester building in Chicago, jostling elbows with the lunch hour crowd hustling down Michigan Avenue. One of the marchers brandished an errantly spelled sign proclaiming, "HITLER WAS AN AMATUER—HEIL HARVESTER!" Since all the marchers were veterans of World War II as well as employees of IH they felt entitled to draw the comparison. "HARVESTER CAN PAY! WE WILL MAKE THEM!" they asserted.[4]

Harvester executives, peering down through their office windows, were surely offended by the sloganeering but were even more affronted by the union's demands. The insistence on a 30 percent pay hike garnered the most press, but FE leaders intended also to amplify the "democratic control over the powers of management" that had gained traction during the war. Thus they committed to fight for a "fair, understandable piecework system" and the retention of company-paid time off for union representatives doing grievance work. The FE pressed for a strong union security clause, meaning workers would have to join the union in order to continue working at IH. The union also sought to replace the company's departmental seniority system in favor of "straight plant-wide seniority." The FE's negotiating committee, headed by Fielde, included five African American workers from IH plants in Chicago. They may have pushed this demand especially forcefully, as plantwide seniority would make it easier for Black employees, who were generally newer hires, to transfer into better jobs.[5]

The FE contended that International Harvester could well afford all of this. "IHC tripled its profits during the war years," the union said, and the postwar forecast, promising "unprecedented profits," looked even sunnier. As always, the rays of good fortune shined especially brightly on one small circle, since nearly two-fifths of the company's stock was owned by just nine members of the McCormick family. It was past time, the FE said, for fairer distribution of this considerable wealth. Not that Jerry Fielde, who had a long memory, actually expected that would happen. "They have not changed their spots," he said in early 1946 about Harvester management, asserting that the company's real intent was "to actually get rid of the union."[6]

Fowler McCormick and Harvester's other top officials would not yet acknowledge publicly that they wanted to get rid of the FE, but they were certainly up front in their willingness to take it on. So not only would Fowler McCormick reject the FE's demands, he was determined to jettison much of what the union had already won. IH officials indicated their primary objectives in postwar negotiations were "to retain our incentive system of wage payment" and "protect the functions of management" and thus, as always, they were less concerned with money per se and more focused on maintaining (or reasserting) their authority. They vowed to eliminate the most glaring examples, all achieved by the FE during the war with the help of government boards, of egregious encroachment on management's turf. Harvester stood opposed to "compulsory unionism" and also sought to vitiate, or at the least substantially reduce, its obligation to remunerate employees moonlighting as union stewards who stirred up plenty of trouble while investigating grievances but "produced nothing."[7]

There was one additional issue that prompted Harvester to draw a line in the sand. "Proper allowances for pieceworkers represent one of the major tasks of the Company for 1946" and therefore the cushy allowance rules workers enjoyed during the war needed to be chucked, by hook or by crook. "If we are to achieve proper costs," read a labor relations department memo, it was deemed "essential" that the company "adopt a sound Allowance Plan through collective bargaining or put it into effect anyway." To outsiders then (and now), Harvester's arcane allowance structure may have seemed an awfully trivial matter to generate such emphatic resolve. But the relaxed allowance provisions struck at the heart of managerial discretion, making it impossible—or at least, prohibitively expensive—for the company to maintain unilateral control over the execution of work. "The power to set [allowance] rules is the power of life and death over our business from a cost standpoint," one IH executive declared. Within International Harvester's headquarters, where Cyrus McCormick II's watchful portrait hung on the boardroom wall, this could be no trifling matter.[8]

Outside in the bracing weather on Michigan Avenue, however, the FE's picket line contingent seemed comfortable about their chances. They were buoyed by the tidal wave of solidarity roiling the postwar economy. Nearly one quarter of a million autoworkers were already on strike against General Motors; walkouts by electrical workers and meatpackers in mid-January added another two hundred and seventy thousand to picket lines across the country. And on the same day the FE strike began, some eight hundred thousand steelworkers began their own walkout. Coal miners, train engineers, municipal employees, and school teachers, among others, would follow suit in short order, with many of these confrontations dragging on for months. This was disruption on an unprecedented scale: nearly five thousand work stoppages involving over four and a half million Americans, more than had ever struck before (or since). The war had imposed much upon workers who had remained at home: grueling schedules, wage limits, uprooted com-munities, rationing and shortages, substandard living conditions in over-crowded defense centers. And many had lost more than could be measured, mourning for those who would never return. But the defense boom had also elevated expectations, as unemployment evaporated, paychecks were con-siderably higher than they had been during the lean Depression years, and union representation instilled confidence in employees who had once known only insecurity on the job. Returning veterans, like those who marched out-side the Harvester headquarters, also felt empowered, and entitled, by their military service. In the meantime, corporate coffers had been spectacularly enriched. So in what one labor economist called the "postwar warfare" of 1946, workers came calling about an overdue debt. They expected to collect what they were owed.[9]

Yet this show of force was met by equal determination from the other side. American industrialists intended to resist wage increases and, more im-portantly, wrest control from upstart unions that had in a few short years grown far too presumptuous. Victory in the "people's war" overseas and visions of a new world order would not, corporate leaders were anxious to reiterate, usher in any profound transformation of the way business was con-ducted back home. By 1946, with Harry Truman in the White House, the New Deal seemed to be degenerating into the same old deal, especially for labor. President Truman made manifest his lack of union affinity when he proved willing to deploy the US Army to break railroad and steel strikes, and the CIO's hopes for federal policy that would promote substantial across-the-board wage hikes and maintain wartime price controls quickly faded. General Motors thus brushed aside the audacious proposal, from razor-sharp UAW Vice-President Walter Reuther, that the company "open the books" to verify its claim that it could not afford the union's demands. GM sat tight on its assets and endured a 113-day strike; autoworkers ultimately settled for a wage increase much lower than had been originally sought while man-agement regained its exclusive right to jack up the sticker prices on its new Buicks. That proved to be the general trajectory for most of the 1946 strikes: unions scored modest financial gains (often offset by postwar inflation) but otherwise achieved little that altered the balance of power between labor and capital. Thus the postwar fix was in: union members could expect regular im-provements in wages and benefits secured through collective bargaining, but in exchange labor leaders grudgingly conceded that management's preroga-tives and issues regarding profit, prices, and productivity were permanently off the table.[10]

That has been the general historical consensus, anyhow, but the Harvester strike of 1946 reveals that both IH and the FE missed the memo regarding such an understanding. In keeping with tradition, Harvester management exhibited its characteristic intransigence during the walkout and, as had also been true in the past, adopted what were at the time sophisticated strikebreaking tactics. In late 1945, as contract negotiations began, and then throughout the strike, Harvester sent out a series of letters to its employees that provided a platform—just as had been the case with its Industrial Council Plan—to highlight "economic laws and facts" that workers seemed unwilling to grasp. The letters stressed that "the Company has the exclusive right to direct the work of employees, to make work assignments and to determine the quality and quantity of production required . . . these are all matters outside the scope of Union authority . . ." And the messages included swipes at the FE leadership's ill-mannered behavior: "There must be an end to the abusive language and the misrepresentations of facts which have so frequently appeared in Union publications and speeches in discussions of the Company or individuals in management." Drop the Hitler comparisons, in other words.[11]

Harvester's direct mail campaign was, at the time, a novel industrial relations concept but one that then came perilously close to violating the law. The outreach drew a stern rebuke from a Department of Labor panel convened to investigate the Harvester dispute. But Harvester continued sending the letters nonetheless, and in addition ignored the panel's recommendations, announced in mid-February 1946, that the company should grant an eighteen-cent-an-hour wage increase and retain the union security and steward pay provisions from its wartime contract. The FE could readily accept these terms, Jerry Fielde indicated, but Harvester would not, though within a few weeks the company consented to the pay hike. "Wages are no longer an issue in this strike," Harvester declared. But that's not the way the union saw it, stressing that promised pay hikes were meaningless absent the other contract provisions. "The company is trying to divert attention," said an FE flyer issued from McCormick Works, "from the fact that it refuses to grant union security and pay for handling grievances and refuses to bargain out agreements on all the other issues which afford our only written guarantee of wages and working conditions, such as wage structure, piecework controls, allowance rules, seniority, etc."[12]

That appeared to be the consensus view within the FE membership, judging by the high level of rank-and-file participation even as the weeks dragged by. "Every day at our Local Union Hall we have a strike meeting at 11:30 a.m. that is attended by two or three hundred people," came a report in late February from the McCormick local. "In fact all the gates at

McCormick are locked up tighter than Fowler's pocketbook!" A few days later, more than seven thousand Harvester workers crammed into a strike meeting at a Chicago auditorium; "the crowd overflowed through the stairways, lobby, and out into the street," as *FE News* photos confirmed. One of the speakers at the rally was Milt Burns, freshly returned to the FE fold after serving with the Marines in the Pacific.[13]

But while these displays of solidarity were crucial they were not the only thing pressuring Fowler McCormick to make further concessions. It turned out that the FE still could find some friends—or at least, some officials not entirely in thrall to International Harvester—in Washington. As farmers clamored for new machinery, the Secretary of Agriculture and the Secretary of Labor jointly concurred that "supplies of equipment are at a disastrously low level," raising the specter of food shortages "not only for the United States but for the suffering peoples of other countries." Due to this "grave emergency" they hinted that a federal seizure of the agricultural implement industry might be in order. Since the government's fact-finding panel had previously recommended a settlement Harvester refused to accept, such a move was not likely to end well for the company. The FE, on the other hand, trumpeted a resolution passed by the National Farmers Union urging a takeover of the struck plants. In late March top IH and FE officials were summoned to Washington; the union immediately complied while Harvester loftily proclaimed that "we see no useful purpose" for the parley and declined to attend. But the company shortly acceded to government pressure, though Fowler McCormick dispatched subordinates rather than make the trek himself. Ten days of round-the-clock negotiations, presided over by Assistant Secretary of Labor (and former Michigan CIO official) John Gibson, finally produced an agreement. The 1946 walkout was over.[14]

"The eighty-day strike," said the FE, "scored the greatest gains for the workers involved in any of the postwar wage and contract struggles." Of course that's what the union's newspaper would say. Certainly the FE was not victorious on every point: eighteen cents an hour was considerably less than its opening demand of a 30 percent pay hike. The paid vacation provision wasn't as generous as what the union had sought. On union security it was a split decision. Harvester successfully fended off "compulsory unionism," as the wartime maintenance of membership provision was replaced with an arrangement more palatable to management, providing for a dues check-off and a seven-day "escape clause" that allowed employees to withdraw from the FE.[15]

In most other respects, though, the *FE News* got it right: Harvester workers won big. The contract did much to democratize shop-floor practice and fortified the union for its future struggles with management. Union stewards would continue to be compensated for their time handling grievances, and at their highest piecework rate, so their earnings would not suffer as they pursued workers' complaints. And there was every reason to believe that FE stewards would henceforth be doing a lot of that: for the first time Harvester workers established the right to challenge their job classifications or piecework prices through the grievance procedure. "The Company may no longer maintain that its book of rules has the standing of the Bible," the FE announced. IH was required to provide advance notice of any impending changes in piece rates and the determination of those rates "shall be fair and reasonable." Harvester had retained the incentive system it so valued but its absolute authority over it had been severely eroded. Moreover, the FE now fielded an army—and the new contract increased the number of stewards allowed—that would be roaming the plants, on company time, reminding management of that inconvenient truth.[16]

The union came out ahead on its other demands as well. Plantwide, rather than departmental, seniority would govern for all workers with more than a year's tenure. "The years a worker applies in Harvester become an investment which cannot be taken away," said the *FE News*. While this protected older employees from arbitrary dismissal, such language, combined with the strong non-discrimination clause included in the contract, also meant that the many hundreds of more recently hired Black workers might transfer into better jobs when openings occurred. "Every American is assured the right to a job in Harvester based on ability—not prejudice," the FE paper declared. This then-exceptional seniority provision would continue over the years to undergird the union's African American support.[17]

But beyond these successes there was another that constituted "one of the biggest contract victories of any CIO union," so much so that the *FE News* boxed it off for singular emphasis. "This is the issue which the company fought bitterly," the paper said, "yielding only on the very last day after trying every trick they could think of." Despite Harvester's determination to be rid of them, the liberal allowances that the FE had secured during the war were preserved entirely intact in the 1946 contract. "The allowance rules were won after a hard-fought battle lasting for over four years, including War Labor Board cases, but it took an eighty-day strike to wring them out of the company," the union insisted. Allowances were a "life and death" matter to Harvester officials, who had declared before the strike that if they could not achieve a "sound" system of allowances at the bargaining table they would "*put it into effect anyway*." Which only underscored the importance of the paid time the union had secured for its steward body. The contract, good as it was, was going to require a lot of policing.[18]

Why, then, did Fowler McCormick and Harvester management concede as much as they did to end the strike? Their eagerness to collect the profits to be made in a booming postwar market and the imperative to maintain Harvester's dominance in the increasingly competitive farm equipment industry were prime motivators. It's also far more difficult to claw back what's already in a contract, as opposed to rejecting new demands. For the most part the FE's victories in 1946 represented a peacetime ratification of what had already been imposed on Harvester during World War II. Federal agencies had been central to establishing those provisions in the first place, and once again such intervention proved helpful for the FE; after the contract was signed, Jerry Fielde wrote to Assistant Labor Secretary John Gibson thanking him for his "fine assistance" during the final round of bargaining. It's not likely that any similar messages were sent by Fowler McCormick. Within a short time—and certainly by November 1946, when Republicans gained control of Congress—the climate in Washington turned decidedly chilly for labor. FE leaders, however, seized the opportunities available while the political winds were still shifting. It would be the last time in a Harvester strike that they could look to federal officials for help, but what had been established in the 1946 agreement provided them with the infrastructure necessary to build strength internally.[19]

For the FE, however, one factor above all had proved decisive: "It was the rank and file, the picket-line solidarity, the hardworking strike committees—the cold and quiet plants—which won the victory." Such was "the great and invincible strength of the workers," Jerry Fielde had said just before the 1946 walkout began, and through that unity they had secured a contract the FE trumpeted as unmatched anywhere else. But Harvester workers, returning to their jobs in late April, were again reminded that their recent achievement had been a long time in the making. On May Day 1946, the *FE News* announced, "special shop meetings" would be held in Chicago's IH plants to "honor the memory of the 1886 martyrs . . . whose mighty efforts paved the way for the standards we take for granted today," and in the afternoon an FE delegation would make a pilgrimage to Waldheim Cemetery to lay a wreath at the anarchists' gravesite.[20]

But this spiritual kinship with the Haymarket martyrs lingered on after the May Day commemorations had concluded. FE leaders regarded the agreement just negotiated with International Harvester, vital though it was, as a document that codified rights and benefits that workers had always been entitled to but did not otherwise serve to delimit their activity. That became crystal clear by September, just a few months into the new contract, when a series of work stoppages took place at Harvester's Farmall plant in Rock Island. In a letter to employees, the plant manager complained that FE officials were endeavoring to "exercise the functions which properly belong to management" and had "disrupted production by attempting to determine the type of work employees should perform and the methods of manufacture." A "cooperative partnership" between the FE and IH could only develop, the letter continued, if the union remained confined to "its proper sphere."[21]

The problem for Harvester was that FE officials, whatever their signatures on the 1946 contract might have suggested, were not especially interested in a cooperative partnership with management and refused to recognize restrictions on where workers could tread: a sentiment August Spies would have been comfortable with. Going forward, however, FE leaders found themselves increasingly at odds on these points not just with the company but with the labor movement they had helped build.

Workers converse on an FE picket line. [Collection of Toni Gilpin]

Part Three

The FE Against the Grain

As the Cold War climate grew increasingly inhospitable for labor radicals, crusading anti-communist Walter Reuther, at the helm of the UAW, asserted jurisdiction over the farm equipment industry. During its "raids" on plants already organized by the FE, the UAW ran ads like this one, insisting that the FE "follows the Communist line." [Collection of Toni Gilpin]

Sterling Neal, a driving force in the Louisville FE, was also an early mentor to noted civil rights activist Anne Braden. [Photograph courtesy of Beverly Neal Watkins and Gerald Neal]

An FE rally outside McCormick Works in November 1945, on the eve of an NLRB election triggered by a UAW takeover attempt. The FE won the election decisively. Note the signs that say: "Two of a Kind: International Harvester Co. UAW Raiders Both Union Busters." [Wisconsin Historical Society, WHS-81734]

FE members and national officials gather outside Tractor Works, prepared to fend off another UAW raid. Included in this photo are Tractor Works Local 101 Vice-President Frank Mingo (holding flyers); Local 101 President Pete Neputy (beside Mingo, in hat); and FE national leaders DeWitt Gilpin (pointing to flyers) and Milt Burns (right foreground, in sports jacket). [UE Archives, University of Pittsburgh Library System]

Between 1945 and 1954, more than one thousand work stoppages took place at International Harvester plants represented by the FE, a fact that did much to solidify the union's radical reputation. Here FE members at Tractor Works have walked out over an unresolved grievance. [UE Archives, University of Pittsburgh Library System]

FE members, like these shown in East Moline, Illinois, during a 1948 strike against International Harvester, were disinclined to allow strikebreakers past their picket lines, and proved willing to employ extreme measures to make their point. [Collection of Toni Gilpin]

At International Harvester's Louisville plant, opened after World War II, African American and white workers came in regular contact with each other. FE Local 236 organized the plant in 1947. This photo of an IH plant is likely from Louisville. [Collection of Toni Gilpin]

Jim Wright was one of the first workers hired at Harvester's Louisville plant and soon became a key leader of the FE local there. Wright would go on to a long career in the labor movement, and is shown here in the early 1970s at a rally for the Equal Rights Amendment in Springfield, Illinois. [Photograph by Syd Harris]

Jim Mouser, shown here on the left, securing groceries with his family during a strike, was also a rank-and-file FE leader at Harvester's Louisville plant. He and Jim Wright became close friends. [UE Archives, University of Pittsburgh Library System]

When two African American local leaders at the Harvester plant in Louisville were fired after instigating a work stoppage, the entire FE membership there—which was 90 percent white—walked out in protest. This action drew favorable notice from the *Louisville Defender*, the city's African American newspaper. [Collection of Toni Gilpin]

12.
A New Adversary Emerges

Atlantic City in the 1940s had sea breezes and glitzy nightclubs and saltwater taffy stands lining its boardwalk. It did not have an International Harvester plant or FE outpost anywhere in the vicinity. Nonetheless, on March 27, 1946, something of great consequence happened there for both the company and the union. At the cavernous Atlantic City auditorium, the delegates at the United Auto Workers convention chose thirty-eight-year-old hard-charging red-headed Walter Reuther to be their president. Reuther's election occurred just a few weeks before the Harvester strike ended, so the FE's leaders were, at that moment, focused on their effort to deliver a good contract. But they took notice of the news coming out of that resort town on the New Jersey shore; with the *Chicago Tribune* declaring, "REUTHER TO OUST REDS IF MADE UAW HEAD," it was impossible to miss. In fact, by 1946 every development within the FE was affected—and not in a good way—by the actions of Reuther's much larger and far better-funded organization. Just at the moment the FE had finally established firm footing in its ongoing struggle with International Harvester, the union would have an additional, and nearly as formidable, adversary to worry about.[1]

As it happened, the 1946 UAW convention took place two weeks after Winston Churchill declared that an "iron curtain" divided the Soviet Union from the "free" world, signaling that the Cold War was underway. With President Truman's avowal to contain Soviet expansion, anti-communism became official US policy. In the November 1946 elections, as part of a sweep that gave Republicans control of both houses of Congress for the first time since 1928, the crusading anti-communist newcomers Joseph McCarthy and Richard Nixon took office. The escalating frenzy to ferret out the "reds" sowed suspicion and stifled speech in classrooms and film studios and factory floors across the country, as thousands lost their jobs—and often much more—when their patriotism was called into question. Few of those accused of being "un-American" were actually radicals of any sort—many had simply defended the American right to dissent—so those with genuine CP ties, like the FE leadership, were clearly in the crosshairs in the anti-communist crackdown. Walter Reuther, however, was more in step with what was rapidly becoming the tenor of those treacherous times.[2]

The FE's left-wing officials, though, did share some common ground with the new UAW president. Like several of the FE's founders, Walter

Reuther was a machinist; as a teenager in the 1920s he began practicing his exacting trade in Detroit's auto factories. Already Reuther's tireless intensity, coupled with his disdain for carousing—he didn't drink or smoke—set him apart. But back then, those who took just a passing glance at Reuther's pale, boyish face might have failed to recognize that he was a young man in a hurry. Initially, however, he wasn't sure just what he wanted to achieve. Reuther's father, a German immigrant, had been an active socialist, and once the Depression hit Walter too flirted with varying left-wing ideologies. In fact, as did Joe Weber, Reuther spent time in the Soviet Union, working for a year at the Gorky Auto Works. Reuther began organizing for the nascent UAW when he returned to Detroit in 1936, and catapulted to national attention for the savage beating he took from Ford Motor Company thugs in 1937.

Reuther was astute and devoted to the union cause, like the FE leadership and so many others who built the early CIO. Increasingly, however, despite (or perhaps because of) the time he spent in Russia, Reuther eschewed Marxist-Leninist principles, and the allegiance to the Communist Party, that guided class warriors like Joe Weber. Reuther still leaned to the left, but tilted away from Moscow. In the late 1930s the UAW was riven by factionalism; as was the case in most CIO unions, Communists had been crucial to early autoworkers' organizing efforts, but there were activists with a range of political convictions vying for power within the union. The announcement of the Nazi-Soviet pact in 1939, which induced CP members to transform overnight from advocates of American intervention in the European conflict into ardent isolationists (only to flip back again a short time later), proved a decisive breakpoint for many in the noncommunist left, Reuther chief among them. He became "a national spokesman for the prodefense, pro-Roosevelt 'right-wing' within the American labor movement" and vowed to purge communist adherents from the UAW. The Communist Party, as far as Reuther was concerned, was an outside agent with a perfidious agenda; one could be faithful to the CP or the UAW but not both.[3]

So Reuther worked relentlessly to isolate his opponents while he steadily broadened his own support both within the UAW and outside it. His proposal for "500 Planes a Day" during World War II and his call to "Open the Books" during the 1945 GM strike burnished his credentials as a labor leader with unusual intellectual heft and vision; given his blue-collar milieu, Reuther's buttoned-down persona (he tended toward three-piece suits and crisply laundered shirts) further underscored his seriousness in the eyes of the press and landed him on the cover of *Time* magazine. He was indeed a trade union politician of the first order: Reuther "deserved much credit," one veteran of the labor in-fighting wryly acknowledged, "and saw that he got it." His margin of victory at the 1946 UAW convention was razor-thin, but by "transform[ing] this narrow victory into an anti-Communist mandate," Reuther ousted the remaining CP partisans and consolidated tight control over the union: loyalty to the UAW had been redefined to mean fidelity to Reuther himself. He had become the head of the largest American labor union and the leading anti-communist within the CIO.[4]

Reuther's ideology, however, was not precisely comparable to that of red-baiters like Joseph McCarthy or Robert McCormick at the *Chicago Tribune*. Reuther never entirely shed those socialist sympathies he'd grown up with, meaning that he was far more than just an adroit political operator or a "bread and butter" union official. He saw the labor movement not simply as an agent for material improvements for its members but as a champion for social justice. Like the FE leadership and other CP-influenced labor activists, Reuther thought systemically and abhorred the inequality generated by unfettered capitalism. He parted company with Marxist analysis, however, in his assessments of how exploitation occurs and what should be done to address it. Reuther "remained convinced that, under the rule of law, competing classes could work for the common good" and defined the fundamental division in American society as between "private privilege" and "the people" rather than that between capital and labor. "I have nothing against free enterprise," he thus maintained. A growing economy, Reuther thought, coupled with an expanded New Deal–style regulatory welfare state, could ensure that the "common good" was served. Combining his ambitious agenda with outspoken anti-communism allowed Reuther to win the admiration of liberal intellectuals and secured for the UAW an increasingly important role within the Democratic Party in the Cold War era.[5]

But Reuther's antipathy toward communism, which was both political and personal—he felt he'd been betrayed during his rise to power by CP members—became no less an obsession for him than it was for reactionaries like McCarthy and McCormick. Nor would he confine his crusade to his own union: he also set his sights on obliterating the Farm Equipment Workers.

From the beginning there had been some tension between the FE and the UAW, springing from obvious jurisdictional overlap. International Harvester, for instance, made trucks as well as agricultural implements, and in 1941, while the FE was engaged in its multiplant battle against IH, the UAW organized Harvester truck plants in Illinois and Indiana. Merger proposals were floated in these early years, but they foundered as the political fault line between the two unions widened, a divide that increased as

Walter Reuther continued his ascent. In 1945 the UAW's executive board announced "an all-out campaign to enroll all farm equipment workers under the banner of the UAW-CIO" and called for representational elections at plants where the FE was the established bargaining agent. (If interest in a competing union is established—usually through petitions—the National Labor Relations Board allows for a vote to be taken to determine which union employees prefer.) The targets in this new organizing drive, in other words, would be workers who were already organized. Though Walter Reuther was not yet in control of the UAW (he was then a vice-president), FE leaders were convinced that his fingerprints were all over this "raiding" scheme. Reuther "was willing to see his union violate CIO unity," proclaimed the FE executive board, and would "endanger the welfare of farm equipment workers in order to strengthen his faction in the UAW." Press accounts and interested parties like the FBI concurred that the Reuther bloc was determined to drive the FE "out of existence because of its communist leadership."[6]

Given that objective, the best place to strike the FE would be at its heart, and so the UAW took aim at the most iconic factory in the farm equipment industry: McCormick Works. The UAW insisted it already had the support of thousands of employees there, despite the fact that they were already members of FE Local 108. So, in March 1945, workers heading into the plant were accosted by UAW staff members passing handbills lauding their organization's superior size and bank balance, while FE loyalists responded with flyers emphasizing their union's "toughness and militancy." Neither side, however, relied solely on the power of the printed word to press their points. One morning "a free-for-all battle," news accounts said, erupted between the feuding unionists, and thus, in addition to leaflets, "black eyes, bruises, and cuts were distributed" that day; six FE members and one UAW sympathizer were arrested. Some seventy-five Chicago police officers regularly patrolled around McCormick Works in an effort to "keep arguments from developing into brawls," an effort that proved only moderately successful. Both unions found ways to make use of the police presence. A UAW supporter swore out arrest warrants for fifteen FE members, claiming he'd been attacked by them on the way to work; the FE retaliated the next week and had fifteen UAW sympathizers brought in for assault and battery.[7]

The FE's leadership relied on other means as well to demonstrate that farm equipment workers, and not just those at the McCormick plant, preferred "toughness and militancy" to whatever the UAW was offering. A poll of the entire membership on the question of UAW affiliation was held in mid-August 1945; more than twenty-nine thousand FE members voted "to maintain their own union," while only some twenty-two hundred expressed a desire to move into the UAW. And on the eve of the November 6, 1945 NLRB election, on an unseasonably warm seventy-degree day, nearly five thousand workers gathered outside the main McCormick gate for an FE rally. The speakers included Bob Travis, the Flint sit-down hero who'd helped engineer the FE's 1941 victory after he'd become an outcast in the increasingly anti-communist UAW.

With those predictors the NLRB election results shouldn't have come as a shock, but they were decisive. With turnout at almost 85 percent, the FE carried the plant by a vote of 3,103 to 1,763, nearly a two-thirds majority. Given the concerted, and costly, campaign they'd waged at McCormick Works, this tally surely proved discouraging to the UAW forces. FE members seemed to have made it convincingly clear that they preferred a union of their own, led by the officers who had founded it.[8]

The vote at McCormick Works, however, did not mean that the effort to subjugate the FE was over: Quite the contrary, for once Walter Reuther solidified his hold over the UAW the battle was guaranteed to escalate. FE officials could thus hardly rest on their laurels, even if they had wanted to, once the 1946 Harvester strike ended. IH management certainly wasn't going to get more cooperative, so regular confrontations would continue at all the company's plants, and with the UAW encroaching on farm equipment turf in an ever-more-ominous Cold War climate, the organizing challenges for the FE would only multiply. But rather than hunker down and defend their existing position, FE leaders launched a new offensive instead. The target once again was an International Harvester facility, but this one was in entirely new territory. IH was heading south, and the FE was going after it.

13.
IH Heads South

Staggeringly wealthy Fowler McCormick, the crown prince of America's industrial royalty, may have felt entitled to make his own rules. In his personal life he made that clear enough when he married his Princeton pal's mother. At the helm of International Harvester, he proved just as willing to defy convention—with the exception, that is, of a few bedrock principles the company would never abandon.

As the peacetime economy took shape, Fowler decided that the McCormicks' august enterprise was overdue for a serious shake-up, and to accomplish that he dipped into coffers made fat from wartime profits. He reshuffled the managerial deck, as he became Harvester's chief executive officer, while former sales manager John McCaffrey took over as company president. Fowler would be the corporate visionary while McCaffrey was tasked with overseeing Harvester's day-to-day operations. Fowler's big game plan included diversifying into consumer goods like refrigerators and air conditioners while capitalizing on the booming agricultural market with innovations to Harvester's traditional product line. Chief among these would be the novel "Cub" tractor. The compact IH Cub was designed for small family farmers, for as late as 1945 most farms in the United States were still under twenty acres, and on nearly a third of them draft animals supplied the only form of locomotion. Fowler was keen to put all those horses out to pasture permanently. Since a large percentage of those smaller farms were in the South, situating Cub production in that region of the country seemed an efficient choice. And there would be no need to build a new factory from the ground up, for in April 1946 IH acquired—at a bargain price—an enormous facility in Louisville, Kentucky, that had been constructed by the federal government during WWII for aircraft production.[1]

Its Louisville plant would be the first International Harvester opened in the South. Those who know the city only from television coverage of the Kentucky Derby might envision white picket fences and rolling hills blanketed in bluegrass. That, however, is genteel Lexington, where thoroughbreds are raised; in Louisville, horses (and gamblers) show up for the races and then go back where they came from. As a river town and vital port Louisville has always been flatter and grittier, and following the Civil War it became known for the "little forest of smokestacks" that marked its increasingly industrial character. As arguably the northernmost city in the South, Louisville's identity has long been somewhat ambiguous, located on the edge rather than in the heart of Dixie—border state Kentucky was not even part of the Confederacy—yet distinctly Southern nonetheless. By the mid-twentieth century Louisville, which then was about fifteen percent African American, had developed a reputation in the region for relative tolerance on racial issues; there were, for instance, no Jim Crow restrictions that prevented Blacks from voting, and streetcars and buses were open to all riders who could sit wherever they preferred.

But the city nonetheless bore the stamp of the pre-civil rights South. "Although it was less complete, rigid, or backed by law," one historian noted, "segregation existed in Louisville and restricted the life choices of African Americans much as it did in other southern communities." Sometimes by actual ordinance or covenants and sometimes through unwritten law, Blacks remained confined to particular neighborhoods; downtown hotels and restaurants refused them service; and schools, parks, and hospitals were kept separate and glaringly unequal. On the job, African Americans faced discrimination as well, and had difficulty getting hired in the first place or securing anything other than menial positions where they worked. Such ingrained racism, even in "progressive" Louisville, served as a regular affront for its Black citizens. But for whites in the city, as civil rights activist Anne Braden noted, "segregation was an accepted part of their lives—unchanged, unchallenged, and unquestioned."[2]

With its move into Louisville, International Harvester had, in a sense, returned to its roots. Cyrus McCormick I was a Southerner, born and raised in antebellum Virginia. It was there that he perfected the mechanical reaper, but not entirely by himself. A man he enslaved, Jo Anderson, a "brilliant artisan and mechanic," was instrumental to its creation, and in fact through the years there were those who insisted—certainly many Black FE members did—that Anderson was the reaper's actual inventor. "Being a slave, the right, title and interest he had in the reaper went to his master," the *Chicago Defender* would proclaim in 1948. "The tragedy of color and the fact that he was chattel prevented Jo Anderson from keeping in step with Cyrus Hall McCormick, the latter climbing the ladder to success and untold wealth." Even after Cyrus I relocated to Chicago to begin amassing that wealth, he remained a proslavery Democrat and an ardent champion of the Confederate cause. There was no small irony, then, inherent in the pivotal role McCormick's machine played in ensuring a Union victory in the Civil War. "The reaper is to the North what slavery is to the South," said Edwin

Stanton, Secretary of War in Abraham Lincoln's cabinet. "By taking the place of regiments of young men in the western harvest fields, it releases them to do battle for the Union at the front and at the same time keeps up the supply of bread for the Nation's armies." Without the reaper, Stanton flatly declared, "the North could not win." This realization caused Cyrus I some despair but no actual discomfort, since the McCormick Company made out handsomely through the war years.[3]

So Fowler McCormick brought his grandfather's company back to the South. But rather than conform to the culture there, Fowler again chose to challenge the status quo, for he had no intention of adopting the segregated hiring practices commonplace in Louisville. He took it for granted that his powerful company should not be constrained by local vagaries; in keeping with the McCormick way of doing things, he would set his own employment rules. But there was more to it than that, for Fowler, consistent with the position he had staked out for International Harvester during World War II, intended the IH plant in Louisville to become an "experiment in biracial industrialism." In 1941 IH pledged to make no distinction between whites and African Americans at any of its factories, a commitment to fair employment practice that went beyond what the federal government then required or what the wartime labor shortage might have necessitated. "We desire to employ as many Negro workers as our business operations will justify," said Harvester's director of public relations in 1944, which was "the attitude of the company's management, from Mr. Fowler McCormick on down."[4]

This policy, bolstered after the war, meant that during the pre-civil rights era Harvester's equal opportunity program was pursued with "an intensity and endurance which were unique in American industry." In many respects its pacesetting position on race represented an extension of the industrial relations innovation and enlightened welfare capitalism that Harvester had nurtured a reputation for since the 1920s. Back then its ambitious welfare programs had served to forestall "outside" interference—whether from organized labor or from government agencies—and similar motivations were embedded in the fair employment practices Harvester adopted in the mid-twentieth century. Equal opportunity should be pursued through "education and individual initiative," Fowler McCormick declared, which were "preferable to legislative methods." Another Harvester executive echoed that sentiment in 1948 when he told a gathering of IH managers: "You know the unfavorable experiences we have had with government intervention in the field of human relations. We don't want it in this phase [minority hiring] of human relations. We think it can all be avoided if all of industry will undertake to resolve this problem

voluntarily." Thus "socially minded" Fowler McCormick's "vigorous leadership" garnered IH widespread recognition "for developing one of the most
progressive racial policies" in corporate America. Fowler, then, had outwardly
cast off the ideology embraced by his grandfather Cyrus McCormick I, the
Confederate loyalist. But his beliefs were entirely consistent with the tenet
that guided his uncle, Cyrus II, who with paternalistic resolve had insisted he
"would treat with men only as individuals." Fowler McCormick also "held a
deep conviction that people should be dealt with as individuals, not as groups."
Fair employment, therefore, could be compatible with anti-unionism. In fact,
as far as Fowler was concerned the two could reinforce each other.[5]

Louisville thus checked various boxes that made it the appropriate
setting to inaugurate Harvester's postwar expansion, and the city afforded
one other critical advantage: the possibility of getting out from under the
troublesome FE. For more than six decades the McCormicks had managed to keep the company union-free; that streak had ended under Fowler's
watch, for the majority of the workforce was now organized, and by the
devoutly intransigent FE no less. The "bad element" within Harvester's existing plants seemed, at long last, too well-rooted to weed out. Faced with
that new reality, Fowler would not throw over the McCormick family's
long-standing anti-union orthodoxy to embrace genuine labor-management cooperation: his nonconformist bent, after all, went only so far. So,
thinking strategically, if the invasive FE couldn't be eradicated, maybe it
could be outrun. Corporations looking to outflank organized labor in the
twenty-first century might move facilities thousands of miles offshore, but
back in 1946 Harvester managers hoped to achieve that same goal just a
half day's drive south from their Chicago headquarters.

At the end of World War II, the still heavily agricultural South remained the poorest region of the country by a long shot. Even its manufacturing pockets were hardly prosperous, except for those who actually owned
the mills and factories. The wave of CIO organizing that had swept through
the American heartland in the 1930s barely made a ripple in the South, and
much New Deal labor legislation had specifically excluded Southern workers.
The defense buildup had stimulated greater industrialization coupled with
government regulation that boosted wage rates above their dismal Depression-era levels, but by the war's end per capita income in the South remained
well below the national average. Thus, manufacturing wages, even for skilled
workers, were far lower than they were for similar work performed elsewhere;
this notorious "Southern differential" reflected the relative powerlessness of
workers in largely non-union Dixie.[6]

This reality was too tantalizing for corporate interests to ignore, and so "capital flight from the unionized North began almost immediately after World War II," as "companies like General Electric, RCA, Thompson Products, Swift, Armour, Alexander Smith, Ford, and J. P. Stevens sought to solve their 'labor problem' by simply replacing one workforce with another." International Harvester, which opened its Louisville plant in 1946 and then one in Memphis a year later, may be added to that list. To be sure, Louisville, which was more industrialized than many Southern cities, was not entirely union-free; the AFL was a strong presence and the city's Ford plant, open since the early twentieth century, had been represented by the UAW since 1941. But union density was far lower in Louisville than in the Midwest, and labor radicalism certainly had no traction there. Fowler and IH management hoped the Ohio River would provide a barrier that the FE could not cross. Harvester would devote nearly $60 million to overhaul the former aircraft factory, and constructed several additions to expand the complex, making the operation in Louisville its largest single investment. Within a few years the plant employed more than six thousand workers, some 15 percent of them African American (the concept of equal opportunity was extended only to men, however, as women were hired only for the plant's offices). Harvester's IH plant had grown to be the biggest factory in Kentucky and the largest wheeled tractor production facility in the world.[7]

One would presume that such a powerhouse of economic activity would have generated nothing but heartfelt gratitude from Louisville's civic leaders. Not quite. "I wish the plant had never come here," one local businessman said in 1949. "The whole outfit can get the hell out, as far as I'm concerned, and good riddance."[8]

For Fowler McCormick, as it turned out, would not manage to escape labor turmoil with the move to Louisville: he succeeded only in importing it into the city. The FE made the leap across the Ohio River as well, as organizers had been dispatched to Louisville before the ink dried on the 1946 FE-IH contact. FE leaders were well aware of the existential threat posed by Harvester's move south, and their escalating rivalry with the UAW made it all the more imperative that they score a win at Harvester's big new facility. Southern soil was unfamiliar ground, but they trusted that the FE's particular combination of militancy and solidarity would resonate with the workforce at yet another IH plant. This would prove to be the case in Louisville—more so than even the FE's organizers had initially imagined.

14.
An Unlikely Friendship

Two men who work at the same place and become close friends: nothing especially remarkable about that. Unless one of them was white and the other was Black. And they both lived in Louisville in the 1940s. Then and there, such an occurrence was indeed out of the ordinary.

The story of these two men and the bond they developed is the story of the FE in Louisville.

Jim Mouser, who was white, was born in Lebanon, Kentucky, a small town located about seventy miles southeast of Louisville. The population of Lebanon was (and still is) overwhelmingly, but not exclusively, white. During the Civil War, Lebanon was the site of a recruiting station for the Northern Army, where many African American soldiers were trained, and eight hundred Union soldiers are buried in the cemetery there. Situated smack in the heart of bourbon country, the town had by the late 1950s established a raucous club scene (the most storied of which were owned by Hyleme George, who had, remarkably, emigrated as a child from Lebanon the country in the Middle East to Lebanon the town in Kentucky) where the likes of Little Richard and Tina Turner were frequent performers. But before that, in the early 1940s, life in Lebanon seemed too tame for fifteen-year-old Jim Mouser, and so after Pearl Harbor he lied about his age to enlist in the Navy.[1]

After four years overseas Mouser returned briefly to his hometown, hoping to re-enroll in high school, but when he was informed that he was too old to play football, he hit the road to look for work. He found his way up to Detroit and into a job at Ford, where the United Auto Workers had won representation only a few years earlier. Not too long after he'd started there, Mouser spent a celebratory night on the town, and was tardy getting to the plant the next morning. What happened then instilled in Mouser a lifelong animosity for the UAW:

> This foreman was all over me—you'd have thought I committed murder or something, you know. I talked to the union steward. I told him, I said, "You know, I don't need all this. I was about an hour late, but they told me to go ahead and punch in anyhow. As long as I was doing my work, the foreman didn't have any business hanging

over me and harassing me the whole day, and I don't want to put up with it." And the steward says, "Well, I can't do nothing about it." The union steward told me that, you know. I didn't stay there . . . I didn't want any part of it.

Looking for another job and a union more to his liking, Mouser headed back down to Louisville, where his family had moved during the war. His father and older brother had snagged jobs at the big new International Harvester factory there, and in short order Jim Mouser did as well. He was then just twenty-one years old.

African American Jim Wright was already employed at the IH plant when Mouser arrived; in fact, Wright was one of the first employees hired there. He was a few years older than Mouser and hailed originally from another small Kentucky town: Russellville, on the far southern edge of the state. Its location, just about twenty miles above the Tennessee state line, ensured that the history of Jim Wright's birthplace contrasted with that of Jim Mouser's hometown. The provisional Confederate government of Kentucky—which never succeeded in replacing the state's pro-Union assembly— was formed in Russellville in 1862 and some one thousand of the town's citizens donned gray uniforms. Russellville still boasts, on its tranquil tree-lined square, a statue of a resolute Rebel soldier, inscribed *Deo Vindice*: With God, Our Defender, the motto of the Confederacy. For Jim Wright, whose grandparents had been enslaved, that monument cast a long shadow he wanted to escape. In 1936 he married young, at seventeen, and while his wife worked as a cook for white families, Wright bounced through a series of jobs around Russellville, eventually finding work washing cars at a Chevrolet dealership in town. There the owners "didn't call you by your name when they wanted you," Wright said. "They called you nigger." He decided he'd had enough and headed north—to Louisville. "I left Russellville on the first day of September, 1941, and I never went back no more," Wright recalls. "I said, I'm going to stay in Louisville if I have to dig ditches, get put in jail, steal somebody, rob, cut their heads off. So I stayed." Things were, as far as Wright was concerned, better there. "Louisville was a progressive little old segregated city," he said. "I liked it."

Wright made good on his vow not to return to his hometown. In 1942, with the defense buildup in full swing, he took a job at a facility opened in Louisville to modify B-24 bombers. At that plant Jim Wright became a UAW member. "The union wasn't much," he indicated, because "it was defense work and you couldn't strike." But, he said, "in all plants, if you work in them, you'll find out that there's some injustice being done to the worker. . . So I joined the union to try and help out the workers." But in less than a year Wright was drafted and sent to Burma. "It was a hell of a deal there for about eleven months, working in the jungle," he said. "They didn't allow Negroes to do much fighting, but you got shot up all the time, they made us build bridges, and they bombed you. Then they said I seemed to be super-intelligent, so they let me fight. And I had tried to act as dumb as possible." Wright was then promoted to sergeant and assigned to supervise Black soldiers who handled the bombs that would be carried by American aircraft. "I don't know why I didn't get killed," he said. "Those bombs weighed a ton, and we had to drop them into a bin. One time one blew up and blew the whole section away. Then they assigned me back to it again." He was later wounded by machine gun fire and spent time in a Japanese prison camp—given all that, his characterization of his time in the service as "a nightmare" seems like an understatement.

When Wright was finally discharged from the service in 1946 he went straight back to Louisville and resumed his search for work. He'd heard about the International Harvester facility on the edge of town and headed out there while still wearing his Army uniform. He was pleased to be offered a job on the spot, but his mood soured when the plant manager approached him. "He said, 'Now I want to break you in right, boy. You can't work in that stuff you have on. You ain't shooting nobody in here. War's over, and we work out here. We don't stand around here with stripes on our sleeves. Hell, I don't care nothing about your stripes.' So I had to take that off him, I had to stand there and listen to him give me a lecture." The manager told Wright to report for work the next day in overalls rather than his uniform. "So I did it," Wright said, "but I didn't put no damn overalls on. I put on pants and a shirt and I went back out there."

Clearly, Jim Wright and Jim Mouser had a good deal in common—beyond their shared first name—not least of which was an inclination to defy authority, or at least regard it with disdain. But nonetheless even once they found themselves employed in the same place, the racism they'd been immersed in growing up in the South and the segregationist reality that defined Louisville made it unlikely that they would become anything more than, at best, cordial coworkers, and even that level of tolerance was hardly a given. It's not as though whites who went to work at the IH plant came from some exceptionally enlightened group. "We had all hillbillies, that's all we had," in Jim Wright's estimation. "Farmers. Guys who wore overalls. Chewed tobacco, spitting on the floor. And those kind of guys were real racist, I mean *real* racist." That Mouser and Wright developed close ties that extended beyond the plant gates to include drinking together after work and socializing in each other's homes challenged what was deemed acceptable in Louisville. "Louisville just wasn't ready for Blacks and whites together," Jim Mouser recalled. "I can remember the first time Val, my wife, and I went to Jim's and his wife's house for dinner. You'd see Blacks look up to say, what's going on here? And vice versa, when they would visit us."

This came about because of something else the two Jims shared: membership in the FE's local in Louisville. For many workers at the Harvester plant, FE Local 236 eroded the prejudices that had been part and parcel of their Southern heritage and fostered relationships that had been previously unthinkable. For Mouser and Wright, who both became leaders within Local 236, the battles they engaged in—inside the plant, on picket lines, and within the city of Louisville—forged a friendship and also engendered a fierce mutual commitment to the FE. "I honestly don't believe, and I'm talking about the Mineworkers, John Lewis and his crew, and how strong they were," Jim Mouser insisted, "I don't believe there was a stronger union in the United States than [the FE] back in those days. From top leadership down to the last rank-and-filer, as a whole." Jim Wright concurred. Though he would, in later years, become a member and an official of other labor organizations, Wright maintained that FE Local 236 was "the closest to the most perfect union" he was ever involved with. That Local 236 might be the epitome of anything worthwhile hardly came to be a universally held sentiment in Louisville, as evidenced by the local businessman who wished the Harvester plant "would get the hell out." But this much is safe to say: in words and deeds, in the shop and in the community, Local 236 became the most perfect embodiment of the FE's ideology.[2]

One essential element of that ideology—an insistence on racial solidarity—became apparent from the moment the FE set up shop in Kentucky.

15.
Organizing Louisville, FE-Style

Jim Wright was hired in the summer of 1946, well before Harvester began production in Louisville. The plant was then still being retrofitted for tractor assembly, so Wright at first "had the job that all Blacks have," he recalled. He was given a broom—"a thousand leg, we called them"—and assigned to cleaning duties in the cavernous plant. At this early point there were fewer than a dozen workers in the IH factory. But it wasn't long before someone who had been closely monitoring activities there knocked on the door at Wright's home. He said his name was Vernon Bailey and he was with the Farm Equipment Workers. And then he said one more thing: "We're trying to get a union in that shop, and we want you to help us."[1]

The squat, ruddy-faced fellow whom Jim Wright invited in that day had been with the FE for several years before he'd been dispatched to Louisville. Bailey's weatherworn visage and misshapen nose suggested that despite his relentlessly chipper demeanor he hadn't backed away from too many fights in his life. He was a skilled metalworker but took up union work in Seattle in the early 1920s and had lived the itinerant life of an organizer ever since. He signed on with the FE in 1941—he was too old for the military—and spent the war years among farm equipment workers in Indiana and downstate Illinois. How Bailey approached his work became evident in the assistance he provided in 1942 to striking railroad workers in Peoria: he enlisted some seventy-five men to reinforce the picket line at the train yard; they then rousted the company guard from his shelter, pushed the small shack into a creek, and set it on fire. Bailey's class-based pugnacity, according to the FBI, derived from his ties to the Communist Party, and that may well have been the case, though he wasn't averse to crossing the Party either. During this period, when the no-strike pledge was in effect, other CP members complained that Bailey skipped important meetings and "did not follow the Party's instructions in union activities" and was guilty of "placing union business before Party interest." His indifference toward CP directives did not seem to undermine his relationship with the FE leadership, and when word came that Harvester would be opening a plant in Louisville, Bailey asked for the assignment, relishing the prospect of yet another battle. He got the job. He may have been an undisciplined party member but there was no question about Bailey's commitment to his union. "He worked," it was said about him, "early and late and endlessly."[2]

Regardless of how much effort he was willing to expend, Bailey recognized that he could not, and should not, take on the mission of organizing the Harvester plant on his own. And so soon after setting up shop in Louisville he squeezed a few dollars out of the FE payroll to take on another organizer. In many respects Frederick Marrero was Bailey's diametrical opposite. Marrero was just in his early thirties, and though he'd been born in New Orleans had spent much of his life in Louisville. He'd worked as a railroad laborer before taking a job in 1942 across the river in Indiana at the Jeffersonville Boat Company (known as Jeff Boat), where the US Navy was manufacturing submarine chasers; he then entered the army in 1944. Marrero was a family man, with three young children, who lived in a small house within walking distance of Churchill Downs. Whereas Bailey could have been cast in a movie as a washed-up prizefighter, young and handsome Marrero, with his high cheekbones and elegant bearing, was leading man material. And there was one other difference between them: Bailey was white and Marrero was Black.

But what they shared proved much more important than what distinguished them. Marrero had already demonstrated his dedication to the labor movement and his willingness to fight, literally and figuratively, for what he believed in. At teeming Jeff Boat—some thirteen thousand were employed there at the height of the war—Marrero had become the local treasurer of the CIO's shipbuilders' union, and also served as vice-president of the Kentucky CIO Industrial Union Council. Factionalism was rife within the shipbuilders' local and racial animosity festered as well, as Marrero was castigated by other officials of the local—all of them white—for endeavoring to "make an issue of 'Jim Crow' policies" within Louisville. But the divisions may have been rooted as much in old-fashioned corruption. Marrero made front-page news in Louisville when he charged that the local's top officers were squandering union dues to line their own pockets and indulge in "wild spending." Tensions boiled over into numerous physical altercations; during one of them a local trustee stabbed Marrero with a knife and threatened to kill him. In September 1944 the national office of the shipbuilders' union intervened, suspending the local's autonomy and ousting its president and vice-president. Marrero, who'd received a draft notice in the midst of all this, was headed overseas, where on balance he might have been safer; he was "glad of the chance to get into the Army," Marrero told the local news, because it "got mighty tough working over in the yard."[3]

Thus when he returned to Louisville after the war, Marrero was already recognized for his courage and his commitment to unions—clean ones, anyhow. He was also an outspoken advocate for the African American community. In response to a 1943 letter to the Louisville *Courier-Journal* insisting that white people prefer "to continue their development as a separate race," Marrero wrote derisively: "If that is so, why has the skin of 90 percent of the Negro population changed color? . . . segregation and discrimination were instituted to hide the sins of white America."[4]

So the fact that Vernon Bailey and Frederick Marrero became a team said a great deal about what the FE intended to accomplish in Louisville. Taking on International Harvester was challenging enough, but in this contest the FE would also be facing off against other unions: the UAW was seeking to gain representation at the Louisville plant, but so too were several different AFL affiliates (the main contender, confusingly enough, was called the United Auto Workers–AFL). In the face of such competition, and in a segregated town, the FE might have soft-peddled the race question, for the moment or perhaps forever. But that was not the course Bailey and Marrero chose: they built a commitment to racial equality into the DNA of the local.

"It makes a tremendous amount of difference," Milt Burns wrote to Vernon Bailey, "where we begin to organize a plant before it opens, and not some months afterwards. . ." Scoping out the situation early on allowed the FE to gain strategic advantage. Bailey encouraged workers who would be likely supporters to seek employment at the Harvester plant, meaning union sympathizers in general but in particular those who might be drawn to the FE rather than its rivals. So Bailey made a point of contacting former stewards, along with "militant rank and file members" from Jeff Boat, which at the war's end downsized drastically. Bailey also looked to the Louisville Ford plant, as many employees there, he believed, were anxious to find work someplace else. "Conditions at the Ford plant are bad" due to the "speed-up schedule agreed to by the UAW," and this "has built up the anti-UAW sentiment," Bailey concluded. By late May, he reported, "we have 60 good honest people contacted to start work the minute they get into the plant; expect to double that within the next two weeks, which will give us a real organizing committee."[5]

The key member of that organizing committee was Fred Marrero, for it was his task to build FE support from within while Bailey worked on the outside. Marrero managed to get hired at IH in June 1946, when at that early point there were only a handful of blue-collar employees in the plant. Within a month, he'd signed up fourteen of the fifteen African American workers there; some time later Marrero reported, "At this time there are fifty-three Colored employees and they have signed F. E. cards only. From day to day we keep this 100% rate of Negro membership in F. E. by signing up the new employees as fast as they are hired." This group, Marrero indicated, contained "five potential leaders" who were "very dependable and try to outdo one another in signing up the new employees. They keep their eyes and ears open and are very resourceful in gaining useful information." This squad of rank-and-file organizers included the man Vernon Bailey had paid an early visit to—Jim Wright—whose methods were indeed resourceful:

> I went and tried to get people signed up, easing, slipping them cards. But my main job, that I created, was since I swept in offices—I was a big shot, I didn't sweep in no shop, I swept in an office—when I emptied the garbage cans, I'd bring the garbage home, and make a file of everything I could find, and there was some valuable information that came out of that. Boy, the union found good stuff—[management would] hold meetings about the union, and tell what the union did last night, and what they planned to do about the union, and all that stuff, and the union always was a jump ahead of them. The union could tell what they would do next.[6]

As Wright and others carried on their clandestine activities, Marrero by early 1947 expressed confidence that Harvester's growing African American workforce was solidly in the FE's corner. "Every attempt of division of the Negro workers at this plant by rivals of FE is met by confirmation of their devotion to FE Local 236," he wrote.[7]

But what, exactly, accounted for this early "devotion" among African Americans to the FE, given that those "rivals" were competing for their attention, and that Harvester's equal opportunity reputation might have undercut their interest in unions altogether?

One critical factor, clearly, was that Black leaders like Marrero played an early and prominent role in the FE's organizing drive, just as had been the case during the 1941 offensive against Harvester. Moreover, since 1941, the FE had increased the presence of African Americans in top positions, distinguishing itself in this regard by comparison to most other unions, even the other communist-influenced ones. This was all the more noteworthy because despite the changes wrought during World War II the FE remained an overwhelmingly white organization; in 1946, African Americans comprised less than 8 percent of the membership.

The FE's executive board had always included one Black member: initially Pleass Kellogg, one of the FE's founders from Tractor Works, held a spot; when he stepped down during the war years Pope Huff, from McCormick Works, was elected to the board. At its August 1946 convention in

Milwaukee—while the organizing campaign in Louisville was underway—
the FE took a step further. By unanimous vote the delegates returned Pope
Huff to his executive board seat but also made twenty-five-year-old African
American Ajay Martin, from the FE's local at the Caterpillar plant in Peoria,
a vice-president of the union. (Not incidentally, the convention also created a
permanent spot on the executive board for a woman.) Thus, two of the eleven
members of the FE's executive board were African American, at a time when
most unions, regardless of their political leanings—including, for instance,
the Steelworkers, the United Electrical Workers, and the UAW—had none.
The *FE News* stressed why such representation mattered. "The 13 million Negro people who want democracy and their constitutional rights . . . have been
wondering about the sincerity of the CIO unions," said the paper's convention
coverage. "And the big companies have hastened to make hay, claiming that
they, and not the unions, have the answers for the Negro people."[8]

That the union would toot its own horn could be expected, but various
outlets in the Black press also heralded what took place at the FE's convention. On August 10, 1946, the national edition of the *Chicago Defender*—
America's most influential and widely read Black newspaper—ran several
separate items about it. "UNION SETS MARK IN RACE INTEGRATION" read
the front-page headline, while an inside photo depicted the crowd of mostly
white delegates "cheer[ing] lustily" for Ajay Martin. The anti-lynching resolution passed by acclimation at the convention—with full-throated support
from "many white workers, some from the South"—was also highlighted, in
an issue that also devoted extensive coverage to recent savage lynchings in
Georgia and Mississippi. And on its editorial page the *Defender* proclaimed
that the FE had "set a pattern for progressiveness" that "some of its larger
brothers could well emulate." By electing Huff and Martin to top leadership,
the editors maintained, "Farm Equipment concretely showed that it does
more than pay lip service to integration."[9]

FE organizers were quick to capitalize on such favorable publicity. Fred
Marrero, who'd been present at the FE convention, reported that "very timely
articles in the *Chicago Defender*, *Bronze Citizen* and *Ebony Magazine*" helped
him "convert [African Americans] into strong proponents of the F.E."[10]

But African Americans in Louisville were not the only ones hearing
about the FE's commitment to integration. Even while other unions were
competing for recognition at the plant, the FE's message was "economic
equality for all," and, Jim Wright indicated, "they refused to compromise
on that." Emphasizing this to Southern whites was a risky proposition, all
the more so because of Harvester's indication that Blacks would be hired

for positions throughout the plant. "The other unions trying for bargaining rights were 'organizing' in the traditional southern fashion," read an FE pamphlet about Local 236. "They were calling the white workers aside and promising them that as soon as they won bargaining rights, the Negroes on machines would be put back on brooms 'where they belonged.'" In his organizer's report, Vernon Bailey wrote that the AFL was "fanning the flames of prejudice," while African American Sterling Neal, another key leader of Local 236 (who, like Marrero, had previously worked at Jeff Boat) also insisted that "red-baiting and Negro-baiting" were central to the efforts of the FE's competitors. But Neal indicated that the FE met these challenges by promoting open discussion about these provocative issues:

> We had meetings during the campaign and at these meetings the workers were encouraged to discuss freely the questions they had on their minds concerning the Farm Equipment union. It wasn't just up front stuff, of the organizer standing up front and making big speeches, but the workers were encouraged to participate on such controversial questions as Negroes working in the plant—[it was] a rare thing in this community for Negroes to hold any position above the status of janitor or laborer—[these] were discussed freely and openly on the floor. Sometimes there was objection openly on the part of the white workers, to the union's policy of no discrimination; on many occasions the white workers who understood this question a little better challenged them on the floor and after some discussion the real basic explanation was given to these people.[11]

"These arguments took all kinds of turns," read an FE pamphlet, "with hundreds of different attitudes being expressed. There were those who said they would work with Negroes, but didn't want them at union meetings, there were those who were in favor of admitting Negroes to the union, but against having union officers and so on." The FE's line, however, remained unwavering: "The only way to beat Harvester's low wages was to unite the Negro and white workers."[12]

While these conversations were ongoing, FE supporters used other means to solidify support among workers, regardless of race. For one thing, they began functioning like union representatives well before any formal recognition had been granted. "We set up a local union," Neal said, "and began to carry on struggles inside the plant and began to handle grievances of the workers in the plant." Bailey, meanwhile, concerned himself with the vital organizing tasks of building committees and fostering communication. He established a veterans' group, for instance, that he believed "will play an important role in this plant." He introduced a shop paper with content that was, he acknowledged, "quite heavy," but on their own "leaflets would not have done the job" of getting the FE message across. And thanks to the intel provided by workers like Jim Wright, Bailey knew that message was being received: "A close check here every week by my efficient janitorial force reveals that not a copy of this paper is thrown away. They read them then take them home with them."[13]

Shortly after arriving in Louisville, Bailey made this prediction about the Harvester plant: "I am sure we can win it if we are given half a chance." He wanted nothing left to chance, however, and so labored ceaselessly to ensure that all the bases in and outside the plant had been covered. The NLRB election was finally held on June 10, 1947, more than a year after Bailey had first begun the organizing drive. The tally gave the FE 578 votes, the UAW 440, and the UAW-AFL 356, meaning no one union had garnered the requisite majority. A runoff election was scheduled for the end of July, and clearly until that date the FE forces needed to redouble their efforts.[14]

But the person who would have been expected to lead that final charge was not around to do it. Vernon Bailey suffered a heart attack in the spring of 1947, and once he was released from the hospital his doctors ordered him to rest and stay far away from the organizing campaign. He didn't. On a sunny Sunday afternoon, Bailey collapsed again, and this time, read the union's obituary, the "straight-shooting, hard-hitting old warrior breathed his last." He was fifty-nine years old, and died on June 1, nine days before the first election.[15]

Perhaps Bailey's untimely death spurred Fred Marrero and the others to pour even more into their last push. The results seemed to reflect that: on July 29 the FE received 1,276 votes to the UAW's 380, while 207 went for the AFL. The FE, then, had captured nearly 70 percent of the workforce, and since turnout (in both elections) ran close to 90 percent, the union could claim a decisive victory. It was the best salute FE supporters might have paid to the fallen "old warrior."[16]

Or, actually, an even more fitting tribute might have been what came next. Because, like Bailey, the leaders of the new FE local in Louisville didn't take time to rest, either: following the election they entered nearly immediately into a major showdown with International Harvester management. The struggle proved deeply significant and profoundly surprising, most particularly to the workers involved. They would emerge from it transformed.

16.
We're Not Going to Be
Second-Class Citizens in the South

Putting aside the small matter of the FE's victory at the new Louisville plant, in 1947 International Harvester's executives were in a celebratory mood. It was the company's centenary year; to mark the occasion Harvester opened a giant public exposition on the Chicago lakefront not far from where the first McCormick factory once stood. The commemoration of bygone days coincided with auspicious future forecasts. One-hundred-year-old IH was "growing like a boy in short pants," said the *Wall Street Journal*, and with the addition of its new facilities "the company is twice its size since Pearl Harbor." Booming postwar demand meant that profit levels, according to Fowler McCormick, were "very satisfactory," and 1947 promised "to be the best in Harvester's history." But to maintain its profitability, given the company's increasingly far-flung network, "cutting costs and stepping up efficiency" would be necessary. So there was only one thing that might spoil the party for Harvester management: "Our success will depend," said IH president John McCaffrey, "on uninterrupted production at reasonable wage levels. This is not a program that can be carried out if it is hampered by strikes or work stoppages."[1]

Given that, Harvester's executives were no doubt disappointed when the Louisville workforce opted for the FE, but they probably presumed it would at least be some time before the new local began causing them major problems. With the plant's overhaul complete, by the late summer of 1947 Cub tractors were rolling off the Louisville assembly line at a steady clip. Company officials were anticipating a long stretch of "uninterrupted production."

They got about a month. And then, on September 17, the two thousand new members of FE Local 236 walked out of the plant and shut it down. It stayed that way for more than forty days.

Vernon Bailey's death, though a blow to the union, did not leave Local 236 without leadership or left-wing influence. For one thing, the local already had a determined corps of African American activists, Fred Marrero (who had been elected the local's secretary-treasurer), Jim Wright, and Sterling Neal among them. But two young white men who also came to the fore during the local's 1947 walkout seemed as though they'd been sent from central casting to fill roles as the perfect antagonists to Harvester management.

Lloyd James, universally called Bud, could play the part of the patrician-turned-radical-firebrand. He came from an affluent family in St. Paul, Minnesota, with a lineage that traced back to the Mayflower. Though most in the James family were steadfast Republicans, from an early age it seemed that Bud was straying from the fold. "Bud is going to be an agnostic and a Socialist, I guess," his mother wrote, when he was just seven years old. "He is very sure that he would arrange the world quite differently if he had the doing of it." She knew her son. In the late 1930s, at the University of Chicago, James became a national leader of the militant American Student Union. While in college he was arrested for the first—but hardly the last—time when he mouthed off to a Chicago cop following a support meeting for the Scottsboro Boys, a group of young African American Alabamians falsely accused of raping two white women. James never managed to get his college degree but he stuck around Chicago and found a place in the burgeoning CIO, initially assisting the packinghouse workers union. He also began writing for the *Midwest Daily Record*, the same Communist Party-connected newspaper that both DeWitt Gilpin and Milt Burns then worked for. No surprise, then, that following World War II—during which he was wounded at Anzio—Bud James joined the staff of the Farm Equipment Workers, and was dispatched in 1947 to take Vernon Bailey's place as the union's rep in Louisville.

In terms of both ideology and work ethic, James was a fitting successor to Bailey. "Bud talked union, figured union, worked on unions, that's all he did, day and night," Jim Wright said. "So I can't give nothing but good accolades for Bud." Wright was aware that James "was an elite guy" but not because that was outwardly apparent. James lived, Wright recalled, in a trailer park across the river in Indiana, and "he never did change clothes for the five years that I knew him." His rumpled appearance and his receding hairline did not distinguish him, but with his "roaring voice and waving fists," as the *Courier-Journal* noted, James knew how to command attention.[2]

But so too did Chuck Gibson, who emerged from the Louisville workforce to take the role, for a brief period, as the bane of Harvester management's existence. Like James, Gibson was not a native Kentuckian, but after overseas service during World War II he also found his way to the state, because during the war he'd married a woman from Louisville. According to his FBI file, Gibson was born in Vermont and was a student during the late 1930s at New York University, where, the FBI contends, he became an active member of the Young Communist League. Jim Wright was sure that Gibson had been a veteran of the Spanish Civil War, which if true somehow escaped the FBI's notice. But the FE leadership knew of Gibson's radical reputation, and it was no accident that shortly after he arrived in Louisville he sought work at the International Harvester plant, and was one of the first men employed on the assembly line there. "He went into the shop at our instigation," Bud James indicated, to help with the organizing drive. Gibson soon proved himself "a tremendously powerful leader," James said. Jim Wright recalls being first introduced to Gibson, in May 1947, by Fred Marrero. "If we ever do win this union," Marrero told Wright, "we want this man to be president."[3]

Both things came to pass: In August 1947, twenty-eight-year-old Chuck Gibson was elected president of Local 236. Though he was a recent transplant, Gibson was readily accepted by the Louisville rank and file, but then he possessed character traits that allowed him to mesh easily with his Southern coworkers. "He was a wild guy, a powerful and courageous guy," Bud James said. "Physically he was a well-built guy and he raised hell. I mean, he'd go out and drink all night . . . and be back the next day just fighting the company like hell and the guys really went for him as a leader."[4]

Not long after taking office, Gibson and the Local 236 leadership decided to challenge Harvester over the very reason the company came to Kentucky in the first place.

IH had long had two pay scales: one for its Chicago plants, and a reduced one for its facilities located everywhere else, based on the rationale that living costs were less outside the big city. With its move to Kentucky, Harvester introduced yet another one. "Our pay scales are set in accordance with the generally prevailing rates in a given community," Harvester announced, in defense of wages that would be the lowest in the chain. It was over this "Southern differential" that FE Local 236 chose to "fight the company like hell."[5]

But before they could take on Harvester management on this issue, the Local 236 leadership needed to convince the workforce that they were owed more than they were being offered. It was in many respects a tough sell. The company's Northern plants seemed a distant abstraction; within Louisville Harvester was paying good money, better than most other employers in the city. But nonetheless the FE hammered away at the differential, insisting that Louisville workers should at least receive Harvester's "out of Chicago" rates. Thousands of leaflets were distributed, and numerous discussions took place in the plant locker rooms and outside the factory gates. "FE-CIO vigorously opposes the practice of plants being established in the South in order to pay lower wages because of the 'lower' standard of living," announced the first issue of Local 236's newspaper, the *Cub*. "We make the same tractors [Harvester] sells to the same farmers; they don't sell a Southern tractor one penny cheaper than they sell another tractor," said Sterling Neal, recalling the arguments the FE used with Louisville workers. "We're not going to be second-class citizens in the South."[6]

Whereas IH claimed that "our company's belief in Louisville and its future" drew it to Kentucky, Local 236 insisted that "bright dreams of cheap southern labor" were the real inducement. The local leadership thus rejected out of hand the sincerity of Fowler McCormick's commitment to "biracial industrialism," even though Harvester's equal opportunity policy was exceptional in the area (at the Ford plant in Louisville, for instance, Blacks were relegated to janitorial positions). African Americans, Neal maintained, were hired at IH so "they would win the support of the Negro people in this community against the union or against any struggle for higher wages." Harvester's continual refrain to its Black employees, Neal insisted, was "why would you turn against us? Aren't you doing better than you would do in any other shop?" So African American workers initially needed some convincing about the necessity of taking on Harvester over the Southern differential, Jim Wright among them:

> To the common guy on the street, that got a job at Harvester, well, you'd think he'd gone to heaven. They give those guys jobs, give them a machine—hell, a Negro couldn't even look at a machine nowhere, wouldn't even let him clean it up—and here they were running it, had all these benefits, and things. If a guy in Indianapolis, or someplace like that, doing the same job like I was on, and I was getting 35 cents an hour less than he was getting, I used to think that was all right. . . . But, see, what the union did was highlight these things for the people, and make them well aware of the difference.

Racial unity, therefore, was a prerequisite if workers in Louisville were to get the higher wages Local 236 leaders said they were entitled to. "The southern bosses for generations had played Negro against white, and white against Negro," read an FE pamphlet. "There was a direct connection between this and the fact that southern workers were the lowest-paid in the country."[7]

The FE leadership in Louisville hoped they had convinced workers there, both Black and white, to challenge their status as "second-class citizens" within the Harvester empire. They had induced most of them to sign a petition calling for the elimination of the Southern differential. Just how persuasive they'd been, however, didn't become apparent until the petition was presented at the plant's front office on September 17. The Local 236 leadership, along with a large contingent of employees who had wandered away from their jobs, were told by the plant manager that the company already paid a "fair wage." That answer proved unsatisfactory. "At that time a lot of the workers spontaneously began to shout, 'let's hit the bricks,'" Sterling Neal recalled. Chuck Gibson then jumped up on a table outside the manager's office. "He told the people, well, let's go down to the union hall and talk it over," Neal said.

"It wasn't supposed to be a strike, it wasn't started as a strike, it was merely a demonstration in the shop," Bud James said, but "the guys were so startled by seeing their own strength that they pulled out together," and the entire plant emptied out. Despite Gibson's directive, because Local 236 had only recently come into official existence it actually had no union hall, and only sixty-one dollars in its treasury. James was at work that day in the FE's small office in Louisville when he got a phone call from Gibson. "He said, 'Hey Bud, they ain't going back to work,'" James recalled. "'Find a hall for us.'" And so the FE's 1947 Southern differential walkout was underway.[8]

James scrambled to find space in a hurry, and managed to secure a run-down empty building near downtown Louisville. Because neither he nor anyone else in the local leadership was entirely sure if what they were doing was legal, Local 236 was said to be merely engaged in a "continuous meeting." And since local officials didn't yet possess a membership roster or a list of employees, the day after the walkout began they put out a call for workers to come by the new union hall to sign up for picket duty—or, rather, to register as "meeting notifiers"—figuring that way they'd at least be able to collect some names. The response stunned even the leadership. "Well, the next day something like two thousand people showed up, and there was a double line," as James recalled. "This double line stretched out into the hall, down the stairs, and onto the sidewalk and clear around the block. They waited all day in line to register for that strike. I'll never forget that line."[9]

With this early demonstration of enthusiasm, the Southern differential walkout became what Jim Wright called "a humdinger." Production was halted entirely at the plant, with contingents of "notifiers" patrolling the gates to ensure that remained the case. The union initially kept even management personnel from accessing the premises; the day after the walkout began the cashier was accosted and the payroll records he was carrying were tossed into the street. When, a few mornings later, a group of forty managerial employees reported to the plant's main entrance, they were met by "some 250 or 300 union pickets," said IH president McCaffrey, while "union sound trucks were driving up and down the highway in front of the plant urging the pickets to stand 'shoulder to shoulder' and refuse admittance" to them. Discretion being the better part of valor, the managers chose to turn back and go home. All this, needless to say, was too much for Harvester to accept; "unlawfully and by force," the company argued in court, Local 236 had effected "a seizure of the Louisville Works [which] resulted in the denial to Harvester of access to its own property except by permission of the union." Ten days into the walkout, IH got the injunction it sought, limiting to two the number of union members at any of the plant's six entrances.

This didn't change things all that much, however, as Chuck Gibson seized on the fact that the judge's order omitted any mention of how often substitutions were allowed. "Nothing can prevent you from replacing a fellow worker every thirty seconds," Gibson told the local's members, and so they still congregated in large groups—sometimes more than one thousand strong—near the gates waiting to take their turn walking the line. Since the area around the Harvester plant at that time was largely vacant countryside, the police were willing to tolerate the throngs, so long as they "stood away from the gates." But they frequently pressed a bit too close. In one two-day stretch in October, for instance, at least thirty union members, both Black and white—including Chuck Gibson, Bud James, Fred Marrero, and Jim Wright—were arrested for various forms of picket line misconduct, most of it aimed at Harvester managers endeavoring to enter the plant. Once out on bail, they went right back at it again: Bud James was hauled in by the police at least six times during the strike. Though Harvester invited production employees to return, few chose to do so; the union claimed only a few dozen white workers ever crossed the picket line, and no African Americans did.[10]

"In Louisville there hadn't been a successful strike in an industry," Sterling Neal indicated, "since anybody could remember . . . it wasn't like Detroit or Chicago or Pittsburgh or someplace where shops had been shut down. It just had never been done here." They may have been new to this, but both the leadership and the rank and file of Local 236 took easily to aggressive, and creative, labor activism. One morning more than eight hundred World War II veterans in the local, wearing their old uniforms, paraded around the plant, led by an African American former marine sergeant. On another occasion, the members of Local 236 parked their cars, three abreast, on the main street leading to the plant; traffic was blocked in both directions as the union conducted a meeting in the middle of the road.[11]

The local also endeavored to convince the broader community of the injustice of Harvester's pay scale, and the rank and file spread the word. "We ran off about ten thousand handbills a day," Neal said, on the lone hand-operated mimeograph machine the local managed to procure (on credit), and had no problem getting them distributed. "There were people waiting around all day to put publicity out on the street . . . we just walked into the hall and asked, give us twenty guys to pass out handbills, thirty guys . . . and people stepped right up and went out into the street corners and threw them in the path of automobiles and left the stuff all over town." Some of the material was distributed even further afield. "Quite a few of the boys had relatives all around through what we call Kentuckiana, between here and Indianapolis and as far south as the Tennessee line, and those fellows making the trips over the weekend while we were on strike, they'd take a lot of those handbills and they'd leave them off in these little hamlets [and] the general stores," Neal recalled. Strikers' spouses, as well, visiting "scores of rural communities," helped circulate flyers pointing out to small farmers—the IH Cub's customer base—"that they would not get the tractor any cheaper if the tractor was made in Louisville but still the company wanted to pay a cheaper wage."[12]

But might this ongoing militant activity have been attributable to a reckless local leadership acting without support from the FE's top officialdom? The reverberations felt well beyond Kentucky suggest otherwise. At various points during the Local 236 walkout, FE members at Harvester plants in Chicago and in downstate Illinois quit work, in some instances for a few hours and in others for a few days. These were, the company insisted, sympathy strikes—and as such unlawful contract violations—citing as fairly convincing evidence FE handbills "supporting the Louisville strike" that were distributed where the walkouts occurred. Sterling Neal's recollections confirm that Harvester management's assessment was indeed correct. "In order to put some heat on the company," he said, "they pulled all kind of wildcat strikes and stoppages in the other plants which were very helpful in forcing this company into some kind of agreement." Finally, on October 18, when the Southern differential walkout was about a month old, the top leadership made it officially clear that the union stood behind Local 236. The FE announced it would seek strike authorization from the thirty-five thousand members at all its IH locals, because the "precedent in Louisville" would allow the company "to cut wages . . . throughout the chain."[13]

A week later, the Southern differential walkout was over. After forty-two days on strike the members of Local 236 returned to work with "two smashing victories in hand," so said the *FE News*, "one over International Harvester, the other over the Mason-Dixon, low-wage line." In fact, the settlement did not entirely equalize Louisville's pay rates with Harvester's other plants, but the union had, in Chuck Gibson's words, "succeeded in winning 75 to 80 percent of our original objectives." All pieceworkers (who constituted two-thirds of the labor force at the plant) and many day-rate workers saw "the paycheck-robbing southern differential entirely eliminated." Workers at the lowest day rate classifications would also get a raise, though they would still be paid somewhat less than those same grades at other out-of-Chicago plants. All the wage hikes were made retroactive to August 21. Even with this impressive victory Gibson indicated the local planned to come back for more. "This is a good win," he said, but promised, "we will knock out the rest of these discriminatory rates in the next go-round."[14]

The cents-per-hour gains, however, were not all that had been achieved through the walkout. "The Louisville situation was of special significance as it represented IH Co's first effort to run away from high northern wages," declared the *FE News*. Harvester's move south—in which it joined the legion of other firms seeking through capital flight to "solve their 'labor problem' by simply replacing one workforce with another"—would afford the company no advantage, if the FE had its way. Heralding the Louisville settlement, Grant Oakes as usual issued a broadside at a familiar target. "It is particularly brazen when a corporation denies its workers pennies while enriching its owners beyond all reason—in this instance the multi-millionaire McCormicks," he said. "International Harvester, now celebrating its hundredth year in a lavish Chicago exhibition . . . would do well to realize the nineteenth century is over . . ."[15]

FE Local 236 had defied the conventional wisdom about what was possible in Louisville. "Everybody was cutting everybody's throat," Sterling Neal said of race relations among workers in the city, and outside the FE "everyone was sure we were going to lose" when the strike began. Yet the 1947 walkout, Jim Wright said, "unified the people" in the nascent local, providing its members with a sense of their own power and a concrete example of what they could achieve when they acted as a cohesive unit. "It was the first strike in Louisville when Negro and white guys were really out on the picket lines battling together," Neal indicated. The membership's heavy involvement not only sustained the walkout but helped subvert ingrained prejudices. "This is a southern town, and the thinking of the guys is southern," Neal said. "But one thing that happened during that strike: the fellows met together in the hall, they ate together, they picketed together and they practically lived together down in the hall, which was an unusual thing."[16]

In the course of these interactions the members of Local 236 no doubt began to discover how much they had in common, and these shared characteristics shed some light on why Harvester workers in Louisville proved so attuned to FE-style militancy and amenable to its insistence on racial unity. They were all men (no women were employed in the plant), and most quite young (in their mid-twenties, on average, in 1947). The vast majority— union sources said about 75 percent—were veterans of WWII, a figure that comports with the biographies of those who've been introduced in this story so far. For African American G.I.s in particular, the service they'd provided their country and the confidence that came from being in uniform made them less likely to tolerate "second-class citizenship." For whites, particularly those from the rural South, their experiences overseas and their participation in a "people's war" dedicated to preserving freedom and equality may have broadened their perspectives. All these youthful former soldiers had been recently schooled in the virtue of discipline and command structure, as well as the value of bravado, when taking on a powerful opponent. This training served the local well during the 1947 strike, and it would continue to do so in the conflicts with Harvester management going forward.[17]

But while most of these workers may have been combat veterans, when it came to organized labor they were largely new recruits. "Ninety percent of our guys," said Sterling Neal, "never belonged to a union before. They were just vets out of the army in many cases and they were guys just off the farms who had come in to work in industrial production for the extra dough and the boys that had been in the union were in the AF of L or the CIO around here that had never done a darn thing." An absence of union tradition within a workforce could be a handicap, but in racially fractured Louisville Neal believed that it had advantages. "All the fellows was green," he indicated, "and if they hadn't been I doubt they would have had such a good experience, and the reason for that is this: each fellow figures he doesn't know a damn thing or how to do anything and so he had better listen to the next guy." And as both the Black and white workers learned from each other, the Local 236 leadership and rank and file came to define their union on their own terms.[18]

An unwillingness to back down became a key component of that definition. "We were a rough crowd to be with," Jim Wright recalls, and the members of Local 236 certainly displayed more than a bit of the contrariness long considered intrinsic to Southern temperament. Their hellraising tendencies along with a visceral resistance to authority (at least, those authorities they didn't respect) synched with the FE's generally combative framework. Wright also believed that the rural roots and transience shared by many of the plant's young workers of both races contributed to this character:

> Didn't nobody really have anything that they owned. Well, they'd come out of the army about two years before, or off a farm or out of

the woods somewhere, and they didn't care what happened. If they struck, they'd go back to the farm, and if the plant didn't continue, they'd go on somewhere else. Just been working there two years, didn't care what they did.[19]

In Louisville, therefore, the FE had pursued International Harvester across the Ohio River and then bested several other contenders, including the UAW, to win over the sizable workforce. Rejecting the company's right to pay its Southern employees less for the same work, the FE had through the 1947 walkout succeeded in significantly eroding Harvester's geographically tiered wage structure. And in both the Local 236 leadership and its rank and file, the FE had gained what looked to be the most willing practitioners yet of its particular form of militant trade unionism. All that was on the plus side for the FE.

But with its incursion into Louisville the FE had rudely crashed Harvester management's party, casting a pall over postwar profit projections predicated on uninterrupted production and "reasonable" wage levels. The 1947 Southern differential conflict in fact constituted a crucial turning point for Fowler McCormick and the top executives at IH, as it marked when the all-purpose anti-unionism that had defined the company's labor relations since the nineteenth century evolved into something far more specific. By the end of World War II, the concept of collective bargaining had been grudgingly accepted by most of corporate America, and International Harvester seemed at long last officially resigned to it as well.

But if unions in some form were the new reality, not all were equally palatable, and one in particular was intolerable. As a result of the 1947 dispute, the smoldering antipathy that IH management felt toward the FE turned white-hot and flared into full public view. In late October, when the Local 236 strike was a month old, all thirty-five thousand workers at the eleven IH factories represented by the FE received a letter from company president John McCaffrey. In his message McCaffrey made no mention of the Southern differential but decried the "situation" in Louisville and the six other Harvester plants where walkouts had recently taken place. He assured his employees that "the Company has no interest in breaking unions. The Company wants good relations with responsible unions." But with the FE that was not possible, McCaffrey said flatly, because the union's officers "are irresponsible radicals, who have no respect for their contracts, and who are more interested in disruption than in labor-management peace." He noted that by this point IH bargained with a number of different unions in the CIO (namely, the UAW at its truck plants) and with various AFL affiliates. "With that in mind," he continued, "consider these facts:"

1. In our fiscal year 1945 at all Harvester operations, there were 163 work stoppages. OF THESE, 129 WERE BY FE LOCALS.
2. In our fiscal year 1946 at all Harvester operations, there were 127 work stoppages. OF THESE, 102 WERE BY FE LOCALS.
3. In 1947 so far there have been 151 work stoppages at all Harvester operations. OF THESE, 144 HAVE BEEN BY FE LOCALS . . .
4. Not only does the FE have more strikes, it has longer ones and bigger ones. Most of the work stoppages in plants represented by other unions were brief and involved few men and not much wage loss.

So the evidence was clear: other unions "get along quite well with Harvester," McCaffrey said. "It looks to us as if it is the FE—not the Company, not the 22 other international unions—that is out of step." McCaffrey concluded with a question to FE members: "Would you like to work without interruption and get your pay regularly?" and offered this advice: "If either your local or your international officers are not properly representing you, see that they change their policies—or get yourself some new leaders." Of course, "these are things for you to decide," McCaffrey assured his employees. "The Company cannot decide them for you."[20]

Those decisions had in fact been up to workers to make since the 1935 Wagner Act went into effect, but brand new legislation freed Harvester to pressure its employees to "decide" that they would be better off without the FE. In the summer of 1947, the US Congress enacted the Taft-Hartley Act, overriding a veto by President Truman to do so. Truman, however, had not previously spoken out against the legislation—which passed with strong bipartisan support—and many in union circles regarded the veto as an empty gesture by Truman aimed at recapturing labor support in advance of the 1948 election. The Taft-Hartley Act, crafted by and for business interests, contained a panoply of provisions that undercut worker militancy and undermined solidarity while significantly strengthening the power of employers. Walkouts when contracts were in place were expressly outlawed, and unions and their officers could be held financially and criminally liable if they refused to squelch such activity, which explains why Local 236 in Louisville dubbed its plant shutdown a "continuous meeting." Closed shops (where union membership was a requirement for employment) and secondary boycotts (where unions refuse to handle or transport goods from businesses involved in labor disputes) became illegal. States were permitted to enact "right to work" legislation, meaning that employees could not be obliged to join a union, or pay dues to one, even in workplaces covered by collective bargaining agreements. The act also required union officers to sign affidavits affirming that they were not members of the Communist Party, which would in short order prove of enormous consequence to the FE and the labor movement in general. Taft-Hartley also restored to employers the free speech rights they insisted the Wagner Act had stripped from them. Henceforth anti-union communications from company officials in any form were permissible, so long as they "contain no threat of reprisal or force or promise of benefits." In other words, bosses should remember to throw in that "these are things for you to decide" even as they make it abundantly clear just what choice they encourage (or expect) their workers to make.

IH, always a pioneer in industrial relations, was the first major employer to exploit this provision in the Taft-Hartley Act. McCaffrey's 1947 letter to FE members became a hot topic for the business press, which ran lengthy analyses devoted to "International Harvester's Attack on Radical Labor" and noted that when "dealing with a troublesome union . . . International Harvester just set an example worth your attention." McCaffrey's missive was praised for being "calm, dispassionate, but hard-hitting with facts." But though it was deemed cutting-edge, the letter was in fact just the latest iteration of the union-avoidance strategy Harvester had utilized as long as it had been in existence. Cyrus McCormick II had bypassed existing labor organizations to "treat directly with the men as individuals" and the Harvester works councils were purposed to allow management to speak directly to (and for) its employees without interference from "outside" groups. The Taft-Hartley Act enabled Harvester to again attempt an end-run around organized labor. The difference this time was that Harvester's message was not anti-union in general, but anti-one-union in particular.[21]

Harvester management may have omitted mention of the company's past practices but Grant Oakes and Jerry Fielde, in their response to McCaffrey, did not. Their lengthy open letter to the IH president, which could not be called dispassionate, began by noting that Harvester's "unique communication" to FE members "could not legally have been written under the Wagner Act." Reaching further back into history, Oakes and Fielde insisted that "the tradition of the McCormicks and Harvester is ruthless anti-unionism, typified in the past by the Haymarket Square brutalities of 1886, at which time the clubbing and beating of Reaper workers established the firm's basic reaction to honest trade-unionism." They disputed McCaffrey's "facts" along with his interpretation of what "responsible" behavior entailed. In Harvester plants, they said,

> . . . jobs are retimed and pay rates cut for frivolous reasons; grievances remain unresolved; foremen ignore, as you do, your own "program

of human relations" and operate in a calculated and arbitrary manner; union members are denied their contractual rights . . . now who, sir, would you say is lacking in responsibility here—the company or the union?"

As to Louisville, the FE officers said that "only a company union" would have tolerated the lower wage scale that IH had hoped to implement. And they pointed to the hefty increase in stock prices Harvester had just registered, a "fact" that McCaffrey's letter, though "it dealt loftily with the wages and welfare of [Harvester] employees," failed to mention.[22]

It might be tempting to say that this bitter exchange signaled that the honeymoon was over, but there had never been anything except irreconcilable differences between the FE and IH. The Southern differential conflict, however, had steeled Harvester management's resolve to send the "irresponsible radicals" packing as soon as possible, and McCaffrey's letter put the FE, along with everybody else, on notice about just how serious that threat was. The satisfaction the union's leaders drew from the favorable terms they had managed to extract in Louisville was tempered by their recognition of the conflict looming ahead.

In the immediate aftermath of the Local 236 walkout, however, the FE would score yet another victory. While the strike was ongoing, Harvester had fired Chuck Gibson, along with three other workers at the Louisville plant, citing as justification their objectionable picket line behavior. Since Gibson had been arrested for overturning the automobile of a foreman, who happened to still be in the car at the time, the company's reprisals were probably anticipated. But the FE contested the dismissals and the matter was sent to arbitration, where union lawyers reasoned that since the activities in question had occurred during the course of a strike, the company had no authority over the men and any punishment meted out could come only from civil authorities. The arbitrator found the FE's arguments persuasive, and in January 1948 Gibson and the other Louisville workers were reinstated, with full back pay. "We're going back in there to keep on fighting as we have in the past," a jubilant Gibson declared, a pronouncement no doubt greeted with gritted teeth in Harvester's front office.[23]

And then, in an instant, the triumph gave way to tragedy. Just a few weeks after the arbitration victory, Chuck Gibson was having dinner with friends at a restaurant near the Local 236 office. Abruptly he stood up, gasped for breath, and then slumped to the floor; when the police arrived they pronounced him dead. FE members in Louisville, and throughout the union, were stunned; to have lost Gibson this suddenly, coming so soon after Vernon Bailey's demise, seemed too cruel to be mere coincidence. "It's the opinion of many people that he was poisoned," Bud James asserted. The death was ruled a heart attack but FE officials insisted that more tests be performed; the coroner concluded that although there seemed to be nothing wrong with Gibson's heart or lungs there was no evidence of foul play. That didn't allay suspicions within the union. "They moved so fast that there was nothing we could do, but it is our opinion that there was skullduggery there," said James. "Of course the company was out to get Chuck with everything they had," he insisted. "The whole thing was so smelly."[24]

Gibson was just twenty-nine years old and the father of two young boys, one of them less than a month old. His funeral, on February 18, 1948, became a massive event in Louisville, as all the production employees at the Harvester plant took off work to attend it, shutting down the factory for the day. Jim Wright remembered the occasion vividly. "We had cars for miles," he said. "Roads blocked, streets blocked. It was just like some kind of phenomenon had happened, you just couldn't believe it. Like Christ or somebody had passed away." Extra police details were assigned to direct traffic. The eulogies delivered at the cemetery have not been recorded, but Wright provided his own of sorts when discussing Gibson decades later. "Chuck was a total committed guy for the union cause. He expressed it, did it, and never veered away from it," said Wright, who found it difficult, even though much time had passed, to talk about Gibson. "He had a short life. But he was committed. Chuck was a good organizer. And I'll—I'll never forget him."[25]

Reflecting on Gibson's leadership during the 1947 walkout, Bud James said that "his personality and his drive were responsible to a large extent of holding a corps of guys together during the strike and instilling in them the spirit that was necessary." After Gibson's death, there may have been some question about whether that spirit would survive him. The answer came soon enough: the IH plant in Louisville became, in James's view, "the most militant in the chain," a fair assessment as walkout and grievance rates there in the late 1940s began to top the company's charts. Much to Harvester management's chagrin, the Bluegrass State provided no safe haven from the "irresponsible radicals" within the FE. Rather, with Local 236, Harvester officials discovered they had a tiger—or perhaps more correctly a wildcat—by the tail, and a very costly one at that.[26]

But workers in Louisville, of course, were affected by events taking place well beyond the city limits. So it would help to draw back for a bird's-eye view of what was taking place within the FE, and the labor movement generally, in the politically charged climate of the late 1940s.

17.
The Shrinking Realm of the Possible

When it secured bargaining rights in 1947 at the IH Louisville plant, the FE added several thousand more workers to its ranks. At that point the union claimed a membership of about sixty thousand, more than half that number from International Harvester. With the farm equipment industry's postwar expansion well underway—Caterpillar, John Deere, Oliver and other firms were also opening new facilities—the FE adopted the slogan "100,000 by '48!" to underscore its hopes for future growth. The victory in the Southern differential strike could have lent the FE valuable momentum and talking points when recruiting workers not yet unionized.

But after Louisville there would be no more big gains for the FE. Plans for new organizing drives in the South and Midwest were shelved. Nearly all the union's resources had to be funneled into maintaining, rather than increasing, its membership.

Yet even that proved too much of a challenge: in one brief moment in early 1948, in Peoria, Illinois, the FE was stripped of nearly one-quarter of its rank and file. What transpired there was emblematic of what was taking place generally as Cold War America became thoroughly inhospitable terrain for home-grown radicals. The FE, widely identified as "communist-dominated," was systematically isolated and beset by a host of enemies. The realm of the possible, for stalwart FE veterans and those headstrong young Harvester workers in Louisville alike, grew ever more constricted.

During the Southern differential strike, IH president John McCaffrey had exploited a provision of the new Taft-Hartley Act when he urged his employees to rid themselves of the "irresponsible radicals" running the FE; it was another piece of that legislation that led to the upheaval in downstate Illinois. Section 9(h) of the act required elected union officials to sign affidavits attesting that they were not members of the Communist Party. Initially, many labor leaders—some of whom were decidedly not Communists—resisted complying, since to do so suggested a validation of Taft-Hartley's draconian anti-unionism, not to mention that the loyalty oath constituted a one-sided affront to their civil liberties (no ideological affirmation of any sort was imposed upon employers). Calling the requirement "a trap," John L. Lewis refused to sign an affidavit and insisted that no self-respecting American would. Not everyone went quite that far. CIO President Philip Murray personally declined to file an affidavit, but emphasized that each union in his organization was free to pursue its own policy on the matter. And while to some section 9(h) looked like a ruse, others saw it as an opportunity. Within the United Auto Workers, which already had language in its constitution barring CP members from holding office, Walter Reuther quickly signed his own affidavit and made sure that everyone else who wanted to remain employed by the UAW did too. By the end of 1947 most union officials, in both the AFL and the CIO, had either reluctantly or willingly conformed to the Taft-Hartley requirement.[1]

Most, but not all: those unions, including the FE, whose top officials were members of, or at least sympathetic to, the Communist Party, held out. This was risky, however, since unions that remained in defiance would not be allowed to participate in National Labor Relations Board elections. Well aware of Walter Reuther's designs on their membership, by early 1948 some FE leaders had reached the conclusion that conforming to the Taft-Hartley requirement had become a distasteful but necessary act of self-defense. But officials of the American Communist Party, along with other left-wing labor leaders—especially those in the sizable United Electrical Workers, the largest of the CP-influenced unions—pressed to maintain a united front against the affidavits. Some mixture of party loyalty, principled objection to section 9(h), and the desire to avoid splintering the labor left caused the FE leadership to continue noncompliance. It was a decision that would cost the union plenty.[2]

Peoria has long been the iconic middle-American city, the harbinger for what will or won't play among what is commonly conceived of as the conservative (and white) heartland populace. Judging by the forces that ran the town—chief among them the monolithic Caterpillar corporation—its reputation was (and is) well deserved. And yet: the sixteen thousand workers at the Caterpillar plant there became members of FE Local 105 in 1941, meaning they were among the first members of the union led by those "irresponsible radicals." From that moment forward the workforce in Cat's single mammoth facility constituted a significant chunk of the FE membership. One of the key leaders to emerge from Local 105 was Ajay Martin, the dynamic young African American man who'd been elected to the FE's executive board in 1946. Peoria's population in the 1940s was less than 5 percent Black, but the African American community had roots there going back to the early nineteenth century—indeed long before that, since Jean Baptiste Du Sable bought land there in 1773. But despite this legacy, and Peoria's location well north of the Mason-Dixon line, segregation there was every bit as pervasive as it was in Louisville. "I am going to Peoria with something like a real dread of the place," Frederick Douglass said in 1882. "The last time I was there I could obtain no shelter at any hotel and I fear I shall meet similar exclusion tonight."[3]

By the mid-twentieth century little along those lines had changed. The Jefferson Hotel bowed to union pressure and allowed African Americans inside when the FE held its 1942 convention in Peoria, but that was only a temporary accommodation. Peoria's public and private facilities, the better ones at least, remained whites-only. Overt discrimination was the rule among employers as well: Caterpillar, in business since the 1920s, refused to hire African Americans until it was obliged to do so during World War II in order to secure lucrative government contracts. These injustices were enforced by the pervasive threat of violence that lingered close by: Pekin, Illinois, just ten miles away, was a Ku Klux Klan stronghold and a notorious "sundown town" where Blacks were not safe after dark.[4]

But there were those no longer willing to accept Peoria's racist reality, regardless of the risks, and Local 105 became active in early challenges to Jim Crow restrictions in the town. Ajay Martin was at the forefront of these struggles. In addition to his position with the FE, Martin was president of the Peoria chapter of the National Association for the Advancement of Colored People (NAACP), and was also a committed member of the Communist Party, though that was not an affiliation he proclaimed publicly. His elevation to an FE vice-presidency in 1946 garnered attention as he became, as a photo spread in *Ebony* magazine noted, "one of the youngest Negro union officials in the nation." In April 1947, Martin's name appeared again in newspapers across the country—especially in the Black press—when Peoria officials barred African American singer Paul Robeson from performing in the city, citing his role as "an active propagandist for un-American ideology." Just as Frederick Douglass had experienced, when Robeson arrived in town for his previously scheduled appearance, he could find no hotel in Peoria open to him. But Robeson was warmly welcomed into the home of Ajay Martin. From Martin's living room Robeson denounced to gathered reporters the "fascist element" that kept him from playing in Peoria. The *Chicago Defender* also condemned the "fascist-soaked town" while saluting the "colored liberal," Ajay Martin, who served as Robeson's "rescuer from the hick police force" in Peoria.[5]

A year later Martin would once more draw national notice, though this time it was because of the "un-American ideology" he and other members of the FE leadership shared. As was the case at International Harvester, Caterpillar executives had not found dealing with the radical FE much to their liking, and they recognized in the recent revisions to labor law just the opening needed to oust their troublesome adversary. As contract nego-tiations approached in the spring of 1948, the company announced there was no point in bargaining with the FE, since its noncompliant status with section 9(h) of the Taft-Hartley Act meant that it might be unseated by a "qualified" organization. Several unions, the UAW among them, took the hint and launched drives to wrest the Cat membership away from the FE. When the Caterpillar contract expired in April, Local 105 went on strike, a move that FE leaders viewed as unavoidable but fraught with peril. During the walkout they would be obliged to take on not only a hostile company, but other unions aggressively courting their rank and file.

Not surprisingly, "the Communist Master Minds who run FE Local 105" served as the primary focus of the UAW's anti-FE campaign. Hysteria was ginned up not just by the encroaching unions but also by the reactionary forces that steered much of Peoria's public opinion. In a speech to the local American Legion that drew front page coverage and rousing applause from the Legionnaires, former FBI agent Paul Ferrin cautioned that communists represented "a more serious threat than even the Nazis." Those evildoers were plotting right next door, Ferrin warned, as he named Ajay Martin, along with another official of Local 105, as sinister hometown subversives.[6]

The NLRB scheduled an election to settle the representation question, but since FE officers had not signed noncommunist affidavits, the union that already represented Local 105 members would not be on the ballot. FE sup-porters thus found themselves in the untenable position of urging workers to vote "no union." The desperate ploy failed. The UAW captured the Caterpil-lar plant on May 20, 1948, a result that FE literature acidly suggested "really made all dead and departed union men like Joe Hill and the Haymarket martyrs turn over in their graves." The UAW's "vulture raid" left FE leaders profoundly shaken, and their wrath had a specific target. "AN ANTI-UNION CORPORATION YELLS FOR HELP," read the *FE News* headline following the election, "AND WALTER REUTHER COMES RUNNING TO THE RESCUE."[7]

The Cat catastrophe had inflicted serious damage, and FE leaders well understood that Reuther was not through with them yet. Continued defi-ance of section 9(h) could be suicidal. Shortly after the Caterpillar vote, the FE's executive board voted to comply with the provision, and in June 1948, Grant Oakes, "with reluctance and repugnance," signed an affidavit, as did the other elected officials of the FE—with four notable exceptions. Secretary-Treasurer Jerry Fielde, Director of Organization Milt Burns, Board Member-at-Large Pope Huff, and Vice-President Ajay Martin all resigned from their posts rather than submit to the noncommunist pledge. The FE thus became the first, and for a full year the only, communist-connected union to meet the stipulations of the Taft-Hartley Act. In the summer of 1949 two other left-led unions moved into compliance, but the UE leadership did not file affidavits until the end of that year.[8]

The FE's decision to strike out on its own on this issue, however, had not been reached easily or unanimously. Burns, Huff, and Martin, in a joint statement carried by the *FE News*, emphasized that they had advocated continued resistance against the Taft-Hartley affidavits; they stepped down from their positions only so as to avoid "any 'split' on this issue" within the union. In their view conforming to section 9(h) represented not a minor bureaucratic concession but a grave political misjudgment. And while in their statement they did not acknowledge whether they were currently, or had ever been, members of the Communist Party, they certainly made their ideological inclinations clear:

> Red-baiting, raiding, support of Wall Street candidates, compliance with the Taft-Hartley Act—all of these measures will weaken the ability of the unions to win higher wages and better conditions for their members; all of these measures will cripple the unions to the point where American fascists and reactionaries can swoop down for the final kill. . . .
>
> After many years in the labor movement we are convinced that labor will suffer depressions, inflations and wars so long as industry—the lifeblood of the nation—is allowed to remain in the private and unrestricted hands of a small group of wealthy families. Only when labor learns to demand that the means of their liveli- hood be owned and operated in the best interest of the majority of the people, and not for wealthy stockholders, will workers be able to look forward to a life of security, abundance and peace for them- selves and their children.[9]

Because, with Martin and Huff, "two of the three signers of this state- ment are Negroes" who have been "proud to be officers of a Union which ac- tively combats racial discrimination," they decried "the serious consequences of compliance upon the struggle of the Negro people for full citizenship rights." In no small measure because of Communist Party policy—and the efforts of Black party members—the FE had been especially aggressive on civil rights issues and reflected comparatively high levels of African Amer- ican leadership. Taft-Hartley's strictures thus seemed a dagger aimed at working-class radicalism within the Black community. Peorian Ajay Martin believed this strongly enough to give up a union office which had afforded him, a young African American, an unusual degree of national recognition. Absorbing the fresh sting of the Caterpillar loss not long after his hometown had vilified Paul Robeson, Martin no doubt felt acutely both the bitterness and defiance expressed in the resignation statement.

Jerry Fielde concurred with the declaration issued by Burns, Huff, and Martin but also offered an individual statement, which spoke to his ten-year tenure as an FE official. Stepping down from his elected post, he indicated, was "not an easy thing for one so intimately connected with the whole struggle we went through in organizing farm equipment . . ." Yet for Fielde, signing an affidavit was not an option either. "The temptation is to 'go along,'" he said, but "the complying sections of the labor movement will discover they have furnished the crosses for their own crucifixion."[10]

Given that these four key members of the union's leadership so opposed the noncommunist affidavits that they quit rather than sign them, why then did the FE move to comply with Taft-Hartley, and long before the other CP-influenced unions? This episode underscores the limits of any Communist Party "control" over the FE. The pressure to comply came from the six district directors on the FE executive board, chief among them John Watkins, the popular and dedicated leader of the crucial Quad Cities region, an area on the Illinois-Iowa border where two Harvester plants (East Moline and Farmall) and other farm equipment factories were located. Watkins was fiercely militant and just as independent, unwilling to follow directives that threatened what he believed were the interests of the workers he steadfastly represented. He had argued, after Taft-Hartley became law, that compliance was requisite to the FE's survival, and after the Cat loss his insistence that the debacle not be repeated was endorsed by a majority of the executive board. Fielde, Burns, Huff, and Martin personally found the affidavit requirement too abhorrent to stomach. But they accepted the decision to move the FE into compliance with section 9(h), however reluctantly, and now, they said, "the question no longer exists as an issue in our Union."[11]

Yet while the FE on paper conformed to the Taft-Hartley Act, within short order the union devised a work-around that flouted the legislation's intent. Jerry Fielde retained his post as chief negotiator with International Harvester and Milt Burns became political action director for the FE: both appointed, rather than elected, positions and thus not subject to the affidavit requirement. Their titles may have changed but Fielde and Burns remained within the FE leadership's high command. Pope Huff and Ajay Martin were also offered FE staff jobs but declined them. Huff left factory work but remained in Chicago and continued to voice support for the FE, particularly on behalf of his former local at McCormick Works. Martin chose to become an employee of the Communist Party—at least, that's what the FBI maintained. He was to focus on "communist organizational work among Negro trade unionists" in the South.[12]

Taft-Hartley, therefore, had succeeded in reconfiguring the FE's leadership but not in ideologically transforming it. Because of that, the union had bought no respite from its enemies. Whatever the stated rationale, failure to comply with the affidavits—or in the FE's case, adhering to the letter but not the spirit of the law—instantly came to constitute one of the principal markers for those unions characterized in this period as "communist-dominated."

But Taft-Hartley, which represented a body blow not just to the labor left but to the entire labor movement, had been crafted in the halls of Congress, and so it appeared to necessitate a political response. This led to another dead giveaway, so it would be claimed, used to identify those unions that were agents of the Communist Party: they supported Henry Wallace rather than Harry Truman in the 1948 US presidential contest. Wallace, who had been FDR's vice-president until he was nudged out in favor of Truman, was an unreconstructed New Dealer and an outspoken critic of the aggressive anti-communism that defined Truman's foreign policy. By 1948, Wallace had abandoned the Democrats to spearhead a new Progressive Party, on a platform that proclaimed, "Never before have so few owned so much at the expense of so many." Because "private power . . . pulls the strings of its puppet Republican and Democratic parties," a third alternative provided the only hope of countering "big business control of our economy and government." The Progressive agenda roundly excoriated Taft-Hartley, Jim Crow laws, and the House Un-American Activities Committee while endorsing "peaceful, hopeful negotiations" with the Soviet Union. And since President Truman had alienated much of organized labor, a third-party effort founded on such principles could generate significant working-class support.[13]

If the Progressive agenda also seemed like one that Communist Party members could get behind, that's because they helped formulate it. Wallace himself was not a communist but some of his influential advisors were, and the CP formally and noisily endorsed him. Many left-wing labor officials, as well, backed the third-party effort, but it was the FE that could claim the most comprehensive level of commitment. The FE's executive board, in December 1947, had urged Wallace to run and was thus the first union leadership to do so publicly. Grant Oakes became the Progressive Party's candidate for governor in Illinois; the FE's district director in Iowa was the Progressive choice for lieutenant governor in that state; and yet another FE executive board member from Chicago ran for a court clerkship. And Homer Ayres, who was the FE's director of farm relations, took a leave from the union to assume that same title with the Wallace campaign.[14]

The FE's involvement with the Progressive Party, however, was more extensive than even all this suggests, which brings someone back into the story who has been missing for a while. DeWitt Gilpin's name was absent from the Taft-Hartley discussion because he was not at that moment an elected official of the FE, or indeed even on the staff of the union. Since early 1948 he was, instead, employed by the Progressive Party, engaged to build "shop committees of Wallace sympathizers in the labor movement." Gilpin was no doubt energized by what then appeared to be "substantial strength for Wallace" evidenced across America. Grassroots organizing secured the Progressive Party a place on the California ballot and a victory in a special Congressional election in New York City. On the stump, Wallace drew sizable audiences; "industrial communities," noted the *New York Times* in May 1948, were turning out "large and demonstrative crowds of workers for Wallace meetings." On his mission Gilpin traveled across the country to solicit Progressive support from the likes of steelworkers and coal miners, but he had a particular affinity for the active Wallace committees established by FE locals in Illinois and Louisville.[15]

In Louisville there was early measurable enthusiasm for the Wallace effort. By January 1948, according to the FBI, Local 236 activists Sterling Neal, Fred Marrero, and Chuck Gibson were already leading the charge for a third-party effort. They would have been buoyed by Henry Wallace's appearance in Louisville a few months earlier, when in November 1947 an overflow crowd of "some 1,600 whites and Negroes sat side by side," making it the largest unsegregated gathering the city had yet experienced. "At 15 points in his speech, they cheered and applauded," reported the *Courier-Journal*. "And at 10:30 when the meeting broke up they were just as enthusiastic about Wallace as they had been at 7:30 when they began to arrive." In mid-February 1948—just a few days after Chuck Gibson's sudden death—the Wallace Committee of Louisville held its inaugural meeting at the headquarters of Local 236. In short order the Louisville FE, or those associated with it, became the main force organizing for the Progressive Party throughout the Bluegrass State. Of the seventeen delegates and observers who made up the Kentucky delegation at the Progressive Party convention, five were members of the Louisville FE, including Fred Marrero and Allen Coones, who had been elected the local's president following Gibson's death.[16]

But the enthusiasm for Henry Wallace was hardly shared by Louisville's labor establishment. Fissures between the left and right factions within the

Louisville CIO were already apparent; the specter of Wallace's candidacy engendered an open split. In January the Louisville Industrial Union Council voted its "opposition to any third party at this time," despite objections raised by left-wing unionists including Fred Marrero, the FE's representative on the council. In March the council reiterated its hostility to the Wallace effort, and this time also ejected Carl Braden, the labor reporter for the *Louisville Times*, from the meeting, citing Braden's "leftist sympathies" as rationale. In response, the FE representatives, along with those from three other smaller left-wing unions, bolted the assembly and decamped to the same 7th Street building where they shared office space.[17]

· That FE members would take such umbrage at Carl Braden's rough treatment by the Louisville CIO was not surprising, since he'd already proven himself their ally. Braden, who'd been named after Karl Marx by his socialist railroad worker father, had cut his teeth reporting on mineworkers' struggles in Harlan County during the Depression. He'd come back to his hometown of Louisville in 1945 to take the job with the *Times*, but his concept of journalism did not preclude involvement with the subjects he wrote about. When FE organizers arrived in Louisville he lent them his expertise, assisting with the publication of the *Cub*, the Local 236 newsletter. In 1948 Carl married Anne McCarty, a young reporter covering education issues for the *Times*. Anne spent most of her childhood in a comfortable Alabama home, steeped in the Southern culture of white superiority, but by the time she met Carl she had developed a visceral antipathy to that noxious brew. Together, the Bradens viewed the Progressive Party as an antidote to the racism and labor oppression they knew well as white Southerners, and they made little effort to mask their enthusiastic support for Henry Wallace.[18]

That was the case as well for others connected to the FE in Louisville. Local 236 member Chris Gastinger, for instance, who then "hated Harry Truman with a passion," from the start threw himself headlong into the Progressive cause, so much so that he was arrested for too loudly blaring entreaties to vote for Wallace from the sound truck he drove through the streets of Louisville. But others did not immediately jump on the bandwagon. At first Jim Wright couldn't understand why his union's leadership was so keen on Henry Wallace, viewing him as "just another white man trying to get into the White House," he said. This was an attitude not allowed to go unchallenged. Indicating just how vested the FE's leadership was in the Wallace campaign, and how much weight they believed Jim Wright carried within Local 236, in the spring of 1948 DeWitt Gilpin and Milt Burns journeyed to Louisville to hash things out with Wright, in what proved to be an epic conversation. From early in the morning until well past lunchtime, without breaks for coffee or food, the three men sat on a park bench and argued about politics. Wright's recalcitrance produced some heated exchanges. "One time, it got so that me and Gilpin was gonna fight," Wright said. Burns, "always the compromiser," settled them down. Their conversation, Wright indicated, focused on civil rights issues, but they also talked about the shackles imposed on the labor movement. "And the right of people to speak out, because they were scared to talk about anything. Said they weren't, but they were," he said. "I agreed with them about that."[19]

As late afternoon set in, Wright had come to agree about Wallace as well. "I said, 'heck, if he can do that much—any white man that can do anything for Blacks, I'm for him, I'll tell you that right now.'" This mollified DeWitt Gilpin, barely. "Well, you didn't act like it, since I had to come all the way down here," a disgruntled Gilpin told Wright.[20]

But Wright proved worth the investment of time, as his commitment to the Progressive cause quickly ramped up. "After a while," he said, "I got really tied up in Wallace—I think I got too tied up; I didn't eat no food or nothing." He was not alone in his crusade. While there were white officials of the Louisville FE, like Gastinger and Coones, who took prominent roles in the Wallace effort, the most intense commitment, in Wright's view, came from among the local's Black leadership. Wright endeavored, along with Sterling Neal, Fred Marrero, and shop steward Robert Mimms, to enlist support within Local 236 and in the broader community; "sometimes we'd block off an area of the plant, shout at them before they went into the plant," Wright said; they also "went to every church, everything . . . we were pounding everywhere we could with leaflets." They were joined in these endeavors by other African Americans with high profiles in the city. Alfred Carroll, an attorney and immediate past president of the city's NAACP, served as an official with the Louisville Wallace committee; Andrew Wade, who would later become prominent for his collaboration with the Bradens to challenge Louisville's segregated housing market, was also active in the campaign. Both Carroll and Wade attended the Progressive Party convention as members of the Kentucky delegation.[21]

And at first, when out campaigning for Wallace, "we got a total response from the Black community" in Louisville, Wright said. This favorable reaction, he believed, pointed to a simmering restlessness within the African American populace. "People were hungry to get from under that bondage some kind of way. The change, the change was coming, but they didn't know the avenue to go through. And here come Wallace."[22]

This initial "total response" that Wright reported was no doubt a reflection of the Wallace campaign's unprecedented outreach—which was not just rhetorical, but actual—to the Black community below the Mason-Dixon line. Paul Robeson, for instance, made risky forays into the Deep South on behalf of the Progressive cause and Henry Wallace refused to patronize segregated establishments. Wallace, who declared segregation "an insult to the dignity of life" and favored repeal of miscegenation laws, was regularly pelted with projectiles and threatened with greater bodily harm by hostile white Southerners. They were evidently unconvinced when Wallace insisted that "the 1,400,000 white tenants and sharecroppers in the South are hurt as badly as the 1,000,000 colored sharecroppers. The big boys are determined to have this reservoir, divided and helpless, as a means of keeping their control." But Wallace found others ready to hear his message. Speaking on a September evening at Mount Olive Baptist Church in Knoxville, for instance, "the candidate had an audience that without reserve was on his side." The large and mostly African American audience "rumbled with the responsive amens" as Wallace proclaimed that "the first function of the law is to see that actions of hate are prevented. They are not being prevented because the promise of the Constitution has not been observed." As though to prove his point, at the same moment on the other side of town, the Ku Klux Klan set ablaze a fiery cross.[23]

In August 1948, when Wallace returned to Louisville—as part of the same Southern campaign that took him to Knoxville—"there were many Negroes and many who appeared to be rank-and-file members of unions" among the audience, press reports indicated. In his address Wallace saluted the members of Local 236 for taking on the Southern differential. They "have declared for all of Wall Street to hear," he said, "that Southern labor is entitled to a fair wage no less than Northern labor." That evening Wallace spent the night not at one of the whites-only hotels downtown, but instead at a far less swanky establishment in the Black section of the city.[24]

But for that Louisville speech, Henry Wallace drew perhaps one thousand people, a smaller crowd than had turned out the previous November. The dwindling attendance reflected the fading hopes of the Progressive Party effort as election day approached. Harry Truman, in part due to Progressive pressure, tacked left, emphasizing his veto of the Taft-Hartley Act and his support for the Democratic Party's civil rights platform. In response noncommunist liberal organizations lined up solidly behind Truman, as did influential African American groups like the NAACP. So too did the labor establishment, as the Louisville FE was well aware: the CIO warned that any unions supporting the third party would face disciplinary action, while the UAW executive board denounced it as "a Communist Party maneuver designed to advance the foreign policy interests of the Soviet Union." That the Wallace effort was in reality a Kremlin plot swiftly became the predominant mainstream narrative, as the "Red Fever" then engulfing America "transformed [Wallace] in the public mind into a wild-eyed fanatic bent on destroying the American way of life." The red baiting was facilitated, to be sure, by the fact that there were in fact reds playing a transparent role in the campaign.[25]

Not that everyone committed to the Progressive cause was a communist; in fact, some were about as far removed from the CP as one might get. The single largest donor to the Wallace campaign was not Moscow but eighty-two-year-old Anita McCormick Blaine, the "multimillionaire heiress to the McCormick Harvester fortune," last surviving offspring of the Reaper King, and thus sister to Cyrus II and Harold McCormick. She was also the widow of Emmons Blaine, whose father James had been a preeminent figure in the nineteenth-century Republican Party and the GOP presidential nominee in 1884. But Anita had drifted from her family's political fold some time before, as she had been a supporter of Franklin Roosevelt and after WWII became an impassioned advocate of world peace. Early on she became one of five national co-chairs of the Wallace for President Committee. Anita was also selected to run for trustee of the University of Illinois, and so she joined the field from her home state that included, at the top of the ticket, Grant Oakes as the Progressive Party choice for governor.[26]

Whoever said politics makes strange bedfellows must have had this scenario in mind. Not only was Anita McCormick Blaine partnered on the Progressive slate with the head of the union regarded by Harvester management—including her nephew, Fowler McCormick—as the company's archnemesis, but thanks to her largesse DeWitt Gilpin was roaming the country stirring up working-class antipathy toward big business. She contributed nearly a million dollars to the campaign and also paid the rent for the Illinois Progressive Party headquarters on Michigan Avenue in Chicago, located just steps from her home, a gabled redbrick mansion on Erie Street that she'd had built in the late nineteenth century. So it's easy to envision aristocratic Anita stopping in at the office to chat with volunteers or confer with her running mate Grant Oakes, though just how their conversations might have proceeded stretches the imagination somewhat. But there's no need to wonder what *Chicago Tribune* editor Robert McCormick thought of his cousin Anita's conduct. To the reactionary "Colonel," the Democrats were bad enough—he was not fond of GOP nominee Thomas Dewey but any Republican was far preferable to Truman—but Henry

Wallace's camp, so proclaimed a *Tribune* editorial, consisted only of "wobblies, Communists, bumpkins and boobs." "Colonel" McCormick put his cousin in at least one of those categories in a *Tribune* story about Wallace's "Red Admirers," charging that the campaign's top donors, including Anita McCormick Blaine, "have records of Communist support and sympathy, if not outright membership in the party."[27]

Confounding the oddsmakers, the *Chicago Tribune*'s preferred candidate did not come in first—Dewey did not beat Truman after all—but Anita's pick finished well out of the money. In November 1948, Henry Wallace chalked up just over a million votes nationally, only 2 percent of the total. As an indication of how the Progressive effort had disintegrated, in early 1948 the *Courier-Journal* predicted that Wallace might capture one hundred thousand votes in Kentucky; instead he garnered less than fourteen hundred. Despite the visibility of FE leaders in the Progressive campaign, clearly most of the union's members—and most workers period—shied away from the red-tinged new party and stuck with the old party of FDR instead. That dismal showing reflected, in part, the power of the political establishment: in Illinois, for instance, the Democratic machine engaged in a series of legal shenanigans that kept the Progressive Party off the ballot altogether, denying the citizens of that state the option of voting for Henry Wallace and Grant Oakes and Anita McCormick Blaine. But a spot on the Illinois ballot would have improved the final result for Wallace only marginally, at best. The historical consensus has it that the quixotic Wallace campaign was an unmitigated disaster, especially for the labor left, as it appeared to achieve nothing beyond allowing for the easy identification and isolation of those unions affiliated with the Communist Party.[28]

Reflecting on the experiences of some Progressive activists, however, makes their participation in this dubious battle more understandable. It's not hard to fathom why Ajay Martin, who was elected to the board of the Illinois Progressive Party, would join his former houseguest Paul Robeson in a political movement that promised a more insistent challenge to the segregated status quo they endured on a daily basis. In Chicago, at McCormick Works, African Americans Harold Ward, Fred Moore, and Bill Smith (who would be elevated to a union vice-presidency in 1949) headed up the FE Local 108 Oakes-Wallace Committee. Though Jim Wright initially had to be nudged (or shoved) into participation, his commitment to Wallace was likewise cemented by the campaign's unprecedented focus on civil rights.[29]

And to judge only by the election's final result misses some of what the Wallace phenomenon represented at the local level. While a good number of the FE activists involved in the Progressive effort had Communist Party ties, many—like Jim Wright—did not. Nonetheless Henry Wallace and his supporters, all of them, were routinely painted with the same broad red brush. The attacks aimed at Wallace, Jim Wright suggested, transformed communism from a sinister abstraction into something more familiar and less threatening. Initially, in Louisville, "what they said about FE, it was just a communist union, just plain communist. People didn't know what communism was, they didn't know, just called you that," Wright said. "But Wallace changed that, so that at least people were thinking of communism as a human being, with a different political thinking: the guy just thinks different." Since red-baiting was often racialized ("they'd say, if he's a communist, he's a nigger-lover," Wright indicated), within Louisville's African American community the anti-communist rhetoric aimed at the Progressive Party often read like a thinly veiled endorsement of white supremacy. Henry Wallace himself, reflecting on the hate-filled white crowds he encountered during his tour of the South, drew that conclusion. "They shouted 'Nigger' and 'Communist' and they looked on both of these ideas as essentially the same thing. Anyone who believes in nonsegregation seems to be a Communist." The Wallace campaign thus inured many rank-and-filers, especially African Americans, to the excesses of anti-communist hysteria before the red-baiting barrage aimed at the FE reached maximum intensity.[30]

And in Louisville in particular, the Wallace campaign sparked a political awakening for many members of Local 236. "I think it was a revolution at the time, for Blacks," Jim Wright maintained. During the campaign, "we got rocks, people almost got hung, and everything else, but we kept fighting," he said. "I remember before that, there wasn't much *fight* in the Blacks." Amending his comment somewhat, he added "I mean, Blacks always had fight in them, but there was nothing, they didn't have no kind of leader to relate to." The Wallace campaign, Wright insists, "started the Blacks a'moving. Blacks began to identify with what was going on in this country, and what they wanted to have happen." The community activities that were pursued by the Louisville FE in the late 1940s and early 1950s "all began to flow from that campaign," he said. Another Progressive Party stalwart, Chris Gastinger, agreed. "More than likely the roots of the civil rights movement in Kentucky came from that campaign," he said. "I suspect a lot of the activists got their ideas in that Wallace campaign."[31]

The failed Progressive effort also connected Carl and Anne Braden to the FE, fostering a relationship that would prove critical to civil rights efforts within the city and the nation. A few months after the 1948 election,

the Bradens established the Labor Information Center, located in the Louisville FE's headquarters, and continued to assist the FE and the other
left-leaning unions in the 7th Street alliance with political and community
organizing. For Anne in particular, her ongoing work with the members of
Local 236 proved pivotal to her understanding of racial and class dynamics
in the South. In 1963 she would be singled out by Martin Luther King, Jr.,
in his *Letter from a Birmingham Jail*, as one of the few whites who possessed
"the vision to see that injustice must be rooted out by strong, persistent and
determined action." She had developed that vision in no small measure
through what she had absorbed years before from Local 236 official Sterling
Neal. Anne described Neal as "a visionary leader" and "a master teacher"
who "pulled no punches with me." She remained immeasurably grateful for
the mentorship he provided her in the late 1940s and early 1950s on matters
of civil rights. "Many of the principles I've tried to live by since, I learned
from him," she said, in her tribute to Neal upon his death in 1997.[32]

Yet whatever positive ramifications the Wallace campaign may have had
at ground level, there is no question that nationally it hastened the day of
reckoning for the CP-associated unions, since the CIO leadership deemed
bucking the directive to support the Democratic Party tantamount to treason.
"You are not going to be tolerated forever," Walter Reuther warned, for "destroying the American labor movement and sabotaging the basic policies of
the CIO." But for one union the clock had already run out: in late November
1948 the CIO executive board gave the FE sixty days to dissolve and affiliate
with the UAW. The UAW promptly initiated a "Drive to Unite All Farm
Implement Workers," as the mandate allowed Walter Reuther to launch an
open crusade against the FE. "From here on out," said UAW Vice-President
John Livingston, "the UAW-CIO is going to take its appeal for unity directly
to the rank and file membership of the FE locals." Translated, this meant
initiating a full-scale UAW raiding offensive on plants already organized by
the FE.[33]

Within the FE this "appeal for unity" was met with defiance. In a testy
mood, FE members gathered in Cedar Rapids, Iowa, in March 1949 for the
union's national convention. "By this time, our union was supposed to be a
dead duck," Grant Oakes told the assembled delegates. But "this convention
is in session," he declared, "because we have been able to forge an unshat-
terable kind of unity in our ranks." Oakes, making clear that recent losses
remained fresh wounds, insisted "the political climate which makes for raids
on FE-CIO and other unions also makes for retention of the union-smash-
ing Taft-Hartley slave-labor law. There is no distinction between an unjust

law to put unions in chains or out of business, and an ultimatum from the top CIO body to do the same thing." The delegates concurred, voting unanimously to reject the CIO's "dictatorial ultimatum" and calling for "an immediate halt to the UAW's union-busting adventure which can only serve to assist the monopoly corporations."[34]

These impassioned arguments, needless to say, left Walter Reuther and the labor establishment unmoved. In May 1949 the CIO executive board indicated that it would, at its convention upcoming in the fall, revoke the FE's charter because of its continuing defiance of the merger edict. With expulsion from the CIO now a foregone conclusion, FE leaders were forced to assess the chances that their small union could survive as an independent organization, especially in the face of a full-scale UAW assault. They thus proposed joining forces with another left-led union, the five-hundred-thousand-member United Electrical Workers, then the nation's third-largest union. The arrangement was less a merger than an affiliation, for, as the FBI noted, the FE would "retain . . . its organizational setup, constitution and autonomy." Grant Oakes would take a place on the UE executive board and chair the newly created FE-UE Farm Equipment Council, while Jerry Fielde would remain the head of the Harvester Conference Board. All other national and local FE officials and organizers would stay on as part of the deal. And in perhaps the most manifest indication of the FE's insistence on autonomy, farm equipment plants would maintain their former local numbers and would henceforth be referred to, for example, as FE-UE Local 236.[35]

The FE membership, polled about the UE affiliation, approved it by an overwhelming margin, though just how many participated in the mail-in vote was not reported. The FE-UE merger was concluded just a few weeks before the CIO's annual meeting in October 1949. Facing certain expulsion itself, the UE, along with its new farm equipment contingent, formally withdrew from the CIO before the convention began. As promised, the CIO executive board banished the FE, and the CIO's constitution was altered to allow for the ejection of other unions "the policies and activities of which are consistently directed toward the achievement of the program or the purposes of the Communist Party. . . ." Though the UE had already quit, the CIO decided, under this new provision, to throw it out anyway, and committees were established to hear "charges" against eight other left-led unions as well. Within two years, all of those organizations, representing nearly one million workers, had likewise been expelled from the CIO.[36]

So by the fall of 1949 the FE seemed primed for a knockout blow. The Caterpillar fiasco, the debilitating struggle over the Taft-Hartley affidavits, the considerable energy expended on the lost Progressive cause: all that had surely discredited the FE leadership. International Harvester's management denounced them as "irresponsible radicals," while the press and politicians of both parties pounded them ceaselessly as "reds" and "commies." Now the FE had been condemned and cast out by the CIO, a loss of power and prestige which the hastily arranged partnership with the UE—another "communist-dominated" organization—could not offset. There was every reason to believe that by this point the FE's rank and file would readily respond to the UAW's "appeal to unity."

But Walter Reuther wanted a sure thing: if the first UAW raid following the CIO expulsion was a success, the remaining FE locals could be expected to quickly jump ship as well. It was imperative to throw every possible resource at a seemingly vulnerable target, one where the FE was not deeply rooted, in a place where workers might be especially amenable to anti-communist exhortations. The logical choice was Louisville.

18.
The Triumph of the Stormy Petrel

Alone the proud,
The stormy petrel
Over the spouting,
Savage sea,
Alone he soars
A prophet crying
Of victory:
Let the storm rage!
Fiercer,
Let the storm break!

> —**Maxim Gorky**, from "Song of the Stormy Petrel," 1901

The outcome was a triumph for the "stormy petrel" union on the scene of
Louisville labor relations.

> —*Courier-Journal*, December 22, 1949

Jim Wright was well aware of the challenge facing Local 236 when the UAW forces set up camp in his hometown in 1949. "They had just beaten us at Caterpillar, in Peoria. Took the shop away from us, took that big plant away, because we couldn't get on the ballot." He knew that in Louisville the FE could not come close to matching its rival's resources. "UAW sent in their whole staff of organizers—I think then they had about seventy-five or eighty organizers on the staff—they sent them all over town, plus all the local union presidents within a five-hundred-mile radius," he said. By this point Wright also recognized that the FE's radical reputation might prove a liability. "Everybody red-baited us to death," and the leaders of Local 236, Wright said, were broadly depicted as renegades run amok: "They strike all the time, they're just rabble-rousers, a bunch of commies, the whole stuff . . . and the newspapers kept saying and kept saying that we were representatives right out of Moscow." Wright maintained that UAW organizers were relentless on that issue, and out at the plant gate the UAW forces "had a picket sign that they painted with a hammer and sickle, carry it around all the time, just carry it around, stay close to us all the time."

And so Wright feared that the local union he had helped build might be overcome. "We thought it was going to be a tough election, really," he said.[1]

There was good reason for Wright's unease. The UAW invested heavily over many months in its effort to win over the thirty-seven hundred employees at Harvester's Louisville plant. "We are not going to stand by and let a union with its top leadership obviously under Communist control sacrifice the interest of the workers," UAW Vice-President John Livingston declared in Louisville in early March 1949, and with that the raid was underway. Big ads appeared often in the local press, stressing that "the Farm Equipment Workers union follows the Communist line" and emphasizing the UAW's superior size and its "vast resources." Switching to the UAW would "stop wildcat strikes," while sticking with the FE meant "failure and insecurity and disillusionment," a forecast of existential despair not generally associated with one's union affiliation.[2]

It wasn't just the paid publicity, however, that favored the UAW. Though Jim Wright took a jaundiced view of the Louisville press, the town's biggest paper—the *Courier-Journal*—was reliably liberal, certainly by Southern standards but even in comparison to many in Northern cities. So it covered union issues more temperately than was true, say, of the *Chicago Tribune*. But through 1949, Local 236 would have preferred less media attention altogether, as the escalating family feud within the labor movement ensured regular stories spotlighting those "Red-Dominated Unions" that were "Defying the CIO," of course referencing the FE. Meanwhile the *Courier-Journal*'s sister publication, the *Louisville Times*, weighed in more expressly, editorializing that the FE leadership should explain why it so often stood on "the Moscow side of all these things."[3]

International Harvester was, on the record, neutral in this contest, but FE supporters believed that the company was doing all it could to tip the balance toward the UAW. "Harvester is taking advantage of the UAW drive to try and get rid of men who favor the United Farm Equipment Workers," one FE member insisted in a letter to the *Courier-Journal*, and in fact in the months after the raid commenced at least seven Local 236 officials were suspended or fired outright. After the expulsion of the left-led unions, in the fall of 1949, IH officials speculated publicly that since the FE was no longer affiliated with the CIO, the company's agreement with the FE might be void. The suggestion to Harvester workers that they might lose their hard-fought contract if they remained in the FE was harmful enough, but company officials, declaring the legal situation "cloudy," began retaining the dues payments that Local 236 was normally allotted through a payroll check-off. The failure to receive their dues money left the local "dead broke"; with weeks to go before the NLRB election—it was scheduled for late December—Local 236 Treasurer Tom DeLong reported they had only 124 dollars in the bank. The UAW, on the other hand, DeLong insisted, was spending "hundreds of thousands of dollars" in Louisville.[4]

With little money or institutional support to mount its defense Local 236 could only keep on operating as it had from the beginning. The hand-cranked mimeo machine in the Louisville office got a workout throughout 1949, churning out "constant leaflets," Jim Wright said, that FE supporters distributed at the plant nearly every day. Fred Marrero, one of the union leaders Harvester had fired (a story to be taken up shortly), and several of the other workers who'd been dismissed by IH utilized their involuntary idleness for "full-time house-to-house organizational work." Those FE leaders still on the job were also fanning out into the community. "We got out there and talked to those people, went to churches," Wright indicated, and "went all over town."[5]

But these personal overtures seemed trifling in the face of the UAW juggernaut, and Local 236's paltry treasury factored into another disappointment it experienced in the run-up to the election. In early 1949 Harvester had inaugurated a new foundry at its Louisville complex, located some distance from the production operation, and its employees would be in a separate bargaining unit. The UAW and the AFL molders' union, along with the FE, endeavored to secure representation there. Focused on retaining its position at the main plant, the FE was too strapped to devote much to this simultaneous effort, and in any event, at least as Louisville FE staffer Bud James saw it, his union never really had a fair shot. Harvester, James insisted, initially hired a mostly white workforce for the new foundry, because "we had such a strong group [of African Americans] in the main shop, that they weren't going to give us a chance to get in there . . . they refused to hire anyone we had any connection with." But "UAW people, known organizers" easily found jobs at the new facility. On November 22, the UAW won the NLRB vote and the right to represent the one thousand workers in the IH foundry. However inevitable that outcome might have seemed to the FE forces, it was another blow for them to absorb at the least opportune time.[6]

And in December, for the big push just before the election at the main plant, the UAW pulled out the stops. "The UAW has opened a field office near the plant and is serving coffee and doughnuts in the morning and beer in the afternoon and night," Tom DeLong reported. "They are paying fifteen dollars a week to anyone willing to wear their buttons and attempt to sign up members." UAW organizers distributed a letter from CIO President Philip Murray urging Harvester workers to abandon the FE, and in the final week, the UAW received crucial endorsements from on high, in a nearly literal sense. Father Charles Owen Rice, Pittsburgh's prominent "labor priest," who was pro-union and anti-communist in equal measure, arrived in Louisville to declare that "every responsible authority considers FE to have been part of the Communist apparatus." From their pulpits a few days later, on the Sunday before the election, priests throughout Louisville—which had a sizable Catholic population—labeled the UAW-FE contest "a straight communist versus anticommunist fight," and advised that "no one can conscientiously have anything to do with communism, whether it is openly professed communism or cleverly disguised communism." Protestants got the same message, as a group of ministers issued a joint denunciation of the FE, and the UAW ferried in African American clergymen from Detroit, Local 236 claimed, in an effort to sway the city's Black congregations.[7]

The next evening, on December 19, Walter Reuther himself appeared to administer the coup de grace; his arrival at the rally in Louisville's twenty-three-hundred-seat Memorial Auditorium was, the press noted, "evidence of the importance UAW attached to the campaign." Reuther's address featured his familiar chastisement of the FE leadership, "who betray the workers whenever the Communist Party dictates." The million-member UAW, which Reuther likened to "a battleship with 16-inch guns," had the obvious advantage in collective bargaining, and made the FE look like "a rowboat armed with peashooters." It would clearly behoove Harvester employees, Reuther insisted, to join with autoworkers to become part of "one powerful union."

All compelling arguments from the man the local press called "one of the nation's most dynamic labor leaders." For the UAW forces, there was just one small problem: few Harvester employees—in fact, not too many people, period—showed up to hear the message. The audience for Reuther's address, the capstone of the all-out assault on the FE he had authorized in Louisville, barely topped five hundred, filling only a fraction of the seats in the cavernous auditorium. "The inference," the *Courier-Journal* noted, "is obvious."[8]

What could be inferred became concrete when the results of the NLRB election were tallied two days later: by a two-to-one margin, and with turnout over 80 percent, the workforce at Harvester's Louisville plant confirmed their support for FE Local 236. "BIG SETBACK FOR CIO," the papers proclaimed, and "a triumph for the 'stormy petrel' on the scene of Louisville labor relations." Their convincing victory left FE supporters jubilant, not to mention relieved, and they took the occasion to blast both the UAW and IH.

"Behind this whole mess," said Tom DeLong, was "the hand of the company, trying desperately to break the workers' own union and company-union-ize the International Harvester company." The failed raid "was a complete setback for the Jim Crow interests that were out to wreck the most effec-tive inter-racial local union in the whole south," said Sterling Neal. "Negro members have shared in the local stewardship and leadership of Local 236 ever since our local was born," Neal insisted, and the FE claimed that only one Black worker had crossed over to vote for the UAW.[9]

In an editorial reflection just after the election, the *Courier-Journal* noted that the FE "has been castigated, disinherited and publicly branded as sub-ject to Communist control." Nonetheless Local 236 "convinced almost two-thirds of [Harvester] employees that it was the union which would protect their interests. The issue is settled." While FE leaders were no doubt pleased to receive such a declaration from Louisville's leading paper, they knew full well that the issue of their union's continued existence was far from settled, inasmuch as either International Harvester management or the labor estab-lishment was concerned. For, in fact, the CIO's "big setback" in Kentucky served as no deterrent whatsoever to Walter Reuther, who initiated thirty-nine separate attempts within the next few years to wrest representation at various farm equipment factories where the FE was already the recognized bargaining agent. These raids were sometimes successful at the FE's smaller locals, and the UAW also managed to splinter off an office unit at one plant, or a toolroom at another. But the heart of the FE, emotionally and numeri-cally, had always been within International Harvester, and those locals would be put to the test time and again. So, through 1953, at McCormick Works (twice), at West Pullman, and at Tractor Works in Chicago; in Richmond, Indiana; in Auburn, New York; and in Rock Island, Canton, and East Mo-line, Illinois, the UAW endeavored to entice Harvester workers away from the FE. Yet the FE—outstaffed, outfinanced, and outcast from the main-stream labor movement—each time emerged victorious, often by margins that matched or exceeded its impressive 1949 showing in Louisville.[10]

The UAW's record of failure in this regard raises the obvious question: why did Harvester workers, in the middle of the Cold War in the middle of America, remain so overwhelmingly loyal to a union "publicly branded as subject to Communist control?" Clearly slapping a bright red label on the FE was not enough to drive them to vote it out. But just what sort of union did they believe they were voting *for*?

"Don't ever play a worker to be a fool," Jim Wright said, recalling his days as a steward for Local 236. He maintained that rank-and-file union members had carefully considered the differences between the FE and the UAW.

> Yes, they talked about that and talked about those things at
> length. . . . A worker's a keen thinker. He's a keen thinker, because
> that's all he's got. All he's got is his machine and his job, his home
> or his house, and his wife and his kids. He thinks about that. . . . So
> the worker would be running the machine, you think that he's using
> the micrometer to check the size of the piece he's about to put in,
> but he's looking out of the corner of his eye and he sees you coming,
> coming down there, and he'll stop you and bring up some kind of
> ideological point about something and stun you . . . I was amazed
> at the workers. I was amazed at the vocabulary—they didn't have a
> good vocabulary, they couldn't use the big words—but then, when
> you work around them a long time, it just looked like the vocabulary
> wasn't necessary.[11]

Local 236 was dubbed Louisville's "stormy petrel"; that seabird, a gutsy
midair maneuverer, is associated by sailors with tempestuous weather and
trouble ahead. It was an apt metaphor, reasonably applied to the FE from
the moment it arrived in Louisville, and by late 1949 those "keen thinkers"
at the Harvester plant fully understood just how disruptive the union was.
That's precisely why they chose to stick with it. And this loyalty to the FE—
demonstrated in Louisville and at the other Harvester plants where the
UAW was rebuffed—was rooted in that slim document that bound all IH
workers together: their contract. It might not have made for riveting reading,
but that agreement contained, in a nutshell, the essence of the modern labor
movement's pivotal ideological conflict.

19.
Pie on the Table or Pie in the Sky?

When UAW Vice-President John Livingston came to Louisville in early 1949 looking to woo Harvester workers there, he touted the groundbreaking contract his union had negotiated a year earlier with General Motors, with its innovative provisions that meant more money for UAW members. Months later, in his election-eve appearance in the city, Walter Reuther promised FE members that if they switched to his union, not only would their paychecks be fatter but the incessant turmoil in their shop would come to an end. "We don't go for wildcatting the year 'round," Reuther assured them. A strike might become necessary when the national agreement expired, he said, but otherwise membership in the UAW meant uninterrupted production, and thus an altogether calmer workplace.[1]

The approach to collective bargaining extolled by Livingston and Reuther in 1949 would achieve great fanfare a year later, when the UAW and GM negotiated what *Fortune* magazine famously dubbed "The Treaty of Detroit." The significance of this agreement, *Fortune's* editors emphasized, was impossible to overstate: "It is the first major union contract that explicitly accepts objective economic facts—cost of living and productivity—as determining wages, thus throwing overboard all theories of wages as determined by political power, and of profit as 'surplus value.'" The key components of the "Treaty," however—a cost-of-living increase and the annual improvement factor (also called a productivity pay increase, designed to reward workers as the company's output levels grew)—were already in place when the UAW raid in Louisville was launched. The 1950 GM contract simply added one additional element: a five-year expiration date. In the accord, the UAW pledged to assist the drive to produce at maximum efficiency, and provided an "ironclad" assurance that it would not seek to re-open the contract. *Fortune* was especially enthused about the productivity pay increase—"this all-important axiom of American progress"—which constituted "the most resounding declaration yet by any big union that the U.S. can grow more prosperous only by producing more." Though the generous wage and benefit provisions included in the contract would cost plenty—over the life of the contract, perhaps as much as a billion dollars—as far as *Fortune* was concerned GM "got a bargain."[2]

GM executives were making the same trade-off that Cyrus McCormick II had made when he spent heavily to uproot skilled molders in his foundry:

the assertion of managerial power was worth a substantial cash investment. But from the other side of the table Walter Reuther was just as keen on the new agreement. He'd seen enough industrial warfare to believe that his UAW constituency—indeed all union members—would be better off with a long stretch of well-compensated peace. "This contract," said *Fortune*, "has become the program on which Reuther hopes to unify American labor under his leadership." Reuther hailed the "maturing relationship between the Union and the Corporation" and the "stability in labor relations" the agreement represented. In his pitch to Louisville workers, Reuther emphasized that by switching to the UAW such stability could become reality within International Harvester plants as well.[3]

But most of those workers, as the subsequent NLRB vote demonstrated, proved immune to Reuther's blandishments. Within the Louisville FE one particular cohort—former UAW members—rejected them with particular vehemence. "I slaved under the UAW for two and a half years," said one-time Ford employee Ralph Self, in an edition of the Local 236 paper issued during the raid. "Whenever the foreman wanted to add more work to an employee, they simply add the work, and the union does nothing. In order to cut the cost of production, they lay off half of their force. That way they get the same amount of production with less men, by making the others half-slave." At the Chevrolet factory where Carl Keithly once worked, "the contract is violated every day of the week and the UAW does absolutely nothing about it," he insisted. "If you want speed-up, vote UAW," said Orville Porter, who had worked at an auto parts plant. "The UAW tells you there won't be any walk-outs if they win. That's true. The company will cut your wages, knock out your seniority and your vacations, and there will be no way you can protest outside of quitting your job. There will be nothing left at the plant but wage cuts and speed-up."[4]

Did Walter Reuther's collective bargaining ethos mean "wage cuts and speed-up" or peace and prosperity for workers? Here was the crux of the deep-seated ideological conflict between the FE and the UAW, differences that came to the fore during the drawn-out 1949 contest between the two unions in Louisville.

"Labor is not fighting for a larger *slice* of the national pie," Reuther had insisted in 1946. "Labor is fighting for a larger pie." That culinary cliché neatly illustrated what one historian termed "the politics of productivity," the emergent postwar ethos postulating that "American society could transcend the class conflicts that arose from scarcity" by "enhancing productive efficiency." Increasing output was deemed universally beneficial, with labor's interests inherently dependent on capital's continued expansion. Such growth would provide rising living standards without the need for any "radical redistribution of economic power": everyone would simply enjoy more on their plate. It was a beguiling philosophy, one that appealed to "labor statesmen" in the CIO and titans of industry alike, and was increasingly the consensus view in post-World War II America.[5]

The implications of this viewpoint were perfectly encapsulated in the "Code of Economic Group Behavior" for business and labor drawn up in 1947 by the National Planning Association, a liberal research group. "We believe unions are here to stay," said the business provision of the NPA "Code," "and that management can successfully develop ways and means of living with them." As for labor, union leaders were obliged to promote "employee practices which will increase productivity and improve the competitive position of the company" and should undertake "informing union members of the responsibilities the employer is facing, the work and competitive position of the company, and the importance of the union to company welfare." Fowler McCormick, whose enthusiasm for productive efficiency ran in his blood, fulsomely endorsed the NPA's credo, since it was "essentially the policy of the International Harvester Company." On the labor side, UAW President Walter Reuther offered his backing as well.[6]

But the "irresponsible radicals" at the helm of the FE, who eschewed the politics of productivity in favor of the politics of class conflict, refused to be parties to the code. To them, the promise that economic growth might provide an all-you-can-eat buffet for both employers and employees was just so much pie in the sky. FE leaders demanded, instead, a larger slice of what was already on the table. Harvester's long-standing practice of fudging its figures, and the incessant chiseling through its purportedly "scientific" pay system, led FE officials to recognize that the "economic facts" of which *Fortune* spoke were mere flimflam. Enhanced "efficiency" was just a euphemism for greater, and more cleverly camouflaged, exploitation. Through their Marxist lens they saw wage levels therefore not as reflective of "objective" realities but of relative power, and they maintained a conviction that profit, in fact, did represent the surplus value extracted from the workforce. For the FE leadership, the equation remained simple and unchanging: for workers to enjoy more, the corporations and the people who controlled them must get less.[7]

Thus FE officials vehemently opposed all the "Treaty of Detroit" represented. "The contract was predicated on the historic lie of labor 'statesmen' that labor can trust big business between contracts; that all that is necessary is to act tough at contract times, come up with a new super plan, and then work out a deal that can help both sides," an FE position paper maintained. "Such an ideology belies the fact that there is only one side for business—its side—and that it operates on the principle of getting as much as it can; it can be deterred in its exploitation only by applying economic and political power 365 days a year."[8]

Even before the "Treaty" was formalized, FE leaders were voicing opposition to its specific tenets. Cost-of-living wage adjustments represent "a policy of maintaining workers on subsistence levels," said a 1949 Officers' Report. "Ours is an obligation to improve the standard of living *over and beyond* mere hand to mouth existence." The cost-of-living concept "assumes that take-home pay was, at the time wages were tied to living costs, sufficient to provide workers and their families with a decent living standard," proclaimed one FE local newspaper. "It fails to relate wages to profits and to recognize that workers are entitled to a larger share of the exorbitant profits being rolled up by the companies."

FE leaders also characterized the productivity pay clause as "collaboration with management to boost production without parallel compensation," and the few cents per hour provided by that provision hardly constituted fair recompense, given that in the postwar years industrial workers had increased their output exponentially. Tying pay to productivity meant that workers would "make more and get less. But the company shows a higher profit," said the 1949 Officers' Report. "It is our obligation to prevent such speed-up which gives the workers the short end of the stick." And the FE leadership resisted the trend toward longer agreements, preferring one-year contracts and a rank and file kept combat-ready by near-incessant negotiations. "We were in constant turmoil, really," former FE organizer Al Verri said. "Of course, at that time we believed in keeping things in turmoil, because we used every opportunity to arouse workers."[9]

In his letter to Harvester workers sent during the 1947 Southern differential strike, IH president John McCaffrey said the FE's officers "have no respect for their contracts." In fact, the FE leadership regarded their hard-won agreements with near-reverence, but defined their purpose quite differently than McCaffrey or McCormick or, for that matter, Walter Reuther did. "We regard a collective bargaining contract as an instrument to protect the *workers'* wages, hours, and working conditions through secure union representation," the FE convention had resolved in 1946. "*A contract is not an instrument to cover false issues of 'company security.'*" Within the FE, the contract was no peace treaty; the brief document instead served as a weapon to be wielded in the 365-day-a-year battle with management.

McCaffrey had also maintained that the FE leadership was "more interested in disruption than in labor-management peace," and on that score he was not entirely wrong.[10]

In any ongoing struggle, frontline leadership makes all the difference, and thus the FE fought to maintain a large and unfettered steward body. Stewards serve as first responders for aggrieved workers in disputes with management, and within the FE, they were from the outset regarded as "rank and file generals" on perpetual duty to keep the membership organized and battle-ready. "Shop stewards are the key to a union's success or failure," the FE had declared back in 1940. "You can take both Oakes and Fielde's word for it that without these lads behind them they couldn't crash the office of the smallest farm equipment corporation." While they looked "just like a thousand other guys who make tractors and combines," FE stewards were nonetheless "the backbone of the union." And "sticking their necks out in good steward fashion" was expected, since "comes company provocation and the necessity of taking drastic action and it's the stewards who do the heavy duty."[11]

FE contracts, therefore, established a sizable steward presence—on average, the union claimed, one for every thirty-five to forty workers—vested with unusual freedom. While there was much in their contract with the FE that aggravated Fowler McCormick and the rest of Harvester management, their indignation increasingly centered on one clause, a holdover from the original 1941 agreement negotiated under the aegis of the War Labor Board: the language that afforded stewards "such time off as may be required for the performance of their duties." FE stewards thus habitually spent much of their workweek not producing farm equipment but handling grievances instead; or, as IH officials saw it, freely roaming the plants to "promote unrest, stir up ill will, harass the company, and convince as many members as it can that labor relations with Harvester is and must be class warfare," and all on the company's dime, no less. In a 1948 arbitration, Harvester officials were rebuffed in their efforts to modify the provision they so reviled: there was a "clear contractual commitment," the ruling held, to paid time off for FE stewards and moreover there was "no limit to the amount of allowable time" they were entitled to.[12]

While Harvester's contract with the UAW—also initially negotiated during WWII—included similar language, IH officials readily offered up evidence demonstrating that the paid-time-off provision was utilized far more, resulting in greater costs to the company, in its plants represented by the FE. FE officials, who believed that "each grievance is legitimate and they are morally bound to do the best they can for the employee concerned," offered little argument on that charge. As "the backbone of the union," a large, mobile and autonomous steward body was integral to the FE's modus operandi. In contrast, the "Treaty of Detroit" sharply limited where UAW officials could go within GM plants and how much time they could spend handling workers' complaints, and allowed for only one union representative on the shop floor for every 250 General Motors workers.[13]

But if "each grievance is legitimate," what, ultimately, should shop stewards be empowered to do if workers' complaints remained unaddressed? Unpersuaded that increased productivity and "stable" labor relations would serve workers' interests, FE leaders resisted any limitations on work stoppages, a distinction evident in the FE and UAW agreements with International Harvester. In 1946 the FE announced its "unalterable opposition" to no-strike clauses. But no corporation, and certainly not International Harvester, would then have acceded to a contract devoid of restrictions on walkouts. Both the FE and the UAW contracts with IH that were negotiated in 1946 contain nearly identical language, stipulating that walkouts during the life of the agreement could be authorized by the national union if, and only if, the grievance procedure had been exhausted. Under both contracts, union officials found responsible for strikes or slowdowns were subject to discipline. But in 1947, shortly after the passage of the Taft-Hartley Act, Harvester and the UAW struck a new, more express, deal: both proclaimed, "it is the desire of the Union and the Company to avoid strikes and work stoppages," and the following year this cooperative ethos was codified with a new clause in the 1948 IH-UAW contract:

> In any case where an interruption of production occurs in violation of this contract, the Union agrees that it will in good faith and without delay exert itself to bring about a quick termination of such interruptions of production, and will insist that the employees involved therein return to work and to normal production promptly. To that end, the Local and International Union will promptly take whatever affirmative action is necessary.[14]

No such provision was ever incorporated into the FE contract with International Harvester.

But on-the-ground realities provided an even greater distinction than contract comparisons might. The FE leadership—from top officials on down to shop stewards—reserved the right, in the face of "company provocation," to take the "drastic action" of interrupting production, which meant they routinely ignored whatever restrictions on stoppages and slowdowns the contract imposed. John McCaffrey made that point in the letter he sent during the Southern differential conflict, and the statistics continued to prove him right. Work stoppages occurred with astonishing frequency at IH plants represented by the FE, far more often than at facilities under UAW jurisdiction. Between 1945 and 1954, more than *one thousand* work stoppages took place at IH plants represented by the FE, as opposed to just under two hundred in IH plants represented by the UAW. (By 1948, because the UAW represented several IH truck plants and had gained jurisdiction over new facilities opened after the Louisville plant, the FE and the UAW represented an approximately equal number of Harvester workers.) These figures are not skewed by one period of particular turbulence; the FE's walkouts outnumbered the UAW's every year. Moreover, though some locations were more troublesome than others, walkouts at every FE-IH plant took place at the drop of a hat, sometimes literally. Jimmy Majors, an FE official at Tractor Works, recalled that when Harvester officials "would try to speed up" he could prompt a work stoppage without saying a word:

> If I went in with my hat on, and came out of the foreman's office with my hat off, with my hat in my hands, that meant we didn't get the thing settled. Guys would start shutting their machines off and stuff like that, and the foreman would want to know what the hell was going on. They didn't know about the signals we had. So we had the damn thing up to snuff.[15]

These walkout statistics, moreover, generally included only those actions that idled whole departments or entire plants, omitting brief stoppages or those involving only a few workers. At many FE plants interruptions to production were even more commonplace, and nowhere was this more true than in Louisville. "A fantastic, pyrotechnic series of disputes" characterized the Louisville IH plant, the *Courier-Journal* declared in mid-1949. In that article Harvester management again blamed FE's "irresponsible leadership" for the recurrent "wildcat strikes," which prompted an indignant response from W. B. Tyler, a member of the Local 236 grievance committee: "In the first place, we of FE do not call them strikes. We call them what they actually are—expressions of pent-up emotions brought on by the company's willful violations of its contract with the union," he explained. "I am sure the membership would soon throw the officers out if they let the company cram stuff down their throats as the company would like to do." And despite (or because of) all the walkouts, Tyler asserted that "we still make more money in a year than workers in other plants here. Where can you find a better job? No place, because FE does not represent workers in any other factory here."[16]

It was in this atmosphere that Walter Reuther announced in Louisville that in the UAW "we don't go for wildcatting the year 'round." Harvester workers soon thereafter made it known that they preferred the union that encouraged however many "expressions of pent-up emotions" deemed necessary to check management's efforts to impose wage cuts and speedup.

The walkout numbers and the contract language don't tell the whole story, though. What did it look like in practice for the members of Local 236 to protect their contract 365 days of the year? The culture of confrontation that permeated the FE from top to bottom served to build solidarity and strengthen the union, in some clear and in other subtler ways. In Louisville and elsewhere, however, that relentless militancy came at a price.

20.
Theory Meets Practice:
The Louisville Shop Floor

J im Mouser got a job at the Louisville Harvester plant just after the Southern differential strike concluded, and so he missed the early turbulence at the plant. But his father and brothers were already IH employees, and Mouser easily absorbed the Local 236 ethos. He was soon elected to be one of the union's "rank-and-file generals," becoming a shop steward on the second shift. He became so adept at his gear-cutting job that he needed only about six hours to make his piecework quota, and "the rest of the time I was all over the plant," he said, doing union business (for which, by the contract, he was paid by the company). Just how such business was conducted within Local 236 looked like this: One night just before the evening break Mouser was approached by a worker who was having trouble producing acceptable parts for a rush job he'd been ordered to perform. The FE-IH agreement stipulated that average piecework earnings were the rule under such conditions, but the worker had been told he would be compensated at a lower rate. Mouser confronted the foreman, the contract in his hand. "You know the contract as well as I do. Here it is, in black and white," Mouser said. The foreman refused to back down. Mouser had a ready response:

> Well, I'll tell you right now. It's not just him, it's the whole department. When that bell sounds at 7:30 and they go on their break, they're going to have a meeting. If you haven't straightened it out, you won't have any pieces from anybody the rest of the night, because they're going to go home. They've already told me that.

Actually, the workers hadn't already told Mouser that, as they hadn't yet heard about this dispute. But it was less a prevarication from Mouser than a prediction. When the break ended, the employees in the department had not returned to their jobs; instead, "they were sitting in the locker room when the plant superintendent came over with the guards to run them out, out of the plant," said Mouser, who took part in the exodus, although he worked in a different department. They all remained out four hours, and Harvester relented, providing the worker whose complaint had sparked the walkout his average piecework earnings, and compensating all the employees who'd quit work for their time lost.[1]

In glossy pamphlets and advertisements, International Harvester often emphasized the cutting-edge technology that characterized its modern Louisville facility. But one critical component of the plant's manufacturing system remained a relic from the past: its incentive pay system. Like everywhere else in the chain, most IH employees in Louisville were on piecework, and company officials there regularly manipulated the system, Jim Mouser said, though "they knew they were wrong in doing it" and in violation of the contract. "They just wanted to see how far they could go," he insisted, and as a steward he saw it as his duty to push back immediately against the company's relentless efforts to get more output for less money.[2]

Jim Wright, also a Local 236 steward, shared that point of view. Wright and Mouser worked in the same department (though Wright was on the first shift), and that overlap contributed to their developing friendship. So did their mutual contempt for Harvester management. "They'd give you a good clean rate on a job, and then they were at work at all times to change that rate," Wright recounted. "Like moving the machine a half an inch, or a quarter of an inch that way. Then they got to retime the machine, and once they retimed it, they'd cut the rate. Any little thing." These struggles were hardly confined to a single section of the plant. "That was the battle in every department," Wright said. "They had these buzzards going around, checking machines and cutting the rates, they'd cut them all the time."[3]

This, then, was how the FE's rejection of the politics of productivity trickled down into the shop. What Harvester dubbed "irresponsible radicalism," the union's local leaders embraced as the most immediate and effective method to ward off management's ever-rapacious "buzzards."

Of course, within the context of a union contract, workers' complaints are supposed to be adjudicated through a grievance procedure. FE members in Louisville and their representatives were certainly not averse to utilizing that system: in late 1949, Local 236 officials claimed they had filed four thousand grievances in the past two years. Harvester management regularly insisted that per employee expenses for stewards handling grievances were far higher in Louisville than they were at any of its factories where the UAW had jurisdiction. But the shop-floor leaders of Local 236 were loath to place much faith in the drawn-out grievance procedure, which provided for arbitration as its final step. "Grievances—you can only win about 10 percent of them," Jim Wright said, "because it sounds like there's a lot of legitimacy in what the company puts forth, when they sit down and argue about a grievance, they argue all the merits, all the particulars about a grievance. We didn't want to hear about any of that." Wright, like Mouser, preferred a more efficient avenue of redress. "We knew if we walked out, heck, if it happened to a worker today, we walk out, and his case will be settled in the morning," Wright insisted. "That's the real results of the walkout. Every walkout, every time we walked out, it got results."[4]

But this tactic necessitated that solidarity be unconditional and widespread. "If something happened to a guy over in Department C and you're working in Department E, which is two blocks [away], it don't affect you," Wright said, but the members of Local 236 had internalized the old adage that an injury to one is an injury to all. Their faith in their stewards, moreover, was such that they required no explanation when directed to quit work. "If that's [the stewards'] opinion on it, well, let's go. Not just one or two of us; we're going to be together" was the attitude among the rank and file, Jim Mouser maintained. "They'd go. They were strong," he said. Often enough, "the workers didn't know what they were going out for, but there was such unanimity among them that they went along with the leadership," Jim Wright recalled.

> I've seen times where we said let's go home, and in ten minutes every car was out of the lot, the parking lot empty, going on home. Whatever we told them, that's what they did, for a long time. If we told them to go out there and jump off that back porch, everybody would jump, on concrete, and they'd be laying out there dead, you know.

Such discipline was essential, Wright believed, for the FE's approach to succeed. "See, if everybody walks out, the whole plant, then the company couldn't fire all of you. That's the only way that works," Wright said. "The unity of the guys, and the sticking together of the guys, kept them from firing, kept mass firings from happening."[5]

Within Local 236, Mouser and Wright were not especially hot-headed; they were simply expressing the Louisville FE's officially accepted wisdom. "Wherever there was price-cutting, the men quit work," acknowledged a Local 236 publication, which meant "instead of wage cuts, the plant average was steadily rising." Local officials charged Harvester with "evading its responsibilities under the union contract" by purposely gumming up the works of the grievance procedure. "NO ONE IN THE PLANT WOULD LIVE LONG ENOUGH TO SEE ALL THOSE PROBLEMS HANDLED BY ARBITRATION," said the *Cub*, the Local's newspaper. "So there is only one answer. YOU WILL HAVE TO BE ORGANIZED IN YOUR DEPARTMENTS STRONGLY ENOUGH TO DEFEND YOUR CONTRACT. YOU WILL HAVE TO FIGHT FOR YOUR RATES."[6]

And pronouncements from Louisville made clear that the FE leadership's contempt for the UAW's cooperative approach had trickled down to the local level. A 1947 issue of the *Cub* cited this clause in the UAW-Ford contract: "'Continued failure of an employee to produce on the basis of established standards shall be considered cause for discipline, *including discharge*'"; therefore, "clearly under this agreement the Union has no power to control speed-up." But, the *Cub* asserted, "NOWHERE IN THE HARVESTER CONTRACT IS THERE A CLAUSE WHICH ALLOWS THE COMPANY TO FIRE A MAN BECAUSE IT IS IMPOSSIBLE TO KEEP UP WITH SPEED-UP OR BECAUSE HE ENGAGES IN AN EFFORT TO BRING THE SPEED-UP UNDER CONTROL. FE would never sign such a clause in any contract!"[7]

So the FE's embrace of shop-floor militancy was on full display in Louisville, certainly in 1949 while the UAW raid was underway and the *Courier-Journal* was reporting on a near-daily basis about the "pyrotechnic series of disputes" taking place at the IH plant.[8] Very often the stories sounded a familiar refrain: repeated walkouts by sheet metal workers in Department 42 were triggered by conflicts over "pay rates for piece work." But other concerns were often bound up in those protests. The troubles in Department 42 began in March 1949 when Harvester management charged five workers with carelessness, suspending them after the critical cutting parts in their machine tools cracked. The men insisted that the damage occurred when they were pressed for increased output from their "worn and out of repair" equipment, adversely affecting their piecework wages and subjecting them to unsafe conditions. Just after the suspensions were issued, another sheet metal worker had his hand eaten up by one of the machines. "The men in Dept. 42 had enough," said a Local 236 publication. "Men would rather work than lose time through stoppages. But there is such a thing as standing up for your rights. Most of us would rather die on our feet than live on our knees." The sheet metal workers left the plant and returned only when the company reinstated the suspended employees. The employees in Department 42 continued their in-and-out ways through 1949 without apology. In a June letter to the *Courier-Journal*, sheet metal worker W. B. Tyler cited Harvester's hefty profits and then declared, "only the most ardent apostle of greed can say that the workers are not entitled to a larger share. FE intends to get it."[9]

Sometimes, however, the members of Local 236 pressed for their "larger share" not by walking out of the plant, but by staying in it. In September 1949, to protest a revision in piecework prices, workers in various departments throughout the Louisville plant began eschewing incentive pay and instead expended only the minimum effort required to earn their base wages. "The employees have refused to give these prices a fair trial," plant manager P. W. Johnson grumbled, and insisted that because of this "deliberate slowdown," production in some parts of the factory "had fallen off by about two thirds of normal." But Local 236 President Allen Coones argued that given the logic of Harvester's piecework system the workers' action was both rational and contractually permissible. "The company is demanding that the men speed up production to incentive level," he said. "The men are not doing it because the company refuses to pay incentive pay." Employees in other departments began slacking off as well, and production on the engine assembly line dropped by 60 percent.[10]

This strategy was not concocted in Louisville or confined to Local 236: in 1949 the FE's top leadership began actively promoting a slowdown policy—or what was dubbed the "strikeless strike"—throughout IH. Since Harvester had designed its piecework system to generate the most profit when workers drove themselves enough to be compensated above—not at or below—what constituted their base wage rates, FE officials encouraged workers to resist the accelerated pace required to earn incentive pay. Concerted efforts of this sort by Harvester workers meant "minimum profit and maximum cost to the company," thus in theory such actions could exert greater pressure on management than work stoppages would. Slowdowns, of course, were a venerable labor tradition: skilled iron molders routinely used them at McCormick Works back in the nineteenth century, and more recently FE members had done so to good effect, for instance, at the IH plant in East Moline during WWII. But slowdowns can be difficult to pull off. They necessitate a strong sense of discipline (to restrain those inclined to simply quit work when provoked) and solidarity (to assure that workers adhere as a unit to the agreed-upon pace, and agree to forego the extra pay allotted for producing beyond the minimum requirements).[11]

Local 236 seemed to possess a surfeit of both qualities. "We declare ourselves in a state of strike without actual stoppage of work," read a resolution approved by the membership in mid-November 1949, openly acknowledging the "strikeless strike" that had hampered production for several months. FE members pledged to refuse all incentive work and "exert no more than normal effort" at their jobs. By this point their objectives had mushroomed well beyond the original piecework dispute. Just before the "strikeless strike" was officially declared, a group of employees had been summoned to the plant's personnel office; union representative Charlie Yates accompanied them, maintaining he had the right "to be present when employees were interviewed for layoff or transfer," since the company, Yates insisted, was routinely violating the contract's seniority clause when making those decisions. When he refused to leave the office, Yates was fired. So the local's demands escalated to include Yates's reinstatement and new policies governing layoff procedures. A few weeks later the membership voted to end the slowdown after the plant manager agreed to negotiations; one result, which the Local 236 paper dubbed "a tremendous victory," was a new process for informing the union about impending layoffs, meaning that stewards could raise objections beforehand. And though it came through an arbitration, Charlie Yates also got his job back.[12]

On the surface, the walkouts and the slowdowns at the Louisville plant were largely concerned with wages and working conditions. But whether these disputes were won or lost, for Local 236 all this rank-and-file activity had more profound effects than could be gleaned from newspaper accounts. In early 1949, two dozen employees from one department, impelled by a time study complaint, quit work and went together to the front office to register their discontent. The two workers Harvester held to be the ringleaders of the protest—Local 236 Secretary-Treasurer Fred Marrero and shop steward Robert Mimms—were promptly fired. Marrero and Mimms were African American; the remaining men in the department were white. When a company hearing the following day confirmed the discharge of the two men, the entire membership of Local 236 responded. "3000 WALK OUT AT HARVESTER AS PROTEST AGAINST FIRING 2," proclaimed the headline in the *Louisville Defender*, the town's Black newspaper. "We believe in the theory of equality and non-discrimination and we put it to work where it counts," said Local 236 President Coones, and he underscored for the *Defender* the FE's ideology:

> At the shop bench and on the assembly line, talk has never accomplished anything. It never will. But actions do. Only through solid unity of all workers can working people hope to meet with the large companies on even terms. Anything to disrupt this unity, be it color prejudice, religious prejudice, or what have you, is a crime against all working people.[13]

From the outset the FE's organizers in Louisville—including Fred Marrero—had made racial solidarity a core tenet of Local 236. Marrero was one of the first officers of Local 236, and though by 1949 there were only about three hundred Black workers in the IH plant, African Americans "were spread throughout the leadership of the union—as stewards, lieutenants, grievance committeemen, and executive board members," said a Local 236 pamphlet. Jim Wright, for example, in late 1949 became an executive board member and editor of the *Cub*. African Americans thus played a highly visible role in the near-daily skirmishes with Harvester

management, and "many skeptical white workers were learning by experience that the Negroes were among the most militant fighters the union
had." Militant enough to risk their jobs, as Mimms and Marrero had, to
battle on behalf of white employees. Regular shop-floor activism, then,
helped workers achieve the "larger share" they deserved in two related
ways. Such resistance was necessary, first of all, to forestall the "constant
chiseling" Harvester was prone to. But because the frequent slowdowns
and walkouts could be effective only when Black and white workers acted
in concert, within Local 236 interracial solidarity became not an abstract
construct but a daily practice that delivered tangible and immediate benefits to the union membership. "Not just one or two of us; we're going to
be together," Jim Mouser had said of the Local 236 rank and file, and the
truer this became, the harder it was for Harvester to extract all that it
wanted out of its Louisville workforce.[14]

Not that the FE leadership in Louisville presumed that demonstrations
in the shop would be enough, in and of themselves, to eradicate the racism
that was second (or first) nature to much of the plant's Southern white workforce. Thus the insistence on interracial unity that had defined the Local
236 organizing drive saw no let-up in ensuing years. Local 236 "carried on a
constant campaign to convince the white workers that only by solidarity of
Negro and white workers could the union be strong," said Anne Braden, and
through the association she began with the Louisville FE in 1948 she was
able to observe that campaign in practice:

> I never went to a [Local 236] meeting where somebody didn't get
> up and make a speech about the reason we're so strong and we can
> win—and they always said they had the highest wages in the South
> and I never saw that refuted anywhere—the reason we got all that is
> because we stick together, Black and white. Let them, they attack a
> Black worker and we're there to do something, we're going to walk
> out of the plant—this is the reason we've got the strong union. And
> they preached that constantly.

In these exhortations, Local 236 leaders would inevitably accuse Harvester management of harboring Jim Crow sympathies and pursuing "divide
and conquer" strategies; they reacted only with derision as Fowler McCormick accumulated accolades for his equal opportunity policies. It was true
that in many respects Harvester's Louisville facility reflected typical discriminatory Southern norms: By 1950 nearly all of the maintenance jobs were
filled by African Americans, and none of the approximately five hundred

foremen in the plant were Black. The FE charged that racist supervisors in the Louisville plant frequently manipulated Harvester's complicated job classification system to block promotions that Black employees were entitled to. And at the insistence of local management, and so as not to "alienate the community resources upon which the plant would have to rely," the Louisville cafeteria retained the segregated seating arrangement that had existed in the original aircraft factory, despite ongoing objections from Local 236 officials. So despite his commitment to "biracial industrialism," Fowler McCormick seemed less dedicated to biracial social interaction.[15]

Yet however loath union leaders were to acknowledge it, Harvester's fair employment policy contributed in no small measure to the Louisville FE's ability to press forward with its own civil rights agenda. That there was an African American presence of any significance within the IH plant in the first place was not a given; though Henry Ford, for instance, had thousands of Black workers on his payroll in the North, until the 1960s Ford Motor Company bowed to "local custom" and maintained a whites-only policy—with the exception of its janitorial staff—at its Louisville factory. In contrast, Harvester not only hired Blacks but required all prospective employees in Louisville to accept its policy of "intergrading the negro employees and eliminating discrimination." This hardly guaranteed that all white workers would comfortably rub shoulders with Blacks on the shop floor and in the union hall, but at least it excluded those who openly refused to entertain the idea. And in Louisville Harvester did make good its commitment to promote African Americans rather than confine them to the common labor pool; Jim Wright, for instance, moved from his maintenance position with the "thousand leg" broom up to truck driver and then to semiskilled machine operator. By 1950, Black employment at the plant had more than tripled, with nearly 40 percent holding semiskilled jobs. About 4 percent of the African American workforce occupied skilled positions. That's not a big number, of course—for comparison purposes, about one-third of the white employees in the plant were skilled tradesmen—but during this era in Southern factories (or Northern ones, for that matter) Black skilled workers were a rare sight.[16]

The "intergrading" of Black employees within the IH plant in Louisville proved consequential for Local 236. Blacks had been hired from the moment Harvester set up shop in Kentucky and had comparable length-of-service records with whites, making the often complicated balancing act between safeguarding seniority rights and advocating equal opportunity on the job less complicated within Local 236. Although the FE's contracts with IH provided for plantwide seniority, at older factories like McCormick Works, the presence of so many white employees with decades of service often stymied advancement for more recently hired African Americans and ensured that some departments remained all white. On the shop floor in Louisville the social terrain was notably different: African Americans operated machinery and assembled tractors alongside white employees in nearly every corner of the facility. Not only was seniority a less provocative issue at the Louisville plant, therefore, but the efforts by Local 236 to promote solidarity were doubtlessly facilitated as interracial interchanges became regular occurrences for the rank and file.

But it was the ways in which Harvester's novel equal opportunity policy melded with long-standing corporate practice that most fundamentally abetted the local's "constant campaign" to unite the Louisville workforce. The company's vexatious wage system was applied without regard to color or creed, and as African Americans moved into all areas of the plant, grievances, which usually affected small groups of men within departments, began to encompass Black and white employees simultaneously. Louisville workers, all equally exploitable in the eyes of their employer, increasingly recognized that racial cooperation was necessary to contend with Harvester management, as was demonstrated by the plantwide walkout on behalf of Fred Marrero and Robert Mimms. It was not just sheer self-interest, however, that fostered the burgeoning sense of solidarity within Local 236; rather, Anne Braden argues, what the rank and file experienced together on the shop floor so often violated their innate sense of justice:

> Whenever just plain white workers in the shop would get up and speak up, when there was some incident or some black workers had been fired or demoted or had his piecework price cut or whatever, not a one of [the white workers] ever said, we got to do this because it's the only way we're going to keep our pay checks high. They'd get up and say, using almost these words, that this just isn't fair. You're not treating that guy right and I'm not going to put up with it.[17]

Just as the favoritism practiced by plant foremen had so galled Tractor Works employees in the 1920s, the racist actions taken by some Louisville supervisors laid bare the limitations of Harvester's ostensibly objective and equitable job classification system. When in early 1951 a foreman denied African American Roger Elliott a position he was clearly in line to get, the men in his department, nearly all of them white, protested through a series of walkouts; IH officials issued the entire department a three-day suspension but upon their return to the plant the workers immediately commenced a slowdown. After several weeks of this unrest Elliott got the job he deserved and the Louisville management was obliged to issue more explicit guidelines about how seniority governed transfers and promotions.[18]

Thus while Harvester may have been lauded for the fairness of its employment practices, it was the inherent unfairness of the company's shop-floor practices that came to dominate daily life for all Louisville workers. And, as the leaders of Local 236 endeavored to enforce fair treatment—as the workers defined it—through the FE's practice of aggressive stewardship, Louisville workers were further bound by their sense of common cause and their participation in common conflict. The recurrent walkouts at the Harvester plant had effects measured well beyond dollars and cents, providing the members of Local 236 "a sense of strength and dignity that the workers in most Louisville plants did not have," Braden insisted.

> They made each man feel temporarily that he was strong enough to deal with his giant employer, and removed some of the helplessness and insignificance that a man often has working each day for a big company. The higher pay that apparently resulted from the militancy removed some of the constant worry of a paycheck too small to cover the bills at home each week. For the white workers, this new sense of dignity and security meant that they no longer needed the Negro as an object of scorn, no longer needed him for the inflation of their own egos and as an outlet for their frustrations and worries; for the Negro workers it meant they could look at the white workers without bitterness.[19]

Perhaps the most profound impact, therefore, of the FE's combative conduct could be assessed not through walkout statistics or wage increases but in the personal transformations such militancy effected within the work-force. The friendship between Jim Mouser and Jim Wright was only one of many that developed among Black and white workers in Local 236, as Anne Braden noted. "It was the usual thing to see Negro and white members sitting together in a union hall discussing their common problems, informally as well as in formal meetings," she said. "The new pattern spilled over outside the union hall, and many of the same white men visited in the Negro unionists' homes, and the Negroes went to white members' homes." [20]

Jim Wright well recalled the attitude that prevailed among the white workforce when the Louisville plant first opened: "those country guys, from out in the sticks, those guys didn't want to integrate." They had been, in

Wright's view, "*real* racists," and he never ceased to be astonished by how membership in Local 236 had redeemed these men:

> They'd go along with [Blacks], eat with them, go places with them, go hunting with them, walk out with them, work on a machine with them, have fun in the shop with them. That was a new thing for [the white workers.] That union had put what people call today some kind of religious—I don't mean a biblical religion—I mean a religious feeling of them sticking together.[21]

What Wright described was quite familiar to Local 236 steward Charlie Yates, who got a job at the Louisville IH plant shortly after it opened. "Well, I don't think that I'm the guy that can say I was never prejudiced against colored people; I grew up down here myself, back in the country and I more or less thought the same thing; the rest of my family is more or less still that way," Yates said in the mid-1950s. He shared the worldview of most of the other white workers at the IH plant, who were "brought up all their life ever since they'd been kids, had it beat into their heads that colored people were always lower than they were." But they could change, Yates knew, because he had. "I realized I was no damn different from a colored person," said Yates, who became a partisan for his union's "constant campaign" to overcome the racial antipathy prevalent among his fellow white Southerners. "It's going to be a hard fight to get it out of their head, [but] I think our fights in the shop have done more to bring people over to our side, to get them to realize that they've got to work along with the colored people and realize that they're no better than a colored fellow working alongside of them," Yates said. "I can't remember a case when a fellow had a grievance in a department and being white or colored, whatever he was, if he had a grievance the rest of the shop had a grievance with him. We learned that in the '47 [Southern differential] strike," he maintained.[22]

Anne Braden similarly recalled a conversation she had with a white member of Local 236, who told her he'd "always thought that colored people were something to look down on. But when I went to work at Harvester I saw something different," he said. "The Negroes were some of the best leaders the union had; they were the ones you could depend on to stick up for you when you got into a fight with the company; they knew what to do and they weren't afraid. You can't help but respect them, and pretty soon you get to like them, and the first thing you know you almost forget they're colored and you think of them as just people like yourself."[23]

But while Charlie Yates and other members of Local 236 were grappling with the racism that was part of their heritage, other white workers

in Louisville—even those in organized shops—were not being asked to.
"Those white guys who went to work in the Harvester plant were no different
from the white people working in the Ford plant here or the distilleries or
the tobacco companies," said Braden. "They were just like everybody else
but they had a different experience when they got [into the IH plant]," she
insisted. "It was something totally different from what workers in the Ford
plant and elsewhere were hearing and therefore they acted in a different
way . . . to me it was amazing, the kind of turnaround in people's minds simply because they were in a different setting and what was acceptable in the
old world was not acceptable when you walked into [the Local 236] hall." In
her view, that distinction was driven by the FE's national leadership. Other
CIO unions "did not take on the race issue," she argued, in a manner that
carried down to the local level. "This I think the FE leadership did."[24]

Fowler McCormick and Walter Reuther may have shared a common
disdain for the "fantastic series of disputes" that set the IH plant in Louisville apart, but within the FE the turmoil was regarded differently. Regularly going toe-to-toe with Harvester management imbued the members of
Local 236 with a visceral understanding of the mechanisms of exploitation
and the virtue of solidarity. And all that activism meant something else too:
life in the plant became about something besides drudgery. Factory labor, as
Anne Braden observed, is generally "oppressive, in what you do all day, not
only the work but having to put up with the foremen and the kind of atmosphere there is." But at the Harvester plant, "people really enjoyed getting
up and going to work in the morning," she said. "You knew there was going
to be something interesting at the gate, there was going to be a leaflet, there
was going to be people out about something, and there was a real esprit de
corps that I think made it bearable to go to work."[25]

Given how much was bound up in the FE's shop-floor militancy, it becomes easy to understand why Walter Reuther's pitch to do away with "wildcatting the year 'round" fell so flat in Louisville. The UAW's abject defeat in
1949 signaled that Local 236 and its disruptive agenda had by then established
overwhelming support from the Harvester workforce. But what about beyond
the plant gates? The leaders of the Louisville FE, in fact, were not content to
contend only with Harvester management: by carrying their "constant campaign" into the community, they sought to transform Louisville as well.

21.
Taking the Constant Campaign into the Community

W hat with tensions running so high inside the Louisville Harvester factory, it might be presumed that during their time off the members of Local 236 would incline toward more relaxing pursuits.

Or perhaps all that shop-floor unrest simply primed them for other contests. Insisting that solidarity had significance that carried beyond plant gates and picket lines, the FE challenged Louisville's segregationist status quo in public spaces, downtown landmarks, and civic institutions. Sometimes these were official activities sanctioned by the Local 236 leadership; on other occasions they were informal forays launched by a band of especially pugnacious rank-and-file activists. But in both cases the community assaults launched by Louisville's "stormy petrel" presaged bigger battles that would later reshape the American South.

There is no question that Jim Wright, already disinclined to accept unfair treatment, felt further emboldened by the FE's civil rights agenda. The 1948 Progressive Party effort, moreover, left him eager to continue the organizing work that he had engaged in around the city. So, in the early 1950s, "each weekend," Wright said, "we mapped out an area of Louisville to do something in we wasn't supposed to, was against the law." The laws they sought to test were those mandating separate, and patently unequal, spheres for Blacks and whites throughout Louisville. The "we" in these instances, as Wright recalled, included a couple dozen African Americans from Local 236 and about seven or eight white members, including Jim Mouser and Charlie Yates. Some white workers, though, joined these excursions not so much because they were up for the fight against segregation, but rather because they were just up for a fight of any sort. One young rank-and-filer named Thomas Pearl "didn't believe in no Blacks, didn't want to know what Blacks did." Nonetheless he frequently accompanied the group because "he liked hanging around to see you break into things, to break down the barriers," Wright said. And when push came to shove, as it literally did often enough, Pearl mixed it up alongside his union brothers.[1]

In this era, there was only one city park open to the Black residents of Louisville: modest Chickasaw Park, outfitted with a few picnic tables, located hard against the bank of the Ohio River on the city's western edge. Whites, however, had dozens of well-equipped, wide-open recreational options. "All the parks for white people—Iroquois, Cherokee, Seneca and Shawnee—were so spacious," civil rights leader Lyman Johnson wrote in his recollections of Louisville. "Negroes could drive by these parks and see how nice they were. We could even drive through the white parks, but if we got out of our cars, we would be arrested for disorderly conduct."[2]

Jim Wright and his compatriots were already experienced practitioners of that sort of behavior. They set their sights on Cherokee Park, originally designed by Frederick Law Olmsted, a bucolic 350-acre expanse enhanced by graceful fountains, a golf course, and stone bridges spanning babbling creeks. But the park's serenity was shattered when the mixed-race delegation from Local 236 set foot there, as within minutes of their arrival they were confronted by a member of the Louisville police force who ordered them to leave. "You know you can't go in this park, I don't know why you communists would come out here," Wright recalled the police officer telling them. The officer, according to Wright, grumbled about the "poor white guys and niggers" who made up the FE contingent and he then declared, "Why don't you leave this town? We didn't have this kind of stuff here until Harvester came here. I wish Harvester would close the plant down and run all of you off." As the union members exited the park, the officer warned them not to return.

Within Local 236, provocations of this sort were not often ignored. The ousted group decided on another foray into Cherokee Park, but this time, Wright maintained, "somebody snitched," because as the union men approached they saw about twenty police cars sitting just inside the park. "Some of the guys started to perspire," Wright said, "because we knew we were going to encounter trouble this time." Jim Mouser, however, would not be deterred. "I said, 'Aren't you scared?'" Wright recalled, but "Mouser said, 'I ain't scared of nothing.'" So the delegation headed in to Cherokee Park, but they didn't get very far. "Those guys just unloaded on us," Wright described the police response. "They beat us, knocked us on the head, knocked us to the ground, and had us running, everything. Drug me to the edge of the park and dumped me on the sidewalk." The officer who hauled Wright out flashed his gun and announced, "we could fix it so you'll never come back no more," and then offered some parting counsel: "I advise you to go down there and integrate Chickasaw. Ain't nothing there but Black people, why don't you go and integrate that?" Wright considered the derogatory suggestion for a few moments, and then decided that it was in fact a pretty good idea, and told the officer so.

"So we went to Chickasaw," Wright said. The Local 236 leadership organized a Sunday outing to the park, and Wright indicated that about two hundred white FE members came along. Though the white workers' entrance into the park surprised some of the Black residents in the area—"we had eyes staring at us down there," Wright said—the integrated picnic drew no response from Louisville authorities. "We went down to Chickasaw, ate, sat around, swam down there, did different things, fished on the river down there, all one Sunday."

But the band of troublemakers within Local 236 had not given up on Cherokee Park. Their next incursion involved just Wright and two other Black men, along with Mouser and Yates and one other white worker, on the theory that a smaller presence might prove less provocative. Heading into Cherokee Park on a crowded Sunday, they encountered no initial hostility, and so they walked up to a concession stand to purchase some drinks. "The lady didn't want to sell it to us, and she looked a long time at us," Wright remembered. "She didn't say it, but I believe she recognized us as being agitators." They did eventually get their sodas, and then "we sat three Blacks and three whites, we sat around there for about two hours. Didn't get thrown out of there. Cops weren't around, wasn't nobody around that Sunday. So then, we thought we'd broken it down."

To test whether they had, in fact, overcome the segregation of Louisville's parks, they led another large excursion into Cherokee Park. An integrated group of some forty FE members, this time along with many of their wives, made themselves comfortable in the park and began to unload the picnic baskets they'd brought with them. Within short order the same police officer who had unceremoniously dragged Jim Wright out of the park once before was on the scene. Because women were present, Wright believed, the policeman refrained from doing the same thing again, but he summoned Wright over to explain what the members of Local 236 seemed unwilling to understand.

> [The officer] said, "Are you from Kentucky?" I said, "Yeah, I'm from Kentucky, born and raised in the *southern* part of Kentucky, but now I'm in the *northern* part of Kentucky." He said, "Northern part of Kentucky, my ass." That's what he said. He said, "You're in Kentucky, and that's the law, that you don't mix in this town. You're violating the law." I said, "We're not violating the law, we're just coming in here as human beings." I said, "If a stray dog wandered in here, wandered into this park, would you run him out of this park?" He said, "That's different. That's an animal." I said, "Well, we're better than animals."

Wright scored a small victory that day, for the officer told him that the FE assembly could remain in the park for one hour, but it was made clear that any repeat visits would be greeted with disfavor by Louisville law enforcement. When the hour had elapsed, the policeman returned as promised and escorted the union congregation out of Cherokee Park.[3]

The parks were not the only segregated Louisville institutions to be visited by interracial FE delegations. After the picnic in Cherokee Park, the local's leaders "left the parks to get a little relief," Wright said. They turned their attention downtown, to the city's whites-only hotels, focusing first on the Earl Hotel, where the union's integrated contingent was repeatedly rejected. But after a time, Wright indicated, the hotel management, desirous of ending the disruption, let Black FE members sit unmolested in the Earl's lobby, and even allowed "one or two of us to sleep in there, overnight." Things did not work out as well at the Brown Hotel. J. Graham Brown "was a rich man, he owned a lot of horses," Wright said—in fact, Brown was reputed to be the wealthiest man in Kentucky—and was determined to keep his hotel open only to whites. Wright dubbed the FE's first interracial foray into Louisville's venerable establishment "the Brown massacre," because the union members had not yet taken seats on the lobby's plush upholstered furniture before the police "just massacred us," Wright said. "Just beat us, just drug us out." Successive attempts were no more successful, for "every time we came in there, they stood there and beat us and drug us out again." The Brown Hotel would not allow African American guests until the mid-1960s, after a Louisville ordinance outlawed segregation in public accommodations.

In addition to these guerrilla-style assaults on whites-only locations, the Louisville FE also took part in the more formal, and less bruising, legal and political struggle against racial discrimination. Local 236 played a prominent role in the Interracial Hospital Movement, a coalition of groups seeking to end segregation within Kentucky's hospitals. In 1951, 150 members of that coalition, carrying petitions signed by more than ten thousand Kentucky residents supporting the elimination of color bars within the state's hospitals, paid a visit to Governor Lawrence Wetherby in Frankfort. Serving as spokesman for the group gathered in the governor's office, Local 236 President Allen Coones, together with Louisville pastor J. Albert Dalton, "made an eloquent plea for State officials to provide hospital facilities for all citizens, regardless of race or creed," the *Louisville Defender* reported. By the mid-1950s, the Kentucky legislature, bowing to pressure from the Interracial Hospital Movement, barred institutions that discriminated in the disbursement of emergency care from receiving state licenses.[4]

And Local 236 brought its "constant campaign" for equality into its solidarity work with other unions as well. In 1949 the woodworkers union struck for recognition at the Bond Brothers railroad tie plant; employees there received poverty wages and lived on company property in virtual servitude, housed in dilapidated shacks and obliged to shop at the company store. Local 236 took the lead in providing support for the Bond Brothers' employees, nearly all of them African American; *Louisville Defender* photos feature white and Black FE members distributing groceries to the strikers. And when in late 1951 Black and white workers at the Brown Hotel and Kentucky Hotel (also owned by J. Graham Brown) went on strike in an effort to secure union representation, FE members rallied in support and joined the integrated picket lines downtown. The Bond Brothers and J. Graham Brown remained steadfast in their anti-union animus (Brown declared he would shut down his hotels before he would consent to collective bargaining) and these lengthy and bitter strikes—the hotel walkout lasted nine months—ultimately fizzled out without securing the workers' demands.[5]

But Local 236 was sometimes pressed by sources closer to home to further broaden its horizons in the struggle for equality. In mid-1949, the spouses of some of the key leaders in Local 236—including Jim Wright's wife Gladys, Sterling Neal's wife Millie, and Thelma Gibson, the young widow of Chuck Gibson—formed a women's auxiliary of the Louisville FE. Anne Braden was enlisted to assist with the group, which was initiated to ease some of the difficulties created by the local's contentious conduct. "They were on strike constantly," Braden said, "and the women didn't always understand. And so there would be a problem on the home front. It's hard on a family if you go on strike once every five years, but if you're constantly on strike that could make a lot of problems." At first the auxiliary concerned itself with "whatever the men wanted us to do," Millie Neal recalled. "Like some women would have time on their hands and so they would go down to the hall and help them with the leaflets [and] stuff the envelopes." But, while Local 236 members were regularly drilled by their union leadership about the necessity for racial solidarity, those lessons were not necessarily carried home. The auxiliary, then, became a vehicle for bridging the racial chasm that separated white and Black women in Louisville. At the auxiliary's inaugural meeting, Braden realized that simply attending an integrated gathering represented a radical step for most of the women present:

> On the night of the first meeting about twenty women appeared, six or seven of them Negroes. As they gathered in one of the smaller rooms in the union hall, I could sense the tensions. The Negro women sat ill at ease. I noticed some of the white women start in surprise when they came in the door and saw the Negro women

there. . . . In any event, no one left. And they returned the next time
a meeting was called. . . . To a certain extent, some of the white
women were influenced by a new kind of social pressure which the
atmosphere in the union hall created; outside, in the atmosphere
of Louisville generally, they were accepted by their friends and ac-
quaintances if they shunned Negroes, for that was the pattern, but
inside the union hall they found that they were accepted by the others if they ignored race bars, because here the pattern was different.[6]

As was the case for workers at the Harvester plant (all of them men),
the "social pressure" brought to bear on the white women in the FE auxiliary was conscious and concerted. Jane Mahoney—whose husband Tom was
an active Local 236 steward—told Anne Braden that at that first meeting,
"I didn't know what to think when I walked in there that night and saw
Negroes sitting there. I'd never been in the room with a colored person in
my life. I almost turned around and walked out." But instead she went in
and found herself seated next to Millie Neal, who made a point of chatting
with her. Neal recalled that Mahoney "would cut me short every time that
I would say different things to her." After that first auxiliary meeting broke
up, however, Neal "told a couple of the other girls that if [Mahoney] was
prejudiced I would break it down." And so Millie Neal began to telephone
the Mahoney household on one pretense or another, in order to talk to Jane.
"Oh, we talked about our families, the kids, the money problem, how to fix
the house, and we also talked about things that were going on in the plant,"
Neal said, and "she found out that my problems were like her problems."
Through this common ground the two women soon established a deep connection, and Jane Mahoney came to regard Millie Neal as her closest friend.
"Jane Mahoney was the most impressive type of woman that I had ever met
because all her life she had been prejudiced," Neal said, but "after she got
to be my friend she wouldn't let anyone say anything against me, Negro
or white. We would plan things together, we would visit each other, [and]
bring our children together." Years later, after the Mahoneys relocated to
California, Millie and Jane continued to exchange letters at least once a
month.[7]

These strengthening relationships encouraged the women in the Local
236 auxiliary to push beyond "whatever the men wanted," as in fact they
embraced activities some men didn't want them to do at all. The auxiliary's
decision in 1949 to hold a dance—integrated, of course—was not, to put it
mildly, well received by everyone within Local 236. "The shit really did hit
the fan when the word got out that we wanted a dance . . . they were furious,"

Anne Braden said, recalling the reaction from many of the local's white members. "Everything else was okay, we'll fight on the job, and you can have an auxiliary—but no, no, we don't dance together." The auxiliary, however, was undeterred, and the occasion proved successful, drawing a good crowd of both whites and African Americans. "Everything went all right," Braden reported. "The roof didn't fall in or anything." Even Jim Wright regarded the events planned by his wife Gladys and the other FE wives with anxiety. "That women's auxiliary about worried me to death," he said. "They'd conduct dances, they were dancing away, and you'd see whites and Blacks dancing together, and the police standing outside the door, ready to arrest you." The police, however, let the dances proceed without interference.[8]

The women's auxiliary trampling on social norms, Jim Wright and his flying squadron disturbing the peace in public places, the Local 236 leadership in the vanguard of the battle to desegregate Kentucky: in these ways the Louisville FE presaged civil rights struggles that would garner national attention some years later. That was a realization that came to Jim Wright only later in his life. "You know, it's kind of ironic. All that stuff we was doing back then, that was prior to [Martin Luther] King's time. I never thought about that," he said.

> We were struggling and fighting and getting put in jail, the same stuff that [King] did. I guess it was ripe for him to grasp it, it was ripe for him to start it. Sure, I never thought of that, but King came in there in '55 after I left [the South], and all the stuff that I was doing, me and Mouser and Neal and everybody else was doing—that was back in '51, '50, '49, '48.[9]

Thus while other FE members (like those in East Moline) may have been just as scrappy, and some (like those at Tractor Works) were as tightly disciplined, Local 236, more than any other, pushed beyond shop-floor struggles to transform the consciousness of both its rank and file and the greater community. From the outset the leaders of the Louisville FE made extraordinary demands of the membership; in the process they built an intensely cohesive and aggressive local that was, just as Jim Mouser insisted, as strong as any union in the country. That was evident not only in the superior wages and shop-floor autonomy established by Local 236, but in the abiding personal bonds that developed between Jim Wright and Jim Mouser, and Millie Neal and Jane Mahoney.

And into the early 1950s there was little indication that Louisville's "stormy petrel" had modified its tempestuous character. As the largest industrial union local in Kentucky, left unchecked Local 236 would surely have continued to contest management's authority, while beyond the plant its "constant campaign" for civil rights would have further eroded the "traditional" norms that perpetuated inequality. The same could be said for the FE in general, since despite the combined best efforts of International Harvester and the labor establishment the union's unrepentantly radical leadership remained in place and retained its penchant for disruption.

But "left unchecked" is, of course, the operative phrase. In 1952 the FE, in Louisville and everywhere else, would be knocked off course and gravely crippled. The union's leaders did not fully anticipate the blow coming their way—but even if they had it's not clear how they could have prevented it.

An arrest during the FE's sit-down strike at the International Harvester's Chicago Twine Mill in 1952. [Collection of Toni Gilpin]

Part Four

Reaping the Whirlwind

FE members crowd the fire escape during their 1952 sit-down strike at International Harvester's Chicago Twine Mill, after the company announced it would close the facility and move it to New Orleans. The mill's closure would mean the loss of 865 jobs. [DN-O-7865, *Chicago Sun-Times/Chicago Daily News* collection, Chicago History Museum]

Workers commandeered the Twine Mill cafeteria during the 1952 sit-down strike. Two-thirds of the mill's workforce was African American; half the employees were women. [Collection of Toni Gilpin]

A heated battle between FE members, Chicago police, and company guards took place when International Harvester began removing machinery from the Twine Mill to ship it south. Sixteen union supporters, including FE official DeWitt Gilpin, were arrested. [DN-O-7919, *Chicago Sun-Times/Chicago Daily News* collection, Chicago History Museum]

FE members at McCormick Works on the picket line as the 1952 strike against International Harvester began. This strike would prove a decisive showdown between the company and the union. [Collection of Toni Gilpin]

FE members and supporters (including members of the Civil Rights Congress) outside Chicago's federal courthouse in 1952, protesting the appearance there of the House Un-American Activities Committee. HUAC summoned FE leaders to testify before it just after the International Harvester strike began. [UE Archives, University of Pittsburgh Library System]

Demonstrators staged a mock burial of the House Un-American Activities Committee. Robert Ray, the president of the FE's local at the McCormick Twine Mill, is shown on the extreme left. [UE Archives, University of Pittsburgh Library System]

International Harvester made good use of
HUAC's interrogation of FE leaders during
the 1952 strike. These ads appeared in
newspapers around the country, particularly
in cities where Harvester plants were located.
[Collection of Toni Gilpin]

During the 1952 strike FE members also made their case outside International
Harvester's headquarters on Michigan Avenue in Chicago. [UE Archives, University of
Pittsburgh Library System]

As the 1952 strike wore on, the FE, with no strike fund to speak of, found it increasingly difficult to meet union members' needs. Here FE members in Louisville put together boxes of food for strikers. [UE Archives, University of Pittsburgh Library System]

Strikers' family members, as shown here in Louisville, supplemented the picket line as more FE members were arrested or enjoined from picketing. [UE Archives, University of Pittsburgh Library System]

WAKE UP!

THE JOB YOU SAVE MAY BE YOUR OWN

Like you, we hoped it would never happen to us.

First International Harvester's plant in Auburn, New York was closed. Then, the McCormick Twine Mill closed down and moved to New Orleans. Harvester's plant closed in Evansville, Ind. Next was the Richmond plant, also in Indiana.

By this time, we could see the hand-writing on the wall. Our plant's buildings were literally falling down. Most of the equipment was ready for the junk pile by modern standards.

We petitioned the company to modernize the equipment, to re-build the plant. So did the Mayor of Chicago and the City Council. Likewise, the community leaders. All to no avail.

McCormick Works, Chicago, the oldest and most historic of International Harvester's plants, is to be closed, its buildings razed, and the land offered for sale.

History was made on the site of our plant. Here began the strike over labor-displacing machinery in 1886, the strike issue being the 8-hour day. Two blocks away at Cook County jail they hung six men in the Haymarket frame-up that followed a strike meeting. Here was the first mass production of the McCormick combine, the machine that revolutionized farm harvesting.

The story of the closing of McCormick, a plant which for 67 years produced profits that made the McCormick family a symbol of Gold Coast wealth and affluence, is the story of what's wrong with our economy.

(Continued on Page 2)

ISSUED FOR THE DELEGATES TO THE 1959 UAW CONVENTION
LOCAL 1308 McCORMICK MIRROR
International Harvester Workers, Local 1308, UAW, McCormick Works
2512 SOUTH OAKLEY, CHICAGO, ILLINOIS

LEONARD CARNEY, President   RALPH MITCHELL, Publicity Director

A portion of a UAW leaflet, written by former FE leader DeWitt Gilpin, that protested the 1959 shutdown of McCormick Works and called for the introduction of a six-hour day. [Collection of Toni Gilpin]

A 30-HOUR WEEK — IN OUR TIME

While improved shut-down agreements will provide greater se-curity to the effected employes, the best guarantee against ensuing hardship is an expanding economy that will provide work for all who need it, regardless of age.

Such an economy can only be guaranteed if a greater percentage of our national income gets into the hands of the people whose labor produces the profits.

We believe that the biggest single step towards an expanding and prosperous economy would be the instituting of a shorter work week, and Local 1308 is on record to this effect in a Convention resolution.

Instituting the shorter work week would create pressures at every level of our economy, and on world economy setting off an era of social change comparable to that which followed the introduction of the 8-hour day in America.

The important thing, we believe, is to give life to the AFL-CIO objective of a shorter work week by having our union, which has established more economic precedents than any other, set a target date for a break-through.

Our doomed plant, which history has now passed by, once heard Cyrus McCormick swear that he would never reduce hours without cutting pay. Like today's defenders of the status quo, Cyrus was bucking the inevitable. In our age of man's mastery of the world and his reach for the universe, scientific and economic progress leaps over centuries. Most of the fruits of man's new knowledge will be enjoyed by our children and their children. But there is one thing we are entitled to in our time—a 30-hour week.

4,000 workers who will be without jobs back the UAW's program for an expanded economy shorter work week, and improved plant shut-down agreements!

EPITAPH: McCORMICK WORKS
BORN IN THE FIGHT FOR 8-HOUR DAY
DIED IN THE FIGHT FOR 6-HOUR DAY

---

issued by Local 1308, UAW, AFL-CIO
McCormick Works, International Harvester

22.
IH Prepares for a Showdown

As the 1950s began, Fowler McCormick had reason to be pleased with himself. His campaign to modernize International Harvester appeared to be paying off, as 1950 profits reached a new high and sales would top the billion-dollar mark for the first time. McCormick, who turned fifty-two in 1950, continued to chalk up accolades for his corporate vision and social consciousness. Among America's CEOs, "he has become a singularly balanced, independent, and philosophic performer," pronounced *Fortune* magazine.[1]

Fowler McCormick enjoyed being the big-picture guy for his family's business. He liked thinking deep thoughts and making bold plans.

He just didn't especially like to do all that in Chicago. After 1946 Fowler was increasingly absent from the IH corporate headquarters, spending months at a time in the Swiss Alps, or at his four-thousand-acre ranch in Arizona, where his wife Fifi doted on her stable of hot-blooded Arabian horses. Maintaining a good distance from the boardroom was preferable, Fowler believed, since "creative ideas are better generated in an atmosphere of quiet than in the hurly-burly of an office." And he could breathe easily since he'd entrusted Harvester's day-to-day operations to his "long-standing team mate," company president John McCaffrey.[2]

Fowler McCormick's trusted lieutenant had, in fact, once been his superior. They had worked closely together for decades; when Fowler finally decided in the late 1920s to focus his attention on Harvester, McCaffrey was one of the managers he apprenticed with. McCaffrey, the son of an Ohio blacksmith, had little formal schooling and was just sixteen when, in 1908, he took a job putting together IH grain binders for the farmers who had purchased them. Within a few years he had moved to Cincinnati to become a truck salesman for the company. McCaffrey, a relentless dealmaker and "a large and canny good mixer" was soon setting sales records in Harvester's truck division and rocketing up the corporate ladder. Once McCaffrey entered management's echelons he tended to surround himself with subordinates similar to himself: "towering men who could crack jokes, crush hands, and intimidate anybody with their sheer presence alone," one analyst said. In 1933 McCaffrey became director of sales for IH, and Fowler McCormick served for a period in Chicago as McCaffrey's assistant. Both were quite tall and only six years apart in age (McCaffrey was older) but otherwise patrician

McCormick had little in common with unrefined McCaffrey. Nonetheless the business press noted how well they worked together—"the two men complement each other as strongly contrasting temperaments"—and within the corporation they were already recognized as a bit of a team.[3]

Of course they weren't really a team of equals. The company was always Fowler's to run if he wanted to, and in 1941 he finally decided he did, and assumed the IH presidency. But he made sure that the influence of his one-time mentor increased as well, and appointed McCaffrey to the Harvester board of directors. And then in 1946, the nature of their partnership was formalized, as Fowler chose to become board chair and the company's chief executive, while McCaffrey took over as Harvester's president. Fowler could thus map out the company's future in picturesque surroundings while McCaffrey remained in Chicago to implement those plans.

There was just one problem with this arrangement: John McCaffrey didn't care for it. And by all accounts—including, ultimately, Fowler McCormick's—McCaffrey possessed "an almost insatiable hunger for power." McCaffrey was not always sold on Fowler's ideas, and resented having to execute corporate policy dictated from afar. Other members of the IH board were also troubled by their chief executive's lengthy absences, and many were ambivalent, at best, about Fowler's more lofty pursuits, like his commitment to African American employment. The corporate restructuring Fowler insisted upon, furthermore, had engendered bruised feelings within some segments of top management. While sales were strong, profits began to slip in 1951, as the company's costs continued to be higher than those of its aggressive competitors. McCaffrey, then, had little trouble coalescing a group of Harvester executives who were loyal to him. Fowler finally realized a palace coup was underway and delivered an ultimatum to the Harvester board—either McCaffrey goes, or he would—confident they would favor a McCormick/Rockefeller heir any day over an uncouth one-time truck salesman. He had miscalculated. In May 1951 the board chose to elevate John McCaffrey to the CEO's position, stripping the board chairman—Fowler's title—of its executive authority. Fowler, "amazed and astounded" and utterly humiliated, promptly stepped down from the chairman's post, retaining only a regular seat on the IH board.

This drama constituted an extraordinary moment in the history of International Harvester, as the press noted. "Mr. McCormick's resignation," reported the *New York Times*, "leaves the giant farm implement company without a McCormick in its top management for the first time since 1831, when Cyrus Hall McCormick, his grandfather, perfected the reaper." An affronted Fowler retreated permanently to Arizona, returning to Chicago for an occasional, and uncomfortable, Harvester board meeting. He remained, however, one of International Harvester's single largest stockholders; other family members also retained sizable IH portfolios. And there was another McCormick in the pipeline: Fowler's cousin Brooks McCormick had been in IH management since graduating from Yale in 1940, and would become Harvester's CEO in 1971.[4]

But in mid-1951 International Harvester was in John McCaffrey's hands, an ominous development for the FE. It was McCaffrey who labeled the FE's leaders "irresponsible radicals" in his widely publicized 1947 letter. McCaffrey, moreover, who "ran Harvester like an autocrat," harbored none of the traditional McCormick paternalism and was utterly uninterested in whether his employees held him in good stead. He was not a "welfare capitalist" but a capitalist pure and simple. There was no love lost for the McCormicks within the FE leadership, but the ascendance of "Hard Nose" McCaffrey—as he was widely known in union circles—posed a more raw existential threat. "McCaffrey's policy of cutting production costs at any cost," DeWitt Gilpin wrote, "was enunciated after he successfully purged from the company chairmanship Fowler McCormick, a soft-nosed Freudian who nursed the fuzzy theory that IH's workers could be mesmerized back into cheap company unionism if he kept playing ball and golf with UAW-CIO President Walter Reuther."[5]

McCaffrey, however, did wholeheartedly subscribe to one tenet that had been promulgated by an earlier McCormick, one who had also been comfortable with hard-nosed conduct. Like Cyrus McCormick II, McCaffrey believed that it was sound management to "weed out the bad element among the men." And he determined the time had come to do that with the FE, once and for all.

Assisting him in this endeavor would be William Reilly, who served as McCaffrey's chief of labor relations. Reilly began his career in 1926 as an electrician at Harvester's Wisconsin Steel Mill on Chicago's South Side; a few years later—just as was true for Grant Oakes and Jerry Fielde in IH plants farther north—Reilly was elected to the mill's management-controlled works council. But unlike Oakes, Fielde and other Harvester employees committed to genuine unionism, Reilly threw in his lot with the company; when in 1937 the NLRB ordered the works councils disbanded, the "Progressive Steel Workers"—with Reilly as president—emerged overnight. Harvester promptly granted the new organization recognition, stymying the Steel Workers Organizing Committee effort then underway.

(Unlike Harvester employees elsewhere, Wisconsin Steel employees in fact never joined the CIO, and were represented by this "independent" union until the mill closed.) Shortly thereafter Harvester management rewarded Reilly for his good work by promoting him to the labor relations staff; he served as assistant director during the 1940s before McCaffrey appointed him to the top spot. As far as Reilly was concerned, the only good unions were docile ones, like the company union he'd once headed, and so he reviled the FE, and one of its leaders in particular. "The reason for the trouble with the FE," he would say after he'd retired from Harvester, "was that DeWitt Gilpin was an out and out Commie."[6]

Of course, Gilpin was hardly the only FE official bedeviling Harvester management, and there were "irresponsible radicals" not just in the union's top leadership but at the local level as well. To oust—or at least break—all of them, McCaffrey and Reilly focused on the document that gave the FE so much power: the contract. "FE-UE boasted that it was 'the best contract in the industry,'" said a company publication. "Harvester management was united in regarding it as the worst contact in Harvester." It was the "worst contact" for a simple reason: under it FE members were getting more and working less than management wanted them to. "We're not going to pay 8 hours' salary for about 5 hours' work," McCaffrey declared. But too often that was the case, as "each attempt by the company to bring realism into the picture with respect to providing a good day's effort was resisted by the union through wildcat strikes, slowdowns and harassment tactics in the grievance procedure."[7]

Thus in 1951, nearly a year before the FE contract was set to expire, McCaffrey put together an internal committee of executives from various departments, along with senior plant managers, tasked with reviewing the agreement in its entirety. The committee concluded that minor adjustments would not suffice; what was necessary was "the complete elimination of those conditions which had given rise to the abuses practiced by this union." Central to those "abuses" was, as always, the pay-for-stewards provision, which "provided good pay and special consideration for FE bosses while they roamed the plant stirring up trouble and dissatisfaction." Also of overarching concern were the various clauses (or lack thereof) that empowered workers to resist speedup. It was imperative to restore "true incentive" to the company's wage system and decisively "mark the end of the gravy train" for pieceworkers; thus "our right to time-study and establish accurate production standards," IH management declared, "[must] be spelled out in the contract with no right to strike over such standards." There should be no tinkering around the edges of the agreement at the next bargaining session. Injecting the necessary "realism," as far as the company was concerned, would require "a complete rewrite" of the contract.[8]

So Harvester management began quietly preparing for a 1952 showdown with the FE many months before contract negotiations were set to begin. FE leaders, though already well acquainted with just what John McCaffrey thought of them, were unaware of the concerted strategizing underway in Harvester's headquarters. But they too were looking ahead to the next contract. They knew just how high the stakes were.

23.
A Fight over Every Job

E ven under the best of circumstances, it's routine for union officials to feel pressured when contracts are coming up for renegotiation. And in 1952 the FE was hardly facing the best of circumstances.

For one thing, the company was not the only antagonist the FE leadership had to be mindful of. During 1952 the FE fended off attempted UAW takeovers at Harvester plants in East Moline and Rock Falls, as well as at McCormick Works. The FE's triumph at McCormick Works, in June 1952—just before the FE and IH began their contract negotiations—marked the sixteenth straight failure for the UAW within the Harvester chain. The victories were sweet but as always defending against the raids drained resources, and the constant competition impelled the FE to deliver more for its membership than the UAW was offering. Given Harvester management's increasingly open preference for the UAW, this would take some doing. Both the UAW and the FE had last negotiated with Harvester in 1950; UAW and Harvester officials had then endorsed the productivity pay and cost-of-living clauses in a new five-year agreement. FE leaders had only reluctantly acceded to those concepts in 1950, though after a two-week strike they were able to rebuff Harvester's demand for contract language lauding the mutual benefits of increased productivity, and settled on a two-year expiration date (the FE had wanted, as always, a one-year agreement). It had been challenging then for the FE leadership to make its case against the particulars of the "politics of productivity," which on the surface appeared to be management gifts to the workforce. But with every raid the UAW touted the extra dollars provided by these provisions, while FE officials endeavored to explain that such short-term gain was purposely engineered to guarantee long-term pain for union members. By rejecting the UAW's overtures, Harvester workers signaled that they grasped, for the moment anyhow, the abstract point their leadership was making.[1]

Despite—or in part, because of—these varied pressures the national FE leadership approached the preparations for the 1952 contract negotiations as an organizing opportunity. Early in the year committees charged with soliciting suggestions from the membership about contract improvements were formed in each Harvester local. Involvement was impressive; in Louisville, Local 236 established a four-hundred-person committee, and other locals also boasted similarly sized groups. The demands thus generated by the rank and file, Jerry Fielde pledged, would not be pared down by the leadership but would be presented in toto to Harvester management when bargaining began. With the UAW nipping at its heels, this grassroots procedure ensured that the FE's top leadership remained in close contact with Harvester workers and cognizant of the issues most pressing to them; union members also became more invested in negotiations and primed for whatever actions might be deemed necessary to achieve a better contract. The locals produced a list of more than 120 demands, including these: elimination of all no-strike and no-slowdown language, the establishment of a guaranteed annual wage "with joint Company-union committee to study the principle of a thirty-hour week with forty hours' pay," formation of another joint committee devoted to the "abolition of race prejudice" in all hiring and promotion procedures, and the appointment of "a full-time 'Union safety man' in each plant to be paid by the Company [who] would have the right to stop any operation he considered unsafe." Such a full-throated assertion from FE members that they were entitled to considerably more—and not just more money, but more control—than they already had must have gratified the union's top officials, as it provided evidence of the trickle-down impact of their ideology. But the bottom-up bargaining process also served to raise, rather than tamp down, expectations at a time when there was good reason to wonder if the FE could deliver big at the bargaining table.[2]

Jim Wright was one of those wondering about that, and in fact his concerns encompassed the FE's viability in general. He could pinpoint the very day when he began to question whether the union had bumped up against the limits of the militancy that had defined it from the start. In the summer of 1952, a grievance dispute broke out in Wright's department. As usual he signaled to the other workers that it was time to quit work. For the first time, rather than receiving instant compliance, Wright fielded questions instead. "What's this about? Why are you taking us out now?" he recalled the men saying. "You ask me what am I taking you out for?" an incredulous Wright replied. "What do you care what I'm taking you out for—let's *go.*" Not all of the workers followed Wright's lead, and those who did went listlessly: "It took them an hour to dribble out of the plant, coming out with their buckets, just walking slow." Management "busted the whole thing that day," and the worker with the grievance lost his argument.

"Hell, we [had] called on them every week, twice a week, let's go," he said. "They had gotten tired." This evolution was perhaps especially marked in Louisville. Once youthful, fiery, and with little to lose, the members of Local 236 had gained some insecurities with the passage of time, Wright noted.

The guys, after they'd been there three or four years, they had started to wonder about those little two-room houses on the side of the road somewhere, and they was trying to raise some kids, all of them had got kids, all of them had bought a car, they were beginning to halfway want to settle down and look toward saving something. And we was still in there pounding away at the grievances, see?

But underlying any attitudinal shift within the rank and file was a more subversive threat: Harvester management, Wright believed, had learned to manipulate the FE's wildcatting ways to its advantage. "The company didn't want peace," he insisted, despite John McCaffrey's protestations to the contrary. "Confusion at first creates unanimity among the workers, but if it's constant confusion, it will break up unanimity too," Wright said. "And nothing's ever done about it, just keep going through the same routine, walkout, stuff like that." He maintained, "The company would practically organize a walkout" by arbitrarily cutting rates. "Sometimes management would know that we couldn't take some of the things that they put out, so they would deliberately plan something on a guy, so we would walk out, and close the plant down," he said. "And that's a mark against us." Harvester frequently retaliated after shop-floor disturbances by suspending or discharging the rank-and-filers who led them, though the contract's less than definitive no-strike language coupled with the FE's aggressive defense sometimes forced the company to back down (with Charlie Yates in Louisville, for example). But often enough the punishments stuck (as was the case with Fred Marrero and Robert Mimms of Local 236, who despite the plantwide walkout on their behalf never got their jobs back) and each loss of a militant local leader weakened the FE that much more.

Most critically of all, Wright had become convinced that the walkouts were no longer inflicting harm where it mattered: on the company's bottom line. "See, we were right in what we were doing," he said, but "we were doing it wrong, to hit the company to hurt them enough. We weren't hurting the company, in them walkouts." Wright, in fact, believed the opposite was true, as Harvester management had learned to stockpile pieces in anticipation of work stoppages. "What the company would do was wait until we had a bunch of pieces all made up, two or three days' work, and then go over there and institute a walkout. And it would save the company ten million dollars in salaries, in wages. And then create another one. And then another one. I saw that. I said, when is this going to end? How can we end this thing?"

Thus, as the Harvester contract neared expiration in the summer of 1952, Wright began to "feel funny" about a potential strike. "I got hold of the guys, white and Black, the leaders of the international union, told them everything, I said, 'we've got something happening here, I don't know what it is, but we'd better take a second look,'" and he urged Jerry Fielde to avoid a chain-wide walkout if at all possible. Fielde, Wright said, argued that they might have little choice: "We can't stay in with no contract—No Contract, No Work." Wright nonetheless continued to express his anxiety to the FE's top leadership. "I told them that this thing just wasn't working out," he said, "and the company had something planned this time to bust us and break us for good."[3]

Yet despite Wright's unease, in advance of the 1952 negotiations the FE by all outward appearances projected its characteristic combativeness at all levels. In Chicago, FE Local 101 proudly proclaimed that at Tractor Works the employees "are still turning out the same number of tractors per man-hour as they were ten years ago" whereas "the UAW-CIO leaders agreed to help the company enforce a new speed-up plan for pieceworkers" in its 1950 contract with Harvester. At a membership meeting in early 1952, Local 101 resolved to "immediately enforce by our collective strength all contract clauses that protect us against speed-up."[4]

Judging by their actions, other FE locals seemed in accord with the sentiments expressed at Tractor Works. Jim Wright may have sensed a downtick in militancy among Harvester workers in Louisville, but there was still plenty of it on display there. In the opening months of 1952, members of Local 236, angry over efforts to speed up the assembly line, engaged in an escalating series of slowdowns and finally a full-fledged one-week strike, authorized by the FE leadership, by the entire local. Around the same time at McCormick Works, some fifty employees—all but three of whom were African American—in the malleable foundry were suspended when they refused orders to perform work that paid less and was more hazardous than their usual jobs entailed. When news of the dispute reached the main plant, Local 108 President Matt Halas, along with two hundred other FE members, confronted the works manager as he was enjoying a bowl of ice cream in the plant cafeteria. Halas demanded that IH management "stop the terrorism in the shop" and rescind the suspensions; when the answer they received was unsatisfactory, the group left the cafeteria and toured the plant, calling workers off their jobs. The entire plant was shut down and picket lines patrolled all the gates for three days before management relented, reinstating the suspended employees and instituting clear separation of tasks in the malleable foundry. And in late February flare-ups at six other Harvester plants prompted John McCaffrey to send yet another letter to all FE members, reiterating that "this company cannot tolerate work stoppages and slowdowns" and insisting that such actions "were not only inspired by, but were ordered by the national headquarters of FE-UE."[5]

But an even more vociferous demonstration of just how far outside the mainstream the FE stood occurred in the summer of 1952. In July, International Harvester began to make good on a decision it had announced some months earlier: the venerable Twine Mill, adjacent to McCormick Works, would be shut down, its machinery shipped to a new facility in New Orleans. Workers at the mill were members of FE Local 141. Closing the facility would mean the loss of 865 jobs, nearly two-thirds of them held by African Americans; women comprised almost half the workforce. Many employees had been at the mill for decades. Harvester indicated it would provide some severance pay to the displaced workers, but was vague about how much, and despite union urgings would not offer preferential hiring at either its new Louisiana mill or at other IH plants in Chicago.

The FE endeavored to draw attention to "the needless loss of an industry to our city and state" that Harvester was instituting. "For years we have heard International Harvester and the millionaire McCormicks boast of their sense of responsibility to employees and the public," one union flyer read. "The truth is that Harvester's long range planning all too clearly indicates relocation of as many plants as possible in low-wage, sweatshop, non-union, Jim Crow areas." Being relegated to "the industrial scrap-heap," FE literature emphasized, would prove especially devastating to the mill's more senior employees—"many of the older men and women will be unable to find other jobs at all"—and the mill closure belied Harvester's purported commitment to African American opportunity. "How can I find another job at decent pay?" asked Alice Scott, a Black woman who'd put in twenty-eight years at the mill. "How can any Negro workers find other decent jobs in Chicago when we are barred from them by Jim Crow methods?" And IH could well afford to modernize the mill and keep it in Chicago, since in the past year the company "reaped $177 million in profits after paying all their production costs and meeting all payrolls," the FE insisted. "At 16 breaths to the minute, that's $21.13 profit every time IH President John McCaffrey draws a breath—awake or asleep, sick or well, in his office, under the shower, or on his yacht."[6]

But for the FE, protestations on paper would not suffice. The president of Local 141 was Robert Ray, an African American with a decade of employment at the Twine Mill, interrupted for a few years during World War II when he served as a sergeant in the Pacific. "We are going to put up a hell of a fight to keep the mill in Chicago," Ray informed UE officials in New

York. That meant more than just a public relations campaign: "We will put up a physical fight to keep the machinery from being moved," he pledged.[7]

Which is precisely what the Twine Mill workers did. "They can't set up the new mill without our machines," Ray told the members of Local 141. "Why don't we try to hold on to them? Most of you spent half your life running them. I figure you got at least half interest in them." In the warm afternoon on Wednesday, July 30, 1952, as the three hundred workers on the day shift were about to quit work, company personnel entered the plant to begin dismantling the valuable machinery IH wanted to send south. Bulldozers pulled into place behind the mill and operators knocked a hole in its back wall to access the equipment.[8]

And then Chicago got to see something that hadn't happened since "the glory days of the CIO": a full-fledged sit-down strike. Robert Ray and a squadron of workers left their jobs and began bricking the damaged wall back up. Other employees "sped through the building, pulling switches and shutting down machinery," letting management officials know that they weren't working but they weren't leaving, either. Two hundred and fifty women and men from Local 141 remained in the building, waving through open windows or crowding together on the multistory mill's fire escape landings. Unfurling a banner that read "No Runaways to the South!" they shouted down greetings to the growing crowd congregating outside the plant fence. That throng included other FE members from neighboring Tractor and McCormick Works, who established a supportive picket line around the mill. Family members brought baskets filled with food and thermoses of coffee that were hoisted up to the sit-down strikers. But they weren't in too much danger of going hungry, for when dinner time approached they settled into the mill's cafeteria and helped themselves to the company's menu de jour. Robert Ray pledged, however, that the workers would do no damage to the facility. "While in the plant, we will protect the property, observe fire hazard restrictions, and police areas we occupy. With many Army, Navy, and Marine vets in our ranks," he said, "we know how to 'police.'" Chicago's actual police, meanwhile, patrolled outside; following Harvester's orders they barred entry to workers on later shifts or anyone else seeking to augment the sit-downers' ranks, but otherwise for the moment made no move to empty the mill.[9]

"SIT-DOWNERS HOLD PLANT," the headlines announced, as the Twine Mill "labor drama" galvanized attention across the country. "Federal and state labor agencies were reported watching the strike closely for any indication it might provide a spark which could set off a conflagration of similar labor tactics on a national scale," said the anxious *Chicago Herald-American*, which defined the sit-down tactic as "a European importation." The *Chicago Daily News* pronounced that "free and unrestricted moving in search of cheaper production is one of the main reasons why the United States is industrially peerless," but the misguided FE, "under left-wing leadership, prefers to take refuge in the radical tenet that a worker has a property right in his job, and can't be deprived of it." One writer, however, evidenced sympathy for just such radical tenets. In his account of the sit-down for the *March of Labor*, DeWitt Gilpin referenced the memory that within the FE remained ever-present, noting that the Twine Mill was located "on the site where 66 years ago the strike began that ended in defeat with the bodies of the Haymarket martyrs swinging from gallows." But the Twine Mill workers also laid claim to more recent history. "There was gaiety and hope amidst grimness," Gilpin wrote, "like the occupied plants in Flint, Michigan, in 1937." In sit-down strikes "the workers temporarily take occupancy of the site of their exploitation and get an insight into the potential of their class," so such actions, he maintained, were uniquely liberating and empowering.[10]

That—and the fact that the only property rights recognized by the state were those belonging to International Harvester—was no doubt why the members of Local 141 were not allowed to remain in the Twine Mill for long. Just over twenty-four hours after the occupation began, Captain George Barnes, head of the Chicago Police Labor Detail, arrived at the mill. He gave the workers two minutes to get out, and traversed the facility with two hundred police officers, billy clubs at the ready, to make his intentions clear. Many of the workers shouted, "we'll stay," in response, but opted not to resist their eviction. Some of them didn't move quickly enough, however, as 102 men—including Robert Ray—and forty-nine women were charged with disorderly conduct and placed under arrest. A few of them were hauled in from the picket line outside the mill, which by then had grown to include several hundred mill workers and other supporters. The officers were "kicked and shoved by protesting workmen" as they led the sit-downers to the twenty police vans waiting to cart them off to jail. One of those workmen protested with a right jab to the nose that sent Captain Barnes tumbling to the ground, an event captured in a widely circulated press photo.[11]

When the mill was set to re-open the following Monday, the members of Local 141—including those now out on bail—met at the nearby FE hall before returning to work en masse. They remained intent, Robert Ray said, on resisting the mill's closure. "Our Mason-Dixon line is the sidewalk in front of the plant," he declared. "The moment the company tries to move any machinery across that line it will be guilty of provoking civil war." John

McCaffrey was not the sort to be deterred by such threats. That afternoon a moving truck rumbled up to the mill and took on a load of equipment. Police cars stood by to escort the truck out through the gates. But then, as Ray had promised, civil war—or at least, a "brief but wild, stone-throwing melee"—ensued. Mill workers poured out of the plant; other supporters and FE organizers joined in and about two hundred protesters massed around the truck, attempting to block its exit. They peppered the truck with bricks, paving stones, and bottles, prompting police officers to plunge into the crowd, and "struggling battles broke out in little groups." It took six officers and a nightstick across his throat to get millworker George Scott into a police van; he promptly kicked out the door and mixed it up with the police again before they threw him into another, better-secured, vehicle. Sixteen others, including DeWitt Gilpin, were also arrested. As the police cleared its path, the moving truck, its windshield fractured by one of the projectiles, inched through the throng and out onto Blue Island Avenue, where at last it roared off "toward Dixie."[12]

Harvester promptly shut down the Twine Mill for a week and suspended Robert Ray and several other members of the Local 141 leadership. Management reiterated that the facility would be closed for good early in 1953. Amidst all its concerns, the FE leadership could now add another one: the impending shutdown of the Twine Mill meant hardship for many longtime members, while the union's dues-paying ranks, and its cadre of militant rank-and-file leadership, would be whittled down some more. But the Twine Mill hubbub and the resultant publicity obliged IH management to run defensive advertisements and make a few concessions: for the first time the company made public the severance packages it would provide, and also agreed that mill workers (those not suspended, at any rate) would be offered preferential hiring at its other plants. And the struggle had galvanized other FE members for the conflicts to come. "The twine mill has already won something for us," said Frank Mingo, the African American vice-president of FE Local 101 at Tractor Works. "You know as well as I do that the company has been talking about moving our foundry south. They'd move anything south if they could get away with it. But the twine mill has shown them what they are in for. IH knows now it'll be a fight over every job."[13]

For the FE, that "fight over every job" was just a few weeks away.

24.
I Didn't See How We Could Lose

The Twine Mill set-to took place at the same time that officials for International Harvester and the FE were sitting down together to, in theory at least, negotiate a new contract.

It's fair to presume that few pleasantries were exchanged across the table at these sessions. There was no actual negotiating either.

Jerry Fielde and the FE's team opened things up by proposing a general fifteen-cent-per-hour wage increase and then presented, over the course of two days, all 122 of the other demands that had been submitted by the local rank-and-file committees. That move was not well received by the company's team. This process "was intended to support a phony 'democracy in practice' philosophy of the union," Harvester officials scoffed, "so that management might understand the 'grassroots' origins of their demands." William Reilly, heading up Harvester's contingent, pronounced the FE's wish list "fantastic" and "wholly unrealistic." But whatever the scope of the union's requests, they were irrelevant in any event. Reilly refused to respond to any of them, and instead unveiled "a complete proposal by the company, covering all phases of the contract." Not only would IH management reject any new demands—whatever they were and wherever they came from—but the FE's old contract would be gutted as well.[1]

The company's proposal entirely overhauled its wage system, reclassifying thousands of jobs into lower pay grades. The favorable allowance rules the FE had fought so hard to establish would be largely eliminated, while new "earning objectives" would be introduced. These "objectives" called for re-timing jobs on the basis of 100 percent efficiency (no fatigue time built into the measurement) and therefore would effectively constitute both the minimum and maximum rate for each job, meaning that management would reap the benefits of incentive work without having to pay real incentive wages. These changes translated to "wage cuts that ranged anywhere from twenty, thirty, forty, fifty cents an hour, and more," said FE staff member Al Verri. None of this, the FE maintained, sprang from any financial duress Harvester was experiencing, since "employment keeps dropping in the company while profits and productivity keeps going up."[2]

But while on paper this promised much greater "efficiency" and consequently bigger profit margins for IH, in practice that wouldn't be the case if

those "free-style troublemakers" in the plants could roam the departments
contesting every reclassification. So Harvester's plan struck squarely at the
power held by FE stewards. They would henceforth be required to secure
passes from company officials before leaving their jobs on union business,
and would be allowed paid time off only for meetings agreed to by management. Union representatives would no longer be required at first-step grievance conversations, providing foremen more leeway to lean on workers when
disputes broke out. Also stricken from the company's new contract was the
language that had entitled the FE to strike once the grievance procedure
was exhausted, replaced with a much more iron-clad no-strike clause. The
agreement was also set to run for three years, so as to expire at the same time
as the UAW's would, and reduce the "turmoil" attendant to negotiations.

"They said, we're going to stop these walkouts," was the way Jim Wright
characterized Harvester management's 1952 position. "The guys have been
walking out for years and years in Tractor Works, McCormick Works,
Twine Mill, Louisville Works, over these grievances. We want to settle
these things across a table, instead of them walking out over these grievances. And if they walk out over a grievance, they're going to lose their job.
That's what they said. And that's what really the big strike was about."[3]

Even the wage hikes Harvester offered were precisely the sort the FE
leadership objected to. There would be no general pay raises, only a continu-
ation of the productivity and cost-of-living increases. These would not begin
to approach what the workforce was due, as "wage gains have not kept pace
with productivity" for years, the FE maintained. And at any rate the modest
wage hikes being tendered would be more than offset, the union believed, by
the job "adjustments" IH planned to impose.[4]

In short, as far as the FE leadership was concerned, Harvester had proposed "a new contract with wage cuts written into it and the means to oppose them written out of it."[5]

But for Harvester officials, this was the "realism" in their relationship
with the FE they'd been preparing to achieve for quite some time. They'd
informed their dealers months earlier that a major strike was in the offing,
urging them to stock up on parts and new equipment. The company ran advertisements while negotiations were ongoing headed "Why Harvester May
Be Struck by FE-UE" in local newspapers where IH plants were located.
"In our opinion, wise and responsible union leadership would not strike," the
ads solemnly intoned. "But that decision is not within the Company's control." If a strike were to occur, IH vowed to keep its plants open and "any
employees who want to work will be welcome." [6]

And then William Reilly gave Jerry Fielde and the FE leadership a choice: sign our proposal, or go right ahead and walk out.

"The company had something planned this time to bust us and break us for good," Jim Wright had warned, if the FE called a strike against International Harvester in 1952. Yet at that moment in Louisville, Jim Mouser was of a different mind than his friend. "As strong as we were, as united as we were," Mouser believed, "I didn't see how we could lose." Many in the FE, some top officials included, shared Mouser's cocksure confidence. Despite the slings and arrows aimed at the FE from so many sources, the Harvester membership had remained undaunted in its loyalty and steadfast in its solidarity. If a union's power was rooted in a militant, engaged, and agitated rank and file—a belief firmly held by the FE leadership—in that regard their organization was second to none. The undersized FE had bested the McCormicks and all Harvester's vast wealth and wherewithal in the past; why not once again?[7]

This time, though, things could be different. Not since the pre-CIO era had Harvester management been as naked in its resolve to crush a union. The "improvements and clarifications" to Harvester's wage system would mean, in reality, pay cuts and speedup for thousands of workers, but as always the complexities of piecework hindered the FE's ability to make that case to the public—or its own members—while IH touted the "substantial benefits" offered through its productivity and cost-of-living clauses. At the same time the isolated and cash-poor FE had few resources to draw on for a long engagement, and its parent body, the UE, had plenty of other struggles already demanding attention. The predatory UAW stood poised to rush in wherever the FE stumbled. And perhaps, as Wright sensed, the union's membership—or at least some segments of it—were not spoiling for a fight quite as readily as had once been the case.

But none of that much mattered. Even if there were those in the union who might have wanted to, there was still too much combativeness embedded in the FE's DNA, at all levels, to ratchet it back at this point. "No Contract, No Work" was a nonnegotiable tenet. And Harvester management had just torn up the union's hard-fought contract and thrown the pieces back across the bargaining table.

So on August 21, 1952, the thirty thousand FE members at International Harvester went out on strike. And the long deep grudge that had been festering since the nineteenth century once again erupted into open class warfare.

25.
A Strong Picket Line Is the Best Negotiator

Though Jim Mouser may have felt comfortable that his union would prevail over International Harvester in 1952, he wasn't about to take any chances. On August 21, the first day of the strike, he arrived bright and early—along with two thousand other members of FE Local 236—for picket duty in front of the Louisville plant. Mouser didn't remain on the line for very long, however. The chief of police, Carl Heustis, had also shown up just after daybreak, along with one hundred of his men. Heustis "lined all the police officers up in the middle of the street, just like he thought it was the army or something, and took roll call," Mouser recalled. Heustis then announced, "We're going to go over and take all those pickets, and put them on the other side of the road."

Mouser felt compelled to acquaint the police chief with the fundamentals of American civil liberties. "I told him he didn't have the authority to do that. He hadn't got an injunction against FE-UE, limiting the number of pickets, and as long as we were in an orderly manner, we could picket, as many pickets as we wanted." Or rather, in Heustis's alternative account, Mouser "charged at me and cursed."

And so in short order Jim Mouser found himself under arrest. He was thrown into a wagon, where an older policeman stood guard in the rear. "This one cop started climbing in, he said, let me get in the back there, I'll work him over with my nightstick," Mouser said. "I told the older officer, let me tell you something, if he starts in that back door, I'm going to kick his brains out, before he gets halfway in the door." The senior officer prevailed upon his younger colleague to back off.

Mouser, however, was not the only member of Local 236 to run afoul of the law that morning. Harvester had reiterated that its plants would remain open during the walkout, and though none of the production workers represented by the FE endeavored to enter the Louisville facility that morning, a sizable contingent of supervisory personnel had gathered at the plant's main gate. "It was a powder-keg situation out there," as Heustis described it, and on that not many would have taken issue with him. The signs the strikers carried underscored how zealously they planned to protect their picket line, not so much through the messages painted on them, but rather because many of the cardboard placards were affixed to baseball bats (quite possibly locally produced Louisville sluggers). Just after Mouser was hauled in those bats began to be put to use, as strikers smashed windshields of the cars belonging to some of the plant's more despised foremen. They also attempted to overturn several automobiles, let the air out of the tires of a few others, and scattered two-inch roofing nails across the driveways leading up to the plant gate. Heustis ordered his officers into the "riotous mob," and seven members of Local 236, in addition to Mouser, were arrested that day.

The aggression practiced by the Louisville pickets was costly for the union—Jim Mouser's bail, at $500, was exceptionally high—but it was also purposeful. Foundry workers, who were represented by the UAW and therefore not party to the strike, accessed the Louisville facility through the same gate as tractor production workers did. The president of the UAW local in the foundry had earlier announced that his union would not as a policy honor the FE's picket line; it would, rather, "be up to each individual member" to determine whether to report for work. The formidable crowd outside the plant would surely be factored into those decisions.[1]

Elsewhere, things were quieter. The only other altercation of note took place at the IH factory in Richmond, Indiana, where the president of FE Local 118 exchanged blows with a worker attempting to cross the picket line—the strikebreaker was eventually escorted into the plant by local police—but no other nonsupervisory personnel sought entry. In downstate Illinois, the FE's presence was substantial but all was calm at the Harvester plants in Rock Island and Rock Falls; at East Moline, where strikers carried signs reading "No Makeum, No Sellum," the local's entire membership either joined the picket line or stayed home. Only a few supervisors sought admission to the plant; the pickets waved the payroll employees through but refused to allow the time study men in. At Harvester's four Chicago facilities—McCormick, Tractor Works, West Pullman Works, and the Twine Mill—picket lines were robust; four hundred strikers patrolled the gates at McCormick Works. The police were out in force too: Captain George Barnes pledged that more than three hundred officers would be detailed to the McCormick and Tractor Works complex.[2]

"A strong picket line is the best negotiator," pronounced an FE flyer from Local 108 at McCormick Works. It was not likely, though, that John McCaffrey would allow the union to continue controlling access to Harvester's plants. Within a week, Harvester obtained the injunction Jim Mouser had pointed out that it lacked in Louisville, stipulating there could be no more than three pickets at any plant gate, and similar orders at several other plants followed. Yet the restrictions did not immediately curb all defiant picket line behavior. Just a few days after the injunction was handed down in Louisville, for example, Sterling Neal and two other members of Local 236 sat down on the railroad tracks leading out of the Louisville plant, blocking passage of a freight train loaded with Cub tractors built before the strike began. The police soon hauled the three men off the tracks and into jail.[3]

International Harvester had already received assists from law enforcement and the courts; next up would be the United States Congress. On September 2, 1952—just two days, ironically enough, after Labor Day—the House Un-American Activities Committee set up shop in Chicago to uncover "how the Communist Party has endeavored to infiltrate and control labor unions" in the area. HUAC, of course, had long had the FE in its sights. During the 1941 IH strike, Congressman Martin Dies, then HUAC's chair, labeled DeWitt Gilpin "a known Communist" and declared the FE to be "a menace we dare not ignore." Three years later a HUAC report insisted that Grant Oakes "has consistently carried out the biddings of the Communist Party." No surprise, then, that the FE would be a principal target of the 1952 HUAC roadshow.

This time, one of the prime movers behind the hearings was Illinois Republican Congressman Harold Velde, a HUAC committee member who would become its chairman in 1953. Velde possessed an odd—or at least mixed—pedigree for someone charged with ensuring America's political purity. Raised in rural Tazewell County, Illinois, Velde got through law school at the University of Illinois before serving in the FBI's counterespionage division during World War II (where he became a wiretap specialist), and then ran for Congress from the Peoria area in 1948. He was the openly backed (and heavily financed) candidate of, as journalist Drew Pearson put it, the "gambling-liquor fraternity," and particularly of the Hiram Walker Corporation, which bottled whiskey in Peoria at what was once the largest distillery in the world. Velde easily defeated his Democratic opponent, a minister whom the liquor lobby feared might favor higher taxes on spirits; it was perhaps not surprising that Velde then launched a campaign to expose communist infiltration of the clergy. He was also opposed to mobile libraries in rural areas, since, he declared, "the basis of all Communism and Socialistic influence is education of the people." Influences of the forty-proof variety were more up small-town-sophisticate Velde's alley, who "frequently posed with a raised glass in his hand as 'a man of distinction.'"[4]

Since Velde had already pronounced before the 1952 hearings began that FE officials were "Communists from top to bottom," it could have been argued that little would be gained by calling them before the Committee. But objective fact-finding was not necessarily HUAC's principal mission, and so Grant Oakes, Jerry Fielde, and DeWitt Gilpin were subpoenaed to testify, as was Ernest DeMaio, president of the UE district covering Illinois. Occurring less than two weeks into the Harvester strike, the timing of HUAC's appearance appeared suspect, to say the least. HUAC chair John Wood, however, took umbrage at the notion that the hearing had been called "for the express purpose of interfering with labor negotiations," and Harvester officials also claimed they "had nothing to do with the Committee's visit nor with the timing of it." That may have been technically true, as Wood claimed that the Chicago hearing had been penciled in for September early in the year, well before the FE-IH negotiations had finally broken down. But the HUAC congressmen, and especially Velde, were well aware that International Harvester would likely be struck by the FE sometime in 1952, so an investigation devoted to "the large concentrations of Communists in the Chicago area" would surely prove helpful to Harvester management at any point that year. The fact that it happened to take place at the worst possible moment for the FE leadership was merely, at least as far as IH and HUAC maintained, a "coincidence."[5]

So on the morning of September 2, the largest and most vociferous FE picket line would be found not outside a Harvester factory but at the imposing federal courthouse in downtown Chicago, where the HUAC hearing was being held. Several hundred people circled the building—which covered a square city block—carrying signs with messages like "HARVESTER and UN-AMERICANS are WORKING TOGETHER" and "WHAT'S RED ABOUT A RAISE?" The sizable crowd, over half of it African American, also suggested better applications of congressional resources, including "INVESTIGATE HARVESTER SUPER PROFITS" and "INVESTIGATE POLICE BRUTALITY AGAINST NEGRO PEOPLE." One young Black woman gripped against her chest a cardboard placard on which was affixed a grisly photograph of an African American man hung from a tree, framed by the handmade letters "INVESTIGATE LYNCHING." Pete Neputy, president of the FE local at Tractor Works, had helped to organize the demonstration, and Robert Ray and many other members of FE Local 141 were also among those present, some of them bearing signs demanding "KEEP THE TWINE MILL IN CHICAGO."

Not content to confine their protest to the sidewalks, after a half an hour outside the contingent headed into the courthouse itself. "Singing and shouting, the marchers poured up the stairs to the second floor and jammed the corridor" near HUAC's hearing room, disturbing the proceedings with "howls of derision and hammering on the doors," said an aghast *Chicago*

Tribune report, which declared the courthouse disruption "unprecedented." The catcalls from the crowd were aimed not just at the congressmen on the committee but at some of the witnesses appearing before them: self-proclaimed ex-communists who willingly provided for HUAC the names of those they knew within the FE and UE who, they asserted, were party members. One of those so identified was Ernest DeMaio; as district chairman of the UE he had, as at least technically, authority over the Harvester strike. DeMaio's testimony came in the afternoon (by which time the hearing room had been cordoned off and the Chicago police roamed the halls armed with riot sticks and shotguns) but he proved to be a far-from-friendly witness. "You are asking me to cooperate with this committee to defeat a strike which is currently taking place at the International Harvester Co., obviously I can't do that and I won't do that," DeMaio said. He certainly didn't, refusing to provide any information about his own relationship with the Communist Party and doing the same as he was asked again and again about the CP affiliations of other union members.[6]

HUAC members had spent several hours grilling DeMaio to get no information; the next day, when the FE leadership appeared before them, they got the same result in far less time. Once sworn in, Grant Oakes, Jerry Fielde, and DeWitt Gilpin all requested that their testimony be postponed since they were involved in ongoing negotiations with International Harvester. Chairman Wood agreed that the FE officials could be called to Washington for interrogation at a later date but first they were individually asked the jackpot question: "Are you now or have you ever been a member of the Communist Party?" All three men asserted their Fifth Amendment privilege and declined to respond, and were then dismissed from the hearing room.[7]

That postponement might have seemed charitable but in those few moments of testimony HUAC had already extracted what it wanted, and what International Harvester needed, from the FE leadership (and in fact the three officials were never recalled before the committee). "UNION CHIEFS DEFY U.S. QUIZ," proclaimed the banner front-page headline of the *Chicago Tribune*, with the subhead "Refuse To Say Whether They Are Commies" running over photos of Fielde, Gilpin, and Oakes. The front pages looked similar in towns around the other struck plants. One of HUAC's friendly witnesses came from the Quad Cities area—where two IH plants were located—and so papers there ran headlines like "Moline Man Testifies—20 HERE WERE COMMUNISTS." All this drew a ferocious denunciation from John Watkins, the East Moline FE leader who was one of the more prominent "reds" to be singled out. The maverick Watkins, in fact, was probably never a card-carrying communist, though his militancy and oft-expressed animosity toward Harvester management led many to presume he was. But he'd had long-standing respectful associations with party members, and moreover he detested stool pigeons, and thus in response to the charges Watkins refused to address his own CP involvement. To do so would validate "the union-busting, strike-breaking committee," he said, and the "conjectural testimony and outright lies of paid witnesses and discredited individuals" who "have been converted into company agents." And characteristically he held nothing back as he accused HUAC of coming to Chicago for one reason only: so that "the committee hearings would be used by the Harvester trust, the newspapers and the radios in an effort to smear the union leadership and interfere with the strike of Harvester workers against the dictatorial, wage-cutting, yellow-dog contract demands of this profit-hungry corporation."[8]

Harvester officials, all the while reiterating they had nothing to do with HUAC's appearance, seized on the negative publicity in precisely the manner Watkins described. In keeping with company custom, IH labor relations head William Reilly had already been sending letters to striking employees about the contract dispute; the hearings provided an opening to weigh in on politics. The FE's demands "are calculated to advance the cause of communism rather than the actual interests of rank and file FE members," Reilly wrote to all Harvester employees on the day the FE leadership appeared before HUAC. To ensure that message reached an even broader audience, within a week Harvester ran three-quarter-page advertisements in a host of newspapers; a collage of press clippings, featuring words like "REDS," "UNION BOSSES," and "DEFY U.S. QUIZ"—and of course the particularly helpful *Tribune* "COMMIE" header—were arrayed around a hammer and sickle, should anyone have missed the point. "It is our belief, and has been for many years," the ad read, "that the most influential leaders of FE-UE are either Communists or Communist sympathizers" and now at long last thanks to the HUAC hearings the general public should know that too. But because IH management maintained such profound respect for the rule of law, "we have no choice" but to deal with the "Communist-dominated" FE. "If we withdrew recognition from FE-UE we would probably be found guilty of an unfair labor practice under the law," the ad concluded sadly.[9]

Only a few weeks into the strike, the FE had already been hamstrung by civil authorities and pilloried by the press, to an extent surpassing anything the union had been subject to before—which was saying something. And the walkout was seriously straining the union's meager resources. FE members "didn't have any true strike benefits," Jim Wright said; the FE treasury was largely tapped out and the UE, itself beset by raids and hostile employers, had little to offer either. Nor could the FE, as might normally be the case, turn to other unions for help, certainly not those in the CIO, whose members were discouraged even from donating individually to the FE strike fund. The local UAW leadership at a plant in Indiana, for instance, declaring that "the CIO kicked [the FE] out of CIO because their international union officers were sympathetic to the Communist cause," prevented its members from aiding IH strikers in nearby Richmond, Indiana.[10]

But the FE, Wright maintained, "was the strongest union I've ever seen in not having any money" and so individual locals scrambled to ensure that their members were fed and the rent was paid. "If they was going to put your lights out, we'd find $100 to keep your lights burning, telephone going to be cut off, we'd pay $50 to keep it going," Wright said. In Chicago, an FE member named Emil Slezak "was head of the mooching committee," said Local 101 member Hank Graber. "We did not have money to supply the soup kitchen. [Slezak] took us out and showed us how to get milk delivered to the kitchen, get vegetables from the South Water Market, and get canned goods and coffee from the wholesale houses, bakery goods—bread, biscuits, and so forth—to go with the coffee."[11]

Despite the many challenges, FE pickets were still finding ways to cause trouble and Harvester's invitation to return to work had largely fallen flat. By mid-September, IH claimed that about eight hundred employees had crossed the picket lines at the struck plants, but that likely was an inflated figure and it included management personnel along with UAW members and other workers not specifically party to the strike. Virtually all of the FE's thirty thousand members remained out, and production at the struck IH plants was entirely halted. All things considered, the FE leadership could be encouraged by the state of affairs.[12]

So John McCaffrey decided to ratchet up the pressure. And Harvester's effort to break the FE transformed into something above and beyond the usual garden-variety union-busting campaign. It became, in FE staff member Al Verri's words, "a crusade."[13]

26.
The Foremen's Crusade

The paltry return-to-work figures meant only one thing, at least as far as John McCaffrey maintained. The explanation could not be the most obvious one: that FE members were overwhelmingly supportive of their union and its demands. No, he insisted, it was the tyrannical control exercised by the FE leadership—that "powerful, well-financed group of union masters"—that was to blame. The FE's "constant propaganda barrage about 'wage cuts'" had led to "confusion as to the issues," and the union's belligerence caused even the most determined strikebreakers to have second thoughts.[1]

Clearly Harvester employees would require more persuasion—and an escort service—to get them across the picket lines. McCaffrey vowed to provide both. To do so, he would not rely primarily on outside agencies, like Pinkerton detectives, that the McCormicks had utilized in the past. Rather, his troops would be mobilized from those already on the IH payroll: the front-line managers. Over the course of a week in mid-September McCaffrey and William Reilly traveled across Illinois and then to Indiana and Kentucky, gathering at lunch and dinner assemblies all two thousand of the company's foremen and lower-level supervisors. Harvester workers, McCaffrey explained, "needed to be told the facts personally," and the foremen were tapped for that assignment. McCaffrey instructed them to visit employees' homes, neighborhood taverns, or "any points where men normally congregate"; the foremen should emphasize that workers returning to the plants would immediately receive the seven cents an hour combined cost-of-living and productivity pay increase Harvester had offered in its contract proposal, an enticing proposition one month into a strike. And they should of course deny that the company's proposed new wage system meant pay cuts and speedup. If the workers themselves resisted these entreaties, the foremen should talk to their spouses. "I don't care how many weeks or months it will take, but so far as I am concerned, this is it," McCaffrey announced, "and we're going to stick." This elicited resolute cheers from the foremen, or at least that's what Harvester's official account claimed.

Harvester made sure the press was in on the excitement, and reporters obligingly wrote about the "organized doorbell pushing campaign" aimed at generating "a wholesale back-to-work movement," dubbing the initiative "unprecedented." Harvester's campaign "is unique in two ways," the *Baltimore Sun* reported. "First, it is carefully organized and systematic, and second, it is organized to reach directly to the lowest man on the line through person-to-person contact." All this was in keeping with an avowal by one IH vice-president, who said, "We are finished with the idea of letting unions tell our story to our people. We are going to do that for ourselves." In essence, however, there was nothing novel here: from early on the McCormicks and Harvester management had sought to maneuver around organized labor in order to disorganize it, seeking at every opportunity to maintain the upper hand by engaging one-on-one with employees. Though by the mid-twentieth century IH officials professed to "sincerely accept the principles of unionism and collective bargaining," in reality there remained nothing about workers' collectivism that they liked.[2]

But however familiar it may have seemed, the intensity of the foremen's campaign constituted a new threat for the FE. "They made house calls on the workers as though they were trying to organize the workers into another organization," said Jimmy Majors, an FE official at Tractor Works. "From what we heard, the company had visited darn near all thirty-five hundred to four thousand workers in [Tractor Works] at that time." One newspaper account described a foreman who by early October had already "contacted some workers half a dozen times." The enthusiasm for the house calls may have varied by location, however. Jim Mouser believed that the contacts in Louisville were done mostly by phone, as visiting strikers at their homes was deemed too hazardous. "If the foreman walked up and wanted to talk to you, like came to my door—I don't think any of them would have got hurt bad, you know, like shot or something," Mouser said, "but some of them would have had some broken noses, or what have you."[3]

In the proposed new contract, Harvester management struck at the locus of the FE's power—its steward body—and the foremen's campaign threatened to undermine the union's other primary sources of strength: its African American leadership and the unity the FE had forged between Black and white workers. For the FE these foundational pillars were interdependent, since in many plants African Americans were prominent in the local leadership and preponderant within the steward body. This was true in Louisville and also at McCormick Works, where the workforce, in the early 1950s, was around 20 percent Black. Of the eighteen members of the McCormick Works Local 108 executive board and grievance committee in 1950, seven were African American—nearly 40 percent, then—and thirty-nine of the eighty-five stewards (more than 45 percent) were Black. "The Negro people," proclaimed Matt Halas, the Polish American president of Local 108, are "the backbone of our organization." In earlier generations when Harvester had sought to "weed out the bad element among the men," Irish and Polish workers had been targeted; in 1952 African Americans were at the forefront of management's effort to cripple the union.[4]

And its foremen's crusade offered Harvester an opportunity, as far as the FE believed, to drive a wedge between the Black and white members of the union. "The Company longs to return to those divide-and-conquer days when it could exploit racial conflicts and play black against white in order to control both," the FE charged. To that end, "company foremen . . . have visited Negro homes, arguing, coaxing and even demanding that Negro workers become scabs and lead the way in breaking the strike and crushing their Union." Thus the semi-isolated malleable foundry at McCormick Works— where the majority of the workforce was African American and which was accessed through its own gate—became, the FE maintained, Harvester's "key back-to-work concentration point in Chicago."

> The company hoped to mass hundreds of scabs at the Malleable Iron gates, who would also be Negroes, and then march them through the picket lines. The aim was to create the impression among its white workers that their Negro brothers were smashing the strike. It would also help create dissension within the ranks of the Negro strikers themselves if Harvester could point to large-scale, successful, smashing of the picket lines led by Negroes.[5]

The back-to-work drive did indeed create some dissension within the ranks, at least judging from one family's story. African American William Lyles had worked for thirty years in the malleable foundry; his two sons, Felton and Twidell, were also employed there. William Lyles decided early on in the strike to return to work, a move that roundly displeased his sons, both union stewards regarded as "FE die-hards" by the company. After the foremen's campaign was launched Local 108 began focusing its picket line activity on the malleable foundry; on the last day of September—there were as yet no injunctions in place at Harvester's Chicago plants—three hundred FE members massed around the malleable gate. William Lyles went through that crowd—and past Felton and Twidell—to report to work. The senior Lyles claimed his sons threatened him and then paint-bombed his home, after which William pledged to "kill any person who tried to harm him or his property" and made clear his intentions by aiming a shotgun at Felton when he next showed up at the house.[6]

But the bad blood wasn't confined to the Lyles family, as Harvester's "wholesale back-to-work-movement" was lighting the fuse under what was

already the "powder-keg situation" around all the struck plants. It was provocative enough that some Harvester employees had already been reporting for
work, but up to that point they had largely been managerial personnel or employees not covered by the FE contract. As the foremen's efforts slowly increased the number of actual FE members attempting to enter the plants, conditions grew even more inflammatory. "They were successful at getting some
workers to cross the picket line," Jimmy Majors recalled, "not to walk across
the picket line, but they were transporting them into the plant in the trunks
of their automobiles, in the back seats covered up with tarpaulins or rugs or
whatever they could cover them up with." IH management "really worked at
it," said FE staff member Al Verri, who spent most of his time at the West
Pullman plant. "They went into the homes, picking up workers, and this was
when they used sightseeing buses picking up those workers, and when they
didn't have the buses they used cars. The cars would have their lights on, they
had flags on the cars, just like a funeral cortege. They would pick them up,
and go with their lights on right on into the plant." And in these efforts the
company was provided invaluable outside assistance. Chicago police officers,
the FE charged, were accompanying foremen on their visits to workers' homes
"for scab recruitment"; policemen were "soliciting workers, on foot and in patrol
cars, to go back to work"; and were "conducting well-organized motorcades of
scabs several blocks, through traffic signals and into the plants."[7]

   The FE put up resistance to this "scabherding" of the forceful, not pas-
sive, variety. In late September, for instance, eleven FE members—as well as
officials DeWitt Gilpin and Milt Burns—were arrested outside McCormick
Works for attempting to overturn an automobile that was conveying strikebreakers into the plant. Some union members even sacrificed their cars for
the union's cause. "I know of a few guys that were tired of driving their old
automobiles," Jimmy Majors remembers, "and they would just turn them
over and burn them around the street car stops at 36th and Western, 26th
and Western, all in those areas." Those considering crossing the picket lines
"thought that somebody's car had been turned over and burned, and they
would get on the streetcar and go back where they came from," Majors said.
"The idea," said Local 108 member Chuck Hall, "was to create a situation
where nobody would want to come around the plant."[8]

   To further drive home that point, as Local 101 member Hank Graber
recalled, the unique talents of a fellow striker, a large man named Leroy, were
put to good use. "He had a 52-inch waistline, which was quite an advantage.
He could put two half bricks underneath his jacket and you would not know if
he had the bricks there or not. He had a neat method of rolling a cigarette—it

was really a masterpiece. I don't know how he did it, but he could roll a cigarette with one hand—his left hand—and with his right hand he could toss a brick through the window of a scab's car," said Graber, admiringly.

> One time in particular this happened, and I was on the other side of Leroy. There was a policeman on my side, and a policeman on his side. There was a squad car at the curb, full of police. I just want to point out that the hand is quicker than the eye. You could look right at Leroy and never see him do anything. All you saw was a brick fly through the window of a car, and he had two hands, and he was moistening the cigarette, with both hands. Captain Barnes, he came by and wanted to know who the hell was on duty and who the hell was at that gate. This cop had one hell of a time explaining why he did not know where that brick came from or who was to blame. It was something to hear. Captain Barnes was fit to be tied that day.[9]

Outside Chicago, confrontations were growing more heated as well. In Richmond a picket line altercation led to an assault and battery arrest of an FE organizer, after which the Indiana state police arrived to supplement the entire Richmond police force which, along with the Wayne County sheriff's department, was already patrolling the Harvester plant there. And the Quad Cities reached a state of near civil war. In Rock Island the window at the FE's local headquarters was shattered by a large rock; a strikebreaker at the East Moline facility, driving down a dirt road early one morning, said he was flagged down by three men who slugged him and threatened him with far worse if he continued reporting for work. As in Indiana, the Illinois state police were called in to augment the city police departments already at full force around the plants.[10]

As usual, though, the FE members in Louisville would take a back seat to nobody in their efforts to enforce respect for their picket line. Sterling Neal, Bud James, and other members of the Local 236 leadership were repeatedly arrested for attempting to obstruct entry to the plant, but Jim Wright may have taken the most dramatic action in that regard. One morning, as some strikebreakers began reporting for work, Wright noticed, some distance away, a train sitting unattended on the rail line that crossed in front of the plant. Wright had once worked in a freight yard, and so he knew how to operate a locomotive, and he determined to back the train down the track far enough to block the plant gate. But just as he reached the train, the engineer returned, and took a dim view of Wright's plan. "He said, 'the hell with you, nigger,'" words which did not have a deterrent effect on

Wright. "I went up in that train, pulled him out of there, threw him off on the ground," Wright recalled, "and put that train in reverse." That achieved, at least momentarily, Wright's objective, as not only did he block entrance to the plant but he damaged some strikebreakers' property in the process. "Knocked cars everywhere you was going, cars all jammed up, wrecked cars." The police were promptly on the scene, and "they grabbed me out of that doggone train," Wright said, "and beat me to a pulp."[11]

Jim Mouser's encounters with the Louisville police may not have been as unpleasant, but they were more frequent. After being arrested on the first day of the strike, "Every time I showed up on the line out there I was locked up," Mouser said. "I'd get out of jail, I'd go out there, I'd just show up, and as soon as I'd show up, they'd pick up the phone, call the main gate, and say 'Lieutenant Dotson, Mouser's out here,'" and he found himself on his way to jail again. At least Mouser made some new friends in the process. "They had me in and out of there so much," he recalled, "the turnkey just called me Jim."[12]

The heavy police presence at the plants and the limitations imposed by injunctions meant that strike-related altercations were often pushed far from the picket lines. That was the case in the Quad Cities and was certainly also true in Louisville, and some of those incidents took on a deadly serious character. FE member Thomas Pearl—the man who had joined the integrated forays into Cherokee Park because, according to Jim Wright, he just generally liked a good fight—was charged with firing a shotgun through the bedroom window of James Coy's single-story house. Coy and Pearl were no strangers: Pearl had been working at the Louisville IH factory since shortly after it opened; Coy, who had been at the plant for less than a year, was a foreman in Pearl's department. The police said that Pearl, the father of four children under the age of six, professed no remorse when he was apprehended. "My babies were beginning to hurt," Pearl said, because of the hardship imposed by the strike, and he held one person especially responsible for that. Coy, who'd been crossing the FE picket line since the walkout began, "was taking my job away from me," Pearl insisted, voicing an ownership right to his position in the plant that would have resonated with the iron molders at McCormick Works in the nineteenth century.[13]

When the shooting occurred, Coy was in his kitchen with his wife and three children; all of them escaped injury. But the bitterness engendered by Harvester's back-to-work effort meant that the violence associated with the strike was likely only to intensify. The ongoing arrests and ever-more-serious charges also ensured mounting expenses for bail and legal fees. There were other costs as well. While the FE had never been able to count on fair press coverage from reactionary outlets like the *Chicago Tribune*, in Louisville the liberal *Courier-Journal* had been less contemptuous. "FE is a democratic union," the paper conceded. "It probably holds more membership meetings than any other union in Louisville, and allows free elections of local officers." That measured tone disintegrated during the course of the 1952 strike. A series of editorials castigated the "thugs and goons" on the FE picket lines who "have disregarded law, orderly procedure and public safety." Nor did the paper confine its criticisms to the current conflict. Local 236 "has been its own worst enemy," responsible for "a repeating pattern of work stoppages" and a "deliberate intention to delay production." All in all, the editors pronounced, the FE "is striving, with some success, to set a record of recklessness and contempt for legal process which is shockingly misplaced in the union movement in the United States." The forms of working-class resistance that even a liberal newspaper deemed acceptable were sharply delineated, and during the 1952 strike the FE had clearly stepped way beyond them. But while the *Courier-Journal* ran a front-page story about Harvester's "Full-Scale Drive to Urge Return of Strikers," the incendiary potential of the foremen's campaign—and with it the company's own apparent disregard for "orderly procedure and public safety"—was left unremarked upon.[14]

Still and all, more than a month into the strike, after the foremen's campaign had been underway for several weeks, the number of workers who'd crossed the picket lines remained fairly low—no doubt attributable both to solidarity within the FE ranks and to the deterrent effect of the forbidding "situation" union activists had created around the plants. In early October, Harvester announced to the press that over 430 employees were at work at the McCormick plant. Even if that figure was scrupulously accurate, and excluded managerial employees and replacement hires, it would have meant about 12 percent of the Local 108 membership: hardly a robust turnout. The company's claims were somewhat better for other plants—at Tractor Works and at Rock Falls, 20 percent of the workforce was said to have returned; at Richmond 30 percent. But only 13 percent of the workforce had shown up at the Farmall plant in Rock Island, and at this point Harvester wasn't releasing information about its West Pullman, East Moline, or Louisville plants, suggesting there was little for the company to brag about in those locations. In total at that point, the company was reporting that seventeen hundred of the striking workers were back—less than 7 percent of the FE membership in Harvester's plants.[15]

And the FE insisted that despite all of Harvester's efforts, the vast majority of African American workers were choosing to emulate Felton and

Twidell Lyles, the "FE die-hards," rather than their picket-line-crossing father. "Of the 1,500 Negroes at Harvester's McCormick Works, only 150 have permitted themselves to be used as scabs," said an FE publication in October. "While of the more than 4,000 Negro workers throughout Chicago the total number of scabs is only about 200." Some Harvester managers acknowledged that the FE's strength among its African American membership remained steadfast. "Our Colored employees, without question, were strongest in their support" of the strike, said an IH public relations official. "Only a relative few of our Negro employees actually joined the back-to-work movement."[16]

Even if the FE's forces remained at this point more solidified than might be expected, however, in its war with International Harvester the union could hardly afford to divert resources to yet another front. But an incident one early morning on a South Side Chicago street would make that imperative. Suddenly the legal difficulty facing Thomas Pearl—accused of malicious shooting with intent to kill—paled in comparison to even graver trouble for another FE member. This particular FE member, moreover, had long been one of the union's stalwarts, dubbed "the key man" in the 1952 strike. On October 10, when the walkout entered its fiftieth day, Harold Ward was arrested for murder.

27.
We Were Gone

"Grudges like heavy hangovers from men and women whose fathers were not yet born when the bomb was thrown, the court was rigged, and the deed was done."

—Nelson Algren

For the historically minded and class-conscious leaders of the FE, it was a given that in their 1952 battle with International Harvester they would invoke a bygone struggle. "The background of this attack on the 30,000 members of the Farm Equipment Workers-UE," read one union publication put out during the strike, "was laid in 1886 when workers were fighting for the eight-hour day. Their fight was made bloody by Harvester controlled cops who attacked them, killing numbers in a vain effort by this world-wide corporation to hold back, by any means possible, the advance of working people toward decent conditions."[1]

But this was meant to be rhetorical flourish, not a real-time report from the field. As the 1952 strike wore on, however, it seemed that what had been long past and largely forgotten (by everyone outside the FE, at least) was growing eerily familiar. And then, in the midst of this latest labor uprising: a mysterious murder, linked again to McCormick Works, and a dragnet that targeted union leaders and threatened their very lives. The specter of Haymarket seemed determined to make a return visit.

In the early morning hours of Friday, October 3, 1952, about a block from his home, fifty-two-year-old William Foster was struck in the head and died in a hospital a few hours later. The attack took place on Chicago's South Side, about five miles from McCormick Works, where Foster was employed. No witnesses came forward immediately and no murder weapon was recovered. Foster had worked for International Harvester for twenty-seven years; he was African American; he began crossing the FE's picket lines early in the strike. Those were the only facts that could be established with certainty in the aftermath of the incident. But as was the case with the bombing in 1886, a paucity of evidence wouldn't stop the company—and those providing it with assistance—from quickly and publicly jumping to conclusions. Before the day was out, and thus in time for the evening papers, John McCaffrey declared that Foster's "only purpose was to earn a living peacefully," and offered $10,000 for information leading to the perpetrators of this "atrocious crime." Harvester's reward helped generate coast-to-coast coverage, and with headlines on October 3 like "STRIKE-DEFIER BEATEN TO DEATH" and "HE WENT TO WORK, NOW HE'S DEAD," the press declared the motive for the crime self-evident without bothering to investigate first. The police did the same. "Police assume that Foster was killed because he crossed a picket line," the *Chicago Tribune* reported, and Commissioner Timothy O'Connor promptly ordered his men to "round up everyone . . . connected with the killing," which translated to a roster of thirty FE officials—nobody not associated with the union made the list—sought for questioning. Actually, bringing them in might take a while, because "Saturday and Sunday were hard days to find union officials," lamented Captain Barnes, who himself spent much of his Sunday at the Bears-Cardinals football game.[2]

But, in fact, that same day many of those officials were in full public view, appearing on live television on local Chicago station WBKB. During a half-hour broadcast, sponsored by the union, Jerry Fielde, Milt Burns, and DeWitt Gilpin, along with leaders from FE locals in Chicago, the Quad Cities, Richmond, and Louisville, presented the union's spin on the 1952 walkout. International Harvester's public relations department summarized the show this way: "It began with harsh criticism of the Chicago police and ended with the singing of the Internationale." Actually, the song at the finale was "Solidarity Forever," but for Harvester the American union ballad and the French communist anthem were pretty much the same thing. During the show William Foster's killing was of course addressed, as DeWitt Gilpin insisted that "the only persons who could have benefited from Foster's death are officials of the Harvester company who are seeking to break our strike."[3]

Those words did not prompt the Chicago police to broaden their focus. Though initial news reports said that Foster provided no information about his attacker before he died, within a day the police claimed that Foster said he had been "hit by a Negro with a three-foot piece of pipe." That suggested that one of the first FE officials detained for interrogation—Local 108 activist Clarence Stoecker—was not the right guy. German American Stoecker had been "seized in his home" on October 4 by police who, the *Tribune* noted, "found a copy of the communist *Daily Worker*" there. After being held overnight Stoecker was released, but not before he was, for unspecified reasons, charged with disorderly conduct. The police then cycled through a few other suspects. African American FE member Roscoe Steele was subjected to a lie detector test before being dismissed, though he also was charged with disorderly conduct on the way out. When "FE die-hard" Felton Lyles conveniently showed up at Commissioner O'Connor's office—along with

Grant Oakes, Jimmy Majors, and forty other union members, to protest the "police terror and intimidation" and the "indiscriminate arrests" they'd been subjected to—he was promptly yanked out of the crowd and handed over to detectives for questioning. Lyles, too, was later released.[4]

But, then, seven days after Foster's death, the authorities decided they had their man, as they arrested Harold Ward, financial secretary of Local 108. His photo, taken at the police lineup, appeared in papers across the country with captions like "ACCUSED AS MURDERER." A "mystery witness" whose identity remained a closely guarded secret had come forward to identify Ward as the killer, the police said. A few days later, when Ward appeared in felony court for his arraignment, so too did three hundred FE members, who made "derogatory remarks" to the state's attorney and were cordoned off by the fifty police officers in the courtroom. The judge was unmoved by the union's show of support and refused to set bail for Ward, who pled not guilty. The judge's decision was also no doubt influenced by the fact that Ward had already been charged with an earlier assault—he was accused of badly beating a non-striker with a baseball bat—for which he would also stand trial. Ward would spend the remainder of the strike in Cook County Jail. If he had a window in his cell he might have been able to gaze out onto his former place of employment, McCormick Works, situated a short distance away.[5]

Harold Ward "is the most important Negro leader of our strike—the key man," said Matt Halas, the president of Local 108. "Harvester Company ordered his arrest in order to cripple the strike and for no other reason." Back in 1886, Cyrus McCormick II had indeed ensured that the labor leader he viewed as the "key man" causing him trouble—August Spies—had been arrested, and it was hardly surprising that FE leaders believed that in 1952, to borrow Yogi Berra's phrase, it was déjà vu all over again. "Just like Foster's death is serving the company's purpose, so did the Haymarket Massacre of 1886 *at these same McCormick Works*," FE literature insisted. Ward, like Spies, was not native to Chicago, as Ward had migrated north as a teenager from his birthplace in Jackson, Tennessee. Both Spies and Ward were just thirty years old when they were taken into custody, and both men were graced with an eloquence and charisma that made them influential leaders. Ward "was a very important guy," said Chuck Hall, who also worked at the McCormick plant. "He was a very handsome, imposing guy. He was extremely active, and he had a following. People listened to him."[6]

Ward, following a long line of troublemakers in the McCormick factory, was an iron molder, employed since 1944 in the malleable foundry. "His militant union activity in fighting to win grievances, in fighting speed-up, and in fighting to win the strikes his union was engaged in," the FE said, earned him the enmity of Harvester management. Ward received at least ten reprimands from IH, including a four-week suspension in 1946 and a three-week suspension in 1950; in both instances the FE secured his reinstatement and back pay. But during the 1952 strike Harvester had fired Ward after his first arrest on the assault charge, and the company hoped, one way or another, to finally be rid of him for good.[7]

And like Spies before him, Ward was an avowed political radical, associated with the movement that in the twentieth century was as feared and loathed by the establishment as anarchism had been in the nineteenth. Ward "has a long list of communist associations," the *Tribune* pointed out. He'd traveled to Warsaw for the Second World Peace Conference in 1950, after which he'd been part of an American labor delegation that visited the Soviet Union. "I found a free, healthy, happy people," Ward said about the USSR, "and in all my life, I never experienced such a feeling of being free from prejudice and discrimination—something that a Negro in America today can never know." During that trip Ward also stopped over in France to meet with workers at the International Harvester factory there. Through that encounter, he saw up close how American foreign policy was underwriting IH and enabling the exploitation of its workforce abroad: "A pack of cigarettes an hour is what a French farm equipment worker earns under the Marshall Plan," Ward said, and upon his return home he made it a mission to tell other union members "the truth about communism and about the Marshall Plan." Though not as widely known as Spies was in his day, Ward was recognized as "one of the most active and prominent Negro unionists in the area," one left-wing paper said.[8]

But to the FE leadership Harold Ward was more than just an exemplar of radicalism: he was a colleague and friend, behind bars and in danger of being dispatched in the same manner that August Spies had been. So the "Committee to Free Harold Ward" was launched, and taking the lead on the public relations front was twenty-six-year-old Chicagoan Oscar Brown, Jr., then known for hosting *Negro Newsfront*, the first national radio news program produced by and for African Americans. Decades later Brown would be widely regarded for his pioneering jazz compositions and hailed by the *Chicago Tribune* as "one of the greatest singer songwriters this city has produced," but in 1952 the *Tribune* would not have been singing his praises. Brown was then, like Ward, a member of the Communist Party. "Harold Ward symbolizes the new Negro," Brown wrote, making a pitch for donations to Ward's defense, "a strong man, unafraid, a strong man getting stronger, a strong man comin' on to full freedom. He symbolizes the growing unity of Negro and white workers; a unity that will rock the foundation of industrial exploitation in every corner of the nation." Brown also authored a one-act play based on Ward's case called *The Scab*. One of the performers enlisted for the four-character production was FE member Ed Dvorak but the others were aspiring professionals: African Americans Fred Pinkard and Beatrice Williams—both of whom later went on to work regularly in theater, film, and television—and white actor Raymond Stough (who had a less successful acting career). Earlier in 1952 Williams and Stough had been married; one thousand guests—including the bride's entire family (from Chicago) and the groom's (from North Dakota)—attended what *Jet* magazine then called "probably the biggest interracial marriage in Chicago's history."[9]

To help raise awareness—and money—*The Scab* was performed at Chicago union halls and community centers during the strike, but it also played out of town, at the National Negro Labor Council's convention in Cleveland. June Ward, Harold's wife, introduced the performance, indicating that her husband "was not guilty of murder but was guilty of going to Russia, and was guilty of fighting for the rank and file." The play was not the only entertainment that evening, as Paul Robeson also sang at the convention. The assembled delegates then passed a resolution calling the prosecution of Ward a "'legal' lynching" and pledged to work "unceasingly to mobilize full financial and moral support" for him.[10]

A considerable portion of the money raised through these efforts would go to William Scott Stewart, retained by the union to defend Ward on both charges pending against him. A graduate of Chicago's déclassé but politically connected John Marshall Law School, Stewart began his career trying cases from the other side; as an assistant state's attorney in the early 1920s he'd become well known as "the hanging prosecutor" for the many convictions he'd obtained in sensational murder trials. But he soon switched to defense work, where he became notorious for his (usually successful) work on behalf of Chicago mobsters like Roger "The Terrible" Touhy and Paul "The Waiter" Ricca. The courtroom finesse of Stewart and his partner W. W. O'Brien earned enduring fame when they scored acquittals in the murder trials of their clients, the seemingly very guilty Belva Gaertner and Beulah Annan—later fictionalized as Velma Kelly and Roxie Hart in the musical *Chicago*. William Scott Stewart may have kept questionable company but he was a master at securing victories against long odds, and Harold Ward's case fit that bill. Expertise of Stewart's caliber, however, did not come cheap.[11]

Ward's arrest, then, had removed from the front lines one of the strike's most effective leaders, and his defense depleted resources badly needed elsewhere. And the widespread presumption that Ward, or somebody in the FE, was responsible for William Foster's death had other deleterious effects on the union. On October 16, International Harvester, citing Foster's killing, finally obtained for McCormick Works what it had already received for its plants elsewhere: a court injunction, stipulating that there could be no more than six pickets at any one gate. The Chicago police, too, stepped up their commitment to "give all the protection we can to those who want to return to work"; all but four of the city's thirty-eight police districts helped shepherd strikebreakers into the plant, and some foremen and scabbing workers received round-the-clock protection. And union officials complained in late October that yet another law enforcement agency was intervening on Harvester's behalf. "People who call themselves FBI agents have been swarming around the Louisville area questioning people about the strikers," said the UE's general counsel, reminding FE members that they had "no legal obligation . . . to discuss any matter whatsoever with any FBI or other police agent."[12]

Despite this heightened interference, violent incidents continued apace as the walkout entered its third month. In Rock Island in late October, some two hundred pickets engaged in a shoving, slugging battle with local police over access to the Farmall plant's main gate; four FE members were arrested. More ominous trouble cropped up away from the plants, as explosions tore apart a strikebreaker's car in Louisville and blew out windows at the homes of two foremen in Chicago. "Bomb Terror," read the banner headlines; "an outrage in civilized society," said Harvester management, calling the attacks "the latest in a series of violent incidents which has marked this radically-led strike." With emotions running raw, and the situation on the ground increasingly difficult to control, FE leaders—however they may have felt, abstractly, about the legitimacy of direct action in the midst of class struggle—had good reason to worry that they might soon have another Harold Ward case on their hands.[13]

Amidst all this travail there was one deeply gratifying moment for the FE. The UAW had initiated a raid at Harvester's Canton, Illinois, plant before the strike began; at the election in late October 1952, despite the barrage of negative publicity it had been subject to, the FE retained its position there with a comfortable 57 percent of the vote. But after its loss in Canton the UAW only stepped up its raiding efforts, filing a decertification petition at the IH plant in Richmond, Indiana, and by November the UAW was "working in practically all other locations" to strip the FE of representation within International Harvester.[14]

So for the FE leadership the anxieties were mounting with each passing day. It may have been "the strongest union in not having any money," but the moochers had exhausted their supplies, and union members were struggling to make ends meet. FE officials grew bitter about what they took to be the failure of the UE's top leadership to "fully understand the viciousness of the strike" and the "refusal or inability of the National [UE] office to understand our financial plight" and properly support the Harvester walkout. "We do not have adequate staff to handle the picket lines and other work," read an urgent letter sent in mid-November to top UE officials. "We have reached a real financial crisis at Farmall and East Moline, where the National Office yesterday refused to give us any further funds and where the locals were compelled to shut off relief, which demoralizes more people in 5 minutes than we are able to strengthen in 2 weeks."[15]

And in terms of demoralizing developments, there were ominous ones afoot that did not bode well for the FE, or for anyone remotely associated with the Communist Party. The strike took place while the Korean War was in full swing, and thus newspapers supplied daily accounts of the "hordes of screaming Chinese Reds" responsible for the mounting number of G.I. casualties. Shortly after HUAC's visit to Chicago, "FBI agents swooped down on suspected Reds in seven states," generating more hyperbolic headlines as eighteen people were charged with advocating the violent overthrow of the government. Slipping out to the movies offered no respite, for films like *My Son John* (a devoted mother is shamed by the discovery that she has raised a communist) and *Big Jim McClain* (John Wayne, playing a HUAC investigator, roots out reds infiltrating Hawaii's labor movement) played in local theaters while the walkout was underway. And then came the general election on November 4: Dwight Eisenhower, attacking "Korea, Communism and Corruption," won a landslide victory over Democrat Adlai Stevenson, who did not carry even his home state of Illinois, and Republicans regained control of Congress as well. In Illinois, Republican William Stratton was elected governor, and the GOP also took all other major state offices and captured a majority in the state legislature. Anti-communist crusader Joe McCarthy won reelection in Wisconsin while his chief antagonist in the US Senate, Democrat William Benton of Connecticut, went down to defeat. Among the power and opinion brokers in the United States, then, corporations like International Harvester had many friends at all levels; the increasingly isolated FE would find only enemies.[16]

Just after the Republicans' electoral triumph, when the strike was twelve weeks old, Harvester claimed that about fifty-seven hundred employees had returned to work: though more than three-quarters of the FE membership remained out, by this point the return to work was gathering momentum, and Harvester said partial production was underway at some plants. IH stepped up the pressure by running advertisements promising "permanent jobs that will continue after the strike is over" to any applicants willing to defy the union. A grim desperation began to settle over the picket lines. "I was standing out there, hungry, ugly, hadn't shaved in a month or something," Jim Wright remembered. "It was a hopeless situation, workers riding in, guys throwing rocks at the cars, hitting 'em, breaking out windows and stuff, police beating 'em and carrying 'em downtown, dragging 'em down the street." The ranks of picket line crashers began to include those who had heretofore been loyal union members, a grave portent not lost on union leaders. In November "the scabs from our own plant went in there and worked, started working, and we had about one hundred or two hundred scabs" that were FE members, said Wright. "I knew then that we were gone. We were gone. When our guys decided to work, when [the company] won them over, I knew we were gone."[17]

"We were gone": by mid-November the rest of the FE leadership had reached that conclusion as well. John McCaffrey and International Harvester's management knew it too. The strike had been lost. All that remained to determine was how much the union would have to give up to end it.

28.
The Big Frame-Up, Revisited

At the end of the 1952 Harvester strike, Jim Mouser found himself exactly where he'd been when it all began: in jail. On Thursday, November 13—the eighty-fifth day of the walkout—Mouser was arrested for violating an anti-noise ordinance, as he refused to stop blaring "We'll never give up!" from a sound truck parked in front of the Louisville plant. Shortly after he arrived at the lockup, Mouser's new old friend the jailer told him that someone had come to see him. "And he opened the door, let me out, and there's Val, my wife," Mouser said. "I says, what are you doing down here? What do you want?" What she wanted, Valerie Mouser replied, was to get out of there, since she too had been hauled in by the police. The picket line that day had been augmented by about fifty strikers' wives along with their children, who held signs like "Don't Take Away My Daddy's Job." True to family form, Valerie Mouser had refused to move aside when ordered to by Police Chief Heustis, and so she was sent to join her husband behind bars. At least Mouser's mother, who had also joined the protest that day, had not been arrested; she took charge of her nine-year-old grandson and they both continued marching by the plant gate. "My Daddy is a Union Man Not a Scab," read the sign carried by young John Mouser.[1]

However disconcerted Jim Mouser may have been by his wife's arrest, he was not as miserable as Jerry Fielde was soon to be. The day after Jim and Valerie Mouser found themselves together in the Louisville jail, IH and FE officials—joined by top UE leader James Matles—gathered at the Congress Hotel in downtown Chicago, though not in the same room. Since the level of animosity by this point meant that face-to-face conversations were unlikely to be productive, the labor and management teams holed up in distant quarters while a federal mediator conveyed messages between them. Believing the walkout was crumbling and their leverage gone, FE leaders nonetheless dug in on two points. The first was an issue that had been central to the 1952 walkout since day one (and indeed to the FE since its founding): the union's desire to retain paid time off for stewards. The other concern was one that had arisen more recently, as FE officials sought the reinstatement of the seventeen workers—all of them key local leaders—who had been fired by Harvester for the "acts of violence or hoodlumism" they had engaged in during the course of the strike. The list of discharged employees included Harold Ward, Jim Wright, and Jim Mouser.

But John McCaffrey and IH labor relations manager William Reilly, sensing blood in the water, would not concede an inch on either point. Stewards "would no longer be paid by the company for roaming the shop 'investigating' grievances and stirring up trouble." As far as the fired FE members were concerned, McCaffrey was emphatic: "They will never work for this company again." These issues, so management maintained, "were of no consequence to rank-and-file employees, but they were vital to the political purposes of the union leaders," which of course ignored the very consequential fact that the decent wages and working conditions enjoyed by the FE's rank and file rested on a bedrock of aggressive and unfettered stewardship. Having made their positions clear, on Saturday, November 15, Harvester officials decamped to IH headquarters, a few blocks north up Michigan Avenue, where they typed up "the contract in the final form the company was willing to sign" and conveyed a copy early that afternoon to the union's leadership. And then they waited. Several hours passed. Finally, at 6:30 that evening, the door to Reilly's office opened and Jerry Fielde, accompanied by James Matles, entered. Without a word the men took seats at the table in the room. The contract was placed in front of Fielde. He signed it. Then the two union officials rose from the table, as silently as they had entered, and left.[2]

Only two days earlier, Jim Mouser had vowed "We'll Never Give Up!" but the FE just had. Union official Al Verri likened the signing of the 1952 IH contract to Germany's acceptance of the Treaty of Versailles after World War I. "I never saw such a look of defeat on [Jerry's] face," Verri said, after Fielde returned from Harvester's headquarters. "If you looked at his signature that day, you'd see it didn't have the clear distinctive features it always had. It was more of a scribble."[3]

There was good reason for Fielde to feel shattered: the contract he signed gave McCaffrey and IH management everything they had sought at the outset of the eighty-seven-day strike, and then some. Harvester's retooled wage system was to be implemented in full, which the FE leadership was convinced would mean retimed jobs, wage cuts and speedup throughout the chain. Under this new pay scheme, the favorable allowance provisions the FE had fought so hard to establish were largely eliminated. Union stewards, as the company had demanded from the outset, would henceforth be compensated only for their time spent in meetings with management, and the no-strike clause was tightened up as well. But the agreement also included brand new language that would further weaken the FE: two "escape periods" which allowed Harvester employees to opt out of the automatic deduction of their union dues or resign from the FE altogether. And the

FE members discharged during the strike, as John McCaffrey had promised, were "through at Harvester." There was no question about which side had prevailed in this contest, as Harvester announced that the union had suffered "total defeat," and even the left-wing press acknowledged that "the new contract is a victory for the company." It was a triumph for the labor establishment as well. Because IH management had largely eradicated the distinctive provisions the FE leadership had been committed to—and added others they opposed—Harvester workers were now covered by an agreement "substantially similar to that of the UAW-CIO."[4]

Nor did FE officials endeavor to provide any sort of positive spin on the settlement, though they did defend the decision to strike in the first place. In an unusually frank public assessment of the walkout written shortly after it ended, Milt Burns argued that Harvester's take-it-or-leave-it stance had dictated the response: "Our union could not be a party to any voluntary agreement on a formula for speedup, worsened conditions, weakened protection." If the FE leadership had capitulated at the start, Burns insisted, the union's integrity would have been irreparably compromised, and to underscore that he invoked the words of a worker from Local 236 in Louisville at the end of the strike: "If our union had accepted the same company proposal we are now forced to take here, without fighting back on the picket lines, I would have called it a damned sell-out. The workers will find out we are right. Sooner or later they'll say, let's take up where we left off."[5]

But if the new contract was so objectionable, why then did the FE leadership agree to it? In fact, not all of them had wanted to. The union contingent that had gathered at the Congress Hotel in the last days of the strike included not just the national officers but representatives from all the striking IH locals. Some of the local leaders present—chief among them the Quad Cities firebrand John Watkins—argued that it would be preferable to return to work without signing the onerous agreement and endeavor to enforce better terms through organized shop-floor resistance. "Several [delegates] honestly held that position," Milt Burns later wrote about the robust debate surrounding the proposal, "especially since signing the contract indisputably meant accepting a weaker agreement than the contract in force since 1946." Watkins was willing to gamble that the FE rank and file's militancy, even without any contractual protection, could match Harvester's power. Others, though, were not willing to take that bet, as Milt Burns insisted:

> History is loaded up with instances of labor moving to improve conditions only to wind up with less than it started with, because of lack of finances, police brutality, etc. Always, however, it has been

the obligation of leadership to provide the maximum umbrella of protection under each new set of conditions.

To send workers back without a contract would have been a form of desertion tantamount to saying, "You had your chance and muffed it. Now you can go back without seniority and with no grievance representation on wages and conditions."[6]

In 1886, of course, labor had taken great strides forward only to be rudely shoved back; the reactionary crackdown and the destruction of the once-formidable iron molders' union meant the workers at the McCormick plant went without any form of organization—and were thus subject to exploitative pay rates, crippling conditions, and arbitrary dismissals—for over half a century. FE leaders were well aware of that reality, given how frequently they referenced Haymarket. Their admiration for their anarchist antecedents found expression in the FE's practice of militant disruption, but for Burns and other officials who sided with him, their syndicalist sympathies had limits. Evidently they proved persuasive, as the majority of the assembled delegates voted to sign the agreement. The instinct to preserve their hard-fought contract—even a watered-down, de-radicalized one—prevailed over Watkins's faith in direct action.

But there were also some immediate considerations at play. Had the FE returned to work without a contact—and so without formal recognition by the company—all IH plants would have been technically devoid of representation and thus subject to immediate poaching from other unions. No doubt James Matles was present during the final round of negotiations to underscore that the UE was unwilling to support a continued strike against IH, and similarly was in no position to defend against a slew of simultaneous UAW raids. If FE leaders had opted to go back to work without a contract, they would have done so on their own.

So in 1952 as in 1886, workers at Harvester had suffered a monumental defeat, but this time around they retained union recognition and the fundamental protections provided by their contract. The other parallel with Haymarket, however—the fate of Harold Ward—had yet to be determined. The wait would not be long, for Ward's consecutive trials—the first for assault, the next for murder—began during Thanksgiving week 1952, less than two weeks after the strike ended. Presiding over both cases was Wendell E. Green, one of Chicago's few African American judges. Green began his career in the early 1920s in a law practice with fellow University of Chicago graduate Earl Dickerson, who would gain fame in 1940 when he won a Supreme Court victory in the *Hansberry* case, which challenged restrictive covenants in Illinois.[7] Green first became a municipal court judge in 1942 and would, in 1950, become the first African American appointed to the Circuit Court of Illinois. By 1952 Green had presided over several high-profile criminal cases and had earned national recognition for his rectitude and evenhandedness. Ward and his supporters must have been relieved that his case would be overseen by Green, who would ensure a fair trial, hardly a given within the city of Chicago. That Green was African American was no doubt also viewed positively by those within the FE. Though there is no way of knowing, the fact that Harold Ward ended up in Judge Green's courtroom may have been no accident: Ward's well-connected lawyer, William Scott Stewart, could have had something to do with that.[8]

Judge Green also ran a tight ship and had a propensity to put in long hours, not something that would work in State's Attorney John Boyle's favor when he requested more time to prepare Ward's murder case. "The best administration of justice lies in a speedy trial," Judge Green said. "This is a simple case, hinging mostly on identification, and almost anybody can prosecute it." Boyle's reminder that Thanksgiving was just a few days away also left Judge Green unmoved. "Lawyers don't get holidays," he replied flatly. Boyle, obviously peeved, insisted there was no urgent need to proceed immediately, unless, he suggested, "Has your honor the feeling that the defendant is not guilty?" This did not go over well with Judge Green, who leaned forward and demanded: "Why do you ask me that question?" Boyle, glowering, remained silent, so Green posed his query again—three times. Finally, Boyle conceded, mumbling an apologetic "Well, I didn't mean it that way," and the judge settled back in his chair.[9]

Thus, on Monday, November 24, Harold Ward's assault trial began. It was over by the next evening. Watson Wright, a McCormick Works employee who had crossed the FE picket line, testified that Harold Ward was the man who had beaten him with a baseball bat, sending him to the hospital with a fractured skull. But on the stand Ward denied the accusation, and attorney Stewart produced witnesses who swore they'd seen Wright somewhere else at the time he said the altercation had occurred. In the end, Stewart argued, this was just one man's word against another's, and he hinted that Wright, who'd been back at work and so was on International Harvester's payroll at the time of the incident, was a "hired witness" who had reason to participate in the frame-up of an innocent man. In the early evening on Tuesday, after the jury had deliberated for two and a half hours, Ward was acquitted on the assault charge. The courtroom, packed with FE members, erupted in "shouts and cheers," which were quickly silenced by Judge Green.

Despite the late hour—and that the following day was the Wednesday before Thanksgiving—Green reminded everyone in the courtroom that his next case would begin promptly in the morning. Procedural details and jury selection took up much of the next few days (in deference to the jury pool, though not the state's attorney, Judge Green did allow everyone to have Thanksgiving and the weekend off) so the trial for the killing of William Foster finally got underway late in the afternoon on Monday, December 1. The prosecutors reiterated that, should they secure a conviction in the case, they would seek a death sentence.[10]

Harold Ward's life now rested in the hands of ten men and two women, all of them white. The jury heard first from the victim's widow, who wept on the stand as she recalled sending her husband off to work at six in the morning and then seeing his crumpled, bloody body on the street some moments later. Ruth Foster had not seen who bludgeoned her husband, but the prosecution at long last produced its "mystery witness" who claimed he had. African American Edward Warren, not a Harvester employee, said he was sitting in his car about thirty feet away when he saw a man strike William Foster with an iron bar. On the stand Warren identified Harold Ward as the assailant, indicating that he had a very clear view of Ward since he was parked such a short distance from the crime scene. After Foster fell to the ground, Warren said, Ward "continued to smash at [the] prone body." Foster's skull, the coroner testified, had been "crushed like an egg shell" and there was no doubt the beating had caused his death.

That was the entirety of the state's presentation, and with such dramatic testimony, including an eyewitness fingering Ward in the courtroom, it seemed airtight. But on cross-examination, William Scott Stewart noted that the description Warren had originally supplied the police—a clean-shaven man with "very dark" skin—didn't much resemble the lighter-complexioned, mustachioed Ward. And since Warren had not come forward until sometime after the murder, Stewart wondered aloud whether the $10,000 reward International Harvester had offered might have helped jog his memory.

Stewart then presented the case for the defense. Harold Ward took the stand, insisting he'd been at home asleep when Foster had been attacked; Ward's wife and her mother (who lived with them) backed up his story. Another Local 108 member said he'd picked Ward up that morning at 8 a.m., and they drove together to the union hall. But while these statements might have been easily discounted, the testimony of the other witnesses Stewart produced could not be. In the days following Foster's murder, three men who lived in the neighborhood also said they'd seen the assault and had provided information when the police had canvassed the area. Stewart put each of them on the stand, and they all indicated that Ward was not the man they had seen attacking Foster. In his "very powerful closing argument," Stewart emphasized these exculpatory statements, along with the fact that the police and state's attorney's office had failed to inform the defense about the existence of these crucial eyewitnesses. Ward's legal team, aided by private detectives and the diligent investigatory efforts of FE members, had ferreted them out.[11]

Judge Green made good on his commitment to ensure a speedy trial, so when the defense rested on Tuesday evening he sent the jury off to deliberate. They came back in less than two hours.

About the recent bitter strike, DeWitt Gilpin had written of "the man Harvester was willing to pay $10,000 to burn." In Cook County Jail, "less than a thousand yards from his own foundry at the McCormick Works across Western Avenue, a Harvester striker sat in murderer's row, framed on a murder charge. He was proof to all Harvester workers that the Big Frame-up always ended, from 1886 to 1952, in the shadow of the chair, whether your name be Parsons, Spies, Lingg—or Harold Ward."[12]

But this time the script played out differently. The verdict was not guilty. Harold Ward would go not to meet the executioner but home to his wife and children.

The jurors had discussed the evidence at length, the foreman indicated, and on their first ballot had voted unanimously for acquittal. "They had much more confidence in the witnesses for the defense than in those for the state," he said. William Scott Stewart, who'd ensured that the big frame-up was a big bust, had proven himself to be worth every penny the union had invested in him. After weeks of headlines devoted to the "strike goon," the *Chicago Tribune* tucked news of Ward's release off its front page, but the story nonetheless still drew national attention. "UNION OFFICIAL ACQUITTED BY WHITE JURY," was the way one Texas newspaper reported it.[13]

So the FE had preserved a contract and saved the life of an outspoken left-wing activist: in those two significant respects, the union's leadership had refused to allow history to repeat itself. But as Haymarket had been for the anarchists, the 1952 strike proved to be a catastrophe from which the FE could never fully recover. In the twentieth century at International Harvester, radical unionism was about to run its course.

29

We Mean Business

L ate one evening, toward the very end of the 1952 Harvester strike, Sonya Burns remembered being awakened by a heated argument emanating from her living room, where her husband Milt was meeting with a small group of men. The others were, she knew, officials of the Communist Party. It was not unusual for Milt to take part in such conclaves, for he was, in her words, "the political commissar" within the FE, serving as the point of contact between the party and the union. This particular conversation, however, was not going well. The CP officials were insisting that the Harvester strike should be continued and workers kept on the picket lines. "And it was at this time that Milt said," as Sonya Burns recalled, "Bullshit! This strike is lost, these guys are starving, we cannot keep them out any longer." She then heard one of the officials say, "'Well, we will'—*we*—'will keep them out another three weeks.'" Infuriated by the presumption, Milt Burns promptly took a swing at the party man and sent him crashing to the floor. A few days after this acrimonious encounter, the FE leadership, obviously ignoring the CP's instructions, terminated the walkout.[1]

The literal collapse of the party official in the Burns's home signified a broader, more consequential breakdown, since the 1952 strike brought about, or at least hastened along, several fundamental transformations of the FE's character. As a result of these changes, how to perpetuate the ceaseless class warfare that had defined the union from the outset—or indeed, whether it was possible to sustain it at all—became increasingly contested questions.

Since its nascent days as a clandestine organizing committee, with the Moscow-trained activist Joe Weber serving as godfather, the FE's principal source of ideological inspiration had been the Communist Party. Yet even among the left-led unions, the maverick FE leadership's relationship with the Party had always been complicated. On some occasions (like the 1948 Progressive Party campaign) the FE had fulsomely embraced positions endorsed by the CP; on others (like the signing of the Taft-Hartley affidavits), the union broke with party policy early and publicly. By the 1950s, though the FE's key leaders remained committed to Marxism in theory, in practice they became increasingly frustrated by the CP's apparent insensitivity to the mounting set of real-life pressures their union faced. The 1952 strike marked the moment when the connection between the party organization and the FE leadership became frayed beyond repair. The dissociation between the FE leadership and the Party was done quietly—none of the union's top officials became vocal anti-communists and all refused to inform on their former comrades—but it was conclusive. In fact, Burns at least formally severed his ties to the CP in the spring of 1953, when in response to an NLRB directive, he signed, for the first time, the Taft-Hartley mandated noncommunist affidavit.[2]

The strike also accelerated the deterioration of the uneasy partnership between the FE and the UE. "I don't think any of us were really happy about that marriage," FE organizer Al Verri said, as the once highly autonomous FE leadership was obliged to adjust to subordinate status in a much larger organization. This conflict found expression in the antagonism between national FE officials and Ernest DeMaio, who as the UE district president in Chicago possessed, at least nominally, authority over them. The hot-tempered DeMaio "had absolute control over his staff," Verri maintained. That was not an administrative style the FE leadership easily adapted to. "We disagreed and we said so," Verri said, who recalled one particularly explosive meeting with DeMaio during the 1952 strike. DeMaio "just couldn't stand our disagreeing with him. He got redder, and huffy about it," and so Verri, along with Jerry Fielde and DeWitt Gilpin, "just walked out on him. We said we're not going to meet with you. Milt Burns followed us out, and had us come back in, and we had to apologize for the kind of language we used."[3]

And outside Chicago, local FE leaders—one in particular, anyhow—harbored simmering antipathy toward the UE that boiled over in 1952. John Watkins, whose signature was on the FE's original 1938 CIO charter, had always been the union's key man in the crucial Quad Cities area and he often played an essential role—which was literally, at least in part, a role—in IH negotiations. "A familiar sight near the close of Harvester bargaining sessions," one management journal reported in 1947, "is Watkins plunging into the smoky room straight from the Rock Island train."

> He listens to an explanation of a settlement that [Jerry] Fielde had convinced company negotiators they should take. Watkins knocks this down, labels it completely unacceptable with his constituents. Then he leans back with an air of daring the others to please him. It is a tough assignment to try and figure out something by which he will not be angered.
>
> A favorite out-of-hours argument among Harvester's labor relations staff is whether the Watkins-Fielde act is spontaneous or pre-arranged. It never seems to generate any sparks between the two livest wires in FE-CIO.[4]

Beyond his part in this bit of negotiating theater, Watkins had been central to the FE's culture of shop-floor confrontation. But he was constitutionally incapable of submitting readily to discipline, whether the entity attempting to enforce it was International Harvester or the Communist Party, and so he was not always on the same page as his union's national leadership. Nevertheless Watkins maintained a positive working relationship with fellow live-wire Jerry Fielde and the FE's other top officials as well, bonded by their marrow-deep mistrust of management and an abiding faith in rank-and-file militancy. And from their long history with Watkins, the FE leadership had learned to do two things: respect the authority Watkins commanded among a significant chunk of the union's membership; and avoid, as much as possible, meddling in the affairs of the Quad Cities locals.

But Watkins's ability to get along with his superiors deteriorated rapidly once those superiors were officials of the UE. "The farm equipment people felt like they were second-class citizens within UE," said one Quad Cities FE member, bitterness Watkins certainly harbored. Before the FE-UE merger Watkins had been the FE's district president in the Quad Cities; after the amalgamation he was relegated to a staff position answering to the UE's district president in the same area. Watkins bristled at what he saw as "the UE campaign to take over FE locals," and his resentment deepened during the 1952 walkout as he believed the UE provided too much interference and too little financial support. UE top official James Matles's sudden appearance at negotiations to ensure the strike's termination—with a signed contract—was for Watkins the last straw. In the immediate aftermath of the strike he remained loyal to the FE, but Watkins began seriously contemplating a move away from the union he had helped found.[5]

Other officials whose names were also on the FE's original charter, however, would beat him to it. In April 1953 Jerry Fielde took an indefinite leave of absence from his position with the union; Milt Burns assumed his duties. The FE's ignominious defeat in 1952 was regarded—by outsiders as well as, no doubt, by the UE leadership—as a personal humiliation for Fielde, a feeling he probably shared. And by mid-1953 Grant Oakes, too, stepped down from the FE presidency. After years of battling International Harvester, Oakes and Fielde may have believed that the new contract so adversely affected the rules of engagement that they preferred to quit the game. More likely, they had both wearied of the fight—or, more correctly, the many fights—altogether. Neither man would be active in the labor movement again, nor indeed live long enough to pursue much else. Fielde sought out the quietude of the north woods of Wisconsin, where he took over a modest fishing resort; he died ten years after leaving the FE, when he was just fifty-one years old. Oakes moved to California but suffered a heart attack shortly thereafter, and his failing health impeded his efforts to secure work as an engineer, his original profession. He passed away in 1967, at the age of sixty-two.[6]

The departure of the FE's two top officials shook the union to its core, but of equal consequence was the loss of local leadership that occurred in the wake of the 1952 strike, as IH fired seventeen union activists during the walkout for acts of alleged "hoodlumism." Harold Ward was one of them, but while the FE at McCormick Works would suffer as a result of Ward's absence, the biggest hit was taken by Local 236 in Louisville, where seven local leaders were discharged. Those men—including Jim Wright, Jim Mouser, Thomas Pearl, and longtime Local 236 official Tom DeLong—"were among the most effective members of the union and were known to the Company to be such," the FE said, resolving to "win back the jobs for our union brothers." John McCaffrey, however, remained adamant, and indeed they were all "through at Harvester." The new contract had simultaneously increased management's ability to get more out of its workforce for less while undercutting the ability of union stewards to address the inevitable grievances that would arise as a result. But for added insurance, IH management made sure—as per tradition—to "weed out" as many shop-floor militants as possible.[7]

Dismissing these activists, of course, was intended to facilitate Harvester's introduction of its revamped wage system. For as Harvester employees began returning to their jobs following the strike, "considerable misunderstanding and resentment was engendered," an arbitrator noted, "by the changes in working conditions brought about as a result of]the application of the new contract": in other words, FE officials had been right about the speedup and wage cuts they saw coming. In response, the FE's national and local leadership, what was left of it, still seemed determined to perpetuate the union's combative legacy. The rank and file as well proved resistant to the "realism" that the reconfigured contract was supposed to introduce on the shop floor.[8]

In many respects the FE was forced to harken back to its early days as a clandestine organizing committee, as DeWitt Gilpin described in an article detailing the impact of the 1952 agreement on the union's original local. As the contract began to be applied at Tractor Works, "stewards for the 5,000 workers were kept so close to their machines that they suggested leg irons. Convoys of foremen followed union leaders every place, even to the washrooms," Gilpin wrote. "Its communications smashed, the union used truckers, oilers, millwrights, any worker who had the run of the plant, to carry messages and instructions." Overcoming the widespread defeatism that followed in the wake of the strike became a tall order. "Convincing the workers they could fight and win took endless meetings, endless leaflets, and—so swore the stewards—endless leadership classes." It also took guts, as when FE Local 101 President Pete Neputy—who managed to keep his job at Tractor Works, though he'd been arrested during the strike—decided in early 1953 to call an in-plant union meeting. "Quick in-plant speeches under harassing conditions take a special technique," Gilpin said in his account. "Make the point and quick. Relate it to something workers can see, feel, hate," and Neputy zeroed in on an especially despised foreman.

> "John Troli's daddy was a coal miner," Neputy told the huge crowd of workers ringed by a thin circle of foremen and bosses. "My daddy was too. Troli worked in the coal mines. So did I. We both grew up in Illinois mining towns. I can go back to those towns and hold my head up. John Troli can't. Somebody might blow it off."
>
> "Why? Because Troli is the foreman who lied and threatened and forced the most workers to return during the strike. He gave them cigars. He gave them whisky. He was bought cheap and he bought some of you cheap. For what? Wage cuts, speedup, and life like a beaten dog."
>
> The crowd stirred. This was it. Pete was telling the bosses off. Pete was pointing his finger.
>
> "There he is," Pete yelled, "standing right among you. Let him answer to you. Let him speak. Let him call me a liar."
>
> Troli didn't. Neither did the company officials.[9]

"The workers began talking with cat-calls, boos, whistles," Gilpin wrote, and then FE Local 101 returned to form, engaging in a series of slowdowns and stoppages. First in the foundry, where fifty-five workers walked out for three days after they were ordered to produce thirty-five additional molds each day for $6 less a week; they returned once Harvester backed off the "adjustments." Then following a pay cut in assembly—Pete Neputy's department—the workers there "wrapped themselves in the tradition of Haymarket and the eight-hour day," as Gilpin saw it, and refused to work more than forty hours a week, "spurning all premium pay while unfinished tractors piled up." They kept up the slowdown for weeks. Finally, in mid-March 1953, the exasperated management issued Pete Neputy a three-week suspension, and in response twenty-two hundred employees—all but a few hundred of those on the plant's first shift—walked out. Few of the fifteen hundred employees on the second shift reported in later that day, either. Tractor Works "became as quiet as a McCormick tomb," as production shut down completely. To get the plant up and running again, IH rescinded the suspensions and the wage cuts, and even gave the assemblers a two-cent raise. "The plant got up off its knees," Gilpin wrote, as the protests "revealed how far along the comeback road the union had traveled" since the strike.[10]

Yet even Gilpin's partisan account remained cautious, indicating only that "the decision on last winter's strike isn't in yet." Harvester management may have made some concessions at Tractor Works, but at every plant IH was vigorously enforcing its new contract and doing its utmost to extract a steep price from those who resisted.

Nowhere was this more evident than in Louisville. As workers began returning to the plant there in November 1952, Harvester announced a revised quota of 367 tractors a day, up from 342 before the strike; "the establishment of adequate production standards," the company admitted, would also mean rate cuts for many piecework employees. Having purged so many militants during the strike, Harvester may have hoped to pull this off without incident, but the officers of Local 236, elected in January 1953, were all experienced practitioners of the FE's combative ideology. And Bud James, the "elite guy" turned radical, was still the FE staff member assigned to Louisville; Sterling Neal, though a UE district president, also devoted much of his time to the Harvester plant. On a Monday morning in late March—about the same time as the Tractor Works walkout—James, Neal, and the officers of Local 236 positioned themselves at the Louisville plant gate while the first shift began reporting in; they urged the workers to report not to their jobs but to an emergency union meeting instead. Two thousand FE members—two-thirds of the workforce—heeded the call, and production at the plant dropped by 60 percent that day. At the meeting the workers voted their support for "any action necessary to protect our contract and win our demands."[11]

IH management may have given some ground at Tractor Works, but not so in Louisville. Ten Local 236 leaders—including the recently elected president and vice-president, along with seven union stewards—were immediately fired for their part in promoting the work stoppage. Though employed by the UE, Sterling Neal technically still had a job at Harvester and was also a Local 236 trustee, and was discharged as well. "We mean business," Harvester said in a letter to its Louisville employees; "the day is gone when [FE leaders] can take matters into their own hands. We lived through that period once. We don't intend to go through it again." The two-day walkout was called off though Harvester agreed to nothing beyond arbitrating the dismissals, and the company expressed little apprehension about that, since "the discharged people were guilty of a deliberate and very serious contract violation."[12]

Harvester's confidence proved well-founded. "It can no longer be doubted," the arbitrator declared in July 1953, that the new contract's language prohibited "the sudden calling of a special membership meeting during working hours as a pressure device and with the obvious intent of causing a substantial interference with a plant's normal rate of production . . ." The FE had argued that Harvester unfairly targeted "the hard core of unionism which had admittedly proven such a thorn in Management's hide during Local 236's existence" but the charge of discrimination against "known active Union leaders," if anything, only strengthened the company's case. Elected local officials, so the arbitrator maintained, were "most certainly to refrain, themselves, from engaging in any activity which counselled resort to self-help instead of to the contract machinery" and moreover they were required to be "mindful of their responsibility as Union representatives to enforce compliance with the contract by their constituents." The arbitrator spared three stewards who had not been directly observed encouraging other employees to skip work, but otherwise the terminations were upheld. Sterling Neal and six other Local 236 officials, like the rest of those fired during the 1952 strike, were now "through at Harvester."[13]

But IH management was not yet finished with its campaign to bring the FE in Louisville to heel. Longtime Local 236 steward Charlie Yates, who had managed to hang on at Harvester through all the other dismissals, was fired in mid-1953 when he objected to an order from his foreman to perform a clean-up job. "Mr. Yates flatly refused to accept the assignment on the ground that he wasn't hired as a janitor and didn't intend to be one," the arbitrator indicated. Yates "had undoubtedly been a militant Union leader during his entire employment with the Company," the arbitrator allowed, but since "the evidence does not support the Union's claim that Yates was discriminated against and discharged for his Union activities" the dismissal was upheld. In all, thirty-five members of Local 236 were fired between January and May of 1953, and no doubt suspensions were being handed out with even greater frequency. The new contract was clearly facilitating Harvester's disciplinary crackdown, for in 1952 there had been a total of twenty-three discharges—including the strike firings—at the plant.[14]

And it seemed that Harvester wasn't satisfied merely with discharging the FE activists. The union claimed that the fired Local 236 leaders—especially those terminated during the strike—were finding it difficult to secure jobs elsewhere in the Louisville area, because other employers had been advised by IH of their "bad union records." To escape the evident blacklist, "some are thinking of moving to California or other areas equally distant," the FE said.[15]

To further underscore that it "meant business," Harvester management also utilized other methods to sabotage the Louisville FE. Regular communications with the membership, maintained largely through the near-daily distribution of leaflets outside the plant, had always been one of the local's defining characteristics and an important source of its power. For years Harvester had tolerated the distribution of literature in the company's parking lot adjacent to the factory, but that long-standing practice was ended after the 1952 strike. Two FE supporters found this out the hard way in March 1953 when they walked onto the lot intending to pass out handbills; Harvester officials promptly had them arrested for trespassing. The men hauled in were—no surprise here—Bud James and Jim Mouser. Mouser remained determined to bedevil his former employer, and two evenings later, armed with leaflets, he went right back onto the parking lot; the police took him right back to jail. Another FE member—one who still had a job at Harvester—who'd assisted Mouser with the leafleting was not arrested but was issued a ten-day suspension by IH, and management made its point: no more union literature on company property. Denied access to the parking lot, FE organizers and Local 236 leaders would find it much harder to keep the membership informed and engaged.[16]

Harvester's get-tough policies were causing Local 236 to erode internally as well. The *Cub* reported in mid-1953 that since the strike nearly seven hundred men—almost one-quarter of the membership—had quit their jobs at Harvester. Many of the workers abandoning the plant, said the union newspaper, were "long seniority men who remember the conditions for the past years, and who are now fed up with the company's new speed-up, wage cut program." Pleading with Local 236 members not to give up, the *Cub* insisted that "the answer is not quitting—it is organization and unity. Build the union in your department; back your union and back each other. Make every man's grievance your grievance and be prepared to defend him. *That is the only real answer.*"[17]

And one new provision of the 1952 agreement was undermining the FE and Local 236 just as the company had intended. In his communications with Harvester employees following the strike, John McCaffrey made sure they were well aware of the "escape clause" now included in their contract, which enabled FE members to discontinue their dues payments or withdraw from the union altogether. With the Local 236 leadership gutted and the FE's ability to respond to mounting frustration on the shop floor severely circumscribed, rank-and-filers began taking advantage of the clause. The *Cub* urged workers to resist Harvester's "campaign to tear apart the Union," but many did not listen. By mid-1953, the local's dues-paying membership stood at eighteen hundred out of twenty-three hundred eligible; by the end of the year the figure had dropped to twelve hundred.[18]

Larger economic forces were also taking a toll on the FE membership. A mid-1953 recession hit farmers, and by extension the agricultural implement industry, especially hard, and Harvester cut back production substantially. By September, one FE source indicated, close to 20 percent of the company's blue-collar workforce was subjected to "temporary" layoffs with uncertain recall dates. At some Harvester plants the situation was even more dire than this overall figure reveals: one-quarter of the employees at McCormick and Rock Falls, and nearly 40 percent at the Farmall plant in Rock Island, were laid off. But at the Louisville plant, the damage went the deepest: between May of 1953 and early 1954 more than 60 percent of the total IH workforce in Louisville received layoff notices.[19]

So on top of everything else, the FE was obliged to confront Harvester over its workforce reductions (grievances related to seniority skyrocketed) and deal with the difficulties faced by its many members now out of work. And in Louisville it would have to do this with unseasoned officials. Because so many of its longtime activists had been picked off, one way or the other, Local 236 was obliged to hold a special election in September 1953 to fill its executive board seats. For the first time, the local's leadership, from the president on down to the grievance committee, was bereft of those names familiar from the union's earlier, and more vigorous, days. Even Bud James was gone by late 1953, transferred from Louisville by the FE to service Harvester's plant in Rock Island, Illinois.[20]

Not all of the original cast, however, had yet left town: after he was fired in 1952, Jim Wright was taken onto the UE staff, assigned to help prop up his struggling former local. One of Wright's gravest concerns was his sense that at the Harvester plant relations between Black and white workers were deteriorating. Gone were the tight-knit group of unionists who from the outset had made interracial solidarity the core tenet of the Louisville FE, and the officers elected in 1953 and afterwards included, in Wright's view, "a lot of racists." In response, Wright sought to repeat the practices the FE had utilized when it first arrived in Louisville. "I think what we need here now is to get some white workers in the shop and have them work part time on the outside with me," Wright suggested to the UE office. "We could visit the key guys and find out what the real base of trouble is at this time. This would also stop any Negro-baiting, which I see coming up now in the local."[21]

But Wright's efforts to return the Louisville FE to first principles failed to make much headway. With its leadership hollowed out and scattered to distant points, Local 236, forced to focus inward, would never again play the transformative role it once had in challenging racism in its ranks and confronting segregation in the community. For this International Harvester bore considerable responsibility. Yet while IH continued to chalk up accolades for its liberal employment practices (in 1954, for instance, the company received the National Urban League's Industrial Statesmanship Award), how Harvester's wholesale crackdown on the FE thwarted progress on civil rights, in Louisville and elsewhere, passed with little notice.[22]

Jim Mouser, Wright's friend and comrade in those earlier desegregation battles, had also been hired as an organizer for the UE. But perhaps to reduce the union's expenditures on bail in Louisville courthouses, in late 1953 the UE sent Mouser out of Kentucky, assigning him to a small Pennsylvania town to assist the effort to unionize a Sylvania electrical factory there. Not long after settling in he ventured out to one worker's house to talk to him about the union, but he didn't get very far—the man's wife barreled out the door and "nearly knocked me clear off her front porch," Mouser recalled. He soon confessed to his superiors in the UE that he didn't think he was making much progress. "You know, they just won't talk," he told them. "They wouldn't even talk to IUE [the right-wing union in the electrical industry]. They didn't want anything to do with anybody." Mouser began to rethink his career options. "I wasn't fond of Pennsylvania anyway," he said. "I couldn't see how I was making any headway at all, on those plants." Unaccustomed to workers devoid even of union inclinations, not to mention militant labor consciousness, Mouser felt discouraged and out of place. He quit the UE, returned to Louisville, and invested some savings in a few bargain-priced thoroughbreds. His horses ran out of the money more often than not, however, and so Mouser eventually found employment as a salesman for a small business. He never again held a union card.[23]

That it proved so difficult for the FE to regain its footing after the 1952 strike came as no surprise to Jim Wright—what astonished him even decades later was that the left-led union gained traction in the first place and had gone on to achieve so much. "We knew, we knew what our destiny was," he said. "We used to sit up in meetings and discuss our destiny. We knew, Bud James, and all of us knew, Neal knew, that eventually we were going to have to go. It would take a miracle for us to work in the plant two years. But I worked there from '46 to '52. That was an extra miracle."[24]

DeWitt Gilpin's article about the post-strike job actions at Tractor Works was called "Comeback," but that title, it was increasingly apparent, had been overly optimistic. The embattled FE, though, still had a few miracles left. Given the corrosive consequences of the 1952 strike—an acknowledged failure for the FE leadership—UAW officials, assuming the pickings would now be easy at International Harvester, launched three quick raids in early 1953. But all the UAW managed to score was major embarrassment: first in January nearly three-fifths of the workers at the IH plant in Richmond, Indiana, voted for the FE, and then in Chicago in early April, 70 percent of the workforce backed the FE at Harvester's West Pullman Works, with participation in both elections topping 90 percent. The UAW then withdrew from the NLRB election scheduled for mid-April at the Farmall plant in Rock Island. No explanation was offered for the abrupt departure, but Quad Cities FE leader John Watkins had one: the UAW left town "to avoid the greatest defeat in the farm equipment industry," he pronounced.[25]

Much to Walter Reuther's and John McCaffrey's chagrin, then, what had always sustained the FE—the fierce allegiance of its rank and file— seemed, despite it all, to be holding. "Unfortunately," an IH labor relations executive grudgingly admitted in reference to the UAW's failed post-strike raids, "some of the employees continued their support of FE-UE because of this union's aggressiveness and because of its ability, in the years past, to secure contract gains." But the "irresponsible radicals" at the FE's helm (which after mid-1953 essentially meant Milt Burns and DeWitt Gilpin) had always understood that the membership's loyalty rested with local officials at least as much as with the union's national leadership. One of those trusted local leaders—John Watkins—was about to jump ship. Once he did, the FE would be unlikely to maintain its united front at International Harvester, and thus the union's ability to protect the workers there, who had remained so steadfast through such adversity, would be diminished all the more. Burns and Gilpin, looking ahead to their next contract negotiation with Harvester in 1955, began to ponder what their most responsible move might be.[26]

30.
We Can't Survive

I n April 1953 John Watkins had laid into the UAW for attempting to take over the Farmall plant in the Quad Cities. Four months later he was sparring with FE officials instead. Quite literally, that is. "Men kicked in the head, beaten to their knees with fists and gouged in the eyes. A pop bottle was hurled by one of the attacking party and shattered in bits in the swirling melee. Chair rungs used as cudgels." Such was the scene as FE and UAW forces squared off in a "bloody brawl" that broke out on the stairway of a Rock Island union hall. Once the dust and the flying glass settled, Milt Burns, who'd been on the other side in this "savage" melee, sought a warrant to have John Watkins arrested for assault.[1]

Watkins could hardly have made it more emphatic that he had abandoned the union he had helped build. Nor could FE officials have demonstrated more convincingly how much his betrayal meant. Following the 1952 strike Watkins had for a while remained nominally loyal to the FE—the UAW's failed Farmall raid seemed evidence of that—but by the summer of 1953 his resentment over UE "interference" would no longer be contained. In late July Watkins openly broke with the UE and urged Harvester workers in the Quad Cities to move into the UAW; he was promptly dismissed from the UE staff. Bitter recriminations were hurled from both sides, as Watkins—who tended to focus his ire on UE, rather than FE, officials—called the UE's James Matles a "company agent" who "forced the contract down Harvester workers' throats." Matles in turn publicly castigated Watkins as a "traitor" and "sellout" who had been engaged in secret negotiations with the UAW for months; Watkins's opposition to the 1952 contract was therefore characterized not as principled but purposed to ensure that the Quad Cities plants were "ripe for secession and raid." (In this scenario the UAW's April 1953 failure at Farmall was due to the ongoing loyalty of the FE membership there; Watkins's anti-UAW statements at the time were merely intended to provide good cover.)[2]

Tensions were thus rising in the Quad Cities in 1953, along with the late summer heat. Temperatures hit the mid-nineties in Rock Island on the last Saturday in August, as Milt Burns and about forty FE leaders from the union's Harvester locals converged on the ornate Labor Temple there for a previously scheduled meeting. Watkins, along with a contingent of about two dozen newly minted UAW supporters from Harvester's East Moline and Farmall plants, attempted to crash the assembly, but the FE members possessed the numerical advantage and held the high ground on the second floor. After an intense but brief skirmish—"exactly 2 minutes and 45 seconds," according to one reporter—Watkins and his troops were driven down the stairs and out of the building.[3]

Milt Burns and his forces won this round, and the UE engaged in a variety of legal actions designed to stymie the effort to deliver the Quad Cities plants to the UAW. But all that just postponed the inevitable. For seventeen years John Watkins had been the face of the FE for workers in the Quad Cities. Like Jerry Fielde and Grant Oakes, Watkins put in his time on the Harvester shop floor, and like them he proved early on that he could not be intimidated by foul-mouthed foremen or smooth-talking McCormicks. His incorruptibility and audacious militancy earned him widespread respect among the rank and file. Moreover, as his condemnation of the 1952 HUAC hearings indicated, Watkins had not previously been a red-baiter, and so his insistence that Harvester workers would now be best served by jumping to the once-hated UAW could not be dismissed as anti-communist hysteria. "The issue has been and remains UE dictatorial control of FE locals for selfish political purposes," Watkins declared when he was fired by James Matles. "My discharge," Watkins vowed, "does not remove me from fighting on the side of the workers against the UE or upon the side of the workers against the company's effort to destroy the wages and working conditions we have won over past years." Unfortunately for the FE-UE, most Harvester workers in the Quad Cities would be likely to take Watkins at his word and follow his lead. It took some time to effect the big switch, but in an NLRB election in May 1954, at Harvester's East Moline plant—where John Watkins got his start—1,326 workers voted for the UAW while only 311 backed the FE. After dozens of raids and many thousands of dollars spent, the UAW had finally wrested an IH plant from the FE. Others might soon follow: the UAW was moving aggressively at Farmall and on the IH plant in Richmond, Indiana.[4]

A month after the East Moline loss, the FE's top leadership gathered for what was surely a grim deliberation. The surviving handwritten notes from this meeting do not always clearly indicate who said what, but they underscore that all those present were grappling to find a way to preserve their vision of left-wing unionism and protect the Harvester workers they represented. They made no attempt to sugarcoat their situation. The FE had made "progress in IH for over 15 years," Milt Burns said, but after the 1952 strike was called off "conditions were taken away, wages worsened, workers speeded up." The restrictions on stewards and the no-strike language meant that "grievances are not being filed or if filed, not being won. Workers are getting no relief—they are looking for a way out." DeWitt Gilpin maintained that the new contract undercut the FE's ability to fend off the UAW. "We do not enjoy the decisive economic edge over the UAW we previously did. Our old handle of economic superiority is gone. The tactic of day-to-day struggle on grievances is mainly gone," he said.

They also acknowledged that their own mistakes following the strike had left them more vulnerable to the UAW. "We failed to fully unify the shops—i.e. strikers and returnees," Burns said. "UAW utilized this split as the basis for raids." Harvester workers who had crossed picket lines could "rationalize their reason for scabbing" by accepting the charges of communist domination leveled against the FE; those workers were all the more likely to succumb to UAW advances. While the UAW offered "pie in the sky promises to workers on the one hand, and concessions to companies on [the] other hand," it nonetheless constituted a more "serious threat" than ever.

And as always International Harvester was still intent on "busting" the FE. The "savage attacks" launched by IH during the strike at least meant that among the workforce "resentment against the company had crystallized." But within the shops management would ratchet up the pressure nonetheless, and the continuing recession made matters exponentially worse. Aware that IH faced "dwindling markets," Burns argued that Harvester's "drive for profits" would impel management to "increase the rate of exploitation" through speedup, while seniority rules governing layoffs were being routinely violated. And as FE leaders attempted in their customary fashion to fight back, they bore the brunt of management's wrath. Though the UAW and the FE at this point evenly split representation at IH, the vast majority of workers disciplined by IH in recent months, someone at the meeting noted, were FE members.

All this meant "we must do everything to guarantee victory in NLRB elections," one person said, "because a loss will lead to direct consequences." But the reports from the locals were not encouraging. At Farmall, though Bud James had recently been assigned to Rock Island, there are "not enough organizers," and "we don't have time to work with stewards." Layoffs were ongoing and grievances were piling up. Nearly half the remaining workforce, it was indicated, had chosen to opt out of the union. In Richmond, also hit by "heavy layoffs," much of the local leadership "went over to UAW." The only bright spot there was that the "bulk of Negroes are still loyal to FE." A recent "Fight Back" meeting in Richmond was sparsely attended; of the eight FE stewards and six other workers who showed up, all were Black. Once layoffs were completed, about one-third of the Richmond workforce would be African American, but Black support alone could not preserve the FE there. "We must win over the returnees" and persuade "more whites." To that end, Sterling Neal had arrived in Richmond to promote "Negro-white unity."

To shore up the FE's dwindling support, Milt Burns suggested "a program that unifies workers" designed to illustrate that the "misery of workers stems from the companies and the government they control." Such a platform would call for a shorter work week, a guaranteed annual wage, guaranteed seniority, strengthened fair employment protection, and higher pensions that would kick in after twenty-five years on the job. Ernest DeMaio, who was present at the meeting, argued for "unity of action from below" and suggested that the UAW's "bureaucracy and lack of rank-and-file democracy" would soon erode its support within Harvester plants. But others were skeptical. FE members, DeWitt Gilpin said, "don't want to be isolated in struggle," and in the aftermath of the strike were increasingly of the view that "things are tough now—why don't we get into one union." Others at the meeting were more blunt. "The UE is broke," one person said. "The UE is dying. We don't want to be the last one out." Someone else said flatly: "We can't survive." Given the Republican sweep in the recent election, another concern was raised: "If we beat UAW, will we then be legislated out of existence?" The central question remained: "Where are we going?"

Jim Wright, also present, was wondering the same thing. "Let us examine ourselves," he said. "Can we win? Are we convinced we can?" In the fight against Harvester "unity" was essential, he said, because "we can't do the job for workers without it. On the other hand, neither can the UAW." So "we need unity," but it must be defined by "democratic rank-and-file unionism, dedicated to the interests and welfare of the workers," Wright maintained.[5]

When the meeting adjourned the officials present continued for the moment to stay the course, but there would be no lessening of the concerns outlined there. While the recession intensified problems within the locals, the hostile Cold War climate meant those in power who might have provided support to struggling Harvester workers closed their doors to the FE leadership. When Milt Burns sought to discuss the layoff crisis with Illinois Senator Paul Douglas, the liberal Democrat responded by telegram with a single sentence: "I believe your union to be communist dominated and therefore will not meet with you." No doubt Burns did not even try for an audience with the other Senator from Illinois, the hardline anti-communist Republican Everett Dirksen.[6]

And in regard to the FE's parent organization, the comment that the "UE is dying" was not hyperbole but rather a realistic assessment of the hemorrhaging inflicted by the CIO's onslaught. While the East Moline defection of more than fifteen hundred workers to the UAW was a blow, it paled in comparison to what the UE suffered a few days later. In early June 1954, workers at the massive GE plant in Schenectady, New York, voted to quit the UE in favor of the International Union of Electrical Workers, and with that the UE lost fifteen thousand dues-paying members. At the time of the FE affiliation in 1949, the UE had boasted more than five hundred thousand members (and it was, before its expulsion, the third-largest CIO union); by 1954 the UE had dipped below two hundred thousand and by the end of the decade would be down to fifty-eight thousand, a 90 percent drop in its ranks in just ten years. In contrast, the UAW's membership grew to one million by the mid-1950s, a figure that was steadily increasing.[7]

Looming over everything, as always, was the recognition that John McCaffrey and International Harvester's management fully intended to "increase the rate of exploitation" of the workforce, and would certainly seek further concessions when the FE's contract expired in June 1955. Though FE leaders voiced the concern, with good reason, that Harvester was looking to "bust" their union once and for all, in fact they also recognized that the post-1952 state of labor relations at IH—two unions, now with essentially equivalent contracts, representing roughly the same number of employees, locked in draining internecine warfare—served the company's purposes quite well. As Jim Wright had argued, neither union alone could "do the job" that was needed for Harvester workers.

So by the fall of 1954, FE officials reached a conclusion: when bargaining sessions began again, it was essential that International Harvester be confronted by a single organization that represented all its production workers. And the painful reality was that there was no chance that union would be the FE. "We would have kept on bleeding," Al Verri said, recalling the conversations held back then, away from the watchful gaze of their UE superiors. "DeWitt Gilpin, Milt Burns, and myself, Jim Wright, we talked about this thing, and we said, we can't wait. It's just a matter of time. We felt the only way we could beat this company back was to unite this chain and take the company on." Thus it was that FE leaders, principally Milt Burns, began under-the-table negotiations with their sworn enemies in the UAW to sound out terms for a possible merger. "To save what was left of a militant struggle, they had to do this," Sonya Burns said, summing up her husband's position at the time.[8]

While these secret discussions were underway, the "bleeding" continued: in January 1955, Harvester workers at Farmall and in Richmond defected to the UAW. The loss of two more locals served as a further spur to the FE leadership. A few months later, the structure for a merger was finalized, which provided for admission into the UAW of the FE's Harvester locals; all FE officials, local and national, would be absorbed by the UAW, as would staff members, who would continue servicing the Harvester locals they had so long been connected to. It might seem surprising that the UAW, which seemed to hold the upper hand, would consent to take on the FE leadership and staff, who had so long and so passionately voiced their utter contempt for Walter Reuther and his agenda. Under the proposed merger Harvester workers who had always been under FE jurisdiction would outnumber those who had been UAW members, meaning that former FE local leaders and staff would dominate the UAW's Harvester Council. But the decision to bring in the FE personnel represented an acknowledgement by the UAW—the recent victories in the Quad Cities and Richmond notwithstanding—that it would prove extremely difficult, and perhaps impossible, to capture the FE's remaining locals over the objections of the union's leadership. UAW officials too were tiring of the raids and the drain in resources—not to mention the bloody noses—imposed by those battles. They were also confronting layoffs at their IH plants, and were well aware that Harvester was looking to exploit the divided loyalties of its workforce even further in upcoming negotiations. So within the UAW the judgement was made that the benefits of unity outweighed the risk that absorbing the FE upstarts posed.[9]

The terms of the merger, then, indicated that despite the vitriol Walter Reuther had aimed at the FE leadership over the years, he had come to recognize the respect they commanded among the Harvester rank and file. Reuther, now fully secure in his control over the UAW—and since 1952 he'd been head of the CIO as well—was astute enough to recognize that experienced and well-regarded union leaders were too valuable to let go. He planned, however, to keep a close eye on these new additions to the UAW staff. And one condition was absolute: they would need to sever any remaining ties with the Communist Party.

Unity, at any rate, seemed to be the watchword for the American labor movement in 1955. In February, the AFL and CIO agreed on terms for an affiliation, to be led by former plumber George Meany, with Reuther in charge of the new AFL-CIO Industrial Department. "I believe in the free enterprise system completely," Meany affirmed. "I believe in management's right to manage." A far cry, surely, from how Milt Burns had once defined the FE's philosophy: "that management has no right to exist." Meany's declaration would seem to settle things, but the agreement also committed the new labor federation to be free "from any taint of corruption or communism." At its formation, the AFL-CIO brought under its umbrella 145 different unions representing sixteen million workers, more than one-third of America's nonagricultural workforce. Even the Communist Party jumped on the unity bandwagon, encouraging the remaining left-led unions to seek reentry into labor's mainstream, advice which James Matles of the UE, who'd broken with the Party some years before, "contemptuously ignored." By this point FE leaders were also estranged from the party hierarchy, but given their former ties they may have drawn comfort from the fact that a move into the UAW comported with CP policy.[10]

So in late March when FE leaders went public with their proposal to bring the IH locals into the UAW, they touted it as a "contribution to the growing movement for labor unity." With both the FE and UAW contracts set to expire in a few months, "the Company has announced open war on wages and contractual conditions," read a statement from the FE leadership. "This is not an idle threat." Harvester workers "know that the Company will stop at nothing in its attacks on all unions." There were traces of regret evident in the announcement. "It is only because of the special situation confronting the FE-Harvester workers—that is, contract negotiations, a split chain, and new and vicious attacks by the Company—that we take this action." The proposed merger, however, was painted not as a defeat but as a way to take what Sonya Burns had called the "militant struggle" into the UAW. "Intact and with head high, proud of their record of fighting at all times in the interests of the membership, the FE-UE locals can move into the UAW determined to make the greatest contribution in the united front against the Harvester Company." And the FE leaders emphasized their "high respect for the UE and our great admiration for its militant record" and preemptively condemned "anyone who tries to use our merger with the UAW in an effort to disrupt the UE."[11]

It was a nice try, but that effusive tribute did not mollify UE officials, who had been kept in the dark about the negotiations with the UAW. An enraged James Matles promptly fired Milt Burns and DeWitt Gilpin, along with other organizers on the UE payroll—like Al Verri and Jim Wright—who promoted the UAW merger. Ernest DeMaio changed the locks and barred the "traitors" from the UE's Chicago office. And there were some FE staff members who chose to remain loyal to the still avowedly left-wing UE, finding an alliance with the organization that had so long endeavored to destroy their union unthinkable. Their bitter opposition was expressed in personal and irreconcilable terms. Sonya Burns indicated that once the UAW merger came out in the open, Bud James and Ken Born, another longtime FE staff member, "never talked to Milt again. Never talked to him again. [They said] he was a sellout. And these were Milt's best friends," she said.[12]

The FE Conference Board stipulated that the merger recommendation would not be final until all remaining FE-UE Harvester locals ratified it by a "clear majority," though with the FE's top officials and most local leaders on board, approval was likely. After years of battling the UAW, however, some salesmanship was required. When Jim Wright first pitched the proposal to the Louisville rank and file, "they really didn't want to do it," he said. "They wanted to take their chances, said you're doing all right in spite of it, hell, [Harvester] fired you two years ago, and you're still living, we're feeding you, and all that stuff, oh man." Wright well understood such defiance—for years, after all, he had helped foster it—but he nonetheless insisted that Louisville's "stormy petrel" could no longer go it alone. "I had to tell them you got to go into the UAW because I don't think FE can make it anymore," he said.[13]

Wright was evidently persuasive enough, as were the other FE leaders who pressed for the deal. In NLRB elections held in May 1955, the nearly twenty thousand members of the last remaining FE-IH locals—at the McCormick, Tractor, and West Pullman Works in Chicago; in Canton and Rock Falls, Illinois; and in Louisville—voted overwhelmingly to move into the UAW. One month later, when negotiations began, all of International Harvester's production employees—for the first time in the company's one hundred-plus-year history—were members of one big union: the United Automobile, Aerospace, and Agricultural Workers of America, AFL-CIO. And the FE was no more.[14]

31.
The Descendants of the FE

"**O**ur union will be in business as long as International Harvester," so the FE leadership had once vowed. That promise could not be kept. Yet despite their move into labor's mainstream, the "irresponsible radicals" who had built the FE resisted for some time the prevailing currents, frustrating corporate executives and making their new colleagues in the UAW uneasy. And for decades onward workers at Harvester clung stubbornly to the belief—contrary to the triumphant hegemony of the politics of productivity—that a union should serve not just to pad their paychecks but to exert control over what sort of work they did and how fast they did it, or even whether they worked at all. IH management and the labor establishment found it a bit harder to wipe the FE's traces clean than had been expected.[1]

Initially the impact of the FE's demise, naturally, was most profoundly registered by the union's leadership. There were major adjustments required, and for some, transferring to the UAW brought with it a change of address as well. Just after the merger was effected, DeWitt Gilpin urged Jim Wright to join him and the rest of the erstwhile FE leadership in Chicago; Gilpin "said get in this car, and go north, got you on the staff of UAW, come up north and integrate some of those spots up here," Wright recalled. So in July 1955, Wright and his family left Louisville, settling across the Ohio River for the first time. "I was out of there," he said. "For good." Wright welcomed the relocation to Chicago, but not so much the cumbersome procedures he needed to learn in the UAW. In the FE, "our strategy was hit 'em, get the case for the man, get him a clean job, get his money that's due him, and move on," said Wright. "Hell, all we had was a plain old brown contract, write the grievance, we knew what we were doing." That spirit of improvisation was frowned upon by his new employer. "Over there in the UAW, you had a department, people to say, well, this comes under this classification, this skill is here, and all this business," Wright recalled. "They had people handling grievances, they had people over here at this desk, so that when we went into the UAW, I said, 'What the hell have all you got in there? Is this an office workers' union, or what?'"[2]

Al Verri also recognized that with the transition to the UAW their jobs had been bureaucratized overnight. "In the FE contract, it didn't have the kind of detailed language that the UAW contract has," he maintained. "As a result, the fight was more what you could get away with. Whoever put on the most pressure, that's who won. Whereas with the UAW contract, it becomes a matter of a system."[3]

To ensure that the former FE officials played by the rules of the larger organization they were now a part of, Walter Reuther kept them closely monitored. "They were not trusted," Sonya Burns said about the new contingent in the UAW. When her husband Milt was required to travel out of town on union business, "Reuther would not let him go alone, for about two years," always assigning a reliable UAW loyalist to accompany him. They would also be required to publicly attest that they had severed all contact with the Communist Party. Thus, when in 1957 Milt Burns and DeWitt Gilpin were subpoenaed to appear before the Senate Internal Security Subcommittee (the higher body's equivalent of the House Un-American Activities Committee), it was made quite clear that if they invoked the Fifth Amendment to avoid testifying—as they had in the past—they would have no future with the UAW.[4]

Fortunately for all those who objected to the civil liberties overreach regularly practiced by these Cold War committees, a third option—beyond clamming up completely or naming names—had recently become available. That was true thanks to Milt Burns's former sparring partner, John Watkins, with assists from the UAW and the United States Supreme Court. In 1954, about a year after he'd defected from the FE, Watkins was summoned before HUAC, in large part because of the earlier testimony against him that had been offered up during the 1952 strike. Before the committee Watkins reiterated that he'd never been a card-carrying party member, but freely acknowledged that he had "participated in communist activities to such a degree that some persons may honestly believe that I was a member of the party." Watkins then indicated he would not utilize his Fifth Amendment shield against self-incrimination—"I will answer any questions which this committee puts to me about myself"—but he was unwilling to act as a fully cooperative witness. "I most firmly refuse to discuss the political activities of my past associates," Watkins said in customarily insubordinate fashion. "I do not believe that such questions are relevant to the work of this committee nor do I believe that this committee has the right to undertake the public exposure of persons because of their past activities."[5]

The committee was unimpressed by Watkins's legal analysis and he was subsequently convicted of contempt of Congress, which carried a possible one-year prison sentence. He appealed, and his defense was paid for by his employer, the United Auto Workers. Walter Reuther, having successfully marginalized, converted, or hounded out of existence the Communist Party elements in his own union and within the CIO—utilizing McCarthyite tactics to do so—could now afford to be magnanimous about the civil liberties of UAW staff members with previous CP ties. So long as there was no question that those associations were confined to the past, that is.

The case wended its way up to the Supreme Court, which in June 1957 overturned Watkins's conviction and held that he could not be compelled to testify about others he knew. The *New York Times* proclaimed the decision "a monument to the return of reason" that "placed fundamental restrictions on a Congressional investigatory power that in recent years has been asserted as all but limitless." Chief Justice Earl Warren, who wrote the 6-1 majority opinion, declared, "There is no congressional power to expose for the sake of exposure where the predominant result can be only an invasion of the . private rights of individuals," citing First Amendment protections for those subject to government interrogations. Warren's opinion generated a torrent of coverage, triggering "more reaction from public and press than any court decision since the court crippled Franklin D. Roosevelt's Blue Eagle early in the New Deal." Though liberal bastions like the American Civil Liberties Union hailed the decision, a bevy of politicians from both parties excoriated it for "lending aid, comfort and assistance" to the communist "enemy." South Carolina Senator Strom Thurmond declared, "The Court has gone power wild," and some members of Congress called for impeaching all the justices at once (of course, many of these elected officials, like Thurmond, were white Southerners and still smarting over the Warren Court's 1954 ruling in *Brown v. Board of Education*). But one thing was certain. With *Watkins v. United States*, a landmark in civil liberties law, the bullheaded blue-collar John Watkins—who'd never even gone to high school—became enshrined in the canon of American jurisprudence.[6]

The *Watkins* case would be seized on by many individuals sparring with the federal government (the playwright Arthur Miller, for one, who had also refused to name names before HUAC), but the UAW staff members summoned before the Senate Internal Security Subcommittee on July 3—just two weeks after the decision was handed down—may have been the first to utilize it. The Subcommittee's chair, Mississippi Senator John Eastland, had already denounced the *Watkins* decision for placing "a cloak of immunity around Communist activity," and witnesses were advised that despite the Supreme Court's ruling the "use of the First Amendment would make them liable for contempt action." It was therefore provocative—and risky—when Milt Burns and DeWitt Gilpin made clear to the committee their intent to "invoke their privilege under the First Amendment as they believe it defined by Chief Justice Warren's decision in the *Watkins* case." They consented to testify, "no matter how irrelevant or unconstitutional these questions may be," only to comply with UAW policy, which required its staff members "to answer all questions put to them by a congressional committee about their own activities." Grilled by committee members, they grudgingly responded to queries about the May Day rallies, Paul Robeson concerts, and civil rights protests they'd attended, but to spare others "public stigma and scorn" they declined to provide such information about anyone else. "You refuse to answer whether or not the officers of the Farm Equipment Workers at the time you were a member were Communists or not?" DeWitt Gilpin was asked, more than once. "That is correct, sir," Gilpin said. "My answer is predicated on pertinence and the First Amendment." Both men maintained that they had fallen away from the Party by the late 1940s—at least in the sense of attending meetings open only to Communists—and affirmed they had no current association with the CP. "One thing is for sure," Milt Burns told the committee, "you cannot be in this union [the UAW] and be a member of the Communist Party." But Burns also noted that "when I went into the UAW, the position of the union was that what you had done before is your own business."[7]

The former FE leaders may have been told that, but they had one more hurdle to jump through before they were deemed fit for UAW service. Because in their Senate testimony they had for the first time publicly acknowledged their communist ties, this appeared to put their employment by the UAW in conflict with the union's constitution, which prohibited party members or supporters from holding elective or appointed positions. That Walter Reuther kept on his payroll such "red dodgers," as Senator Eastland dubbed them, provided fodder for reactionary anti-unionists in high places. Reuther had, however, recently established a "watchdog" entity for such situations: the UAW's Public Review Board, a "citizen appellate body" composed of scholars and jurists, tasked with adjudicating internal disputes and enforcing "ethical practices" within the union. The review board burnished Reuther's liberal bona fides, as had the underwriting of John Watkins's Supreme Court case, while conveniently allowing him to deflect criticism from both in and outside the UAW. Thus, in its inaugural decision, the review board declared that since there was apparently nothing in the UAW constitution "barring *former* communists from office," Milt Burns and DeWitt Gilpin could keep their jobs. Since the ruling was issued on December 26, 1957, they could regard it as a Christmas present of sorts from Walter Reuther.[8]

But while the former FE leaders performed the rituals required to demonstrate their distance from the Communist Party, they nonetheless retained the adversarial approach to collective bargaining that they had developed when they had been close to the CP. They made that clear right after they signed on with the UAW, as the 1955 contract negotiations with International Harvester got underway. At that moment the recession that marked the beginning of the decade was over, laid off employees had been called back to the plants, and Harvester's profits were climbing again. Leonard Woodcock, then chair of the UAW's Agricultural Implement Department, served as the union's chief negotiator, but several of the former FE leaders just brought in through the merger were part of the bargaining team as well. "Woodcock was not accustomed to the FE guys at Harvester," Al Verri reported about that negotiating session. "He could see how rough they were when they wanted to go beyond the pattern—the pattern was what they had negotiated with the auto companies in Detroit—and we weren't supposed to go beyond that." Each night when the bargaining sessions broke up, Woodcock, in an effort to escape from his insistent fellow negotiators, retreated to the bar of Chicago's Knickerbocker Hotel, "and he lined up about half a dozen Manhattans," Verri said, "trying to drown them out."[9]

Woodcock soon found that the local union leaders who had recently morphed into UAW officers at the Harvester plants were no less demanding. Several days before the 1955 contract expired, the four thousand members of UAW Local 1301—formerly FE Local 101—walked out of Tractor Works and began picketing the plant. They "jumped the gun," local president Pete Neputy freely admitted. "The workers got tired of speedup, low wages, lousy seniority," he said, indicating they would keep the plant shut down until their issues had been resolved. Within hours the new UAW members at McCormick Works, in the Quad Cities, and in Louisville followed suit. A few days later, when no settlement had been reached, the UAW called an official strike of its forty thousand members within International Harvester. "We have met, or more than met, the so-called 'Detroit pattern,'" IH labor relations head William Reilly grumbled, seven days into the strike. The walkout continued for another three weeks, however, ending when Harvester ponied up hefty wage and benefit increases in a three-year agreement. And with the FE vanquished, the company consented to a full union shop in all its plants. "We gained a better deal from Harvester than we got from Ford and General Motors," said a UAW staff member, not one who had previously been in the FE.[10]

So the aggressiveness of "the FE guys" paid off, literally, for Harvester employees, as did, no doubt, the fact that the entire workforce was now represented by one union. But the 1955 strike differed conspicuously from those that came before, the Louisville *Courier-Journal* noted, as "no rocks were thrown, no insults exchanged" on the orderly, subdued picket lines. That Harvester workers were now represented by the UAW, which is "firm but conciliatory in all its negotiations," was the "obvious reason" for the "remarkable" change, and the newspaper applauded the "responsibility" demonstrated by UAW leaders. "They respect their agreements, and the workers who were forever breaking into wildcat demonstrations under FE will now stay at work unless an approved strike vote calls them out." Even William Reilly praised the "considerably improved" climate at the 1955 bargaining sessions, but his positive feelings extended only to Woodcock and the other top UAW negotiators. "On the part of the local leaders and many union members," he complained, there remained "this bitter, intolerable attitude."[11]

But whatever "bitter" feelings may have been retained by former FE members and their leaders, the new regime they now operated under constrained their ability to act on them. While the 1955 UAW contract meant more money for Harvester employees, those fatter paychecks came at a price extracted on the shop floor. The restructured wage system and ramped-up production standards the company had imposed in 1952 were unchanged by the new agreement, so there would be no lessening of the speedup Pete Neputy had complained about. Harvester continued to enforce its steward restrictions and its hardline no-strike policy, while at the same time the UAW regimentation that had so confounded Jim Wright and Al Verri replaced the guerrilla-style immediacy that had characterized the FE. That meant that Harvester workers, and their local UAW representatives, had only one option open to them to resist management's exploitation: file a grievance. And so they did. From 1954 through 1959, Harvester workers lodged some sixty thousand grievances—an extraordinarily high figure within American industry—with more than 48,500 of them appealed on up through arbitration, meaning they "had about a one-in-a-thousand chance of being heard," one UAW official acknowledged.[12]

This, then, was the dynamic that governed labor relations at International Harvester in the ensuing decades. Each new three-year agreement—often following strikes that might last a few days or several weeks—brought significant pay and benefit improvements for the UAW membership at IH. But between contracts, the company's ongoing efforts to rake back those expenditures through the manipulation of its incentive wage system fueled festering shop-floor resentment. In an effort to address the mounting backlog of complaints, Harvester management tinkered at various times with its grievance machinery, but left the wellspring of discontent—its relentless drive for "efficient" production—in place.[13]

Harvester's push to cut costs and increase profits would, in the latter half of the twentieth century, begin to take a more outwardly apparent toll as well. In 1952 the McCormick Twine Mill had been shut down; in 1959 it was the main plant's turn. The factory where Cyrus McCormick's farm equipment empire had originated was to be torn down, its four thousand employees to lose their jobs. Delegations of UAW officials and Chicago's recently elected Mayor Richard J. Daley pleaded with the company to overhaul the plant or rebuild on the site, but IH executives would not budge. The company was looking to unload its older facilities and shed workers, certainly its well-paid unionized ones; the bottom line left no room for sentimental attachment to either historic buildings or longtime employees. "The story of the closing of McCormick, a plant which for 67 years produced profits that made the McCormick family a symbol of Gold Coast wealth and affluence, is the story of what's wrong with our economy," read a leaflet issued by UAW Local 1308 to protest the McCormick Works shutdown. Written by UAW staff member DeWitt Gilpin, it reflected more than a little of the perspective he brought with him from the FE. "A prosperity that is based on fewer workers and farmers each year will lead to social chaos unless a greater share of the profits derived from improved production methods goes to the people who buy the tractors and the cars."

Yet the solution Gilpin proposed in the leaflet—a thirty-hour week without wage reductions—was one that had been roundly rejected by Walter Reuther months earlier at the UAW's 1958 convention. Reuther dismissed the call for a shorter work week as unobtainable and, given in his view the need to maintain full production due to the ongoing Soviet threat, quite possibly un-American. Gilpin, however, thought there were relevant lessons to be drawn from the past. "Our doomed plant, which history has now passed by, once heard Cyrus McCormick swear that he would never reduce hours without cutting pay. Like today's defenders of the status quo, Cyrus was bucking the inevitable," he wrote. "There is one thing we are entitled to in our time—a 30-hour week." The leaflet concluded with a black-framed "epitaph" for McCormick Works: "Born in the Fight for the 8-Hour Day. Died in the Fight for the 6-Hour Day."[14]

But if the six-hour day was "inevitable," it had still not arrived before IH shut down more plants: Richmond, Indiana. Rock Falls in central Illinois. And then in 1969, on the same day the papers reported "IH Profits, Sales Climb," the company announced it would shutter the Chicago factory where the FE had been born: Tractor Works. DeWitt Gilpin penned a leaflet that served as obituary for yet another Harvester plant—"every agitator who had a cause took it to Tractor," he said—and expressed particular concern for the twelve hundred African American employees, out of the workforce of thirty-five hundred, "many of whom can't transfer to plants in suburbs where no housing is available for blacks." But the flyer also included a tribute to stalwart Tractor Works local president Pete Neputy, who was felled by a sudden heart attack just two weeks after his plant's closing was announced, and died at the age of fifty-nine. "To Pete there wasn't such a thing as a bad grievance. Every grievance was a scream for justice," Gilpin wrote, and concluded with a resolute, if melancholy, pledge: "Old unionists don't die. Neither do their Local Unions. They just apply for a transfer to carry on in a new place."[15]

International Harvester would cycle through a number of chief executives in the 1960s and '70s, all of them dedicated to increasing profit margins by trimming expenditures. Such thriftiness, however, did not apply to their own salaries. Brooks McCormick, who headed Harvester for most of the 1970s, hand-picked a successor—Xerox executive Archie McCardell—who would be the first president ever hired from outside the company.[16] McCardell was lured to Harvester in 1977 with an "unprecedented compensation package" that combined an extravagant signing bonus and annual salary with a hefty portfolio of IH stock, ushering in the modern era of lavish CEO remuneration. Once McCardell took the helm at IH, "cost-cutting quickly emerged as the No. 1 priority," and he "saw Harvester's contract with the UAW as a perfect target for his cost-cutting campaign." McCardell determined to revamp many of the work rules that he believed undermined Harvester's competitiveness. He had three particular objectives: to limit seniority-governed transfers between jobs when openings occurred; to rescind the right of pieceworkers, if their regular jobs were unavailable, to go home rather than accept a lower-paying assignment; and—most important of all—to introduce mandatory overtime. Though John Deere and Caterpillar—indeed, most employers—could require employees to work past their regular hours or on weekends, at Harvester overtime had long been arranged on a voluntary basis. All these practices—which spoke to what sort of work union members would do or whether they had to do it at all—had been first established under the FE. In 1979 IH, ranked twenty-seventh among the Fortune 500, posted record sales and impressive profit margins, but as contract negotiations began in the fall McCardell demanded that Harvester workers cede some of the rights they had exercised for decades. And why not? This marks the moment, after all, when the American labor movement stopped making gains and started giving back: in October 1979, to stave off Chrysler's threatened bankruptcy, UAW President Doug Fraser offered up "significant concessions" promising that "any reasonable request will be fulfilled."[17]

But McCardell made a grave miscalculation. He "completely discounted the militant vestige within Harvester's union ranks," one business publication noted. "The philosophical descendants of those FE leaders still held sway at the local level in 1979." In fact, some were literal descendants: Dave Boynton, employed in 1979 at Harvester's Farmall plant, was the son of a longtime (and many years retired) FE activist. McCardell "wanted to cut us back to where Dad and them were in 1954 or before," Boynton said, which for him and the other thirty-five thousand UAW members at IH was a no-go. "How long must the workers struggle and sacrifice in order to win what they already had in the past?" asked another Harvester worker. "That's what the company must learn. You can't treat human beings like this." McCardell's demands, said a UAW leaflet, are "an attempt to take every Harvester worker back thirty years," and so "Harvester workers in every Local Union are willing to make any strike that we have had in the past look like basic training," which, given what had happened in 1952, was saying something.[18]

Thus on November 1, 1979, workers at Harvester's seventeen farm equipment and truck manufacturing facilities went on strike. "We'll stay out until hell freezes over if we have to," said one UAW member from the IH plant in Louisville. "Mandatory overtime? HELL NO!" proclaimed the buttons worn on the picket lines, as overtime quickly emerged as the focal point of the strike. "I don't want to live in that stinking factory," said one East Moline striker. Another UAW member from the IH plant in Canton, Illinois, agreed. "I work a lot of Saturdays 'cause I want the money, but maybe there's a Saturday I don't want to work, that I want to be home with my family," he said. "I want the freedom to choose." With mandatory overtime the plants "would become nothing more than a penitentiary for every Harvester worker," a UAW flyer insisted. "We Refuse to be Slaves," declared a sign carried at a strike support rally in East Moline. "My Daddy Spends His Weekends with Me," read another.[19]

With Harvester executives adamant about their demands, the strike dragged past Christmas and into 1980. Financial pressures mounted for union members and their families—though as opposed to what had been true for the FE, the UAW had a healthy strike fund—but their resolve did not diminish as the snow piled up along with the bills. "We've gone this far and we're going to stick it out no matter how badly it hurts," said a striker in February. "All I saved up was determination and that's still with me," said another in March. As the bitterness deepened the picket lines became less orderly and began to take on the militancy reminiscent of struggles from the past, particularly in Louisville. Strikers there hurled rocks, eggs, and Christmas ornaments filled with yellow paint at company officials' cars, and shotgun blasts damaged the homes of two plant managers.[20]

The strike didn't last until hell froze over, but it came close. On April 21, 1980, after nearly six months, a settlement was finally reached, and the strike became one for the record books: the longest against International Harvester (eclipsing the three-month 1952 walkout) and the longest ever waged by the UAW against a major multistate employer (surpassing the 1945 117-day General Motors strike by a full fifty-nine days). The determination that Harvester's rank and file had in reserve provided the UAW a "smashing victory," the business press agreed, as management dropped all its concessionary demands. There would be no mandatory overtime, seniority would still govern job transfers, pieceworkers whose machines broke down could go home if they felt like it. Even those Louisville workers who'd been fired for their misconduct on the picket lines got their jobs back. All Archie McCardell had achieved through his attempt to "take Harvester workers back thirty years" was to chalk up a $580 million loss for the company and rekindle among the "descendants of the FE" that long deep grudge that had lain dormant for a while. "There'll be sabotage, all right," warned Cletus Williams, a UAW local leader at the IH plant in Canton, indicating how the strikers would act on their pent-up resentment once they returned to the plant. And he issued this reminder to Harvester management: "The worker always controls the quality [and] how much is produced. The company can invent and engineer and put on an ad campaign, but when all is said and done, the decision of how many pieces will be made and how good they'll be is up to the employee." Those words could well have graced an FE leaflet from decades earlier.[21]

When FE leaders had pledged in 1952 that their union would be in business as long as International Harvester, the underlying assumption was that mighty IH would survive well into the next century at least. But, in fact, for decades fault lines had been undermining Harvester's foundation, and by the early 1980s it was teetering toward collapse. The multimillion-dollar loss incurred as a result of the 1979 strike obviously was no help to its bottom line, but even business analysts who lacked union sympathies argued that Harvester's problems were more attributable to the "disastrous mismanagement" and unfocused leadership that had plagued the company since the end of World

War II. IH had failed to anticipate the emergence of larger, more mechanized farms that required new types of equipment. Through the 1950s John McCaffrey favored truck production at the expense of the company's more profitable, and also more complex, agricultural implement division; engineering blunders and questionable modifications of IH machinery—even painting some tractors yellow—allowed competitors to make inroads on farms that had been loyal to "Big Red" for generations. In 1958 Harvester lost its lead in farm equipment sales to John Deere and never got it back. In the ensuing decades, forays into tenuously related markets and risky technologies drained resources, while factories that turned out the company's core products deteriorated from lack of capital investment. By the early 1980s, with Archie McCardell ousted, a new executive team ratcheted up the cost-cutting—Harvester's Louisville plant was closed, along with several other factories—but the company remained in deep financial trouble. In late 1984, IH sold off its farm equipment division to J.I. Case, a subsidiary of Tenneco Inc. (though Case was uninterested in acquiring some operations, like the Farmall factory in the Quad Cities, which was then shut down). Harvester's pared-down truck division was rebranded with the new name Navistar.[22]

Thirty years after it had vanquished the FE, International Harvester, a "founding giant of modern industrial America," was out of business too.[23]

32.
The Rank and File Loved That Union

M y father, DeWitt Gilpin, did not live to see the collapse of International Harvester, his old nemesis. He retired from the staff of the UAW when he was sixty-five and died three years later, a few months before the record-breaking 1979 Harvester strike began. Many of the FE's national and local leaders who figured in this story also passed away before IH did. Jim Wright, however, outlasted the company that had once fired him. He rose through the UAW ranks and in 1980 was elected director for the union's Region 4, headquartered in Chicago. Wright thus became one of the UAW's few Black regional directors and was the first (and so far only) African American to head the union's Midwestern region. In the 1980s the *Chicago Tribune*, ironically enough, lauded him as "one of the nation's top black labor leaders"; among Wright's many accomplishments in his later career was to serve as an early supporter and close advisor to the first African American to be elected mayor of Chicago, Harold Washington. Jim Wright died in Chicago in 1999, at the age of 80.[1]

Now nearly all those with any direct memory of the FE are gone; the McCormick family, though many descendants remain exceptionally wealthy, is no longer in the public eye; and even the company is remembered mostly by a small but passionate fan club of farmers (or former farmers) who collect IH paraphernalia. Keeping in mind historian David Brody's admonition—that deriving what's important comes not from speculating about what might have been but from "a closer examination of what did happen"—what of value can be extracted from the FE's brief existence and the history of this long deep grudge, now that it has been largely covered up by the passage of time?[2]

The fact that the FE's leadership never abandoned its conviction that it had a grudge against the McCormick family and International Harvester's management would be the place to start. Contrary to the cooperative ethos that has for decades defined the American labor movement, the "irresponsible radicals" who headed the FE nurtured the hostility they felt toward the corporate executives on the other side of the bargaining table, and that sense of ceaseless conflict found expression in the contracts they negotiated and the shop-floor conduct they countenanced. John McCaffrey got a lot of things at IH wrong, but he'd been correct that the FE leadership was "more interested in disruption than in labor-management peace" and he was right that such unabashed belligerence was distinct from what was being championed by Walter Reuther, the labor movement's premier statesman. It was once commonplace for scholars to assert that a leadership's ideological orientation had no bearing on day-to-day union operations, but in this particular instance John McCaffrey knew what he was talking about.

Yet what also matters here is not just that FE officials talked tough—plenty of union leaders do that—but that they thought differently than did their noncommunist counterparts. The resolutely class-conscious FE leadership viewed the accumulation of profit—or what they obstinately regarded as "surplus value"—not as a pathway toward general prosperity but as the crucial mechanism by which management maintained its ongoing power. FE leaders believed that Harvester workers were being purposely shortchanged every minute of every day they were on the job, a reality that a collective bargaining agreement could ameliorate but not eliminate. The company's piecework system revealed this exploitation in an especially naked form, as without ongoing resistance the output required for each task would be nudged up and employee compensation thereby decreased, but FE officials recognized this widening gap between wages and profits not as a bug peculiar to Harvester's byzantine wage scheme but a feature inherent to capitalism. In their Marxist worldview no good, for workers anyhow, could come from a labor movement that aided and abetted such corporate plunder, for as International Harvester's history made clear enough, employers really ought not be trusted with any excess cash. In the pre-CIO era the McCormicks used the staggering wealth they had amassed (and kept partially hidden away) to acquire mansions and diamonds and divorces, and also labor-displacing technology and Pinkertons and lawyers and industrial relations consultants, all for the purpose of weeding out those employees who had the temerity to suggest they deserved more than the company deemed they were worth. Even the expenditures on the welfare programs that garnered IH such good press were designed as much to control as to reward. When industrial unionism at last forced management to fork over more to its workers, Harvester executives sought to regain what they had lost with speedup and piecework-rate chiseling. In the post-World War II years, the captains of industry who ran IH squandered the tremendous surplus the company had in reserve through a series of poor decisions that antagonized its workforce and disrespected its customer base. And inevitably, as management prioritized cost-cutting above all else, IH—like all other industrial firms—pursued that objective by chasing cheaper labor or by closing plants altogether.

The FE's radicalism, therefore, was evident not only in walkout statistics but also in what the union's leaders fought to include—and exclude—in their contracts. To the FE leadership the postwar labor-management "bargain" epitomized by the 1950 UAW-GM contract—laced with come-ons like productivity and cost-of-living wage hikes—was no bargain at all but an especially clever swindle, the kind where the con artist has long since left town before the marks realize they've been had. Refusing to accede to "management's right to manage," the FE successfully rebuffed Harvester's effort to pad its profit margins by imposing a lower wage scale at its Louisville plant, but once the labor establishment endorsed the politics of productivity—and cast out the left-led unions that opposed it—challenging the company on such prerogatives became increasingly difficult. As historian Steve Rosswurm has noted, "Capital mobility was an important part of the corporate postwar counteroffensive" against union power, but "the CIO responded lamely to this capital mobility because it was trapped in a web of ideological and institutional commitments that closed off its options." So the independent FE's full-on assault in 1952 against Harvester's relocation of its Chicago Twine Mill received no outside support and failed. A few years later, when FE officials signaled defeat and accepted the terms offered them by Walter Reuther, they joined an organization that, as Nelson Lichtenstein has underscored, "reflected a technological determinism that saw productivity growth as an autonomous process divorced from the character of class relations." Those former FE officials did their best—which was very good—to continue delivering for those Harvester workers who remained employed. But as UAW staff members operating within the confines of a labor movement that accepted "economic growth" as a value-neutral objective and equated "efficiency" with progress, they could do little besides issue despondent press releases when yet another factory shut down.[3]

Long-term vision, however, was not all that distinguished the FE leadership from labor's mainstream: the rejection of the politics of productivity also generated a different conception of what effective day-to-day union representation looked like. Because FE leaders believed they had a duty not to bolster but to claw back as much corporate wealth as possible, they were obliged to thwart Harvester at every turn, so they resisted schemes that linked compensation to productivity and noisily challenged the company's efforts to reduce labor costs by fleeing to the American South. And, most visibly, they sought to directly undermine in a myriad of ways management's ceaseless drive for greater "efficiency" on the shop floor. "The creation of a normal working day," Karl Marx maintained, is "the product of a protracted civil war, more or less dissembled, between the capitalist class and the working-class." FE leaders concurred that continual combat was necessary to prevent Harvester management—through the manipulation of its deliberately dissembled piecework system—from encroaching on the limits of the agreed-upon "normal working day"; the frontline troops were the FE stewards, whose primary mission was to ensure that union members got paid what they were owed and didn't have to work themselves to exhaustion to get it. Even once they'd conceded defeat and entered the UAW, former FE leaders like my father clung to the notion, in keeping with what the anarchists had insisted back in 1886, that to "reduce hours without cutting pay" should remain a prime directive for the labor movement. But the productivity bargain struck by Walter Reuther and the CIO mainstream meant that "the shorter workweek movement had been decisively defeated within the industrial union movement," as historian Jonathan Cutler has noted. As a result, "the discourse of shorter hours—the vision of less work and more pay—has vanished from the horizon of possibility" and the right to define what constitutes a "normal working day" has been handed back to the employers.[4]

All this helps explain one of the extraordinary elements of this story: the fierce and sustained loyalty of the FE's rank and file. Within the plants, FE local leaders advocated for their members only; workers were not encouraged to assist management in meeting the latest production targets. Thus, they not only regarded "every grievance as a scream for justice" but could act on that sentiment immediately, instigating walkouts or slowdowns that enforced fair treatment of the workforce. Assessments of the left-led unions have often argued that the ongoing allegiance of their memberships sprang not from an any identification with the national leadership's ideology but was instead rooted in the respect commanded by officials at the local level, most of whom were not card-carrying communists. But one was a necessary prerequisite for the other. Certainly Harvester workers held the FE in high regard because their local officials represented them so aggressively, but that conduct was made possible by the precepts of proper trade unionism as defined by the CP-influenced national leadership.

Yet while FE leaders purposely refrained from pushing their members to help pad Harvester's profits, they were quite willing to risk alienating them on other fronts. One of the FE's fundamental tenets was a genuine commitment to all-inclusive unionism, something labor organizers confronting the McCormicks' dominion had been grappling toward since the nineteenth century. FE officials thus challenged rather than conformed to the racism prevalent within the majority-white membership, insisting that solidarity brooked no exceptions. This approach deepened African American support for the union, but it also transformed many whites as well, and as Black and white workers recognized their common interest in the struggle against the company they developed personal affinities that carried past the plant gates and into their homes. The risk, in other words, paid off, and as a result the FE transcended what comes from the isolating "where's mine?" school of unionism that makes no demands on its members. "The rank and file loved that union": that's what Frank Mingo, an African American leader at Tractor Works, said about the FE, and the depth of that sentiment made the small union uncommonly powerful, allowing it for a while to best Harvester management and the UAW both. Where the cohesion derived from the commitment to racial unity proved the strongest—in Louisville—the FE leveraged its "constant campaign" for solidarity into a drive for equality in the larger community.

The FE's hyper-militancy, promoted by the leadership and practiced by the rank and file, therefore, was a key source of strength—until, it must be noted, such militancy (or one particular form of it, anyhow) began to undermine the union. The concerns Jim Wright raised about the diminishing returns reaped from the FE's trigger-happy walkout policy were shared by Jerry Fielde and other top officials; hence the attempt to shift toward slowdowns—or what was dubbed the "strikeless strike"—as a tactic that would better restrain Harvester's profit-taking and more successfully shield workers (and the union) from retribution. Slowdowns, however, require more coordinated discipline and can take longer to pay off than walkouts might; once the wildcats were out of the bag it proved difficult for FE leaders to nudge the membership towards other forms of resistance. And the UAW's ever-present threat further narrowed the room to maneuver, as the FE could ill afford even the suggestion that it had backed away from responding aggressively and immediately to workers' grievances. But actions by FE members that occurred shortly after the disastrous 1952 strike offer a worthwhile comparison: at Tractor Works they slowed down and extracted concessions from Harvester management; in Louisville they walked out and achieved nothing beyond getting nearly the entire local leadership fired. It's important, then, to recognize that walkouts are not the only marker of labor militancy, and in fact there may be better ways to pressure management. Since, though, employers and government agencies often track work stoppages but not slowdowns, the evidence for the seemingly less dramatic inside operations is harder to uncover.

If, however, the FE could have redirected its militancy—or made any number of other course corrections—it still may not have been enough. For this story is not just about labor but is also a cautionary tale about the fearsome power of American capital, as represented by one of its premier entities: International Harvester. Historian Stephen Meyer invoked the 1928 writings of early labor historian Selig Perlman as a reminder that capitalism is "not simply an economic and political arrangement where one class owned 'the means of production, exchange and distribution'; it was rather a social organization presided over by a class with an '*effective will to power.*' The capitalist class 'defend[ed] its power against all comers' and 'convinced other classes that they alone, the capitalists, know how to operate the complex economic apparatus of modern society upon which the material welfare of all depends.'"[5]

Harvester serves as the epitome of this "effective will to power," with no one's will more effective in this regard than that of Cyrus McCormick II, who maintained management's upper hand for half a century with increasingly sophisticated strategies that maximized exploitation of the workforce and obliterated organizing efforts within it, all cloaked by "economic laws and facts" that were purportedly immutable but were in fact often fabricated out of whole cloth. The pioneering schemes developed at Harvester under Cyrus II's watch in the then-emerging field of industrial relations permeated outward and armed capital with new weapons to fend off "all comers." The anti-union culture promulgated by Cyrus II long survived him, and the full brunt of Harvester's considerable resources were deployed against the FE, because it—as opposed to the UAW—vehemently challenged the by-then hegemonic notion that the elites of the sort running IH were uniquely entitled to "operate the complex economic apparatus of modern society." Of course, during the Cold War era Harvester could also count on assistance from opinion makers and government officials at all levels (not that all outcomes were guaranteed, as evidenced by Harold Ward's trial). Once the labor establishment, as well, joined the full-court press, it was, as Al Verri once said, "just a matter of time" for the FE.

But as Jim Wright had pointed out, what is remarkable is not that this union with its militant orientation was eventually overcome, but that against such concerted, formidable might the FE nonetheless, on the strength of its determined leadership with devoted rank and file support, accomplished what it did. For FE leaders like Wright, Verri, and my father, the move into the UAW in 1955 was certainly a capitulation but by no means an indication of abject failure. Preserving the superior pay and benefits that had been wrested at great cost from a seemingly invincible company was not an insignificant achievement. Because of that, tens of thousands of Harvester employees were able to take vacations, receive quality medical care, buy houses, put their children through college, and retire with dignity. What they were denied, following the destruction of radical unionism in the United States, was the opportunity for any real influence over "the complex economic apparatus of modern society."[6]

Now that the good-paying industrial jobs in this country have been largely eliminated, and with them the labor movement that had developed out of those factories and mills, how much that bargain really cost has again become a salient question. For more than just the unions were decimated, as Steve Rosswurm has noted: "Capital mobility destroyed and destroys—for the process is an endless one—history: the working-class institutions, communities, and organizations that were the product of years of struggle." That their battle with Harvester management was one that went well beyond pay and benefits and reached into the realm of history itself would have been a sentiment fully appreciated by the FE leadership. As the repeated invocations of Haymarket made clear, possibly no other union was as animated by its own history as was the FE, or more cognizant of how struggles from distant decades laid the groundwork for later triumphs. FE leaders remained devoted to maintaining that lifeline to the past. Days before his sudden death in 1969, Tractor Works local president Pete Neputy "spoke out publicly trying to right an old wrong," my father said in his eulogy for his longtime friend, "calling for the erection of a memorial to the leaders of the first strike at Harvester, the Haymarket martyrs who led a strike for an eight-hour day and were framed and hung in Chicago for such audacity." (It would not be until 2004, however, before such a monument at Haymarket Square was unveiled.) And because of their conscious connection to their own history, those FE leaders would understand that, despite the demolished plants, the company's demise, and the deterioration of the labor movement, this story, which began in the mid-nineteenth century with the demands made by a handful of iron molders at the McCormick Harvesting Machine Company, is not yet finished. The subterranean fire that August Spies spoke of smolders still; it only remains to be seen where, among working people, its flames will blaze up again.[7]

Hanging on a wall in my home is a black-and-white photograph that I discovered among my father's papers after he died. Though it does not depict a well-known or especially dramatic event, I became instantly fond of it. I'm not sure exactly when it was taken, but most likely in the late 1940s; it's of a group of about twenty people walking on a picket line in front of the gate at

Tractor Works. They were not there, clearly, in relation to a chain-wide strike called after a contract expiration, but rather were engaged in one of the FE's innumerable "unauthorized" walkouts. About half the workers in the group are white, and the rest African American. It must have been a relatively warm day, as they are in shirt-sleeves. Several are wearing hats: a few fedoras, along with some baseball-style or traditional workers' caps. One of the things I like so much about the picture is that it exposes what filmmakers almost always get wrong when they stage strike or protest scenes: in the movies the signs carried by demonstrators, even when they're intended to look handmade, are spelled and spaced correctly. The two signs visible in my photograph, however, were clearly painted by the strikers themselves. One reads, in jagged lettering:

**WE SHALL
NOT
BE MVE**

and the other says:

**WE DEMAND
REINSTATE
OUR COM
MITTEE**

But there's something even more affecting about this photo that made me want to display it so I might look at it often: the people in it look like they are having a good time. Certainly the two men toward the front of the line do: one is my father, the only man in the picture wearing a tie, as he was generally apt to do, and which marks him as the union staffer in the group. There's a cigarette dangling from his mouth, and the way his hands are positioned he was likely holding a book of matches, about to strike one for a light. He is smiling. So too is the man next to him—Pete Neputy—who bears a broad grin and appears to be engaged in some banter with my father. Several of the other workers are also chatting with each other and all seem at ease. They look like happy class warriors. Perhaps I am reading too much into one photograph, but it appears to illustrate what Anne Braden found to be true at the Harvester plant in Louisville, where, she said, "people really enjoyed getting up and going to work in the morning," because of the FE. "You knew there was going to be something interesting at the gate, there was going to be a leaflet, there was going to be people out about something, and there was a real esprit de corps that I think made it bearable to go to work." And it is also evocative of what Frank Mingo—who does not appear to be in the photo, but as a Tractor Works leader was probably on that picket line somewhere—said about the FE: "The rank and file loved that union."

And so: this is a tale about a long deep grudge, and how that anger and resentment prodded workers to demand what was justly theirs and to win at least a larger portion of it. But it is also a story about love: about workers who genuinely loved their union, and thus each other, as they had developed the deep bonds of affection and solidarity that uplifted them and energized them to fight on together. To build a successful labor movement—and thereby a fair and equitable society—the grudge needs to be acknowledged and acted upon. But the love must be there too.

Acknowledgments

T*he Long Deep Grudge* has its origins in a dissertation about the Farm Equipment Workers that I wrote decades ago at Yale University. I was fortunate there to join an extraordinarily supportive cohort of graduate students, all of us mentored by the late David Montgomery. David's breadth of historical knowledge was legendary, but as a former machinist and left-wing labor organizer he possessed a bone-deep understanding of class conflict and solidarity. I remain grateful for all I learned from him and from my grad school comrades, who have honored David through their own scholarship and activism.

This book, however, owes its existence to Louisville residents Walter and Kay Tillow, themselves also longtime labor activists. After stumbling across my dissertation online back in 2011, they tracked me down—through their old friend David Montgomery—and urged me to get it published. I initially put them off, since I was busy with other political work and wasn't convinced there would be much current interest in the FE. But Walter and Kay kept prodding me, and as our economic crisis deepened, I finally recognized what they had all along: that the FE's story is exactly what those endeavoring to revitalize the labor movement need to know. I am indebted, therefore, to Walter and Kay for their persistence, as well as for the support and generosity they have continued to extend to me.

Once I embarked on this project, I reconnected with Steve Rosswurm, who had been my college thesis advisor when I first started looking into the FE's history. Steve urged me to go beyond simply tinkering with my dissertation, suggesting that I start from scratch to create something with both scholarly integrity and broad appeal. Thus I jettisoned my old framework, expanded my scope, did additional research, and worked much harder to craft an engaging narrative than I might have otherwise. The book took longer, but is far better thanks to Steve's belief that I should do more. Steve also provided ongoing commentary on each chapter, and his deep understanding of the subject matter much improved my manuscript. I am very thankful for all his advice.

My friend Dana Frank—one of my grad school pals—also read a good chunk of the manuscript. Dana's tireless work with trade unionists in Central America leaves me humbled, and so I much appreciate that she took time away from her vital efforts to provide me valuable commentary. Thanks also to our good friends Toby and Penelope Sachs for their cogent advice on early chapters and enthusiastic support throughout. Their input helped me shape the FE's story so that it could interest a varied audience, and not just academics or labor history devotees.

I am profoundly gratified that Haymarket Books chose to publish *The Long Deep Grudge*, which seemed poetically appropriate given that the Haymarket legacy plays a central role in my book. At all points in the publishing process I felt valued and respected, in part because of the press's cooperative ethos, but also because everyone on the staff is just genuinely nice. So my heartfelt thanks to everyone at Haymarket, especially those whom I worked with most closely: Dana Blanchard, Nisha Bolsey, Julie Fain, Eric Kerl, Maya Marshall, and Ashley Smith.

My mother, Mimi Gilpin, does not appear in the story I've told here but is integral to it nonetheless. My parents met after WWII (my father's first marriage ended in divorce) and their devoted—if sometimes tempestuous—relationship fortified my father through his many draining battles involving the FE (and later, the UAW). Despite all she experienced, my mother, a union and community activist in her own right, somehow retained an entirely uncynical commitment to social justice until her death, at 93, in 2015. I wish she were still around to read this book, for she influenced me more than she realized.

And now comes the part where words fail me, because expressing how much I owe my husband and best friend Gary Isaac is beyond my ken. Ours was a genuine picket line romance (our first date took place after we were both arrested for participating in a union protest) as Gary wowed me with his fiery orations and his strategic prowess during the 1984 Yale clerical workers' strike; he is still my hero every day and the best organizer I know. He shares my passions, gets my jokes, and occasionally wins an argument with me. He is my everlasting love, and everything I do—writing this book being a prime example—is made easier and better thanks to him. And our dazzling whip-smart daughters, Amy and Esther Isaac, have awed me from the start and still keep me on my toes. My work is enhanced by what I regularly learn from them. They have no tolerance for inequality, are unimpressed by authority, and don't easily back down from a fight. I regret that my father, DeWitt Gilpin, never got to meet his granddaughters, for he would have recognized them as kindred spirits.

Select Bibliography

ncluded here are many of the books consulted for *The Long Deep Grudge*. Other sources—including interviews, government documents, dissertations, primary documents from archives and personal collections, and newspaper, journal, and magazine articles—are referenced in the endnotes.

Adams, Luther. *Way Up North in Louisville: African American Migration in the Urban South, 1930–1970*. Chapel Hill: University of North Carolina Press, 2010.

Andrews, Wayne. *The Battle for Chicago*. New York: Harcourt Brace and Company, 1946.

Ashby, Steven K. and C. J. Hawking. *Staley: The Fight for a New American Labor Movement*. Urbana: University of Illinois Press, 2009.

Avrich, Paul. *The Haymarket Tragedy*. Princeton: Princeton University Press, 1984.

Bergreen, Laurence. *Capone: The Man and the Era*. New York: Simon and Schuster, 1994.

Bernstein, Irving. *The Lean Years: A History of the American Worker, 1920–1933*. Boston: Houghton Mifflin, 1960.

Bernstein, Peter and Annalyn Swan. *All the Money in the World: How the Forbes 400 Make—and Spend—Their Fortunes*. New York: Random House, 2008.

Bogart, Ernest Ludlow and Charles Manfred Thompson. *The Industrial State*, Vol. 4 in *The Centennial History of Illinois*, edited by Clarence Walworth Alvord. Chicago: Illinois Centennial Commission, 1920.

Boyle, Kevin. *The UAW and the Heyday of American Liberalism 1945–1968*. Ithaca: Cornell University Press, 1995.

Braden, Anne. *The Wall Between*. Knoxville: University of Tennessee Press, 1999.

Brock, Pope. *Charlatan: America's Most Dangerous Huckster, the Man Who Pursued Him, and the Age of Flimflam*. New York: Broadway Books, 2009.

Brody, David. *Labor Embattled: History, Power, Rights*. Urbana: University of Illinois Press, 2005.

Cameron, Rondo and V. I. Bovykin, eds. *International Banking 1870–1914*. New York: Oxford University Press, 1992.

Casson, Herbert N. *The Romance of the Reaper*. New York: Doubleday, 1908.

———. *Cyrus Hall McCormick: His Life and Work*. Chicago: A.C. McClurg, 1909.

Chandler, Alfred D. *The Visible Hand: The Managerial Revolution in American Business*.

Cambridge: Belknap Press, 1977.

———. *Scale and Scope: The Dynamics of Industrial Capitalism*. Cambridge: Harvard University Press, 1994.

Cherney, Robert W., William Issel, and Kieran Walsh Taylor, eds. *American Labor and the Cold War: Grassroots Politics and Postwar Political Culture*. New Brunswick: Rutgers University Press, 2004.

Chernow, Ron. *Titan: The Life of John D. Rockefeller, Sr.* New York: Random House, 1998.

Cochran, Bert. *Labor and Communism: The Conflict That Shaped American Unions*. Princeton: Princeton University Press, 1977.

Cohen, Lizabeth. *Making a New Deal: Industrial Workers in Chicago, 1919–1939*. Cambridge: Cambridge University Press, 1990.

Commons, John R. *History of Labour in the United States*. Vol. 2. New York: Macmillan Company, 1918.

Cowie, Jefferson. *Capital Moves: RCA's Seventy-Year Quest for Cheap Labor*. New York: Cornell University Press, 1999.

———. *Stayin' Alive: the 1970s and the Last Days of the Working Class*. New York: New Press, 2012.

Craypo, David and Bruce Nissan, eds. *Grand Designs: The Impact of Corporate Strategies on Workers, Unions, and Communities*. Ithaca: ILR Press, 1993.

Culver, John C. and John Hyde. *American Dreamer: A Life of Henry A. Wallace*. New York: W. W. Norton, 2001.

Currarino, Rosanne. *The Labor Question in America: Economic Democracy in the Gilded Age*. Urbana: University of Illinois, 2011.

Cutler, Jonathan. *Labor's Time: Shorter Hours, the UAW, and the Struggle for American Unionism*. Philadelphia: Temple University Press, 2004.

Darby, Edward. *The Fortune Builders: Chicago's Famous Families*. New York: Doubleday, 1986.

Davenport, Russell Wheeler. *USA: The Permanent Revolution*. New York: Prentice-Hall, 1951.

Davis, Mike. *Prisoners of the American Dream: Politics and Economy in the History of the U.S. Working Class*. New York: Verso, 1986.

Delton, Jennifer. *Racial Integration in Corporate America, 1940–1990*. Cambridge: Cambridge University Press, 2009.

Dennis, Michael. *The Memorial Day Massacre and the Movement for Industrial Democracy*. New York: Palgrave Macmillan, 2010.

Derber, Milton. *The American Idea of Industrial Democracy.* Urbana: University of Illinois Press, 1970.

Devine, Thomas. *Henry Wallace's 1948 Presidential Campaign and the Future of Postwar Liberalism.* Chapel Hill: University of North Carolina Press, 2013.

Donner, Frank. *Protectors of Privilege: Red Squads and Police Repression in Urban America.* Berkeley. University of California Press, 1990.

Dubofsky, Melvin. *Hard Work: The Making of Labor History.* Urbana: University of Illinois Press, 2004.

Early, Steve. *The Civil Wars in U.S. Labor: Birth of a New Workers' Movement or Death Throes of the Old?* Chicago: Haymarket Books, 2011.

Evans, Sterling. *Bound in Twine: The History and Ecology of the Henequen-Wheat Complex from Mexico to the American and Canadian Plains, 1880–1950.* College Station: Texas A&M University Press, 2007.

Feurer, Rosemary. *Radical Unionism in the Midwest, 1900–1950.* Urbana: University of Illinois Press, 2006.

Filippelli, Ronald and Mark McColloch. *Cold War in the Working Class: The Rise and Decline of the United Electrical Workers.* Albany: SUNY Press, 1995.

Fine, Sidney. *Sit-Down: The General Motors Strike of 1936–1937.* Ann Arbor: University of Michigan Press, 1969.

Fink, Gary, ed. *Biographical Dictionary of American Labor.* Westport: Greenwood Press, 1984.

Fones-Wolf, Elizabeth A. *Selling Free Enterprise: The Business Assault on Labor and Liberalism, 1945–60.* Urbana: University of Illinois Press, 1994.

Fones-Wolf, Ken and Elizabeth Fones-Wolf. *Struggle for the Soul of the Postwar South: White Evangelical Protestants and Operation Dixie.* Urbana: University of Illinois Press, 2015.

Forbes, B. C. *Men Who Are Making America.* New York: Forbes Publishing Company, 1916.

Fosl, Catherine. *Subversive Southerner: Anne Braden and the Struggle for Racial Justice in the Cold War South.* New York: Macmillan, 2002.

Freedland, Richard. *The Truman Doctrine and the Origins of McCarthyism.* New York: Knopf, 1975.

Freeman, Joshua. *In Transit: The Transport Workers Union in New York City, 1933–1966.* New York: Oxford University Press, 1989.

Garraty, John R. *Right-Hand Man: The Life of George W. Perkins.* New York: Harper Brothers, 1957.

Glaberman, Martin. *Wartime Strikes: The Struggle Against the No-Strike Pledge in the UAW during World War II*. Detroit: Berwick Editions, 1980.

Gourevitch, Alex. *From Slavery to the Cooperative Commonwealth: Labor and Republican Liberty in the Nineteenth Century*. Cambridge: Cambridge University Press, 2015.

Green, James R. *The World of the Worker: Labor in Twentieth-Century America*. New York: Hill and Wang, 1980.

———. *Death in the Haymarket: A Story of Chicago, the First Labor Movement and the Bombing that Divided Gilded Age America*. New York: Anchor Books, 2006.

Greenhouse, Steven. *The Big Squeeze: Tough Times for the American Worker*. New York: Knopf, 2008.

Gross, James A. *The Reshaping of the National Labor Relations Board: National Labor Policy in Transition, 1937–47*. Albany: SUNY Press, 1981.

Hall, Wade, ed. *The Rest of the Dream: The Black Odyssey of Lyman Johnson*. Lexington: University Press of Kentucky, 1988.

Harrison, Gilbert. *A Timeless Affair: The Life of Anita McCormick Blaine*. Chicago: University of Chicago Press, 1979.

Haycraft, William. *Yellow Steel: The Story of the Earthmoving Equipment Industry*. Urbana: University of Illinois Press, 2000.

Hersh, Seymour. *Reporter: A Memoir*. New York: Random House, 2018.

Hicks, Clarence J. *My Life in Industrial Relations: Fifty Years in the Growth of a Profession*. New York: Harper Brothers, 1941.

Higdon, James. *Cornbread Mafia: A Homegrown Syndicate's Code of Silence and the Biggest Marijuana Bust in American History*. Guilford: Lyons Press, 2013.

Hope, John II. *Negro Employment in Three Southern Plants of International Harvester Company*. Washington, DC: National Planning Association, 1953.

Hounshell, David. *From the American System to Mass Production, 1800–1932: The Development of Manufacturing Technology in the United States*. Baltimore: Johns Hopkins University Press, 1984.

Hutchinson, William. *Cyrus Hall McCormick: Harvest, 1856–1884*. New York: D. Appleton-Century Company, 1935.

Jacoby, Sanford. *Employing Bureaucracy: Managers, Unions, and the Transformation of Work in the Twentieth Century*. New York: Columbia University Press, 1985.

Kampelman, Max. *The Communist Party vs. the CIO*. New York: Praeger, 1957.

Keeran, Roger. *The Communist Party and the Auto Workers Unions*. Bloomington: Indiana University Press, 1980.

Kelley, Robin D. G. *Hammer and Hoe: Alabama Communists during the Great Depression*. Chapel Hill: University of North Carolina Press, 1990.

Kennedy, David. *Freedom from Fear: The American People in Depression and War, 1929–1945*. New York: Oxford University Press, 1999.

Kimeldorf, Howard. *Reds or Rackets?: The Making of Radical and Conservative Unions on the Waterfront*. Berkeley: University of California Press, 1988.

Kleber, John, ed. *The Encyclopedia of Louisville*. Louisville: University Press of Kentucky, 2001.

Klehr, Harvey. *The Heyday of American Communism: The Depression Decade*. New York: Basic Books, 1984.

Klepper, Michael and Robert Gunther, *The Wealthy 100: From Benjamin Franklin to Bill Gates—A Ranking of the Richest Americans, Past and Present*. New York: Citadel Press, 1996.

K'Meyer, Tracy. *Civil Rights in the Gateway to the South: Louisville, Kentucky, 1945–1980*. Lexington: University Press of Kentucky, 2009.

Korstad, Robert. *Civil Rights Unionism: Tobacco Workers and the Struggle for Democracy in the Mid-Twentieth-Century South*. Chapel Hill: University of North Carolina Press, 2003.

Lamoreaux, Naomi and Daniel M. G. Raff, eds. *Coordination and Information: Historical Perspectives on the Organization of Enterprise*. Chicago: University of Chicago Press, 1995.

Leffingwell, Randy. *Farmall: The Red Tractor that Revolutionized Farming*. Minneapolis: Voyageur Press, 2007.

Levenstein, Harvey. *Communism, Anti-Communism and the CIO*. Westport: Greenwood Press, 1981.

Levin, Meyer. *Citizens*. New York: Viking Press, 1940.

Lichtenstein, Nelson. *Labor's War at Home: The CIO in World War II*. Cambridge: Cambridge University Press, 1982.

———. *Walter Reuther: The Most Dangerous Man in Detroit*. Urbana: University of Illinois Press, 1995.

———. *State of the Union: A Century of American Labor*. Princeton: Princeton University Press, 2002.

MacDougall, Curtis. *Gideon's Army*. New York: Marzani and Munsell, 1965.

Marsh, Barbara. *A Corporate Tragedy: The Agony of International Harvester Company*. New York: Doubleday, 1985.

Marx, Karl. *Capital*. Vol. 1. New York: International Publishers, 1967.

McCormick, Cyrus III. *The Century of the Reaper*. Cambridge: Riverside Press, 1931.

McTighe, John. *The Barefoot Boy on the Parkway: A History of UAW Local 862*. Louisville: UAW Local 862 publication, 1988.

Messer-Kruse, Timothy. *The Trial of the Haymarket Anarchists: Terrorism and Justice in the Gilded Age*. New York: Palgrave Macmillan, 2011.

Metzgar, Jack. *Striking Steel: Solidarity Remembered*. Philadelphia: Temple University Press, 2000.

Meyer, Stephen. *"Stalin over Wisconsin": The Making and Unmaking of Militant Unionism, 1900–1950*. New Brunswick: Rutgers University Press, 1992.

Miller, Donald. *City of the Century: The Epic of Chicago and the Making of America*. New York: Simon and Schuster, 1996.

Miller, Earl J. *Workmen's Representation in Industrial Government*. Urbana: University of Illinois Press, 1921.

Mitrani, Sam. *The Rise of the Chicago Police Department: Class and Conflict, 1850–1894*. Urbana: University of Illinois Press, 2013.

Montgomery, David. *Workers' Control in America: Studies in the History of Work, Technology, and Labor Struggles*. Cambridge: Cambridge University Press, 1979.

Moody, Kim. *U.S. Labor in Trouble and Transition: The Failure of Reform from Above, the Promise of Revival from Below*. New York: Verso, 2007.

———. *On New Terrain: How Capital is Reshaping the Battleground of Class War*. Chicago: Haymarket Books, 2017.

Murolo, Priscilla and Ben Chitty. *From the Folks Who Brought You the Weekend: A Short, Illustrated History of Labor in the United States*. New York: New Press, 2001.

National Industrial Conference Board. *Experience with Works Councils in the United States*, Report No. 50. New York: Century Company, 1922.

Nelson, Bruce. *Workers on the Waterfront: Seamen, Longshoremen, and Unionism in the 1930s*. Urbana: University of Illinois Press, 1990.

Nelson, Daniel. *Managers and Workers: Origins of the Twentieth-Century Factory System in the United States, 1880–1920*. Madison: University of Wisconsin Press, 1995.

Nugent, Daniel, ed. *Rural Revolt in Mexico: U.S. Intervention and the Domain of Subaltern Politics*. Durham: Duke University Press, 1998.

Ottanelli, Fraser M. *The Communist Party in the United States: From the Depression to World War II*. New Brunswick: Rutgers University Press, 1991.

Ozanne, Robert. *A Century of Labor-Management Relations at McCormick and International Harvester*. Madison: University of Wisconsin Press, 1967.

———. *Wages in Practice and Theory: McCormick and International Harvester,*

1860–1960. Madison: University of Wisconsin Press, 1968.

———. *The Negro in the Farm Equipment and Construction Machinery Industries*. Philadelphia: University of Pennsylvania Press, 1972.

Pacyga, Dominic A. *Chicago: A Biography*. Chicago: University of Chicago Press, 2009.

Perry, Douglas. *The Girls of Murder City: Fame, Lust, and the Beautiful Killers Who Inspired Chicago*. New York: Penguin, 2011.

Perusek, Glenn and Kent Worcester, eds., *Trade Union Politics: American Unions and Economic Change, 1960s–1990s*. Atlantic Highlands, NJ: Humanities Press, 1995.

Phelan, Craig. *Grand Master Workman: Terrance Powderly and the Knights of Labor*. Westport: Greenwood Press, 2000.

Phillips, Lisa. *A Renegade Union: Interracial Organizing and Labor Radicalism*. Urbana: University of Illinois, 2013.

Pierce, Bessie Louise. *The Beginning of a City, 1673–1848*. Vol. 1. In *A History of Chicago*. Chicago: University of Chicago Press, 1937.

———. *The Rise of a Modern City*. Vol. 3. In *A History of Chicago*. Chicago: University of Chicago Press, 1957.

Piketty, Thomas. *Capital in the Twenty-First Century*. Cambridge: Harvard University Press, 2014.

Pomerantz, Charlotte, ed. *A Quarter-Century of Un-Americana, 1938–63: A Tragico-Comical Memorabilia of HUAC*. New York: Marzani and Munsell, 1963.

Portelli, Alessandro. *They Say in Harlan County: An Oral History*. New York: Oxford University Press, 2011.

Roderick, Stella Virginia. *Nettie Fowler McCormick*. New Hampshire: Richard R. Smith, 1956.

Roediger, Dave and Franklin Rosemont, eds. *Haymarket Scrapbook*. Chicago: Charles H. Kerr, 1986.

Rosenfeld, Jake. *What Unions No Longer Do*. Cambridge: Harvard University Press, 2014.

Rosswurm, Steve, ed. *The CIO's Left-Led Unions*. New Brunswick: Rutgers University Press, 1992.

Russell, Thaddeus. *Out of the Jungle: Jimmy Hoffa and the Remaking of the American Working Class*. New York: Knopf, 2001.

Saposs, David. *Communism in American Unions*. New York: McGraw Hill, 1959.

Saul, Scott. *Becoming Richard Pryor*. New York: HarperCollins, 2014.

Schatz, Ronald. *The Electrical Workers: A History of Labor at General Electric and*

Westinghouse, 1923–1960. Urbana: University of Illinois Press, 1983.

Schmidt, Karl. *Henry A. Wallace: Quixotic Crusade, 1948*. Syracuse: Syracuse University Press, 1960.

Selekman, Benjamin, Sylvia Selekman, and Stephen Fuller. *Problems in Industrial Relations*. New York: McGraw Hill, 1958.

Serrin, William. *The Company and the Union: The "Civilized Relationship" of the General Motors Corporation and the United Automobile Workers*. New York: Random House, 1970.

Shaw, Brent. *Bringing in the Sheaves: Economy and Metaphor in the Roman World*. Toronto: University of Toronto Press, 2013.

Shulman, Bruce. *From Cotton Belt to Sun Belt: Federal Policy, Economic Development, and the Transformation of the South, 1938–1980*. New York: Oxford University Press, 1991.

Sinclair, Upton. *The Jungle*. 1904. Edited by James Barrett. Urbana: University of Illinois Press, 1988.

Spies, August. *Autobiography: His Speech in Court and General Notes*. London: Forgotten Books, 2012. First published by Nina Van Zandt, 1887.

Smith, Merritt Roe. *Harpers Ferry Armory and the New Technology: The Challenge of Change*. Ithaca: Cornell University Press, 1977.

Starobin, Joseph. *American Communism in Crisis, 1943–1957*. Berkeley: University of California Press, 1972.

Stein, Judith. *Pivotal Decade: How the United States Traded Factories for Finance in the Seventies*. New Haven: Yale University Press, 2011.

Steinbeck, John. *The Grapes of Wrath*. New York: Viking Press, 1939.

Stepan-Norris, Judith and Maurice Zeitlin. *Left Out: Reds and America's Industrial Unions*. Cambridge: Cambridge University Press, 2002.

Storch, Randi. *Red Chicago: American Communism at Its Grassroots, 1928–35*. Urbana: University of Illinois Press, 2007.

Stromquist, Shelton. *Labor's Cold War: Local Politics in a Global Context*. Urbana: University of Illinois Press, 2008.

Terkel, Studs. *Hard Times*. New York: Random House, 1970.

Tifft, Susan and Alex Jones. *The Patriarch: The Rise and Fall of the Bingham Dynasty*. New York: Summit Books, 1991.

Topik, Steven and Allen Wells, eds. *The Second Conquest of Latin America: Coffee, Henequen, and Oil During the Export Boom, 1850-1930*. Austin: University of Texas Press, 1998.

Tuttle, William. *Race Riot: Chicago in the Red Summer of 1919*. New York: Athenium, 1970.

Weinstein, James and David Eakins, eds. *For a New America: Essays in History and Politics from Studies on the Left, 1959-1967*. New York: Random House, 1970.

White, Ahmed. *The Last Great Strike: Little Steel, the CIO, and the Struggle for Labor Rights in New Deal America*. Berkeley: University of California Press, 2016.

Notes

Preface: Heavy Hangovers

1. The greater Detroit area was broken into several different UAW regions at the time, which also factors into why Region 4 was then larger than any other in the union.

2. Joe Flaherty, "Working People Talk Back," *Nation*, October 18, 1980, 377. Many less biased observers have also expressed the opinion that the UAW's agricultural implement contracts outpaced its contracts in other industries, including auto; see William Serrin, *The Company and the Union: The "Civilized Relationship" of the General Motors Corporation and the United Automobile Workers* (New York: Random House, 1970), 183–84; Barbara Marsh, *A Corporate Tragedy: The Agony of International Harvester Company* (New York: Doubleday, 1985), 213.

3. "Harvester Union Hails New Pact," *Atlanta Constitution*, April 20, 1980; David Shepardson, "UAW Loses 33,000 Members in 2008," *Detroit News*, April 1, 2009; Bureau of Labor Statistics, "Major Work Stoppages in 2013," February 12, 2014 (both these sources include statistics from earlier decades). In terms of union density—the percentage of the workforce that is organized—even the 1979 20 percent figure represented a decline for the labor movement. In the mid-1950s union density in the United States peaked at more than 30 percent, meaning that in 1954 one out of every three workers in the country was a union member. Union membership as a percentage of the workforce (as opposed to union membership expressed in absolute numbers) has been declining ever since. Gerald Mayer, *Union Membership Trends in the United States*, (Washington, DC: Congressional Research Service, 2004).

4. Bureau of Labor Statistics, "Economic News Release, Union Members Summary," January 18, 2019, www.bls.gov/news.release/union2.nr0.htm; Keith Laing and Ian Thibodeau, "UAW Membership Dropped by 35,000 in 2018," *Detroit Free Press*, March 29, 2019, https://www.detroitnews.com/story/business/autos/2019/03/29/uaw-membership-dropped-last-year/3314861002/. In another reflection of the altered economic landscape, the UAW has taken up organizing on college campuses, and white-collar workers now comprise nearly one-third of the union's membership. "2018-01-28 Companion Page Regarding UAW Membership Percentages," January 28, 2018, https://workin4alivin.com/2018/01/28/2018-01-28-companion-page-regarding-uaw-membership-percentages/.

5. Bureau of Labor Statistics, "Major Work Stoppages (Annual) News Release," February 8, 2019, www.bls.gov/news.release/wkstp.nr0.htm.

6. Patricia Cohen, "Paychecks Lag as Profits Soar, and Prices Erode Wage Gains," *New York Times*, July 13, 2018, www.nytimes.com/2018/07/13

/business/economy/wages-workers-profits.html; Chad Stone, Danilo Trisi, Arloc Sherman, and Roderick Taylor, "A Guide to Statistics on Historical Trends in Income Inequality," Center on Budget and Policy Priorities, May 15, 2018, www.cbpp.org/research/poverty-and-inequality/a-guide-to-statistics -on-historical-trends-in-income-inequality. Widespread attention to the scope of economic inequality owes much to the Occupy Wall Street movement and its focus on the wealth controlled by "the one percent," and to Thomas Piketty's *Capital in the Twenty-First Century* (Cambridge: Harvard University Press, 2014) which provides exhaustive detail on this point: "Since 1980 . . . income inequality has exploded in the United States" (294). The Economic Policy Institute also provides ongoing analysis of the continuing wage and wealth gap in America, see for instance Estelle Sommeiller and Mark Price, "The New Gilded Age," Economic Policy Institute, July 19, 2018, www.epi .org/publication/the-new-gilded-age-income-inequality-in-the-u-s-by-state -metropolitan-area-and-county/; and Lawrence Mishel, Elise Gould, and Josh Bivens, "Wage Stagnation in Nine Charts," Economic Policy Institute, January 6, 2015 (one of these charts starkly depicts how wages for American workers uncoupled from rising productivity after 1979), www.epi.org/publication /charting-wage-stagnation/. For a chart detailing the sharp post-1979 split between rising profits and declining wages, see Seth Ackerman, "Piketty's Fair-Weather Friends," *Jacobin*, May 29, 2014, www.jacobinmag.com/2014/05 /pikettys-fair-weather-friends/. For a wealth of statistics on how unions raise working-class living standards generally, see Josh Bivens et. al., "How Today's Unions Help Working People," Economic Policy Institute, August 24, 2017, www.epi.org/publication/how-todays-unions-help-working-people -giving-workers-the-power-to-improve-their-jobs-and-unrig-the-economy/.

7.   For more on labor's decline from the 1970s onward, see Kim Moody, *On New Terrain: How Capital is Reshaping the Battleground of Class War* (Chicago: Haymarket Books, 2017); Jake Rosenfeld, *What Unions No Longer Do* (Cambridge: Harvard University Press, 2014); Jefferson Cowie, *Stayin' Alive: the 1970s and the Last Days of the Working Class* (New York: New Press, 2012); Steve Early, *The Civil Wars in U.S. Labor: Birth of a New Workers' Movement or Death Throes of the Old?* (Chicago: Haymarket Books, 2011); Judith Stein, *Pivotal Decade: How the United States Traded Factories for Finance in the Seventies* (New Haven: Yale University Press, 2011); Steven K. Ashby and C. J. Hawking, *Staley: The Fight for a New American Labor Movement* (Urbana: University of Illinois Press, 2009); Steven Greenhouse, *The Big Squeeze: Tough Times for the American Worker* (New York: Knopf, 2008); Kim Moody, *U.S. Labor in Trouble and Transition* (New York: Verso, 2007); Nelson Lichtenstein, *State of the Union: A Century of American Labor* (Princeton: Princeton University Press, 2002); Jefferson Cowie, *Capital Moves: RCA's Seventy-Year Quest for Cheap Labor* (New York: Cornell University Press, 1999); Glenn Perusek and Kent Worcester, eds., *Trade Union Politics: American Unions and*

Economic Change, 1960s–1990s (New Jersey: Humanities Press, 1995); Mike Davis, *Prisoners of the American Dream: Politics and Economy in the History of the U.S. Working Class* (New York: Verso, 1986).

8.   David Brody, *Labor Embattled: History, Power, Rights* (Urbana: University of Illinois Press, 2005), 87.

9.   Thomas Piketty, in *Capital in the Twenty-First Century*, argues that "the history of inequality is shaped by the way economic, social, and political actors view what is just and what is not, as well as by the relative power of those actors and the collective choices that result" (20). He concludes with this invocation: "Yet it seems to me that all social scientists, all journalists and commentators, all activists in unions and in politics of whatever stripe, and especially all citizens should take a serious interest in money, its measurement, the facts surrounding it, and its history. Those who have a lot of it never fail to defend their interests. Refusing to deal with numbers rarely serves the interests of the least well-off" (577). Though Piketty himself ignores the labor movement and its influence on the distribution of wealth, I'd argue that the FE-UAW debate represents an ideological dispute about money (or wealth) and how best to increase the share of it that goes to the working class, and so falls within Piketty's call to add some detail to the history of money, wealth, and inequality. For more on Piketty and on the issue of inequality generally, see also Paul Krugman, "Why We're in a New Gilded Age," *New York Review of Books*, May 8, 2014; Jeff Faux, "Thomas Piketty Undermines the Hallowed Tenets of the Capitalist Catechism," *Nation*, April 18, 2014; Branko Milanovic, "The Return of 'Patrimonial Capitalism': review of Thomas Piketty's Capital in the Twenty-First Century," *Journal of Economic Literature* (June 2014); Jacob Hacker, Paul Pierson, Heather Boushey, and Branko Milanovic, "Piketty's Triumph," *American Prospect*, March 10, 2014. For Piketty's failure to focus on the labor movement, see Thomas Frank, "The Problem with Thomas Piketty: 'Capital' Destroys Right-Wing Lies, but There's One Solution it Forgets," *Salon*, May 11, 2014; Toni Gilpin, "'Them That's Got Are Them That Gets': Piketty's Lessons for Activists," *Labor Notes*, July 3, 2014.

Introduction: Undried Blood on the Pavement

1.   Just how uninterested the establishment press then was in the tragic and/or violent deaths of African Americans was something Sy Hersh learned early on as a cub reporter in his hometown of Chicago in the late 1950s. Shortly after landing his first reporting job, Hersh arrived at the scene of a tenement fire that had killed several people, including three children, and phoned one of his editors with what he saw as a big, important story. "There are traumatic events we remember all of our life," Hirsch wrote, "and I remember every word he said: 'Ah, my good, dear, energetic Mr. Hersh. Do the, alas, poor unfortunate victims happen to be of the Negro persuasion?' I said yes. He said, 'Cheap it out.' That meant that my City News dispatch would report the following, give

or take a phrase: 'Five Negroes died in a fire last night on the Southwest Side.' It might also have included an address. I thought, having worked for years in a family store in a black area, that I knew something about racism. [My editor] taught me that I had a lot to learn." Seymour Hersh, *Reporter: A Memoir* (New York: Random House, 2018), 21–22.

2.   "30 Union Chiefs Sought for Quiz in Pipe Slaying," *Chicago Tribune*, October 5, 1952; "Harvester Firm Employe Slain; Seek Murderer," *Sarasota Herald-Tribune*, October 4, 1952; *Herald-American* editorial quoted in "International Harvester's Frame-up of Harold Ward," National Committee to Free Harold Ward, October 1952, United Electrical Workers Archives, University of Pittsburgh, (hereafter, UE Archives); "Which Prosecutor?" *Chicago Tribune*, October 10, 1952. In a similar editorial the *Chicago Sun-Times* also presumed the FE responsible for Foster's death: "Murder is the Payoff," *Chicago Sun-Times*, October 7, 1952. The Chicago Police Department's Labor Detail was formed in 1940, and Captain George Barnes was its first commander. "Chicago Police Labor Detail, At Work For A Year," *Chicago Tribune*, February 9, 1941. The labor detail worked in tandem with the CPD's industrial squad—also known as the "Red Squad"—which shadowed and infiltrated left-wing organizations and labor unions, particularly those in the CIO. "[The] industrial squad played an important role in collaborating with employers in strikebreaking, not only by assaulting picketers and protecting scabs, but in supplying dossiers (usually for a fee) to the right-wing press (the Hearst *Chicago American* and the *Chicago Tribune*), discrediting unions and their leaders. Well into the strife-torn forties, the labor detail served as a defense corps for AFL unions embraced in 'sweetheart' contracts with employers to repel CIO organizing efforts, as well as combating rank-and-file revolts against repressive AFL union leadership." Frank Donner, *Protectors of Privilege: Red Squads and Police Repression in Urban America* (Berkeley: University of California Press, 1990), 51. No doubt the information the *Tribune* printed regarding Harold Ward's communist associations—see below—was supplied to the paper by the Chicago police.

3.   *Chicago Tribune*, October 5, 6, 1952.

4.   *Milwaukee Sentinel*, October 11, 1952; "International Harvester's Frame-up," October 1952, UE Archives.

5.   "International Harvester's Frame-up," October 1952, UE Archives; *Chicago Tribune*, October 11, 1952.

6.   *Chicago Tribune*, October 11, 1952.

7.   John McCaffrey to all Harvester employees represented by the FE, letter, October 20, 1947, file 5212 DE1-02, International Harvester (now Navistar) Archives (hereafter, IHA).

8.   IH, *The Unstoppable*, pamphlet, 1952, in author's possession, also in IHA; H. C. Baker, (IH Assistant Manager of Labor Relations), address before the fourteenth training course in industrial relations, June 1953, IHA; *Chicago*

Daily News and *Chicago Tribune*, September 8, 1952.

9. "Grant Oakes," in *Biographical Dictionary of American Labor,* ed. Gary Fink (Westport, CT: Greenwood Press, 1984), 272–73; Sonya Burns, interview with author, April 17, 1986.

10. For evidence of the role of skilled workers in the early organization of the electrical industry, see Ronald Schatz, "Union Pioneers: The Founders of Local Unions at General Electric and Westinghouse, 1933–1937," *Journal of American History* 66 (December 1979): 586–602. Verri quoted in Barbara Marsh, *A Corporate Tragedy: The Agony of International Harvester Company* (New York: Doubleday, 1984), 82 (Marsh renders Fielde's shortened first name as "Gerry" but I've changed it to "Jerry," as that's the spelling he used); Sonya Burns, interview with author, April 17, 1986.

11. DeWitt Gilpin, "Fired for 'Inefficiency,'" *Social Work Today,* November 1935; "Larry Van Dusen," in Studs Terkel, *Hard Times* (New York: Random House, 1970), 105–8 (Larry Van Dusen was a pseudonym for DeWitt Gilpin); Sonya Burns, interview with author, April 17, 1986.

12. Alan P. Herrmann, "Westfield By the Book," Westfield, New York website, August 2010, westfieldny.com/living-here/westfield-book.

13. Al Verri, interview with author, January 29, 1981; Milt Burns is quoted in Robert Ozanne, *A Century of Labor-Management Relations at McCormick and International Harvester* (Madison: University of Wisconsin Press, 1967), 214.

14. FE Local 108 Flyer, September 1952, included in Complaint for Injunction, International Harvester v. UE Local 108, David Rothstein papers, Chicago History Museum Archives (hereafter, CHMA); *Chicago Daily News*, September 29, 1952; *Chicago Tribune,* September 4, 1952.

15. "International Harvester's Frame-up," October 1952, UE Archives.

1: The Reaper Kingdom

1. William Hutchinson, *Cyrus Hall McCormick: Harvest, 1856–1884* (New York: D. Appleton-Century Company, 1935), 687–88.

2. B. C. Forbes, *Men Who Are Making America* (New York: Forbes Publishing Company, 1916), 244–45; Hutchinson, *Cyrus Hall McCormick*, 751. Cyrus Hall and Nettie Fowler McCormick had seven children—Cyrus Hall II, Mary Virginia, Robert, Anita, Alice, Harold Fowler, and Stanley Robert. Robert and Alice died as children.

3. Before McCormick's horse-drawn reaper made its appearance, farmers collected grain in the same arduous manner they'd employed since the dawn of agriculture: on foot, slicing through their fields with hand-held tools (initially, sickles; by the sixteenth century, with two-handled scythes, which at least offered an improvement because they were designed to be used in a standing, rather than a stooping, position) while others followed behind gathering the felled crop into bales. Because harvesting was the most labor-intensive

step involved in crop production, and had to take place quickly, farmers were obliged to limit how much they planted, or sometimes watched grain rot in the fields when they lacked enough hands to bring it in.

4.   Chicago in the 1840s already displayed its characteristic raw energy, but was certainly short on creature comforts, except insofar as that term applied to actual creatures. "Not only did large numbers of dogs run at large in the streets, but also hogs and cattle. The last, especially, were a source of complaint since they not only injured the elms set out along the streets for shade-trees and discouraged the planting of more, but sometimes used the sidewalks more than did the people, often lying upon them or being driven upon them to be milked. Alleys were rendered loathsome by these bovine inhabitants, who added to other charges lodged against them the plundering of grain and bags left in the farmers' wagons and the 'hooking' of children." Bessie Louise Pierce, *A History of Chicago, Vol. I: The Beginning of a City, 1673–1848* (Chicago: University of Chicago Press, 1937), 205.

5.   Herbert N. Casson, *Cyrus Hall McCormick: His Life and Work* (Chicago: A.C. McClurg, 1909), 154. McCormick's real estate investments paid off handsomely, but not all of his financial decisions were as savvy. He could have been an even richer man, as in 1864 he passed on the opportunity to advance a loan to a former dry goods clerk, Marshall Field, who had an idea for a new retail store. He was also prone to speculation and lost money on schemes that never paid off, like a gold mine in South Carolina and a railroad in Georgia. Wayne Andrews, *The Battle for Chicago* (New York: Harcourt Brace and Company, 1946) 44–45; Edward Darby, *The Fortune Builders: Chicago's Famous Families* (New York: Doubleday, 1986), 240–43.

6.   B. C. Forbes, *Men Who Are Making America*, 244; see also Stella Virginia Roderick, *Nettie Fowler McCormick* (New Hampshire: Richard R. Smith, 1956), 99.

7.   Roderick, *Nettie Fowler McCormick*, 119; Hutchinson, *Cyrus Hall McCormick*, 666.

8.   Roderick, *Nettie Fowler McCormick*, 120. The Princeton class of 1879 was an especially influential one, including, among others, future president Woodrow Wilson; he and Cyrus McCormick II remained lifelong friends.

9.   This description is drawn from Hutchinson, *Cyrus Hall McCormick*, 694, and from an article describing McCormick Works in *Scientific American*, May 14, 1881, 307–8; David Hounshell believes the *Scientific American* article was written by Cyrus McCormick II, see *From the American System to Mass Production, 1800–1932: The Development of Manufacturing Technology in the United States* (Baltimore: Johns Hopkins Press, 1984), 180.

10. *Scientific American*, May 14, 1881; see also Hutchinson, *Cyrus Hall McCormick*, 695. David Hounshell, in *From the American System*, indicates that from the company's founding through 1880 "there is little evidence" that the McCormicks had "expanded [their] technical horizons to encompass the developments known as the American system of manufactures. The

McCormick factory employed almost no special or single-purpose machinery, and there is little evidence that Leander [McCormick, brother of Cyrus I, who supervised day-to-day operations at the factory before 1880] knew of the techniques of special gauges, jigs, and fixtures which distinguished the arms industry. Handwork and skilled machine work appear to have prevailed during this period. Moreover, the output of reapers and mowers was surprisingly small." *American System*, 7; see also 154.

11. For more on foremen and their power in nineteenth-century factories, see Daniel Nelson, *Managers and Workers: Origins of the Twentieth-Century Factory System in the United States, 1880–1920* (Madison: University of Wisconsin Press, 1995), 35–55.

12. More about the McCormick molders union can be found in Robert Ozanne, *A Century of Labor-Management Relations at McCormick and International Harvester* (Madison: University of Wisconsin Press, 1967), 3–28; and Timothy Messer-Kruse, "Strike or Anarchist Plot? The McCormick Riot of 1886 Reconsidered," *Labor History* 52, no. 4 (November 2011): 483–510. For more about foundry work in this era in general, see James Horner, "The Equipment of the Foundry," *Cassier's Magazine*, June 1903, 496–97.

13. Quotes are from David Montgomery's rich discussion of early craftsmen's conduct: "Workers' Control of Machine Production in the Nineteenth Century," in *Workers' Control in America* (Cambridge: Cambridge University Press, 1979), 9–31.

14. Robert Ozanne, *Wages in Practice and Theory: McCormick and International Harvester, 1860–1960* (Madison: University of Wisconsin Press, 1968), 31; Ozanne, *Century*, 5, 7. Ozanne, in his exhaustive examination of wage data at McCormick Works, is clear on the trickledown impact of the molders' strikes: ". . . the bargaining gains of this small band of skilled molders was passed along to the unskilled foundry workers (equal in number to the molders) and usually to the entire plant, within a week or two." *Century*, 4. This contradicts Timothy Messer-Kruse's argument that strikes by the self-interested molders typically affected the rest of the McCormick workforce only adversely: the molders "won concessions and conducted strikes on behalf of roughly 10 percent of the factory's employees, the other 90 percent suffering unemployment when the molders struck, but not necessarily reaping any benefits when the molders won." Messer-Kruse, "Strike or Anarchist Plot?," 484. Since Messer-Kruse's source on this point is Ozanne's *Century*, it's difficult to see how he makes his case here for the 1860s and 1870s. For a few years in the early 1880s, however, Ozanne's other study does note that wage increases won by the molders were not passed on to common laborers in the plant. Ozanne, *Wages*, 28.

15. Hounshell, *American System*, 179. Quote is from Hutchinson, *Cyrus Hall McCormick*, 689. Cyrus II was an adept mechanic: as a teenager, he had already devised innovations that contributed to the creation of a twine binder, one of the more significant technological leaps forward in the development of farm

equipment. For more about the origins of the American System, see Merritt Roe Smith, *Harpers Ferry Armory and the New Technology: The Challenge of Change* (Ithaca: Cornell University Press, 1977).

16.   Hounshell, *American System*, 180; *Scientific American*, May 14, 1881, 307; Ozanne, *Century*, 11.

17.   Hutchinson, *Cyrus Hall McCormick*, 690, 699; statistics are drawn from Hutchinson, *Cyrus Hall McCormick*, 699; and from tables from Ozanne, *Wages*, 27, 112; and Hounshell, *American System*, 161.

18.   Quotes from Hutchinson, *Cyrus Hall McCormick*, 689; wealth assessments from Michael Klepper and Robert Gunther, *The Wealthy 100: From Benjamin Franklin to Bill Gates—A Ranking of the Richest Americans, Past and Present* (New York: Citadel Press, 1996), 261; Darby, *Fortune Builders*, 240. Cyrus McCormick I left an estate of $10 million in 1884. There is, of course, no exact way to compare the value of money across centuries, but using the standard Consumer Price Index metric, $10 million in 1884 would be worth the equivalent of $260,000,000 in 2019. Another measure, which assesses the relative share of gross domestic product, would equate $10 million in 1884 to over $20 billion in 2019. For methods of calculation see www.measuringworth.com/calculators/uscompare/.

19.   In his assessment of Cyrus McCormick II, Robert Ozanne has suggested that the protracted 1885 and '86 labor altercations at McCormick Works resulted in part from blunders made by the inexperienced, Ivy-League educated company president, who, Ozanne argues, spent most of his time at the downtown office, far removed from the factory, and thus made critical decisions during those turbulent years "with little understanding of the issues or possible consequences. Nothing at Princeton or in his four years as understudy to his father had given him any insight into the feelings or temper of the fourteen hundred men who labored in his factory." This interpretation has often been repeated by historians detailing the Haymarket affair, especially because (not surprisingly) many of them rely on Ozanne's meticulous study when discussing Cyrus McCormick's role in the Haymarket-related strikes. But William Hutchinson's account of Cyrus II's role in the business upon his return from Princeton makes clear that he was at the plant much of the time—as noted above, Hutchinson reported that Cyrus II was often at the Works until after midnight—and Hutchinson also quoted company officials who in 1880 and 1881 said that Cyrus II "was carrying the whole load," "looks after the factory more than anyone else," and that because of Cyrus II's efforts the factory "was in better working trim than it has ever been." And David Hounshell also emphasizes Cyrus II's year as the Works's assistant superintendent under Charles Wilkinson, from 1880–81, when he spent extensive time in the shop under Wilkinson's tutelage, after which Cyrus II took over as Works superintendent, the position he held until he took over the company presidency in 1884. Cyrus II, then, had clearly served as something more than

an understudy to his father (who spent a good portion of the early 1880s in New York and Europe) and was by 1885 well acquainted with the factory and the men who worked in it. He had by then developed a clear sense of how he wished to accelerate growth at the company and what he thought were the impediments standing in the way. The misjudgments he made in 1885 and 1886 were tactical in nature, but did not derive from any unfamiliarity on his part with the factory or the workforce, or stem from a lack of clarity in his own mind about his mission there. See Ozanne, *Century*, 10, 13; Hutchinson, *Cyrus Hall McCormick*, 689; Hounshell, *American System*, 178–82.

2. Birds of the Coming Storm

1.   Z. L. White, "Western Journalism," *Harper's Monthly* (October 1888); 687; statistics from Walter Nugent, "Demography," *Encyclopedia of Chicago*, 2005, www.encyclopedia.chicagohistory.org/pages/962.html.

2.   Quotes from Bessie Louise Pierce, *A History of Chicago*, Vol. 3: *The Rise of a Modern City* (Chicago: University of Chicago Press, 1957), 269–70; wage-cut information from Robert Ozanne, *A Century of Labor-Management Relations at McCormick and International Harvester* (Madison: University of Wisconsin Press, 1967), 13.

3.   *Chicago Tribune*, April 4, 1885.

4.   *Chicago Tribune*, March 28, 1885.

5.   Cyrus McCormick III, *The Century of the Reaper* (Boston: Houghton Mifflin, 1931), 89–90.

6.   Ozanne, *Century*, 15; *Chicago Tribune*, April 6, 1885 and April 9, 1885.

7.   Craig Phelan, *Grand Master Workman: Terrance Powderly and the Knights of Labor* (Westport: Greenwood Press, 2000), 88–91. Irishman McPadden was also active in the Clan na Gael, a furtive association dedicated to establishing, by any means necessary, an independent Ireland. For a recent consideration of the Knights' philosophy, see Alex Gourevitch, *From Slavery to the Cooperative Commonwealth: Labor and Republican Liberty in the Nineteenth Century* (Cambridge: Cambridge University Press, 2015).

8.   *Chicago Tribune*, April 8, 9, 1885.

9.   *Chicago Tribune*, April 11, 1885.

10.   *Chicago Tribune*, April 10, 1885.

11.   *Chicago Tribune*, April 12, 1885.

12.   Ozanne, *Century*, 18, 20.

13.   Ozanne, *Century*, 18–21, 25–27.

14.   Ozanne, *Century*, 19.

15.   "Capital" quote is from Donald Miller, *City of the Century: The Epic of Chicago and the Making of America* (New York: Simon and Schuster, 1996), 468. See also Paul Avrich, *The Haymarket Tragedy* (Princeton: Princeton University Press, 1984), 73–74, 143–49; James Green, *Death in the Haymarket: A Story*

of Chicago, the First Labor Movement, and the Bombing that Divided Gilded Age America (New York: Anchor Books, 2006), 113, 130; John R. Commons, *History of Labour in the United States* Vol. 2 (New York: Macmillan Company, 1918), 388; Floyd Dell, "Bomb-Talking," in Dave Roediger and Franklin Rosemont, eds., *Haymarket Scrapbook* (Chicago: Charles H. Kerr, 1986), 74.

16. Timothy Messer-Kruse, "Strike or Anarchist Plot? The McCormick Riot of 1886 Reconsidered," *Labor History* 52, no. 4 (November 2011): 488.

17. August Spies, *Autobiography: His Speech in Court and General Notes* (London: Forgotten Books, 2012; first published by Nina Van Zandt, 1887), 1.

18. It is worth noting that both men were members of the Knights of Labor and remained active in that organization as well.

19. Ozanne, *Century*, 11; Spies, *Autobiography*, 18. B. C. Forbes, *Men Who Are Making America* (New York: Forbes Publishing Company, 1916), 242. Cyrus McCormick purchased land—ultimately about three thousand acres—in what is now part of the Ottawa National Forest in Michigan's Upper Peninsula. The land was deeded to the US Forest Service in 1967 by the McCormick family, and is still designated as the McCormick Wilderness. Even today, according to the Ottawa National Forest website, "The Wilderness is fairly rugged, isolated, unspoiled, and relatively difficult to access."

20. Ozanne, *Century*, 21.

21. Miller, *City of the Century*, 473; Ernest Ludlow Bogart and Charles Manfred Thompson, *The Industrial State*, In Clarence Walworth Alvord, ed., *The Centennial History of Illinois*, Vol. 4 (Chicago: Illinois Centennial Commission, 1920), 464.

22. Ozanne, *Century*, 22.

23. Bogart and Thompson, *The Industrial State*, 166.

24. *Chicago Tribune*, March 1 and 2, 1886; Ozanne, *Century*, 22. The Chicago Police Department had changed considerably between 1885 and 1886, as had McCormick's relationship with Chicago Mayor Carter Harrison. For more on the evolution of the Chicago police and their role at McCormick Works, see Sam Mitrani, *The Rise of the Chicago Police Department: Class and Conflict, 1850–1894* (Urbana: University of Illinois Press, 2013), especially chapter 6.

25. Ozanne, *Century*, 23; Robert Ozanne, *Wages in Practice and Theory: McCormick and International Harvester, 1860–1960* (Madison: University of Wisconsin Press, 1968), 116; *Chicago Tribune*, March 5, 1886.

26. Avrich, *The Haymarket Tragedy*, 188.

27. Spies, *Autobiography*, 39; Ozanne, *Century*, 23.

28. Robert Ozanne found little evidence to suggest that there were many McCormick strikers involved in the assault on the plant, a conclusion echoed by Timothy Messer-Kruse in his evaluation of the event. But Ozanne nonetheless reiterates, "There can be no doubt that the company's ruthless actions toward unions in the strikes of 1885 and early 1886 had aroused substantial resentment among its employees, certainly enough to have inspired such an attack," which

seems a reasonable reading of the fury unleashed on May 3. See Ozanne, *Century*, 24; Timothy Messer-Kruse, "Strike or Anarchist Plot?"

29.   Spies's quotes from these paragraphs are drawn from his autobiography and from his article for the *Arbeiter-Zeitung*, May 4, 1886, entitled "Blood!" included as People's Exhibit 63 from the Chicago History Museum Haymarket Digital Archives, www.chicagohistoryresources.org/hadc /transcript/exhibits/X051-100/X0630.htm.

30.   McCormick's words to the press are recounted in Spies's *Arbeiter-Zeitung* article, "Blood," May 4, 1886.

31.   *The Haymarket Speeches As Delivered On The Evening Of The Throwing Of The Bomb, At Haymarket Square, Chicago, May 4, 1886* (Chicago: Chicago Labor Press Association, 1886).

32.   Green, *Death in the Haymarket*, 189; "A Hellish Deed: Dynamite Thrown into a Crowd of Policemen," *Chicago Tribune*, May 5, 1886; "Anarchy's Red Hand: Rioting and Bloodshed in the Streets of Chicago," *New York Times*, May 6, 1886; *Chicago Tribune*, May 6, 1886. In addition to Spies and Parsons, the others arrested were George Engel, Samuel Fielden, Adolph Fischer, Louis Lingg, Oscar Neebe, and Michael Schwab. For a discussion of the impact of Haymarket on the labor movement, see Green, *Death in the Haymarket*, 274–300. For a recent, and controversial, reassessment of the anarchists' connection to the Haymarket bombing, see Timothy Messer-Kruse, *The Trial of the Haymarket Anarchists: Terrorism and Justice in the Gilded Age* (New York: Palgrave Macmillan, 2011).

33.   Spies, *Autobiography*, 51, 54.

34.   *Chicago Tribune*, May 6, 1886; Pierce, *History of Chicago*, Vol. 3, 281; Avrich, *Haymarket Tragedy*, 223.

35.   Green, *Death in the Haymarket*, 270; *Chicago Tribune*, August 20, 1886. Oscar Neebe, whose connection to the incident was especially tangential, was sentenced to fifteen years in prison. Of those sentenced to death, Samuel Fielden and Michael Schwab had their sentences commuted to life imprisonment by Governor Richard Oglesby on November 10, 1887. Louis Lingg committed suicide in his cell that evening. Spies, Parsons, Adolph Fischer, and George Engel were hanged the next day. In 1893 Governor John Altgeld pardoned Neebe, Fielden, and Schwab.

36.   Ozanne, *Century*, 24; Pierce, *History of Chicago*, Vol. 3, 289; Avrich, *Haymarket Tragedy*, 126, 430; see also Green, *Death in the Haymarket*, 204–5, for the demise of the eight-hour movement in Chicago after the bombing.

3: The Difficult Birth of a Behemoth

1.   Such assessments of comparative wealth are somewhat subjective but Rockefeller comes out on top on most such lists; see, for instance, Grant Suneson, "The Thirty Richest Americans of All Time," MSN, May 9, 2018,

www.msn.com/en-us/money/savingandinvesting/30-richest-americans-of -all-time/ss-AAvnXqa. Peter Bernstein and Annalyn Swan insist that "if John D. Rockefeller were alive today, his wealth would be many times greater than Bill Gates"; *All the Money in the World: How the Forbes 400 Make—and Spend—Their Fortunes* (New York: Random House, 2008), 17. The Fifth Avenue Baptist Church—located at the corner of 46th Street and 5th Avenue—commonly called "Rockefeller's Church," became the site of protests against Rockefeller interests; socialist minister Bouck White, for instance, interrupted services there in 1914 to protest the recent massacre of miners at the Rockefeller-owned Ludlow Mine in Colorado; "Why I am in Prison," *Independent*, October 26, 1914. When the liberal Reverend Charles Frederick Aked from England was appointed to head the church in 1917, he hoped to end the designation. "It is not a millionaire's church," he insisted. "I want the shop girl and the workingman to come to the Fifth Avenue Baptist Church"; "Not Rockefeller's Church, Says the New Pastor," *Pittsburgh Press*, April 21, 1907. The Fifth Avenue Church would be replaced in 1930 by a larger "Rockefeller Church," the Riverside Church in upper Manhattan.

2. Descriptions of the planned wedding and the actual ceremony come from the *New York Times*, November 26, 1895, and the *San Francisco Call*, November 27, 1895.

3. Alfred D. Chandler, Jr., *The Visible Hand: The Managerial Revolution in American Business* (Cambridge: Belknap Press, 1977), 332.

4. Company founder William Deering was a dry-goods salesman with an eye for a good investment; he made his best one in 1879 when he put his money into what became the first saleable twine binder. His son Charles took over the firm in 1901. Cyrus McCormick insisted that Charles Deering "has a natural talent for intrigue and his long ambition . . . has been to supplant the McCormicks in the leadership of the harvesting machine industry." Notes attributed to an undated memorandum from the Stanley McCormick papers, cited in International Harvester Chronology, year 1903; McCormick-International Harvester Collection, Wisconsin State Historical Society (hereafter WSHS).

5. Helen Kramer, "Harvesters and High Finance: Formation of the International Harvester Company," *Business History Review* 38, no. 3 (Autumn 1964): 293. George Perkins's close relationship with J. P. Morgan was reflected in the title of his biography: John R. Garraty, *Right-Hand Man: The Life of George W. Perkins* (New York: Harper Brothers, 1957).

6. Herbert N. Casson, *The Romance of the Reaper*, (New York: Doubleday, 1908) 94–95.

7. The Illinois Northern Railway was a company wholly owned by the McCormicks, and consisted of the seventeen miles of track within the McCormick Works complex, along with an additional ten miles or so of track outside the plant; this railway became part of International Harvester and remained so until it was sold to the Santa Fe Railroad in 1950. The railway had

several of its own locomotives and employed about one hundred people. The railway's principal function was to move loaded cars to and from McCormick Works, but as the only railroad in the immediate area it also hauled freight for the many other factories around the McCormick plant (and was of course paid for the service) to and from Chicago's switching yards, where freight cars would be switched to national railways for transit beyond Chicago. This process also involved a fee, and in 1904 the Interstate Commerce Commission declared that the Illinois Northern Railway—and thus International Harvester—was considerably overcharging for its switching fees; *18th Annual Report of the Interstate Commerce Commission*, December 19, 1904, 19–21.

8. Garraty, *Right-Hand Man*, 144; *New York Times*, July 7, 1914. American capitalists, no less than European monarchs, cemented connections and augmented fortunes through marriage. This was certainly true for the McCormick family, and the familial alliances with the Rockefellers and Deerings were not the only examples: for instance, in 1876 Robert Sanderson McCormick (cousin to Cyrus II) married Katherine van Etta Medill, the daughter of Joseph Medill, owner and editor of the *Chicago Tribune* and mayor of Chicago from 1870 to 1873. Their son Robert Rutherford McCormick became the controversial arch-conservative owner/publisher of the *Chicago Tribune* from the 1920s through the mid-1950s. Another son from that union, Joseph Medill McCormick, married Ruth Hanna, daughter of the Ohio Senator, political kingmaker, and multimillionaire Mark Hanna.

9. "In 1901 and 1902 [John D.] Rockefeller had made large loans to the McCormick organization, and he had helped play an important role in the successful merger talks of 1902. He then contracted to lend the McCormicks up to $14 million to finance their required contribution to International Harvester's initial operating capital. He also was a close ally of the McCormicks in their ongoing struggles with the Deerings, George Perkins, and Judge Elbert Gary, including his stockholdings with theirs in calculations of which faction controlled a majority. While Rockefeller insisted that the loans to the company were strictly business, he clearly wanted the McCormicks to control the company; moreover, he constantly supported long-term strategies to strengthen the company." Rondo Cameron and V. I. Bovykin, eds., *International Banking 1870–1914* (New York: Oxford University Press, 1992), 515. For more detail on the founding of International Harvester and the McCormick-Deering-Perkins struggle for supremacy, see Carstensen, "'. . . a dishonest man is at least prudent': George W. Perkins and the International Harvester Steel Properties," *Business and Economic History* 9 (1980): 87–102; Kramer, "Harvesters and High Finance"; Robert Ozanne, *A Century of Labor-Management Relations at McCormick and International Harvester* (Madison: University of Wisconsin Press, 1967), 104–115; Barbara Marsh and Sally Saville, "International Harvester's Story: How a Great Company Lost Its Way," *Crain's Chicago Business*, November 8, 1982.

"McCormick descendants" is from Michael Klepper and Robert Gunther, *The Wealthy 100: From Benjamin Franklin to Bill Gates—A Ranking of the Richest Americans, Past and Present* (New York: Citadel Press, 1996), 261.

10.   Cameron and Bovykin, *International Banking*, 516; United States Bureau of Corporations, *The International Harvester Co.*, March 3, 1913, Washington, DC: Government Printing Office, xx.

11.   Ozanne, *Century*, 71; Barbara Marsh, *A Corporate Tragedy: The Agony of International Harvester Company* (New York: Doubleday, 1984), 46; Casson, *Romance of the Reaper*, 96–97. There is considerable historical literature on International Harvester's influential role in Mexico and Latin America; see, for instance, Sterling Evans, *Bound in Twine: The History and Ecology of the Henequen-Wheat Complex from Mexico to the American and Canadian Plains, 1880–1950* (College Station: Texas A&M University Press, 2007); Steven Topik and Allen Wells, eds., *The Second Conquest of Latin America: Coffee, Henequen, and Oil During the Export Boom, 1850–1930* (Austin: University of Texas Press, 1998); Daniel Nugent, ed., *Rural Revolt in Mexico: U.S. Intervention and the Domain of Subaltern Politics* (Durham: Duke University Press, 1998).

4: Fair and Square Fifty-Fifty

1.   Walter S. Hubbard to Cyrus McCormick II, March 23, 1916, IHA.

2.   Herbert N. Casson, *The Romance of the Reaper*, (New York: Doubleday, 1908), 104–5; Robert Ozanne, *Wages in Practice and Theory: McCormick and International Harvester, 1860–1960* (Madison: University of Wisconsin Press, 1968), 47. Some women had been employed at McCormick Works, and the other plants in the Harvester chain, since the nineteenth century. The first women were employed as stenographers and file clerks, but by the time IH was founded women worked in industrial departments as well. They were confined, however, to those departments where the labor was deemed "women's work"—so, the Twine Mill, where the work was similar to that in textile mills; the core room in the foundries, where women packed foundry "flour" and sand—"like the mud pies of childhood"—into molds for small castings after which the molds were carried off to ovens for baking; and the canvas department, where the stiff fabric used in harvesting equipment was stenciled, cut, riveted, sewn and hemmed. Some of these "women" were in fact young girls, as through the 1920s those as young as fourteen were eligible for employment at McCormick Works. *Harvester World*, September 1912, WSHS.

3.   Upton Sinclair, *The Jungle*, ed. James Barrett (Urbana: University of Illinois Press, 1988), 193. Despite the ruinous pace, Sinclair posits that compared to the stockyards, McCormick Works for Jurgis was "a kind of a heaven to him." But just as Jurgis allows himself to imagine a decent future for his family, the factory abruptly closes "until further notice"—one of the seasonal layoffs common to farm equipment manufacturing. "There was not half an hour's

warning—the works were closed! . . . that was the way of it; and thousands of men and women were turned out in the dead of winter." Jurgis never returns to McCormick Works.

4.   Sinclair, *The Jungle*, 192; *Chicago Evening Post*, May 2, 1916, in clipping book, IHA; *Chicago Tribune*, April 28, 1916.

5.   *Chicago Examiner*, May 7, 1916, in clipping book, IHA; Robert Ozanne, *A Century of Labor-Management Relations at McCormick and International Harvester* (Madison: University of Wisconsin Press, 1967) 107; *Chicago Tribune*, May 13, 1916.

6.   Among those most strongly urging the need for a comprehensive labor policy was Morgan partner George Perkins, who at this point was still on the Harvester board. Ozanne, *Century*, 112.

7.   Cyrus McCormick II, memorandum, July 13, 1916, IHA.

8.   Cyrus McCormick II, memorandum, July 13, 1916, IHA; *National Association of Corporation Schools Bulletin* 5, no. 1 (January 1918): 466; *Harvester World*, September–October 1922, WSHS.

9.   Alfred Chandler, *The Visible Hand: The Managerial Revolution in American Business* (Cambridge: Belknap Press), 345.

10.   Sanford Jacoby, *Employing Bureaucracy: Managers, Unions, and the Transformation of Work in the Twentieth Century* (New York: Columbia University Press, 1985), 87.

11.   McCormick quotes from *Harvester World*, December 1919, WSHS; *Chicago Tribune*, July 18, 1948 (the story details Harvester's ongoing efforts to recoup its losses in Russia). IH and the Singer Sewing Machine Company were "the two largest integrated commercial enterprises in imperial Russia." Before the Revolution Harvester had two thousand workers in Moscow, producing machines sold through branches in eleven cities, controlling 80 percent of the dealerships in Russia. Alfred Chandler, *Scale and Scope: The Dynamics of Industrial Capitalism* (Cambridge: Harvard University Press, 1994), 200.

12.   The SCC was a purposely small group meant to represent those companies predominant in their fields; the other companies on the original roster included U.S. Rubber, Westinghouse, and Bethlehem Steel; AT&T joined in 1925 and U.S. Steel in 1934. Clarence J. Hicks, *My Life in Industrial Relations: Fifty Years in the Growth of a Profession* (New York: Harper Brothers, 1941), 136–37; US Senate Subcommittee of the Committee on Education and Labor (the LaFollette Committee), *Violations of Free Speech and the Rights of Labor*, 1939, 76th Congress, 2nd Session, (16781, 16785), Washington, DC: Government Printing Office. $13 billion in 1939 translates to between $241 billion and nearly $3 trillion in 2019 dollars, depending on the calculation used.

13.   Hicks, *My Life*, 138. "The very existence, method of operation, and regular functioning of the Special Conference Committee throughout two decades are evidence of a high degree of collaboration on labor matters by key corporations," as Robert Ozanne notes, in *Century*, 160. In fact, because many

of these industrial relations directors hopped from company to company, the SCC was made up of a very small group of tightly connected men. Clarence J. Hicks, chairman of the committee until 1934, had been with International Harvester before joining Standard Oil in 1915. John D. Rockefeller, following the Ludlow Massacre, had Hicks devise one of the original employee representation plans for the Colorado Fuel and Iron Company. Arthur Young came from the Rockefeller organization to head Harvester's Industrial Relations Department in 1918. When Young resigned from Harvester in 1924 to head the consulting firm of Industrial Relations Counselors, Inc., he was asked to remain on the committee as a personal member, despite the fact that he no longer had a formal company connection. George Kelday, who replaced Young as Harvester's director of industrial relations, became Harvester's representative on the committee. Young became a vice-president of U.S. Steel in 1934, and it was then that that company was added to the Special Conference Committee. US Senate, *Violations of Free Speech and the Rights of Labor,* 16781–2. As an example of how influential these firms were, Massey-Harris, a Canadian farm equipment firm, adopted Harvester's employee representation plan outright in late 1919; see Industrial Relations Association of America (IRAA), *Proceedings,* May 19, 1920, 369–70.

14. For a thorough examination of Harvester's forays into "welfare capitalism," and how those programs were used as much to control as they were to reward, see Ozanne, *Century,* 71–95. And Sanford Jacoby, in *Employing Bureaucracy* (198–99), confirms the limited application of such magnanimity: "But one should not make too much of these programs. The new welfare work did little to relieve popular pressure for social legislation because it affected so few workers. . . . International Harvester's paid vacation plan was so restrictive that not a single production worker at the firm's plant in Fort Wayne in the early 1930s qualified for it." See also Rosanne Currarino, *The Labor Question in America: Economic Democracy in the Gilded Age* (Urbana: University of Illinois, 2011), 111.

15. IRAA, *Proceedings,* May 19, 1920, 6; "New Harvester Officers: Cyrus H. McCormick Jr. Takes Charge of Company's Plants," *New York Times,* November 5, 1922. The three generations of Cyrus McCormicks, because they were all involved in the family business (often during the same periods) and because of the odd way in which they handled their names, are with some regularity confused for each other in accounts of Harvester history. The first one—inventor of the reaper—was Cyrus Hall McCormick, who generally used all three names to identify himself. His son Cyrus, who took over the company in 1884, was originally named Cyrus Rice McCormick, but he later changed it legally to Cyrus Hall. Within the family and on most company documents he is referred to as Cyrus H. (using the initial, not Hall), and was sometimes identified as Cyrus II, but he never referred to himself as Junior. For obvious reasons, however, Cyrus II is often identified in historical accounts as Cyrus Jr. Cyrus II's son Cyrus, born in 1890, was in fact Cyrus III

but was referred to within the family and on company documents as Cyrus
Jr. He overlapped in Harvester management for some years with his father,
Cyrus II. Confusion about which Cyrus McCormick is which is therefore
understandable. See Edward Darby, *The Fortune Builders: Chicago's Famous
Families* (New York: Doubleday, 1986), 258.

16. US Senate, *Violations of Free Speech and the Rights of Labor,* 16798. General
Motors and U.S. Steel were the exceptions; U.S. Steel adopted employee
representation later in the 1920s and GM did so in the early 1930s.

17. The final plan is presented in *Harvester World*, March 1919, WSHS.
Discussion of the preparation of the plan can be found in IRAA, *Proceedings*,
May 19, 1920, 379; and in the many drafts of the plan itself that were retained
in International Harvester's archives. Young revised the plan twenty-six times,
and twelve drafts of the evolving Works Council Plan are still extant, complete
with the notes of management officials asked to comment on them, and
they reveal some conflicts among these executives and how the plan evolved
along the way. The plant superintendents were anxious to underscore that
"the actual conduct of the work [and] the responsibility for the efficient and
proper operation of the shop are wholly vested in the management," which
they did not want to see affected by the councils' existence. For his part,
Cyrus McCormick proved particularly interested in defining the requisite
qualifications for employees who might serve on the works councils, insisting
that potential representatives needed at least two years in a Harvester plant:
"Less service than that does not give the employee time to get the spirit of
the company." IH vice-president H. F. Perkins (no relation to Morgan partner
George Perkins), however, argued for a shorter requirement; ultimately, they
agreed on one year's employment. First draft, Industrial Council Plan, n.d.
[summer of 1918]; Fourth draft, Industrial Council Plan, October 18, 1918;
Tenth draft, Industrial Council Plan, February 5, 1919. All drafts from IHA.

18. The percentage of foreign-born employees can be found in Ozanne,
Century, 131. Harvester's age and citizenship requirements were much more
stringent than those at other firms that introduced ERPs. At IH, employee
representatives needed to be at least twenty-one years old, though most other
ERPs created during this era established no minimum age requirement.
Harvester's stipulation that employees had to have one year of continuous
employment to be eligible to serve on the councils was also a much stiffer
requirement than that specified in most other plans. The Colorado Fuel
and Iron Company, for instance, had no minimum age requirement and
required only three months employment for workers to be eligible to serve
as representatives. At IH the average age for the first group of employee
representatives was thirty-eight years, with an average length of service at
Harvester of seven years; 85 percent of the representatives were married. By
1922 the average age had increased to thirty-nine years and the average length
of service to almost nine years. National Industrial Conference Board (NICB),

Experience with Works Councils in the United States, Report No. 50 (New York: Century Company, 1922), 126. Most ERPs introduced at other firms contained no citizenship requirement, while a few required employees to have at least begun the naturalization process to serve as representatives. The Bureau of Industrial Research, in its 1919 report *American Shop Committee Plans*, found only one other plan that made full citizenship requisite for employee representatives. Given the restrictions IH imposed it was not surprising that the first workers to serve on the councils were praised as "responsible and mature men" by Arthur Young. In fact, if company officials "had been permitted to name the employee representatives," he said, "their choice would have been no more conservative and no more representative than the selection of the workers themselves." National Implement and Vehicle Association, *Proceedings of the 26th Annual Convention*, October 16, 1919, 66, Farm and Industrial Equipment Institute Archives, Chicago.

19. *Harvester World*, March 1919 and September–October 1922, WSHS.
20. Ozanne, *Century*, 117.
21. *Harvester World*, August 1919, WSHS; *New Majority*, (published by the Chicago Federation of Labor), August 2, 1919. John Kikulski, a well-known union organizer from the stockyards and a member of the Chicago Federation of Labor's executive board, coordinated the Harvester strike activities. General discussions of 1919 in Chicago can be found in Lizabeth Cohen, *Making a New Deal: Industrial Workers in Chicago, 1919–1939* (Cambridge: Cambridge University Press, 1990), 38–51; and William Tuttle, Jr., *Race Riot: Chicago in the Red Summer of 1919* (New York: Athenium, 1970).
22. Young quoted in IRAA, *Proceedings*, May 19, 1920, 365; see also *Harvester World*, September 1919, WSHS; Ozanne, *Century*, 126–31.
23. *New Majority*, August 9 and 23, 1919; Chicago Federation of Labor, minutes, August 17, 1919, CFL Records, CHMA.

5: With the Men It Is Actual Experience

1. Interestingly, Becker's "district" in McCormick Works did not include any of the heavy manufacturing or foundry departments. Elected from the Fire and Watch Department, he also represented the Inspection and Paint Departments, from which Jerry Fielde, a leader of the Farm Equipment Workers, would emerge several years later.
2. McCormick Works Council minutes (hereafter McWC), *Harvester Industrial Council Minutes of Regular Meetings*, July 8, September 8, October 21, October 28, 1921, IHA. Management representatives on the councils were generally the plant superintendent (who did not always attend the meetings), and some number of assistant superintendents and plant foremen. Arthur Young served as chair and was often present at the council meetings at the various plants.
3. McWC, August 7 and 17, 1922. Though when IH introduced its Industrial

Council Plan, its arbitration provision was widely heralded as an indication of how committed IH was to genuine power-sharing, during the eighteen years the councils were in existence the option of arbitration was never utilized. Earl J. Miller, *Workmen's Representation in Industrial Government* (Urbana: University of Illinois Press, 1921); National Labor Relations Board, *Decisions and Orders* 2, July 1, 1936–July 1, 1937, 328, Washington DC: Government Printing Office.

4.   McWC, February 3, 1923.

5.   IRAA, *Proceedings,* May 19, 1920, 368; McWC, March 10, 1922, February 13, 1925. This was the general trajectory for most employee representation schemes devised during this era. "Statements of employers . . . show that whereas employees were inclined to use the works councils at the time of their initiation principally for airing their grievances, after the plans had been in place for some time the airing of grievances gave way to a utilization of the councils for the consideration of questions of efficiency and economy." National Industrial Conference Board, *Experience with Works Councils in the United States,* Report No. 50 (New York: Century Company, 1922), 54–55. And the role employee representation could play in promoting "efficiency" was a particularly attractive feature for those companies that utilized piecework. "The employer who desires to cut [piece] rates can use the same [works council] machinery . . . then a gradual reduction of the piece rate, without loss of efficiency, can be accomplished by placing able leaders on the council, who persuade the workers' representatives that adverse business conditions and the consequent dire straits in which the company finds itself necessitate reduced rates." Miller, *Workmen's Representation,* 85–86. This certainly was the case at Harvester, and one contemporary study noted that these practices were having an effect at IH, where employee representatives "have suggested ways of saving labor and materials," and the councils thus helped the company "reduce costs." Sumner Slichter, "The Current Labor Policies of American Industries," *Quarterly Journal of Economics* 43 (May 1929): 401–2.

6.   McWC, May 11, January 12, and February 13, 1923. There was no provision in the Industrial Council Plan calling for a vice-chairmanship, but the McCormick Council had established the six-month position.

7.   McWC, October 28, 1921. Since employee representatives were elected from particular "districts" in the plant, if they were transferred to another area they were obliged to surrender their seats.

8.   McWC, March 13, 1925; June 11, 1926 (McCormick's speech was reprinted in the works council minutes). Robert Ozanne documented much the same reality within the works council at Wisconsin Steel; *A Century of Labor-Management Relations at McCormick and International Harvester* (Madison: University of Wisconsin Press, 1967), 141.

9.   The existence of this secret reserve was disclosed not by some muckraking journal but by *Fortune* magazine in 1933. Having this cash on hand did allow

Harvester to offset some of its early Depression losses. *Fortune*, August 1933, 22. See also Barbara Marsh, *A Corporate Tragedy: The Agony of International Harvester Company* (New York: Doubleday, 1984), 57; Robert Ozanne, *Wages in Practice and Theory: McCormick and International Harvester, 1860–1960* (Madison: University of Wisconsin Press, 1968), 49. Harvester's net profit in 1920 was $17 million, but for the following two years—which were a recession period and particularly hard on farmers—the company's profits averaged about $5 million annually (this was the period when Harvester pressed its works councils to accept wage cuts). For the rest of the decade through 1930, however, profits soared, averaging $22 million a year, peaking at its record $37 million in 1929, and in 1930, a year after the stock market crash, the company still netted $26 million. (These figures do not include the millions stashed away in its reserve fund.) Not until 1932 did the Depression cause IH to take a loss (of $8 million). To put this in perspective, Harvester's record profit in 1929 of $37 million would be worth anywhere from $556 million in 2019 (measured in terms of the standard of living) to nearly $8 billion (measured in terms of economic power). IH's net profit for the entire 1920s of $182 million would be worth from $3 billion to nearly $42 billion in 2019.

10. Through the 1920s unemployment remained a serious problem (running between 10 and 13 percent through the decade) and most working families failed to bring in enough annual income to maintain the "American standard" of decent food, housing, and clothing with a modest reserve for recreation. Irving Bernstein, *The Lean Years: A History of the American Worker, 1920–1933* (Boston: Houghton Mifflin, 1960), 47, 59, 64–65. For exhaustive statistics regarding the disproportionate gains made by the top 1 percent and top .01 percent during the 1920s, see Emmanuel Saez and Gabriel Zucman, "Wealth Inequality in the United States Since 1913: Evidence from Capitalized Income Tax Data," (working paper 20625, National Bureau of Economic Research, October 2014). The statistical parallels between the 1920s and more recent decades in which benefits have accrued to the top 1 percent are striking: from 1920 to 1929, GNP increased 42 percent, and physical output in manufacturing increased 48 percent. There were, however, the same number of factory employees in 1929 as there had been in 1920 (10,702,000), while the number of hours worked declined by only 7 percent. Thus, the output per man-hour shot up by 63 percent over the course of the decade (from 1900 to 1909, output per hour increased 17 percent; from 1910 to 1919 it increased 14 percent, by comparison) but "industrial money earnings [for workers] were practically stationary, and real earnings for the employed rose only because of a decline in prices." Milton Derber, *The American Idea of Industrial Democracy* (Urbana: University of Illinois Press, 1970), 201.

11. Ozanne, *Century*, 238; Ozanne, *Wages in Practice and Theory*, 51. In his thorough assessment of the available data Frank Stricker notes Harvester's failure to raise wages during the "prosperity decade," and also emphasizes

that workers in general did not fare all that well during the 1920s: "It is clear 1) that during the 1920s while wages were generally at a higher level than before World War I, gains made during the decade, especially the long period of prosperity from 1923 to 1929, were not exceptional and in some cases nonexistent; 2) that unemployment was much higher than we have been led to believe and a continuing worry for most workers; 3) that the wages of millions of workers—and perhaps a third of all non-farm *family* incomes—were at or below the poverty line in 1929; 4) that the lower sections of the working class, such as unskilled railroad workers, probably had insufficient incomes for a nourishing diet; and 5) finally, taking one vaunted symbol of the decade's prosperity, that the proportion of working-class families owning automobiles was probably less than half. In short, our picture of the 1920s as a period of prosperity for workers must be radically qualified." "Affluence for Whom? Another Look at Prosperity and the Working Classes in the 1920s," *Labor History* 24, no. 1, (Winter 1983): 8. Emphasis in original.

12.   *Forbes,* March 2, 1918. Cyrus II's net worth in 1918 would be the equivalent of from $1 billion (standard of living) to over $17 billion (economic power) in 2019. John D. Rockefeller, with personal wealth of more than $1.2 billion in 1918, was of course in first place on the *Forbes* list. Cyrus McCormick II and Harold McCormick owned a combined total of 332,000 shares of IH common stock in 1936, and IH was identified by the nascent Securities and Exchange Commission that year as being one of the American corporations—along with General Motors, DuPont, and Chrysler—in which a disproportionate share of stockholdings were held by company officers or directors. "Big Share Holdings Summarized by SEC," *New York Times,* July 17, 1936.

13.   The quote is from *Fortune,* August 1933, 28. More details of Harold McCormick and Edith Rockefeller's marriage, and Harold's later relationships, can be found in Wayne Andrews, *The Battle for Chicago* (New York: Harcourt, Brace and Company, 1946), 257–62; and Gilbert Harrison, *A Timeless Affair: The Life of Anita McCormick Blaine* (University of Chicago Press, 1979), 188–96.

14.   One of Edith Rockefeller's sons died young, which some said contributed to her eccentric behavior. The divorce did not result in a split between the Rockefellers and the McCormicks, as both John D. Rockefeller and John, Jr. were sympathetic to Harold during his difficulties with Edith. "Fowler McCormick: Self-Made Man," *Fortune,* September 1946.

15.   "Deny Human Glands Used in McCormick Operation," *Lewiston Daily Sun,* June 24, 1922. This procedure—the Viagra of its day—was of course just quackery but many of its practitioners became quite wealthy. See Pope Brock, *Charlatan: America's Most Dangerous Huckster, the Man Who Pursued Him, and the Age of Flimflam* (New York: Broadway Books, 2009).

16.   "Walska the Bride of H. F. McCormick," *New York Times,* August 12, 1922; Mitchell Owens, "Garden of the Slightly Macabre," *New York Times,* August 22, 1996.

17.   Harrison, *A Timeless Affair*, 193. After divorcing Harold in 1931 Walska would go on to marry twice more (for a total of six husbands). "Men always propose to me the minute they meet me," Walska is purported to have said to a society matron. "Ah, but just what do they propose?" was the rejoinder.

18.   "Harold McCormick Quits as President of Harvester Firm," *New York Times*, June 3, 1922. Cyrus McCormick I's third son, Stanley (Cyrus II's and Harold's brother, then), who had been active in the company in the early twentieth century and was involved with the negotiations to put together International Harvester, had become mentally unstable and was institutionalized by this point. Had the times been different, Cyrus I's daughter Anita (seven years younger than her older brother Cyrus II) would certainly have been considered for the company presidency. Anita was diligent, smart, and serious, but two things disqualified her for corporate leadership in the early 1900s: her unorthodox politics (she became involved in a number of liberal causes, beginning with settlement houses in Chicago; in later years, as this narrative details, she became a prominent supporter of Henry Wallace's Progressive Party bid for the presidency), and of course the fact that she was a woman.

6: The ABCs of Industrial Unionism

1.   "Quite obviously an implement for which there is a trade demand of five thousand a year cannot carry the burden of special manufacturing equipment, assembly chains, and like which can desirably be supported by a production of a hundred thousand units." Cyrus McCormick III, *The Century of the Reaper* (Cambridge: Riverside Press, 1931), 257.

2.   Cyrus McCormick III, *Century of the Reaper*, 255; International Harvester, untitled document, n.d. [1923], IHA. Also essential to Harvester's ability to drive Ford out of the tractor market was IH's superior sales and dealership structure. Harvester dealerships, which had been a long-standing presence in rural communities, were able to offer the service and specialized expertise that Ford could not easily re-create; customer feedback communicated through these dealerships allowed Harvester to further refine its tractor designs to better meet farmers' needs. Alfred Chandler, *Scale and Scope: The Dynamics of Industrial Capitalism* (Cambridge: Harvard University Press, 1994), 203–4. Plow manufacturer John Deere moved into tractor production in the 1920s and would, by the late 1930s, emerge at Harvester's chief competitor.

3.   International Harvester (IH), "Report on the Study of the Background and Development of the United Farm Equipment and Metal Workers Union," April 25, 1952, 26–28, IHA. Minutes of the Tractor Works Council were not preserved, so the names of these representatives cannot be retrieved from those records.

4.   Robert A. Margo, "Employment and Unemployment in the 1930s," *Journal of Economic Perspectives* 7, no. 2 (Spring 1993): 43; David Kennedy, *Freedom from Fear: The American People in Depression and War, 1929–1945* (New York:

Oxford University Press, 1999), 87; Dominic A. Pacyga, *Chicago: A Biography* (Chicago: University of Chicago Press, 2009), 251–52; Laurence Bergreen, *Capone: The Man and the Era* (New York: Simon and Schuster, 1994), 400–401; *Chicago Tribune*, November 27, 1930; John Steinbeck, *The Grapes of Wrath* (New York: Viking Press, 1939), 298.

5. Nelson Lichtenstein, *Walter Reuther: The Most Dangerous Man in Detroit* (Urbana: University of Illinois Press, 1995), 61.

6. Among the books that have considered the issue of communism in the CIO generally are: Max Kampelman, *The Communist Party vs. the CIO* (New York: Praeger, 1957); David Saposs, *Communism in American Unions* (New York: McGraw Hill, 1959); Bert Cochran, *Labor and Communism: The Conflict that Shaped American Unions* (Princeton: Princeton University Press, 1977); Harvey Levenstein, *Communism, Anti-Communism, and the CIO* (Westport: Greenwood Press, 1981); Steve Rosswurm ed., *The CIO's Left-Led Unions* (New Brunswick: Rutgers University Press, 1992); Judith Stepan-Norris and Maurice Zeitlin, *Left Out: Reds and America's Industrial Unions* (Cambridge: Cambridge University Press, 2002). Among those that focus on specific CP-associated unions (or factions within unions) are: Roger Keeran, *The Communist Party and the Auto Workers Unions* (Bloomington: Indiana University Press, 1980); Ronald Schatz, *The Electrical Workers: A History of Labor at General Electric and Westinghouse 1923–1960* (Urbana: University of Illinois Press, 1983); Howard Kimeldorf, *Reds or Rackets?: The Making of Radical and Conservative Unions on the Waterfront* (Berkeley: University of California Press, 1988); Joshua Freeman, *In Transit: The Transport Workers Union in New York City, 1933–1966* (New York: Oxford University Press, 1989); Robin D. G. Kelley, *Hammer and Hoe: Alabama Communists during the Great Depression* (Chapel Hill: University of North Carolina Press, 1990); Bruce Nelson, *Workers on the Waterfront: Seamen, Longshoremen, and Unionism in the 1930s* (Urbana: University of Illinois Press, 1990); Stephen Meyer, *"Stalin over Wisconsin": The Making and Unmaking of Militant Unionism, 1900–1950* (New Brunswick: Rutgers University Press, 1992); Ronald Filippelli and Mark McColloch, *Cold War in the Working Class: The Rise and Decline of the United Electrical Workers* (Albany: SUNY Press, 1995); Robert Korstad, *Civil Rights Unionism: Tobacco Workers and the Struggle for Democracy in the Mid-Twentieth-Century South* (Chapel Hill: University of North Carolina Press, 2003); Rosemary Feurer, *Radical Unionism in the Midwest, 1900–1950* (Urbana: University of Illinois Press, 2006); Shelton Stromquist, *Labor's Cold War: Local Politics in a Global Context* (Urbana: University of Illinois Press, 2008); Lisa Phillips, *A Renegade Union: Interracial Organizing and Labor Radicalism* (Urbana: University of Illinois, 2013).

7. IH, "Report," 31–32; *Local 101 News*, April 18, 1950, copy in author's possession. A similar operation was utilized in the late 1920s and early 1930s by the organizers of the Transport Workers Union in New York City, many of whom had emigrated from Ireland and had been members of the IRA there,

and so for them maintaining an elaborate and secretive underground network was second nature. Freeman, *In Transit,* 69. The ABC-type resistance structure is also succinctly described in *The Battle of Algiers,* the classic film depicting the insurrection against French colonial occupation.

8. Hank Graber, interview with author, January 3, 1981.

9. Quotes from *CIO News, Farm Equipment Edition,* November 16, 1952. Lawson remained an FE stalwart for decades; he held various local offices within the FE organization at Tractor Works and also became an FE district vice-president in 1942.

10. *Local 101 News,* April 18, 1950.

7: Red Breakthrough

1. Most of this applied to the other CP-connected unions as well. See Ronald Filippelli and Mark McColloch: "The loosening of the ties between the party and the trade unionists, and particularly the elimination of Party caucuses in the unions [in the late 1930s], ended what little effort had been expended in the CIO unions to convert the rank and file to communism and to seriously recruit new party members. Even the open party members in the shop, many of them stewards, did little to propagate communism, recruit new members for the party, or explain Communist political positions. Selling the *Daily Worker* at the plant gates, often at a plant other than their own, was often as far as it went. It has proven easier to become leaders of masses than to build a mass base." *Cold War in the Working Class: The Rise and Decline of the United Electrical Workers* (Albany: SUNY, 1995), 8. See also Joshua Freeman: "Lacking a mass Communist base, the TWU leadership maintained its position through a combination of effective economic unionism, charismatic leadership, some internal political education, and a tailoring of style and policy to the culture and perspective of the membership." *In Transit: The Transport Workers Union in New York City, 1933–1966* (New York: Oxford University Press, 1989), 130.

2. As Ellen Schrecker has noted about the CP-associated unions generally: "It is hard to assess the extent to which the party shaped the unions it controlled. Many of the Communists who rose to positions of leadership were trade unionists first and party members second. It was not unusual for these people to ignore party directives that clashed with union priorities, and in fact some of these labor leaders actually left the CP when they felt that its demands were contrary to the interests of their unions. They had, after all, joined the party in large part because they felt it would help them build a strong labor movement. None of them even tried to transform their unions into revolutionary organizations." From "Labor and the Cold War: The Legacy of McCarthyism," in Robert W. Cherney, William Issel, and Kieran Walsh Taylor, eds., *American Labor and the Cold War: Grassroots Politics and Postwar Political Culture* (New Brunswick: Rutgers University Press, 2004), 9.

3.   Bill Sentner of the UE was one of the few prominent union leaders who
      openly acknowledged his CP affiliation; see Rosemary Feurer, *Radical
      Unionism in the Midwest, 1900–1950* (Urbana: University of Illinois Press,
      2006).

4.   The machinations of the American Communist Party and its relationship (or
      fealty, depending on one's point of view) to the Soviet Union have been the
      subject of fierce and extensive historical debate. One survey that explores much
      of what has been written on this subject is Bryan Palmer's "Rethinking the
      Historiography of United States Communism," and the response from James
      Barrett, "The History of American Communism and Our Understanding of
      Stalinism," both in *American Communist History* 2, no. 2 (2003): 139–82. My
      study focuses less on the policy dictates from on high to explore instead a
      central question Barrett raises in his essay: "What role do all these local and
      personal stories, what importance does the rank-and-file perspective have
      in . . . [the] understanding of American Communism as an indigenous social
      movement, a genuine reflection of class conflict in the USA?"

5.   For a similar reflection related to African American party members in
      Alabama, see Robin D. G. Kelly: "Though they knowingly bucked national
      leadership decisions on a few occasions, local cadres tried their best to apply
      the then current political line to the tasks at hand. But because neither Joe
      Stalin, Earl Browder, nor William Z. Foster spoke directly to them or to their
      daily problems, Alabama Communists developed strategies and tactics in
      response to local circumstances that, in most cases, had nothing to do with
      international crises." *Hammer and Hoe: Alabama Communists During the Great
      Depression* (Chapel Hill: University of North Carolina Press, 1990), xiii–xiv.

6.   *Harvester World*, December 1919, WSHS; Fraser M. Ottanelli, *The Communist
      Party in the United States: From the Depression to World War II* (New Brunswick:
      Rutgers University Press, 1991), 15.

7.   Ottanelli, *Communist Party*, 128; "Larry Van Dusen"—a pseudonym for
      DeWitt Gilpin—in Studs Terkel's *Hard Times* (New York: Random House,
      1970), 107–8.

8.   Terkel, *Hard Times*, 106.

9.   *Midwest Daily Record*, March 12, 1938; *Chicago Tribune*, August 11, 1944.

10.   From testimony provided by Vern Smith, who identified himself as a "publicity
      man for workers' organizations," but was a long-standing correspondent
      for the *Daily Worker*. US Senate, "Conditions in Coal Fields in Harlan and
      Bell Counties, Kentucky," *Hearings Before a Subcommittee of the Committee
      on Manufacturing*, 1932, 72nd Congress, 1st session (76), Washington, DC:
      Government Printing Office.

11.   Alessandro Portelli, *They Say in Harlan County: An Oral History* (New York:
      Oxford University Press, 2011), 195, 199; US Senate, "Conditions in Coal
      Fields in Harlan and Bell Counties," 38; American Civil Liberties Union,
      The Kentucky Miners' Struggle, May 1932; Workers' International Relief,

Kentucky Miners Fight, 1932 (copies of both pamphlets in author's possession); "Tennessee to Probe Red Kidnapping Case," *Pittsburgh Press*, January 20, 1932.

12.   In early 1937 some 150 workers at Fansteel Metallurgical Corporation, frustrated by the company's refusal, in defiance of the Wagner Act, to recognize their union, occupied the plant (located in North Chicago, which is not a section of the Windy City but rather a town that lies about 30 miles north) and unfurled banners declaring, "Union recognition or bust." Some ten days later the workers were ousted from the facility following a tear gas barrage launched by police and sheriff's deputies; Joe Weber was among those arrested during the assault. Fansteel fired the workers who had been involved with the sit-down, but the NLRB ordered them reinstated because the company had been "guilty of gross violations of law, violations which in fact were the moving cause for the conduct of the employees." The dispute made its way to the Supreme Court; the 1939 decision *NLRB v. Fansteel* overturned the NLRB's ruling, upheld the discharges, and declared that sit-down strikes were illegal, a major setback for labor and for the authority of the NLRB. The ruling in effect encouraged employers to engage in unfair labor practices, as labor's—and the NLRB's—recourse was limited in light of *Fansteel*. See James A. Gross, *The Reshaping of the National Labor Relations Board: National Labor Policy in Transition, 1937–47* (Albany: SUNY Press, 1981), 25; "Sit Down Strikes Illegal!" *Chicago Tribune*, February 28, 1939; "Six Hurt in Battle as Sheriff Tries to Oust 'Sit-Downs,'" *New York Times*, February 20, 1937; "Gas Barrage Ousts Fansteel Strikers in a Short Battle," *New York Times*, February 27, 1937.

13.   "Quite an orator" from Joe Germano, quoted in Randi Storch, *Red Chicago: American Communism at its Grassroots, 1928–35* (Urbana: University of Illinois Press, 2007), 171; Meyer Levin, *Citizens* (New York: Viking Press, 1940), 168. The novel is a lightly fictionalized depiction of the 1937 Memorial Day Massacre, detailed below. "Facts Concerning J. W.," n.d. [1945?], David Rothstein papers, CHMA. Weber had much in common with John Santo, a Hungarian immigrant and convert to communism who was one of the founders of the Transport Workers Union, another CP-influenced union. Santo's "lingering Hungarian accent and origins outside the industry served to demarcate him from the mass of workers.... But initially it was Santo who was the clear leader of the union drive and for a short while even the head of the union. It was he who coordinated the various elements of the emerging union, who knew of the full range of activity, who pulled in key local leaders. And it was Santo who was the liaison between the CP and the union, and the main Party representative inside the TWU." Change the accent slightly and the union involved and this could be Joe Weber's biography. Freeman, *In Transit*, 51.

14.   The four members figure from *Party Organizer*, September 1934; Harvester's internal report contends that there were no party members among the original ABC activists, and the company probably would have said differently if there had been clear evidence to the contrary. IH, "Report," 34. S. Yandrich,

"Open Letter an Instrument for Penetrating into the Basic Industries," *Party Organizer* 7, March 1934, 24. Joseph Weber, interview with author, January 4, 1981. The CP's TUUL period of "dual unionism," during which time communist organizers were to abandon their work inside the AFL in order to build separate, revolutionary unions, has often been judged by historians to have been a tactical disaster, dictated by misguided directives from Moscow. Evidence about the SMWIU at Harvester is too scanty to either entirely support or refute that thesis, but Weber's work at Harvester—in which he worked with the (at least initially) noncommunist ABC apparatus while simultaneously endeavoring to build the SMWIU—suggests that TUUL organizers were willing to adapt to their circumstances, and by doing so were able to be successful at enlisting union and (to a lesser degree) party members. The ABC organization, of course, was not an AFL affiliate, with no hierarchy controlling it, which made it more feasible for Weber to work with it, rather than against it. It's also worth noting that in companies like Harvester where the playing field was open—there was no active AFL presence—the work done to build the TUUL simply evolved into the organizing effort just a few years later for the CIO. According to Joe Weber, "There was set up the TUUL—we had a nuclei of left-wing people in and around all the plants in Chicago—such as Crane, such as International Harvester, in the packinghouses, in Western Electric, etc. The work with the TUUL and its affiliate, which was the Steel and Metal Workers Union, of necessity had to be underground. . . . Now, when the CIO came on the scene the left in the labor movement had skeleton organizations in all the major industries. . . . so we were able to swiftly move to organize." For works criticizing the CP's TUUL strategy see Harvey Klehr, *The Heyday of American Communism: The Depression Decade* (New York: Basic Books, 1984), 38–48, 118–134; Bert Cochran, *Labor and Communism: The Conflict that Shaped American Unions* (Princeton: Princeton University Press, 1977), 44–45. For a more nuanced assessment, see Edward P. Johanningsmeier, "The Trade Union Unity League: American Communists and the Transition to Industrial Unionism: 1928–1934," *Labor History* 42, no. 2 (2001).

15.   IH, "Report," 34, 37. The importance of Cavorso and Kellogg to the organization of Tractor Works is cited in "FE-UE News: Voice of Local 101," FE local newspaper, April 18, 1950, copy in author's possession. Kellogg was a FEWOC executive board member and became the educational director for the FE's Tractor Works local in 1944. *Midwest Daily Record*, February 28, 1938; *FE News*, October 2, 1944.

16.   "Actual Experiences in Building the Party in International Harvester Co.," *Party Organizer*, September 1934; IH, "Report," 35–36.

17.   US Senate Committee on Education and Labor, *Hearings on the Creation of a National Labor Board*, 1934, 73rd Congress, 2nd Session (917–18), Washington, DC: Government Printing Office.

18.   John Matuszyk to Charles Shrock, November 30, 1936, Local 57 collection,

Archives of Labor History and Urban Affairs, Wayne State University (hereafter WSU); IH, "Report," 41.

19. IH, "Report," 41; Hank Graber, interview with author, January 3, 1981.

20. Benjamin Stolberg, "Big Steel, Little Steel, and the C.I.O.," *Nation*, July 31, 1937; "Facts Concerning J.W.", CHMA; US Senate Subcommittee of the Committee on Education and Labor (the LaFollette Committee), *Violations of Free Speech and the Rights of Labor*, 1939, 76th Congress, 2nd Session, (4916–24), Washington, DC: Government Printing Office; IH, "Report," 47.

21. FEWA minutes, April 10, December 9, 1936; February 28, May 17, May 25, May 31, July 27, August 8, September 12, October 10, October 26, 1937, David Rothstein papers, CHMA; FEWOC minutes, August 8, 1937, Local 57 collection, WSU; SWOC minutes, April 26 1937, District 31, United Steelworkers of America papers, CHMA.

22. National Labor Relations Board, *Decisions and Orders*, "In the matter of International Harvester Company and Local Union No. 57, International Union, United Automobile Workers of America," Case No. C–41, November 12, 1936, Washington DC: Government Printing Office.

23. IH went from taking in $26 million in net profits in 1930 to only a $1 million net in 1931, and then saw losses in 1932 (of -$8 million) and in 1933 (of -$2 million). But for the rest of the Depression Harvester's net profits were in the black, showing a steady increase from $4 million in 1934 on up to $32 million in 1937. Harvester's profits drooped some during the downturn in the late 1930s (an $18 million profit in 1938 and $13 million in 1939) but then picked up again with the onset of World War II. Data from Robert Ozanne, *Wages in Practice and Theory: McCormick and International Harvester, 1860–1960* (Madison: University of Wisconsin Press, 1968), 117. See also Barbara Marsh, *A Corporate Tragedy: The Agony of the International Harvester Company* (New York: Doubleday, 1985), 71.

24. See National Labor Relations Board, *Decisions and Orders* 29, January 16– February 28, 1941, 456–514, Washington, DC: Government Printing Office.

25. "Tractor Workers," flyer, n.d. [1938]; "The Employee's Mutual Association," flyer, August 2, 1937; David Rothstein papers, CHMA. Emphasis in original.

26. *Midwest Daily Record*, February 25, 1938.

27. Joseph Weber, interview with author, January 4, 1981.

28. *Midwest Daily Record*, April 30, 1938.

29. *Midwest Daily Record*, April 30, 1938.

30. This phrase was used in 1937 by Benjamin Stolberg to describe the leadership of the sit-down strikes in the auto industry but seems quite apt for the FE leadership as well. Stolberg, "Big Steel, Little Steel, and C.I.O."

31. Quotes from US Senate, *Violations of Free Speech*, 31. See also Ahmed White, *The Last Great Strike: Little Steel, the CIO, and the Struggle for Labor Rights in New Deal America* (Berkeley: University of California Press, 2016); Michael Dennis, *The Memorial Day Massacre and the Movement for Industrial Democracy*

(New York: Palgrave Macmillan, 2010).

32. *Chicago Tribune,* June 6, 1937.

33. *Chicago Tribune,* August 8, 1944, March 8, 1946, March 9, 1946.

34. Information on Weber's legal battle can be found in the file marked "Joe Weber" in the papers of the American Committee for the Protection of the Foreign Born, University of Michigan Special Collections Library; see also the *FE News,* September 3, 1945; October 4, 1946; the antilabor *Chicago Journal of Commerce,* January 23, 1947; and the *Chicago Tribune,* April 28, 1950.

35. Lizabeth Cohen, in her examination of industrial workers in Chicago during the 1920s and '30s, argues that welfare capitalism established the framework for the CIO's emerging unions: "Enlightened industrialists provided workers with a new set of standards for evaluating a good job: steady work, high wages, opportunity for advancement, decent conditions, generous benefits. . . . This belief in the potential for a 'moral capitalism,' born out of the promise of employers' welfarism in the twenties, would shape the political character of workers' union movements in the thirties." *Making a New Deal: Industrial Workers in Chicago, 1919–1939* (Cambridge: Cambridge University Press, 1990), 206, 209. But a look at how the FE emerged at Harvester makes that thesis problematic. Many IH workers did avail themselves of company initiatives introduced in the 1920s—stock options or company insurance, for instance—but participation in such programs (which offered financial benefits or may have been deemed necessary to demonstrate proper company loyalty) in and of itself tells us nothing about what workers thought of them. Workers may accept wage increases, for instance, while remaining convinced that their employers could afford far more. Moreover, since the demands issued by the FE during its organizing drive echoed, almost exactly, what Harvester workers had been agitating for since the nineteenth century—higher wages, job security, and the abolition of the exploitative and punishing piecework system—that agenda clearly had not been first established in the 1920s by "enlightened" IH managers. Workers at Harvester didn't need the tenets of welfare capitalism to define for them what constituted a "good job"; their own experience taught them that. And finally, in the combative rhetoric employed by FE's leaders during their organizing drive, there are no hints of any belief in the "potential for a 'moral capitalism.'" In its organizing drive the FE didn't take on capitalism per se, but it certainly denounced "welfarism" generally, and Harvester management and the McCormick family specifically, and these arguments proved persuasive enough to win over thousands of IH employees. I wouldn't argue that the anticapitalist feelings of the left-wing FE leadership can be extrapolated to apply to the entire Harvester workforce, or even to any large percentage of it. But it is at least as difficult to support the presumption—at IH, at any rate—that workers retained an abiding faith in the "moral capitalism" that management had peddled in the 1920s.

8: New Feet under the Table

1. *Midwest Daily Record,* March 24, 1938.
2. National Labor Relations Board, *Decisions and Orders* 29, January 16–February 28, 1941, 456–914, Washington, DC: Government Printing Office. International Harvester was represented in the NLRB proceedings by Pope & Ballard, one of the nation's first law firms to concentrate, in the wake of the Wagner Act, on representing management interests in labor relations. In 1945 several lawyers from Pope & Ballard moved to form Seyfarth Shaw, which became (and continues to be) the country's most notorious management-side (or, put another way, union-busting) law firm. International Harvester moved its business to Seyfarth Shaw when it was founded and became one of the firm's most important clients.
3. *Chicago Tribune,* March 6, 1941; "Statement of the Farm Equipment Workers Organizing Committee Concerning Issues in Dispute with the International Harvester Company," n.d. [May? 1941], FEWOC file, CIO papers, Catholic University of America (hereafter CUA).
4. *CIO News, Farm Equipment Edition,* May 13, 1940; "International Harvester and Crane Co. Lay Off Thousands in Huge Chicago Metal Shops," *Daily Worker,* November 19, 1937.
5. Quotation from Sidney Fine, *Sit-Down: The General Motors Strike of 1936–1937* (Ann Arbor: University of Michigan Press, 1969), 92.
6. Travis discusses his knowledge of sit-downs elsewhere and the role of the CP in providing that information in an interview with Neil Leighton, December 13, 1978; University of Michigan-Flint Archives, http://www.umflint.edu/archives/bob-travis.
7. Clarence Stoecker, interview with author, July 20, 1986. See also *CIO News, Farm Equipment Edition,* October 10, 1940.
8. *CIO News, Farm Equipment Edition,* February 3, 1941; Robert Ozanne, *A Century of Labor-Management Relations at McCormick and International Harvester* (Madison: University of Wisconsin Press, 1967), 198; *Chicago Tribune,* February 23, 1941; *CIO News, Farm Equipment Edition,* March 5, 1941. Lucy Parsons's exact birthdate is unknown, but she was probably eighty-eight years old when she addressed the rally.
9. Stoecker's quotes from interview transcript, Julia Reichert with Clarence Stoecker, October 20, 1978 (copy in author's possession); *International Harvester Company v. Local 108, FEWOC,* 41S-4090, Superior Court of Cook County, Chancery Division (March 24, 1941), Ben Meyers papers, CHMA; see also Ozanne, *Century,* 199.
10. *Chicago Tribune,* March 1, 1941; *CIO News, Farm Equipment Edition,* March 10 and 17, 1941.
11. "Fowler McCormick: Self-Made Man," *Fortune,* September 1946; Ron Chernow, *Titan: The Life of John D. Rockefeller, Sr.* (New York: Random House, 1998), 649; Gilbert Harrison, *A Timeless Affair: The Life of Anita McCormick*

Blaine (Chicago: University of Chicago Press, 1979), 163; the "goofiness" quotation comes from the *Chicago Tribune Sunday Magazine* section, October 23, 1983.

12. Possible Anne Stillman engagement: *New York Times*, April 6, 1921; "notorious litigation": "Fowler McCormick: Self-Made Man," *Fortune*, September 1946; details of the Stillman divorce and reconciliation: *New York Times*, March 11, 1921, January 14, 1944; "just friends": *Milwaukee Sentinel*, June 6, 1931; Fifi-Fowler wedding, *Chicago Tribune*, June 6, 1931. Fifi's actual first name was Anne, as was her daughter's, which can lead to some confusion in the historical record.

13. *CIO News, Farm Equipment Edition,* March 10, 1941; Press Release, FEWOC, n.d. [March 1941], in author's possession.

14. *Chicago Tribune*, March 21, 1941.

15. Injunction Writ, Superior Court of Cook County, *International Harvester Company v. Local No. 108 of the Farm Equipment Workers Organizing Committee* (March 22, 1941), Ben Meyers papers, CHMA; *Chicago Tribune*, March 24, 1941; *CIO News, Farm Equipment Edition*, March 31, 1941.

16. Grant Oakes to "The Twelve Members of the McCormick Family," telegram, March 20, 1941, IHA, also contained in Ben Meyers papers.

17. *Chicago Tribune*, March 23 and 26, 1941; Statement of Bruno Zei, March 1941, Ben Meyers papers, CHMA; advertisement in *Chicago Sunday Times*, March 23, 1941, IHA; Ozanne, *Century,* 201.

18. Ozanne, *Century,* 202.

19. *Chicago Tribune*, March 29, 30, and 31, 1941.

20. "Statement of the Farm Equipment Workers Organizing Committee," CUA. Lizabeth Cohen has argued that CIO unionists did not seek "a fundamental redistribution of power such as a role in hiring, firing, work and wage assignments, and production decisions," *Making a New Deal: Industrial Workers in Chicago, 1919–1939* (Cambridge: Cambridge University Press, 1990,) 315. I'd suggest that the FE's piecework demands were, in fact, designed precisely to achieve a fundamental redistribution of power, and what the union sought would have affected the company in all these areas except, perhaps, hiring; that's why IH management so strenuously resisted them. (See the discussion of piecework in a later chapter for more on the power dynamics of Harvester's piecework system.)

21. Ozanne, *Century,* 204.

22. Grant Oakes to Allan Haywood, July 24, 1941, with attached copy of summary and findings on the NDMB Harvester case, FEWOC file, CIO papers, CUA; Ozanne, *Century,* 204–5.

23. The initial election results were, at West Pullman, FE: 1,138, AFL: 887, no union: 206, challenged: 10; at East Moline, FE: 815, AFL: 630, no union: 46; at Rock Falls, FE: 101, AFL: 97, no union: 1, challenged: 9; at Rock Island (Farmall), FE: 1,383, AFL: 1,692, no union: 92, challenged: 36; at Milwaukee,

FE: 910, AFL: 2,067, no union: 92, challenged: 43. At McCormick, the FE garnered 2,682 votes, and the AFL 2,671, with 206 voting no union and 78 challenged ballots. The close vote at Rock Falls might have necessitated a runoff as well, but the NLRB sided with the FE and held that the challenged votes affirmed the CIO victory there. *Chicago Tribune*, June 19, 1941; Ozanne, *Century*, 207.

24. *People's Press*, March 19, 1938, David Rothstein papers, CHMA; *CIO News, Farm Equipment Edition*, April 24, 1939.

25. The "equal rights" quote comes from Fraser Ottanelli, *The Communist Party of the United States, from the Depression to World War II* (New Brunswick: Rutgers University Press, 1991), 36–37. See also Ellen Schrecker, who indicates: "During the 1930s and 1940s, the Communist Party was the only political organization not specifically part of the civil rights movement that was dedicated to racial equality. At a time when workplace segregation was common, the party pressed its labor cadres to fight discrimination. Such an agenda was not always popular with the rank and file. . . . Though these measures did not increase the left-led unions' popularity with the large majority of white workers, they did appeal to minority ones"; from "Labor and the Cold War: The Legacy of McCarthyism," in *American Labor and the Cold War*, eds. Robert W. Cherney, William Issel, and Kieran Walsh Taylor (New Brunswick: Rutgers University Press, 2004), 9. For a thorough exploration of the CP's appeal to, and strength among, African Americans in the South see Robin D. G. Kelly, *Hammer and Hoe: Alabama Communists During the Great Depression* (Chapel Hill: University of North Carolina Press, 1990). Other quotes in this paragraph are from *Harvester Worker*, November–December 1937 and January–February 1938, both in David Rothstein papers, CHMA; *CIO News, Farm Equipment Edition*, December 23, 1940; "The Labor Front," *Chicago Defender*, November 9, 1940.

26. "The Labor Front," *Chicago Defender*, March 1, 1941 and July 19, 1941; *CIO News, Farm Equipment Edition*, April 7, 1941.

27. "Harvester's Going CIO," FEWOC flyer, June 1941, David Rothstein papers, CHMA; "Expect Heavy CIO Vote at Harvester Co.," *Chicago Defender*, June 14, 1941; *CIO News, Farm Equipment Edition*, April 7, 1941; "Vote AFL," *Chicago Defender*, June 14, 1941; "An Open Letter to the Negro Workers in Harvester," *Chicago Defender*, June 14, 1941. For examples of *Defender* stories on the AFL, see "Warn A.F. of L. on Jim Crow Labor Groups," *Chicago Defender*, February 22, 1941; "A.F.L. Oppose Bill to Outlaw Jim Crow Unions," *Chicago Defender*, March 15, 1941.

28. *Chicago Defender*, February 8, 1941; "Speech by Grant Oakes" and "Speech by Richard Kelly," February 27, 1941, file 5201-DE102, IHA.

29. Press Release, FEWOC, n.d. [March 1941], in author's possession.

30. *CIO News, Farm Equipment Edition*, March 24, 1941; "Speech By Grant W. Oakes," February 27, 1941, file 5201-DE102, IHA. In its 1941 Report

on Agricultural Machinery and Tractors, the Securities and Exchange Commission indeed noted that IH had recorded a profit increase of more than 35 percent between 1940 and 1941. *Survey of American Listed Corporations,* December 31, 1941, Washington, DC: Government Printing Office.

31   *CIO News, Farm Equipment Edition,* May 18, 1942; Ozanne, *Century,* 208. .

32.   National Implement and Vehicle Association, *Proceedings of the 26th Annual Convention,* October 16, 1919, 66, Farm and Industrial Equipment Institute Archives, Chicago.

9: The People's War

1.   Joe Clark, "Windy City Walkout," *The Review* (Young Communist League), February 17, 1941. "Lightning" is from Steve Nelson, quoted in Fraser Ottanelli, *The Communist Party of the United States, From the Depression to World War II* (New Brunswick: Rutgers University Press, 1991), 182. In its opposition during the Nazi-Soviet pact period to direct American involvement in the war, the CP did not differ from the rest of the labor movement, or for that matter from the then largely isolationist American public. But the AFL and CIO, along with US opinion generally, supported federal aid to Great Britain during this period, while the CP did not. And prior to the pact the CP had been aggressively anti-Nazi; many American communists had, for instance, volunteered to fight fascism in Spain and hundreds of them died there. So it was the change of course dictated by the pact that proved particularly jarring at the least for individual party members.

2.   These quotes and others below come from the US Army Intelligence Files pertaining to Sergeant DeWitt Gilpin, obtained through a FOIA request in 1983. The file is in the author's possession.

3.   I have a series of letters that my father wrote to his parents and sisters during the war. This is not an exhaustive collection, as he undoubtedly also wrote to other people, including his wife (his first wife, who was not my mother) but if those letters still exist they are not in my possession.

4.   A newspaper account from late November 1944—"*Rain and Floods Fail to Stop Men Under Patton in Metz Advance*"—confirmed Gilpin's assessment of the weather in France and included his description of the "quickie" bridges constructed by his engineering battalion to straddle the swollen Lorraine River. "'There was German machine gun crossfire at the bridge site,' said Sergeant DeWitt Gilpin of Chicago. 'But that bridge was passed across the river in exactly twenty minutes working time. The tanks rolled across . . . and the town was ours.'" *St. Petersburg Times,* November 20, 1944.

5.   *CIO News, Farm Equipment Edition,* September 14 and September 21, 1942; *Chicago Defender,* October 10, 1942.

6.   *CIO News, Farm Equipment Edition,* January 18, 1943.

7.   *CIO News, Farm Equipment Edition,* May 18, 1942.

8.   *CIO News, Farm Equipment Edition*, August 31, 1942.

10: The Nefarious System

1.   War Labor Board, Case No. 11–4, International Harvester Company and
       United Farm Equipment and Metal Workers of America, Local 108, April 10,
       1943, file 5211 DE1-02, IHA. In 1941 IH indicated that military contracts,
       worth $60 million, comprised 20 percent of the company's total output; *New
       York Times,* May 20, 1941. Overall, for the six Harvester plants that had been
       represented by the FE since 1941, employment increased 25 percent during
       the war. Detroit, however, saw an overall increase in employment of 76 percent,
       while employment in Los Angeles increased by 33 percent. "Results of Vote on
       Maintenance of Union Membership Held in Eleven Harvester Plants by War
       Labor Board," July 28, 1942; "International Harvester Company Bargaining
       Unit, Union, and Number of Employees in Unit as of October 1, 1945, 1946,
       and 1947," n.d., both documents from IHA. See also Martin Glaberman,
       *Wartime Strikes: The Struggle Against the No-Strike Pledge in the UAW during
       World War II* (Berwick Editions, 1980), 26.
2.   In late 1944 total employment at Tractor Works was 7,700; at McCormick
       Works 7,000; and at the Twine Mill, 750. Figures on female and African
       American employment at IH come from "International Harvester Plants
       with Bargaining Groups Represented by U.F.E. and M.W.—CIO," company
       chart, November 30, 1944, IHA; IH labor relations letter No. 616, February
       20, 1945, IHA; War Labor Board, Case No. 111-2193-D, August 16, 1944,
       Report and Recommendations, 55, IHA; Robert Ozanne, *The Negro in the Farm
       Equipment and Construction Machinery Industries* (Philadelphia: University of
       Pennsylvania Press, 1972), 25. The Twine Mill and the West Pullman plant in
       Chicago were the only IH plants that historically had any significant level of
       female employment.
3.   Hank Graber, interview with author, January 3, 1981; "Work Stoppages,
       January 1, 1943 to December 31, 1943," February 15, 1944, "Work Stoppages,
       January 1, 1944 to December 31, 1944," January 22, 1945, "Work Stoppages,
       January 1, 1945 to December 31, 1945," January 21, 1946, company charts,
       IHA. It should be noted that according to these charts, which include a
       brief description of the reasons for each walkout, none of the walkouts
       were triggered by white employees objecting to the hiring or promotion
       of Black workers, which was a source of unrest in other industries. And of
       course walkouts represented the most extreme expression of discontent, but
       piecework complaints were rife generally within Harvester. FE sources often
       indicated that 90 percent of the grievances pursued by their stewards were
       piecework related; see, for instance, *CIO News, Farm Equipment Edition*,
       November 11, 1940. This would remain true after the war as well. "About the
       only point on which [FE officials and IH management] agree is that the vast

majority of FE grievances relates to piecework prices." US Congress, Joint Committee on Labor-Management Relations, *Labor–Management Relations: Report Pursuant to Section 401 of Public Law 101*, 80th Congress, 2nd Session, March 15, 1948 (123), Washington, DC: Government Printing Office.

4.   The impact of the no-strike pledge has been explored most fully in Martin Glaberman's *Wartime Strikes* and Nelson Lichtenstein's *Labor's War at Home: The CIO in World War II* (Cambridge: Cambridge University Press, 1982). Both books posit that the CIO leadership's full-throated support of the pledge (voiced especially enthusiastically by the CP-affiliated unions) widened the gap between increasingly bureaucratized labor officialdoms and restive union memberships, quelling rank-and-file militancy and thus weakening labor's position heading into the postwar era. Within the FE, however, the no-strike pledge played out differently, suggesting that at least in some unions the reality of the pledge's impact may have been more complicated. As Hank Graber and the wildcat strike statistics at IH indicate, there is no doubt that many FE members took a dim view of the pledge and were willing to defy it despite the union's support for it. But, as the discussion below of the FE leadership's behavior during WWII suggests, there was often a disconnect between the FE's "official" stance on the no-strike pledge and what the union's leadership countenanced (or encouraged) in reality in the shops. And the FE leadership clearly intended to offset its support for the pledge by aggressively utilizing the war labor boards to challenge Harvester's authority. As demonstrated below, FE members emerged from the war financially better off and the union was substantially strengthened, with no measurable lessening of the FE's commitment to shop-floor militancy.

5.   Cyrus McCormick III, *The Century of the Reaper* (Cambridge: Riverside Press, 1931), 254. McCormick acknowledges the company's debt to Frederick Taylor in his description of how IH revamped its factories in the 1920s. For more discussion regarding the introduction of Harvester's incentive pay plan in the 1920s, see: an address by George Kelday, Harvester vice-president and assistant manager of industrial relations, to the American Management Association Convention, 1922; "Job Analysis—Occupational Rating," Committee Reports and Addresses, *Proceedings of the American Management Association Convention*, 1922; A. J. Kramer (production manager, IHC), "Calculating Piece-Work Wages," *Michigan Manufacturer and Financial Record*, December 30, 1922. "Compensation schemes can function as important mechanisms of control in factories in which production is carried out by many independent decision-makers (that is, workers)": Daniel M. G. Raff, "The Puzzling Profusion of Compensation Systems in the Interwar Automobile Industry," in *Coordination and Information: Historical Perspectives on the Organization of Enterprise*, eds. Naomi Lamoreaux and Daniel M. G. Raff (National Bureau of Economic Research, University of Chicago Press, 1995), 14.

6.   War Labor Board, Case No. 111-2193-D, August 16, 1944, *Report and*

Recommendations, 24–34, IHA; "Comments of the Company on Report and
Recommendations of the Panel," September 12, 1944, IHA; *Cub* (FE Local
236 newspaper), November 25, 1946, copy in author's possession; "Report and
Recommendations of the Fact-Finding Board in the International Harvester
Case," February 1, 1946, papers of John W. Gibson, Harry S. Truman Library.

7.   There were various technical reasons why IH (and other farm equipment
      manufacturers) retained incentive pay systems when other large
      manufacturers—like the auto companies—were abandoning them. As the
      auto industry matured, in the 1920s and '30s, its plants were increasingly
      characterized by large assembly lines, devoted to a single product. With
      Ford-style production, workers were obliged to adhere to the pace set by the
      assembly line. There was less need to motivate workers to drive themselves:
      the technology itself provided the discipline. Moreover, as factories grew
      larger and all activities came to be carefully coordinated around that assembly
      line, it grew less cost-effective if some employees—those who produce parts
      that are assembled by the line, for instance—produced more than necessary,
      since an oversupply of inventory is wasteful. In such a situation it is preferable
      for management to "simply tell the effort suppliers [i.e. workers] what to
      do, paying them compensation based on obedience rather than on output
      per se. If workers keep the centrally determined pace, they are paid for their
      time. If not, they are fired." Daniel M. G. Raff, "The Puzzling Profusion of
      Compensation Systems," 18. But despite Harvester's long-standing interest in
      innovative technology it could not entirely conform to the auto manufacturers'
      model. Most plants—McCormick Works, for instance—turned out not one
      product but hundreds of different ones, with a variety of modifications on
      its many pieces of equipment. Within those plants there was no assembly
      line production remotely approaching the scale seen in the auto industry.
      In addition, Harvester workers were called on to manufacture an array of
      replacement parts—for late-model equipment but also for machines built
      decades before—on a continual basis, because IH dealerships in far-flung rural
      areas needed to keep them readily available. Farmers have a very short window
      to plant or harvest crops, and if a machine breaks down at a critical moment—
      and the replacement part cannot be immediately supplied—that could mean
      the loss of a customer (and possibly an entire community) for life. So in most
      Harvester plants, workers performed much smaller-batch manufacture than
      was the case in auto plants; they labored individually or in small groups; and
      flexibility was required in order to quickly shift them from one task to another.
      Thus an incentive pay system—despite the shop-floor conflict it engendered—
      proved more cost-effective for Harvester. Even in Harvester's tractor and truck
      facilities, where assembly lines did exist, this was also the case (though group
      piecework was generally the rule), as more models with differing modifications
      were produced than was typically the case in auto plants. Certainly Harvester's
      incentive pay system contributed to its ability to contain labor costs. At its

Farmall plant (in Rock Island, Illinois) wage rates at the plant increased 21.5 percent between 1929 and 1937, but labor costs per tractor produced there *declined* by 15.2 percent. And in general at IH "although wage rates were higher in 1937 than in 1929, unit costs of factory labor did not increase proportionately to the increase in wage rates." United States Department of Labor, Temporary National Economic Committee, *Investigation of Concentration of Economic Power; Industrial Wage Rates, Labor Costs and Price Policies: the International Harvester Company*, 1940 (Washington, DC: Government Printing Office), 137, 71. Such cost containment cannot be attributed entirely to its incentive pay system, of course: technological improvements and manufacturing reorganization were also factors. But figures like those certainly led Harvester management to believe in the efficacy of its piecework system, regardless of what was happening in other industries, and despite what its workers might have preferred. For FE quote see WLB, Case No. 111-2193-D, August 16, 1944, *Report and Recommendations*, 27–29, 43; *Report and Recommendations of the Fact-Finding Board in the International Harvester Case*, February 18, 1946, file 5205-DE501, IHA.

8. War Labor Board, Case No. 111-2193-D, August 16, 1944, *Report and Recommendations*, 85, IHA; *Local 108 Union Reaper*, March 19, 1942, contained in FBI file 100-71906-25, in author's possession; "Piecework—the Harvester Squeeze Play," FE document, n.d. [1941?], IHA.

9. *CIO News, Farm Equipment Edition*, May 26, 1941; *CIO News, Farm Equipment Edition*, January 16, 1939; Statement of the Farm Equipment Workers Organizing Committee Concerning Issues in Dispute with the International Harvester Company n.d. [May? 1941], FEWOC file, CIO papers, CUA. Ridley Bell, a longtime FE activist at the West Pullman plant, grew up in a southern Illinois coal town just a stone's throw down a dirt path from John L. Lewis.

10. Grievance quote is from "a union official" in Robert Ozanne, *A Century of Labor-Management Relations at McCormick and International Harvester* (Madison: University of Wisconsin Press, 1967), 224; Benjamin Stolberg, "Big Steel, Little Steel, and the CIO," *Nation*, July 31, 1937.

11. Aaron Cantor, interview with author, October 20, 1986; "Harvester Row is Youth vs. Age," *Chicago Daily News*, February 2, 1946.

12. IH labor relations letter No. 225, July 15, 1943; IH weekly labor relations letter No. 20, September 23, 1944, both in IHA; *FE News*, September 18, 1944.

13. IH labor relations letters No. 598, January 29, 1945, and No. 491, July 28, 1944, IHA.

14. The other plants were West Pullman, Richmond, East Moline, Rock Falls, and Bettendorf.

15. Quote from *FE News*, August 13, 1945.

16. WLB, Case No. 111-2193-D, *Report and Recommendations*, August 16, 1944, 52–3, IHA.

17. WLB, Case No. 111-2193-D, *Report and Recommendations*, August 16, 1944,

82; "Comments of the Company on Report and Recommendations of the Panel," September 12, 1944; IHA.

18. Strike reported on in *Chicago Tribune,* June 20 and 23, 1945; telegram quoted in IH labor relations letter No. 678, June 19, 1945, IHA; *FE News,* July 30, 1945; WLB, Case No. 111-2193-D, "Majority Opinion," n.d. [October 10, 1945], IHA.

19. WLB, Case No. 111-2193-D, "Majority Opinion"; "Company's Petition to the National War Labor Board," Case No. 111-2193-D, November 13, 1945, 4, both in IHA.

20. IH weekly labor relations letter No. 31, December 9, 1944; "Superintendent to All Employees of East Moline Works," January 5, 1945, both in IHA.

21. IH weekly labor relations letters No. 30, December 2, 1944; No. 31, December 9, 1944; No. 34, December 29, 1944; No. 36, January 15, 1945; No. 39, February 2, 1945; Labor relations letters No. 564, December 11, 1944; No. 714, September 13, 1945 (contains arbitration award with Cantor's signature), letter, plant superintendent to all employees of East Moline works, January 4, 1945; all in IHA.

22. Aaron Cantor, interview with author, October 20, 1986.

23. Aaron Cantor, interview with author, October 20, 1986; Lichtenstein, *Labor's War at Home,* 111; IH labor relations letter No. 498, August 4, 1944, IHA.

24. *FE News,* September 18, 1944.

11: Postwar Warfare

1. *FE News,* January 16, 1946; January 21, 1946; April 24, 1946.

2. *FE News,* January 16, 1946.

3. *FE News,* January 21, February 4, 1946; IH weekly labor relations letter No. 80, November 19, 1945, IHA; *Daily Times* (Davenport, Iowa), June 9, 1944. The struck plants included McCormick, McCormick Twine, Tractor, West Pullman, and Deering (all in Chicago, where more than half the strikers were located); Rock Falls, East Moline, and the Farmall plant, all in Illinois; Richmond, Indiana; and the IH binder plant in Auburn, New York.

4. *Chicago Herald-American,* January 25, 1946.

5. *FE News,* January 16 and January 21, 1946.

6. *FE News,* January 16, 1946; "Harvester Background Material," n.d. [1945], IHA; *IHC Spotlight* (an FE-Harvester Council publication) n.d. [October 1945], IHA. "Changed their spots" from Fielde's testimony on February 5, 1946, before a US Conciliation Service Fact Finding Panel, quoted in Robert Ozanne, *A Century of Labor-Management Relations at McCormick and International Harvester* (Madison: University of Wisconsin Press, 1967), 210. In addition to his considerable stock portfolio, the FE also noted, IH president Fowler McCormick also received a salary of over $180,000 in 1945 (the equivalent, depending on how the measurement is assessed, of anywhere from

nearly $3 million to more than $17 million in 2019 dollars.)

7. *New York Times*, January 22, 1946; *Chicago Tribune,* February 9, 1946.

8. IH labor relations letter No. 773, January 29, 1946, IHA; *Chicago Tribune,* March 29, 1946. The "life and death" quote came from then IH vice-president, and future company president, John McCaffrey.

9. 1946 strike statistics: James Green, *The World of the Worker: Labor in Twentieth-Century America* (Hill and Wang, 1980), 194; "postwar warfare": George Soule, "Profits by the Billions," *New Republic*, January 7, 1946. According to Soule, "The United States Department of Commerce estimates that the profits of all corporations in the United States, after deduction of taxes (including excess-profits taxes), were $8.5 billion in 1941, $8.7 billion in 1942, $9.8 billion in 1943 and $9.9 billion in 1944. In 1944 they were more than twice as large as in 1939, the last year in which World War II did not affect profits, and were $3 billion higher than in 1929, the greatest year of business boom hitherto experienced in this country. These estimates, say the government statisticians, may be too low, since they are based on the records of the larger concerns, and it is believed that the smaller ones made even greater advances."

10. See, for example, Nelson Lichtenstein's *Labor's War at Home: The CIO in World War II* (Cambridge: Cambridge University Press, 1982), 203–32; Green, *World Of the Worker,* 194–96. In an earlier essay Green argued that ". . . it is important to see how these strikes [in 1945–46] focused on regaining real wages lost in the war far more than they focused on extending workers' control over the means of production"; "Fighting on Two Fronts: Working Class Militancy in the 1940s," *Radical America* (July–August 1975), 32.

11. IH letter to all employees of McCormick Works, January 31, 1946, IHA. At least seven other letters (addressed either to specific plant workforces or to all IH employees) were sent from November 1945 through April 1946. All are in the IHA and several of the letters can also be found in the William H. Brown collection at the Yale University Library.

12. *Chicago Tribune,* February 7, 1946; *Report and Recommendations of the Fact-Finding Board in the International Harvester Case*, February 1, 1946, papers of John W. Gibson, Harry S. Truman Library; *Chicago Tribune*, February 20, 1946; IH letter to employees, March 21, 1946, IHA; *Daily Worker,* April 5, 1946, contained in FBI file 10071906 Sub. A, in author's possession; Local 108 Flyer, March 13, 1946, IHA; "The Public is Entitled to the Facts," [FE advertisement], *Chicago Sun,* February 9, 1946, in David Rothstein papers, CHMA. Under the original Wagner Act, communications of the sort IH engaged in from employers to workers were defined as an unfair labor practice and were thus prohibited. The 1947 Taft-Hartley Act changed that by inserting a "free speech clause" into the National Labor Relations Act that allowed employers to express their opinions about unions freely using any medium, so long as they did not overtly threaten to fire workers for union activity. Following the passage of Taft-Hartley IH stepped up its letter-writing

efforts and also included in them more direct attacks on the FE leadership.

13. *FE News,* February 27, March 4, and April (Victory Issue) 1946.

14. Joint telegram from Clinton Anderson, Secretary of Agriculture, and L. B. Schwellenbach, Secretary of Labor, to Fowler McCormick et. al., March 27, 1946, attached to *Report and Recommendations of the Fact-Finding Board in the International Harvester Case,* February 1, 1946, papers of John W. Gibson, Harry S. Truman Library; *FE News,* March 13, 1946; *Chicago Tribune,* March 20 and April 10, 1946.

15. *FE News,* April 1946 (Victory Edition). Under this contract, Harvester workers with one year seniority got one week paid vacation; those with five years got two weeks; and those with fifteen or more years got three weeks.

16. "Contract Between Richmond Works, International Harvester Company, and Local 118, UFEMWA-CIO," April 15, 1946, in author's possession; *FE News,* April 1946.

17. *FE News,* April 1946 (Victory Issue). The FE's early fight for plantwide seniority would become an especially important point of contrast in later years as the FE's battle with the UAW heated up. The UAW, which gained recognition at Harvester's engine plant in Melrose Park, Illinois, in 1942 (as UAW Local 6), did not push for plantwide seniority there: "When the plant reopened for civilian production in 1946 . . . black workers were initially confined to janitorial jobs, mostly below the shop floor cleaning washrooms. The left caucus, which had the allegiance of the majority of black workers, led the successful fight for opening machining and assembly-line jobs to black workers. The nearby left-wing Farm Equipment Workers Union (FE) local at IHC's Tractor Works in Chicago, which had a better civil rights record and a far more aggressive stance on such issues, won complete plantwide seniority for job bidding and layoffs at an early time. Local 6, despite UAW rhetoric, never won or fought for full plantwide seniority." Glenn Perusek and Kent Worcester, eds. *Trade Union Politics: American Unions and Economic Change 1960s–1990s* (Atlantic Highlands, NJ: Humanities Press, 1995), 89.

18. *FE News,* April 1946 (Victory Issue).

19. *FE News,* April 24, 1946; Ozanne, *Century,* 212. Gibson had been the lead organizer of the United Dairy Workers union in Detroit in the 1930s and also served as president of the Michigan CIO in the early 1940s before his appointment to the Department of Labor. He was a social democrat in the Reuther-Hillman mold, with important connections within the Democratic Party, and was largely animated by his long-standing animus toward Jimmy Hoffa and the Teamsters' corrupting influence on the Michigan labor movement. Gibson was no communist but in 1946 would have been sympathetic to the FE's objectives and was undoubtedly irritated by Fowler McCormick's high-handed efforts to subvert his authority. For more on Gibson see Thaddeus Russell, *Out of the Jungle: Jimmy Hoffa and the Remaking of the American Working Class* (New York: Knopf, 2001).

20.   *FE News*, April 1946 (Victory Issue); April 24, 1946.
21.   IH labor relations letter No. 810, September 18, 1946, IHA.

12: A New Adversary Emerges

1.   *Chicago Tribune*, March 23, 1946.
2.   Roger Keeran, *The Communist Party and the Auto Workers Unions* (International
      Publishers, 1980), 257–58.
3.   Nelson Lichtenstein, *Walter Reuther: The Most Dangerous Man in Detroit*
      (Urbana: University of Illinois Press, 1995), 123, 157. Lichtenstein's book is
      the most comprehensive exploration of Reuther's career and his ideology.
4.   Kevin Boyle, *The UAW and the Heyday of American Liberalism* (Ithaca: Cornell
      University Press, 1995), 22; Lichtenstein, *Walter Reuther*, 184, 248; Daniel
      Nelson, "How the UAW Grew," *Labor History* 35 (Winter 1994): 5.
5.   Boyle, *Heyday*, 23–27.
6.   *United Automobile Worker*, March 15, 1945; FE International Executive Board,
      "Report to the Membership on the Raid by the UAW..." June 22, 1945,
      Walter Reuther papers, WSU; "The 'Rescue' Squad," FE leaflet, n.d. [1945], in
      author's possession; FBI Chicago field report 100-71906-102, May 11, 1945,
      in author's possession; *Chicago Tribune*, February 20, 1945. The *Peoria Star*
      indicated that Walter Reuther "heads a large faction which seeks post-war
      power for control of the union by organizing agricultural implement workers
      and other wartime members who will be later lost to the union rolls." *Peoria
      Star*, February 12, 1945, contained in scrapbook, Ernest DeMaio papers,
      CHMA.
7.   *Chicago Daily News*, March 1, 1945, and March 12, 1945, contained in Irving
      Meyers papers, CHMA; IH weekly labor relations letters No. 43, March 3,
      1945, No. 44, March 12, 1945, IHA; *Chicago Sun*, March 5, 1945, contained in
      FBI Chicago field report 100-71906, in author's possession.
8.   *FE News*, August 13, 1945; *Chicago Sun*, August 13, 1945; Fielde to "Sir and
      Brother" (letter with FE executive board resolution attached), August 1, 1945,
      Walter Reuther papers, WSU; *Chicago Sun*, November 6, 1945; IH weekly
      labor relations letter No. 79, November 12, 1945, IHA; FBI Chicago field
      report 100-71906-127, date obscured [1946], in author's possession; *FE News*,
      October 26, 1945.

13: IH Heads South

1.   Randy Leffingwell, *Farmall: The Red Tractor that Revolutionized Farming*
      (Voyageur Press, 2007), 193–94; *Louisville Times*, April 12, 1946. Harvester
      paid $6.7 million for the facility, which had cost the federal government $13
      million to build.
2.   Tracy K'Meyer, *Civil Rights in the Gateway to the South: Louisville, Kentucky,*

1945–1980 (Lexington: University Press of Kentucky, 2009), 5; Anne Braden, *The Wall Between* (Knoxville: University of Tennessee Press, 1999), 52; Wade Hall, ed., *The Rest of the Dream: The Black Odyssey of Lyman Johnson* (Lexington: University Press of Kentucky, 1988), 127; Luther Adams, *Way Up North in Louisville: African American Migration in the Urban South, 1930–1970* (Chapel Hill: University of North Carolina Press, 2010), 39–40; John Kleber, ed., *The Encyclopedia of Louisville* (University Press of Kentucky, 2001), xxi.

3.　The McCormicks in Virginia enslaved people and Jo Anderson, under their ownership, had grown up with Cyrus I as his boyhood companion. When Cyrus I moved to Chicago in 1848 he left Anderson behind and rented him out to nearby landowners; after the Civil War McCormick bought Anderson a small farm and cabin. The McCormicks, in their writings about the company, all acknowledge Anderson's assistance in the reaper's development and paint a gauzy portrait of the warm friendship between master and slave. The reality for Anderson, who of course never shared in the McCormick family's wealth that derived from the machine he at the least helped perfect, and who remained in bondage after Cyrus I left Virginia to make his fortune, was likely different. The centrality of slavery both to the reaper's invention and the generation of the McCormicks' wealth was underscored by Brent Shaw, who notes, "Through the felicitous veils of paternalism and self-congratulatory praise that cover [the McCormick accounts] we see not only the central role played by a slave, Jo Anderson, in the process of invention but also the whole background of the institution of slavery in antebellum Virginia. . . . Slavery is ever present in the production of the wealth out of which McCormick himself arose and which helped create the large-scale agriculture that provoked the invention in the first place. Not unimportantly, it was also central to the position of men who could sustain the free time and the fiscal burdens required by the invention. The two big financial backers that McCormick specifically notes . . . were slaveholders and plantation owners in the Virginia Piedmont. As members of families of considerable social standing in Virginia society, both men provided monetary support for McCormick's invention, surely because his technical efforts converged with their own agricultural and economic interests." *Bringing in the Sheaves: Economy and Metaphor in the Roman World* (Toronto: University of Toronto Press, 2013). The Stanton quote is from Cyrus McCormick III, *The Century of the Reaper* (Cambridge: Riverside Press, 1931), 63; the *Chicago Defender* quotes are from the December 11, 1948 issue. More information about Jo Anderson can be found in *Century of the Reaper,* 11; George Reasons, "They Had a Dream," *Pittsburgh Post-Gazette,* September 1, 1970.

4.　Dale Cox to Claude Barnett, February 15, 1944; Claude Barnett papers, CHMA.

5.　McCormick quoted in "Fowler McCormick Describes His Firm's Approach to Equal Job Chance for Negroes," *St. Louis Post-Dispatch,* April 23, 1948;

"Unfavorable experiences" is from Ivan Willis, Harvester's vice-president of industrial relations, quoted in Jennifer Delton, *Racial Integration in Corporate America, 1940–1990* (Cambridge: Cambridge University Press, 2009), 61. See also Robert Ozanne, *A Century of Labor-Management Relations at McCormick and International Harvester* (Madison: University of Wisconsin Press, 1967), 188–89; Delton, *Racial Integration*, 130–52; John Hope II, *Negro Employment in Three Southern Plants of International Harvester Company* (Washington, DC: National Planning Association, 1953).

6. For comparative information on the income standards of Southern workers in the period see the National Emergency Council, *Report on Economic Conditions of the South*, Washington, DC: Government Printing Office, 1938; Andrew Seltzer, "The Political Economy of the Fair Labor Standards Act of 1938," *Journal of Political Economy* 103, no. 6 (December 1995); Bruce Shulman, *From Cotton Belt to Sun Belt: Federal Policy, Economic Development, and the Transformation of the South, 1938–1980* (New York: Oxford University Press, 1991).

7. Nelson Lichtenstein, *State of the Union: A Century of American Labor* (Princeton: Princeton University Press, 2002), 114.

8. *Welcome to International Harvester's Louisville Works*, company pamphlet, n.d. [1950], IHA; *Louisville Times*, April 12, 1946, (contained in Carl and Anne Braden papers, WSHS); *Courier-Journal*, June 26, 1949. The *Courier-Journal* was (and is) Louisville's leading newspaper, but its masthead did not include the city's name.

14: An Unlikely Friendship

1. Lebanon, Kentucky, had a population of about four thousand in the mid-1940s. For more on the remarkably rich history and latter-day notoriety of this town, see James Higdon, *Cornbread Mafia: A Homegrown Syndicate's Code of Silence and the Biggest Marijuana Bust in American History* (Guilford: Lyons Press, 2013).

2. All quotations in this section are drawn from interviews by the author with Jim Mouser, October 17, 1987; and Jim Wright, January 8, 1986 and October 20, 1987.

15: Organizing Louisville, FE-Style

1. Jim Wright, interview with author, January 8, 1986.

2. Allan Haywood to Vernon Bailey, July 8, 1941, Carl and Anne Braden papers, WSHS; *Globe-Gazette* (Mason City, Iowa), March 12, 1942; *Courier-Journal*, March 12, 1942; *Palladium-Item* (Richmond, Indiana), July 13, 1944; Vernon Bailey's FBI files 100-190362-6, July 26, 1943, 100-71906-47, January 17, 1944, in author's possession; *Cub*, June 1, 1947, copy in author's possession; *Courier-Journal*, March 2, 1947.

3.   *Courier-Journal*: April 21, April 22, September 9, and September 20, 1944; May 8, 1948.
4.   *Courier-Journal*, May 1, 1943. Marrero wrote frequently to the *Courier-Journal* about issues of the day and other letters from him can be found on January 17, 1943; February 16, 1947; December 20, 1947; March 1, 1949; and February 18, 1950.
5.   Milt Burns to Vernon Bailey, January 7, 1947; Vernon Bailey to Milt Burns, May 13, 1946, and May 28, 1946; all contained in Carl and Anne Braden papers, WSHS.
6.   James Wright, interview with author, January 8, 1986; Vernon Bailey to Milt Burns, July 24, 1946; Fred Marrero to Milt Burns, February 1, 1947; both letters contained in Carl and Ann Braden papers, WSHS.
7.   Fred Marrero to Milt Burns, February 1, 1947; Carl and Anne Braden papers, WSHS.
8.   *Midwest Daily Record*, February 2, 1938; *FE News,* October 30, 1944; *FE News*, August 21, 1946. The FE's convention that year was originally planned to take place in the Quad Cities (on the Illinois-Iowa border) but the executive board chose to move the convention to Milwaukee when the hotel association in the Quad Cities refused to require all accommodations be open to African Americans. *FE News*, May 22, 1946.
9.   *Chicago Defender*, August 10, 1946, 1, 3, 14.
10.   Fred Marrero to Milt Burns, February 1, 1947, Carl and Anne Braden papers, WSHS.
11.   Sterling Neal and Bud James (n.d.), joint interview, Carl and Anne Braden papers, WSHS; Vernon Bailey to Milt Burns, November 23, 1946, WSHS; FE, *The Louisville Story*, pamphlet, n.d. [1953] in author's possession; James Wright, interview with author, January 8, 1986.
12.   *The Louisville Story.*
13   Sterling Neal and Bud James (n.d.), joint interview; Vernon Bailey to Milt Burns, August 26, 1946, and November 23, 1946; Carl and Anne Braden papers, WSHS.
14.   Vernon Bailey to Milt Burns, May 27, 1946, Carl and Anne Braden papers, WSHS; *Courier-Journal*, June 11, 1947.
15.   *Courier-Journal*, June 2, 1947; *Cub*, June 1, 1947, copy in author's possession.
16.   *Courier-Journal*, July 30, 1947.

16: We're Not Going to Be Second-Class Citizens in the South

1.   *Chicago Tribune,* October 18, 1947; *Wall Street Journal*, May 9, 1947; *Indianapolis Star*, May 13, 1947.
2.   Oliver Jensen, "Young Pink," *Life,* September 23, 1940; *Courier-Journal*, March 13, 1952; Jim Wright, interview with author, January 8, 1986.
3.   FBI reports 122-246-6, September 29, 1953; 100-213-630, February 26,

1948, in author's possession; Bud James, interview, n.d. [1951], James Wright, interview, December 12, 1951, both contained in Carl and Anne Braden papers, WSHS.

4.   Bud James, n.d. [1951], interview, Carl and Anne Braden papers, WSHS.

5.   "To Set the Record Straight," International Harvester advertisement, n.d. [1947], IHA.

6.   *Cub*, September 17, 1946, copy in author's possession; Sterling Neal and Bud James, interview, n.d. [1952?], Carl and Anne Braden papers, WSHS.

7.   *Welcome to International Harvester's Louisville Works*, company pamphlet n.d. [1950], IHA; FE, *The Louisville Story*, pamphlet, n.d. [1953], copy in author's possession; Sterling Neal and Bud James, interview, n.d. [1952?], Carl and Anne Braden papers, WSHS; Jim Wright, interview with author, January 8, 1986.

8.   Sterling Neal and Bud James, interview, n.d. [1952?], Carl and Anne Braden papers, WSHS.

9.   Sterling Neal and Bud James, interview, n.d. [1952?], Carl and Anne Braden papers, WSHS.

10.   Jim Wright, interview with author, January 8, 1986; *Courier-Journal*, September 18, 24, 25, 27, 28, 29, and October 7, 9, 10, 1947; Letter, John McCaffrey to the Harvester management group, September 24, 1947, IHA; *The Louisville Story*; Sterling Neal and Bud James, interview, n.d. [1952?], Carl and Anne Braden papers, WSHS. In the *Courier-Journal* on October 7, 1947, IH claimed that forty-two production employees had returned to work, so the truth, in terms of how many workers crossed the picket lines, probably lies between several dozen and forty-two: still a small number. Neal was adamant, however, that no African Americans crossed the line, and there is no reason to doubt that claim.

11.   Sterling Neal and Bud James, interview, n.d. [1952?], Carl and Anne Braden papers, WSHS; *The Louisville Story*.

12.   Sterling Neal and Bud James, interview, n.d. [1952?], Carl and Anne Braden papers, WSHS; *The Louisville Story*.

13.   Sterling Neal and Bud James, interview, n.d. [1952?], Carl and Anne Braden papers, WSHS; *Daily Clintonian* (Clinton, Iowa), September 29, 1947; *Chicago Tribune*, September 30, 1947; John McCaffrey to all Harvester employees represented by the FE, October 20, 1947, IHA; *Courier-Journal*, October 18, 1947.

14.   *FE News*, November 1947; *Courier-Journal*, October 27, 1947.

15.   *FE News*, November 1947; FE press release, October 28, 1947, copy in author's possession.

16.   Sterling Neal and Bud James, interview, n.d. [1952?], Carl and Anne Braden papers, WSHS; Jim Wright, interview with author, January 8, 1986.

17.   Characterizations of the percentage of veterans and the youth of the Louisville workforce come from *The Louisville Story*; FE press release, October 28, 1947,

copy in author's possession; author's interview with Harvester worker and Local 236 leader Chris Gastinger, April 11, 1991; and Sterling Neal and Bud James, interview, n.d. [1952?], Carl and Anne Braden papers, WSHS.

18. Sterling Neal and Bud James, interview, n.d. [1952?], Carl and Anne Braden papers, WSHS.

19. Jim Wright, interview with author, January 8, 1986.

20. John McCaffrey to all Harvester employees represented by the FE, October 20, 1947; IHA. To put the FE's strike behavior in perspective and provide a sense of how much has changed for organized labor, the Bureau of Labor Statistics reports that for the *ten-year period* from 2007 to 2016, there were a *total of 143 work stoppages* in the entire United States. Now this figure only includes major strikes of over one thousand workers, and most of the FE's work stoppages would not have involved that many workers, but quite a few did. In the United States between 1947 and 1956, there were 3,438 work stoppages all told, and the FE contributed its share to that much higher figure. So these statistics speak to the decline of workplace militancy and the taming of the labor movement that has taken place since the end of WWII.

21. *Business Week,* November 1, 1947; *Factory Management and Maintenance,* December 1947; Research Institute of America Executive Policy Letter, November 7, 1947, IHA.

22. Grant Oakes and Jerry Fielde to John McCaffrey, November 6, 1947, IHA. The letter, which ran as an advertisement in various Midwestern newspapers, was also said to be distributed to "all FE-CIO members, every union in the American labor movement, [and] farmer and cooperative organizations." *Daily Times* (Davenport, Iowa), November 15, 1947.

23. *New York Times,* October 21, 1947; Arbitration, *FE Local 236 v. IH,* December 22, 1947, IHA; *Courier-Journal,* November 8, 27, 1947, January 24, 1948. The arbitrator in this case was renowned sociologist Herbert Blumer. Blumer, who originated the concept of symbolic interaction in sociological theory, was a fascinating character: Born in 1900, he grew up on a farm in Missouri and worked his way through the University of Missouri. While pursuing his doctorate at the University of Chicago, he played professional football for the Chicago (now Arizona) Cardinals. He became a professor of sociology at the University of Chicago in 1927, where he remained until he moved to the University of California, Berkeley in 1952. So he would have been a professor at the U of C when Bud James was a student there. How much the two may have crossed paths is unknown, but it's interesting to note that Blumer was providing an assist to a union connected to James, a former U of C student who was already well known during his time on campus for his radical views.

24. *Courier-Journal,* February 15 and 19, 1948; Bud James, interview, n.d. [1951], Carl and Anne Braden papers, WSHS. Other indications of the widespread feeling that there was something "smelly" about Gibson's sudden death come from Local 236 member Jim Mouser, who said that his father and older

brother—who worked at the Louisville plant longer than he had—were convinced that someone must have "put something in his drink he was served, or what have you," and Anne Braden, who said "There always was some suspicion that there was something strange about [Gibson's] death . . . there was a feeling, whether it was verified or not, that somebody had killed him." Mouser interview with author, October 17, 1987; Braden interview with author, March 9, 1991.

25. Jim Wright, interview with author, January 8, 1986; *The Louisville Story*, *Courier-Journal*, February 19, 1948.

26. Bud James, n.d. [1951], interview, Carl and Anne Braden papers, WSHS.

17: The Shrinking Realm of the Possible

1. "Annual Conventions of the AFL and CIO," *Monthly Labor Review* 65 (November 1947): 528; Joseph Starobin, *American Communism in Crisis 1943–1957* (Berkeley: University of California Press, 1972), 168–69. In 1965, the noncommunist affidavits were struck down by the Supreme Court in *United States v. Brown* (381 U.S. 437).

2. Max Kampelman, *The Communist Party vs. the CIO* (New York: Praeger Press, 1957), 69–70.

3. Lucius Harper, "From Fred Douglass to Robeson, Peoria Hasn't Improved," *Chicago Defender*, May 3, 1947.

4. "Pekin Wasn't Always a Welcoming Place," *Pekin Daily Times*, June 21, 2013. While circumstances have changed since the mid-twentieth century, Peoria remains an inhospitable place for African Americans. "Group Names Peoria Worst City in Nation for Black Americans," *Journal Star* (Peoria), October 16, 2016. For more about Peoria's race relations and labor history see Jason Kozlowski, "Will Globalism Play in Peoria? Class, Race and Nation in the Global Economy, 1948—2000" (PhD diss., University of Illinois, 2011); see also Scott Saul, *Becoming Richard Pryor* (New York: HarperCollins, 2014). Pryor was a Peoria native.

5. For the FE's early challenges to Peoria's Jim Crow, see "Kluxer's Kin Defies Jim Crow, Sets Town on Ear," *Chicago Defender*, October 7, 1944. Martin is featured in a photo spread about Black labor leaders in the February 1947 issue of *Ebony*. He is identified as the Peoria NAACP president in the *San Antonio Register* (a Black newspaper), August 22, 1947, in a story about the American Legion's expulsion of the "Negro" post of the Legion in Peoria for "giving comfort to ideologies opposed by the Legion, namely communism." Coverage of Robeson's appearance in Peoria, and his stay with Martin, was widespread; for examples see Harper, "From Fred Douglass"; *New York Times*, April 19, 1947; *Minneapolis Star*, April 19, 1947; *Pantograph* (Bloomington, Illinois), April 19, 1947.

6. "Master Minds" from a UAW ad in *Pantograph* (Bloomington, Illinois), May

10, 1948; Ferrin quoted in *Peoria Journal and Transcript*, March 19, 1948.

7. *FE News*, June 1948; *United Automobile Worker*, June 1948; "'Cat' Workers Tangle," *Business Week*, April 24, 1948, 114–16; James Shaughnessy to Walter Reuther (letter with news clippings enclosed), February 20, 1948, Walter Reuther papers, WSU; FE, *Why We Fight Back*, pamphlet, 1949 [in author's possession].

8. "Tactical Switch," *Business Week*, June 12, 1948; *Battle Creek Enquirer*, June 3, 1948; see also James Peneff, "Reluctant Surrender," *New Republic*, August 30, 1948; US Senate Committee on Labor and Public Welfare, *Hearings on Communist Domination of Unions and National Security*, 82nd Congress, 2nd Session, 1952, Washington, DC: Government Printing Office, 512–13. That the FE broke ranks among the party-connected unions was not generally acknowledged at the time, at least by anti-communists. In a 1950 article, Albert Epstein and Nathaniel Goldfinger said, "[u]ntil the spring of 1949, [party followers within trade unions] refused to resign from their posts or to sign the non-Communist affidavits required by the law if the procedures of the NLRB were to be used. This policy was followed by all Communist-line unions, regardless of the consequences to the membership or the organization"; "Communist Tactics in American Unions," *Labor and Nation* (Fall 1950): 41.

9. *FE News*, June 1948.

10. *FE News*, June 1948.

11. Watkins indicated in his later testimony before the House Un-American Activities Committee (HUAC) that he had supported compliance with the Taft-Hartley Act; *Hearings on Investigation of Communist Activities in the Chicago Area –Part 3*, 83rd Congress, 2nd Session, 1954, Washington, DC: Government Printing Office, 4268.

12. "Statement by Pope Huff," FE handbill, April 15, 1949, Holgate Young papers, WSU. It is this statement by Huff that indicates that both he and Martin were offered international representative positions with the FE; Memo, June 18, 1948, FBI Chicago field report 100-7879, section 5, in author's possession. At its next convention, in 1949, the FE elevated Bill Smith, a Black local official from McCormick Works, to a vice-presidency, thus retaining African American presence on the FE executive board. Following the FE-UE merger (see below) Sterling Neal, from FE Local 236 in Louisville, was also promoted to a national leadership position in the UE.

13. "Peace, Freedom and Abundance," platform of the Progressive Party, 1948, http://credo.library.umass.edu/view/pageturn/mums312-b121-i298/#page/1/mode/1up.

14. "FE 'Trib,'" FE leaflet, September 15, 1948, Carl and Anne Braden papers, WSHS; *New York Times*, May 28, 1949. A recent treatment of the Wallace campaign is Thomas Devine's *Henry Wallace's 1948 Presidential Campaign and the Future of Postwar Liberalism* (Chapel Hill: University of North Carolina Press, 2013). Much earlier Curtis MacDougall, who was Grant

Oakes's running mate in Illinois, wrote the three-volume *Gideon's Army* (New York: Marzani and Munsell, 1965) about the campaign. Homer Ayres was a South Dakota rancher, cowboy poet, and radical rabble-rouser, first with the communist-associated United Farmers League and then with the left-wing National Farmers Union before he became the FE's farm relations director in 1946; the FE was the first CIO union to create such a position. Ayres wrote a column for the *FE News* called "The Farmer's Angle," which was widely syndicated; Ayres and the FE leadership directed considerable attention to fostering alliances between factory workers and farmers in the immediate post-WWII years. But those outreach efforts, like so much else, foundered after 1948 as FE resources were increasingly stretched thin. For more on Ayres and the FE's farm relations efforts, see William Pratt, "The Farmers Union and the 1948 Henry Wallace Campaign," and Warren J. Wilson, "The 'People's Century' in Iowa," both from *Annals of Iowa* 49 (1988).

15. MacDougall, *Gideon's Army*, 623; "Wallaceites Hear Robeson and Pressman," *Pittsburgh Press*, April 20, 1948; Richard Freedland, *The Truman Doctrine and the Origins of McCarthyism* (New York: Knopf, 1975), 298, 301; Cabell Phillips, "Why They Join the Wallace Crusade," *New York Times*, May 23, 1948; *Courier-Journal*, September 5, 1948.

16. *Courier-Journal*, November 22, 1947; FBI Louisville field report 100-213-630, February 26, 1948, in author's possession. Herbert Monsky, a labor lawyer whose client list included Local 236, served as director of the Kentucky Wallace campaign; Chris Gastinger, a Harvester worker and Local 236 official, was a co-chair of the campaign; while Thelma Gibson, Chuck Gibson's widow, became its secretary.

17. *Courier-Journal*, January 7, February 17, March 17, 1948, July 23, 1949; FBI Louisville field report 100-71906-171, February 18, 1948, in author's possession. The other unions in the 7th Street Coalition were the United Public Workers, the Transport Workers Union, and the Furniture Workers Union. The Transport Workers union represented Louisville's bus drivers, while the United Public Workers represented the city's garbage workers. The garbage workers' and furniture workers' locals were predominantly African American.

18. Details of the Bradens' lives can be found in Anne's autobiography *The Wall Between* (New York: Monthly Review Press, 1958), and in a biography of Anne by Catherine Fosl: *Subversive Southerner: Anne Braden and the Struggle for Racial Justice in the Cold War South* (New York: Macmillan, 2002).

19. Chris Gastinger, interview with author, April 11, 1991; *Courier-Journal*, November 3, 1948; Jim Wright, interview with author, May 13, 1987.

20. Jim Wright, interview with author, May 13, 1987.

21. Jim Wright, interview with author, May 13, 1987; FBI Louisville field report 100-213-659, April 17, 1948, in author's possession; "Negroes Play Prominent Role at New Party's Convention," *Chicago Defender*, July 31, 1948.

22. Jim Wright, interview with author, May 13, 1987.

23. Richard Freedland, *The Truman Doctrine and the Origins of McCarthyism* (New York: Knopf, 1975), 298, 301; Phillips, "Wallace Crusade;" *Courier-Journal*, September 5, 1948.

24. *Courier-Journal*, August 25, 1948; Jim Wright, interview with author, October 20, 1987.

25. *Courier-Journal*, August 25, 1948; the *Courier-Journal* reported that auditorium officials estimated the audience at 800, while the Kentucky Wallace Committee put it at 1,200. *United Automobile Worker*, April, 1948; "wild-eyed fanatic" from John C. Culver and John Hyde, *American Dreamer: A Life of Henry A. Wallace* (New York: W. W. Norton, 2001), 472.

26. "Harvester Heiress on Wallace Ticket," *Palladium-Item* (Richmond, Indiana), May 7, 1948; "700 Wallace Backers Mobilize to Call 3rd Party Convention," *Baltimore Sun*, March 26, 1948; "Progressives' Ticket Names Blind Lawyer," *Decatur Daily Review* (Decatur, Illinois), May 7, 1948. The four other co-chairs of the Wallace for President committee were Paul Robeson; UE President Albert Fitzgerald; Rexford Tugwell, an economist who had been part of FDR's "Brain Trust"; and Jo Davidson, a prominent sculptor. Other candidates on the Progressive ticket in Illinois included *Chicago Defender* columnist Rebecca Stiles Taylor, the choice for Illinois Secretary of State; and Donald Hesson, a blind lawyer nominated to run for Attorney General.

27. Gilbert Harrison, *A Timeless Affair: The Life of Anita McCormick Blaine* (Chicago: University of Chicago Press, 1979), 220–28; *Chicago Tribune*, July 27, 1948. Anita's one-million-dollar contribution to the Wallace campaign would be the equivalent of about $10 million in today's dollars.

28. *Courier-Journal*, March 7, 1948; November 4, 1948. The fight over Progressive Party access to the ballot, in Illinois and elsewhere, has application to third-party efforts today. For an examination of that battle in Illinois, see "Legal Barriers Confronting Third Parties: The Progressive Party in Illinois," *University of Chicago Law Review* 16, no. 3 (Spring 1949): 499–523. The best examination of the ballot fight in the various states comes from Karl Schmidt, *Henry A. Wallace: Quixotic Crusade, 1948* (Syracuse: Syracuse University Press, 1960). The '48 election, though it affirmed the Democratic Party's strength among union members, could also be taken as a repudiation of the Taft-Hartley Act. Truman regularly denounced it and, as the *Courier-Journal* noted, "Labor organizations, with few exceptions, put on all-out vote drives against those who voted for the controversial act." As a result, of the fifty-four House members who lost their seats in November 1948, fifty-one had voted for Taft-Hartley. Despite that fact, and Truman's pledge to overturn the law, in the next few years only tepid efforts were mounted to overturn Taft-Hartley and it was never repealed. *Courier-Journal*, November 4, 1948.

29. For participation by Black FE members in the Progressive Party, see "FE 'Trib,'" FE leaflet, Carl and Anne Braden papers, WSHS; "Illinois Progressives Elect Eight to Board," *Chicago Defender*, March 7, 1948.

30.   Jim Wright, interview with author, May 13, 1987; *Courier-Journal,* September 5, 1948.
31.   Jim Wright, interview with author, May 13, 1987; Chris Gastinger, interview with author, April 11, 1991.
32.   FBI field report 100-71906-209, March 13, 1950, in author's possession; *Courier Journal,* June 8, 1997.
33.   Harvey Levenstein, *Communism, Anti-Communism, and the CIO* (Westport: Greenwood Press, 1981), 281; *United Automobile Worker,* February 1949.
34.   "Opening Statement of FE-CIO President Grant Oakes," March 25, 1949; FE, *The Rank and File Said NO!* pamphlet, April 1949; both from FEWOC file, CIO papers, CUA.
35.   *United Automobile Worker,* June 1949; FBI Chicago file 100-7879, section 11, in author's possession; "Proposed Relationship Between UE and FE," FE leaflet, n.d. [1949], FEWOC file, CIO papers, CUA.
36.   "Proposed Relationship Between UE and FE," FE leaflet, n.d. [1949], FEWOC file, CIO papers, CUA; *UE News,* November 14, 1949; "Eleventh Convention of the CIO," *Monthly Labor Review* (December 1949): 644; Bert Cochran, *Labor and Communism: The Conflict that Shaped American Unions* (Princeton: Princeton University Press, 1977), 291, 312–15; Kampelman, *The Communist Party vs. the CIO,* 160. Among the other unions expelled by the CIO were the International Longshoremen's and Warehousemen's Union; the Mine, Mill and Smelter Workers' Union; the United Office and Professional Workers' Union; the Fur and Leather Workers' Union; the United Public Workers; and the Food, Tobacco, Agricultural, and Allied Workers' Union.

18: The Triumph of the Stormy Petrel

1.   Jim Wright, interview with author, January 10, 1986.
2.   The UAW's intention to displace the FE at the Louisville IH plant was first reported in the *Courier-Journal* on February 16, 1949; Livingston was quoted in the *Courier-Journal* on March 2, 1949. The UAW ran quarter-page ads in the *Courier Journal* frequently, for instance on March 2, March 6, March 20, March 30, December 17, and December 19, 1949 (the FE ran no such ads).
3.   *Courier Journal,* October 11 and October 25, 1949; *Louisville Times,* April 22, 1949. The Bingham family of Louisville, owners of the *Courier-Journal* and the *Times* from the mid-nineteenth century through the mid-1980s, rivalled the McCormicks for demonstrations of the foibles of the well-to-do, and surely surpassed them in terms of ruinous sibling animosity. See Susan Tifft and Alex Jones, *The Patriarch: The Rise and Fall of the Bingham Dynasty* (New York: Summit Books, 1991).
4.   *Courier-Journal,* March 24 and November 3, 1949; Thomas DeLong to James Matles, November 23, 1949, UE Archives.
5.   Jim Wright, interview with author, January 10, 1986; *UE News,* January 9, 1950.

6.   Bud James, interview, [1952?], Anne Braden papers, WSHS; *Courier-Journal*,
      November 23, 1949.

7   Thomas DeLong to James Matles, November 23, 1949, UE Archives; *Courier-
      Journal*, December 16 and 19, 1949; FE, *The Louisville Story*, pamphlet, n.d.
      [1953], in author's possession. In *Struggle for the Soul of the Postwar South:
      White Evangelical Protestants and Operation Dixie* (Urbana: University of
      Illinois Press, 2015), Elizabeth Fones-Wolf and Ken Fones-Wolf have
      suggested that Rice's visit backfired, as it allowed Local 236 leaders to "spread
      rumors that CIO President Philip Murray was an emissary of the Pope,"
      which led Baptists within the local, "fearing Rome more than Moscow," to
      choose the FE over the UAW (p. 201). But it's hard to believe that it was
      merely fear of Papism that led to the UAW's defeat. For one thing, the
      FE's margin of victory was too large to explain by last-minute defections
      engendered by Rice's appearance. The suggestion that the FE was engaging
      in Catholic-baiting came from a professor of theology in Louisville who was
      sympathetic to the CIO, so as was the case with many noncommunists he may
      have presumed there must be some explanation for a left-leaning union victory
      besides the obvious one: that the workers just preferred it. But one wonders
      how many workers in Louisville would have been so spooked by the specter of
      Catholicism, given its significance not just in the city but in the surrounding
      area (Catholics played a prominent role in Kentucky's bourbon industry, for
      instance). There were also a fair number of Catholics within the Local 236
      rank and file and its top leadership included Catholics, like Leo Wright
      (described by Anne Braden as "a big Catholic"); Wright (who was white and
      no relation to Jim Wright) was an early FE supporter and the elected Local
      236 delegate to the IH Conference Board at the time of the raid. So it's
      unlikely that the Louisville FE promoted anti-Catholic rumor-mongering,
      particularly since such behavior would have run contrary to the message of
      equality the union otherwise emphasized. And given the heavy Catholic
      presence within its Chicago locals, it would have been dicey for the FE to do
      so, as those messages might filter back north. But there is no question that the
      UAW did itself no favors with its zero-hour religious assault. Relying on out-
      of-town figures like Rice and John Ramsay (a former steelworker official who
      became co-chair of the National Religion and Labor Foundation and was the
      CIO's leading point man on religious issues) to castigate the FE for its godless
      communism was seen as "heavy handed and inept," as the *Courier-Journal* put
      it (December 23, 1949). The FE was able to capitalize on the UAW's effort
      to inject religion into the contest, as Local 236, "mildly and reproachfully," so
      the *Courier-Journal* said, emphasized that it "never questioned or doubted any
      man in this plant because of religion, race, creed, or politics." So to the extent
      that religion played a part in explaining the FE's margin of victory, I'd argue
      that the UAW's misstep in that regard came in underestimating how much
      Harvester workers in Louisville, regardless of where they attended church,

resented being told what to do, especially by outside "authorities."

8. *Courier-Journal*, December 20 and 23, 1949.
9. The exact election results were: FE: 1,908; UAW: 1,049; no union: 26, *Courier-Journal*, December 22, 1949; *UE News*, January 9, 1950; *The Louisville Story*; *The Daily Worker*, December 23, 1949. The "stormy petrel" reference was no doubt an allusion by the literate reporters at the *Courier-Journal* to Maxim Gorky's revolutionary anthem, said to be one of Vladimir Lenin's favorite poems.
10. *Courier-Journal*, December 23, 1949; "How to Win in 1955," n.d. [1954], FE position paper, in author's possession.
11. Jim Wright, interview with author, January 10, 1986.

19: Pie on the Table or Pie in the Sky?

1. *Courier-Journal*, March 2 and December 20, 1949.
2. "Economic facts" from Russell Wheeler Davenport, *USA: The Permanent Revolution* (New York: Prentice-Hall, 1951), 94; other quotes from *Fortune*, July 1950, 54.
3. Davenport, *Permanent Revolution*, 95; "Agreement between General Motors Corporation and the UAW-CIO," May 29, 1950, contract collection, WSU; *United Automobile Worker*, June 1950.
4. *Cub*, December 19, 1949, copy in author's possession
5. Walter Reuther, "GM v. The Rest of Us," *New Republic*, January 14, 1946, 42; Charles Maier, "The Politics of Productivity: Foundations of American International Economic Policy after World War II," *International Organization* 31 (Fall 1977): 613; see also Ronald Radosh, "The Corporate Ideology of American Labor Leaders from Gompers to Hillman," in *For a New America: Essays in History and Politics from Studies on the Left, 1959–1967*, eds. James Weinstein and David Eakins (New York: Random House, 1970). References to pies seemed requisite to the politics of productivity, as Elizabeth Fones-Wolf makes clear: "In this vision, corporate leaders claimed the right to control America's economic destiny without significant interference from unions or the state while acknowledging their responsibility to make the benefits of industrial capitalism available to all. Economic growth rather than the redistribution of income proposed by unionists would allow business to hold up its end of the bargain. The key, as the Committee for Economic Development's research director pointed out in 1947, was productivity. He asserted productivity was 'a vitally needed lubricant to reduce class and group frictions. As long as we get more by increasing the size of the pie there is not nearly so much temptation to try and get a bigger slice at the expense of others.' In short, the business vision linked economic success with freedom, individualism and productivity." *Selling Free Enterprise: The Business Assault on Labor and Liberalism, 1945–60* (Urbana: University of Illinois Press, 1994), 5. For more on the pie metaphor in post-WWII economics, see Oren Cass, "The

Working Hypothesis," *American Interest*, October 15, 2018,
www.the-american-interest.com/2018/10/15/the-working-hypothesis/; for
more on labor's embrace of increased productivity, see Kim Moody, *U.S. Labor
in Trouble and Transition: The Failure of Reform from Above, the Promise of
Revival from Below* (New York: Verso, 2007).

6.   "For Harmony in Industry," *Harvester World*, April 1947, WSHS. Among the
       other labor leaders who signed the "code" were Clinton Golden of the United
       Steelworkers of America; Marion Hedges of the International Brotherhood of
       Electrical Workers; James Carey of the CIO; Emil Rieve of the United Textile
       Workers; and George Meany, Secretary-Treasurer of the AFL.

7.   Other left-wing unions also challenged the underlying premises of the politics
       of productivity. See for example Rosemary Feurer, *Radical Unionism in the
       Midwest, 1900–1950* (Urbana: University of Illinois Press, 2006), 72–73,
       223–26; and Judith Stepan-Norris and Maurice Zeitlin, *Left Out: Reds and
       America's Industrial Unions* (Cambridge: Cambridge University Press, 2002),
       especially 159–88.

8.   "How to Win in 1955," n.d. [1954], FE position paper, in author's possession.

9.   "Officers' Report to the 4th Constitutional Convention," March 25–29
       1949, FEWOC file, CIO papers, CUA (emphasis in original); *FE Local 115
       News* (Charles City, Iowa), April 14, 1949, contained in DeMaio scrapbook,
       CHMA; Al Verri, interview with author, January 29, 1981.

10.   *FE News*, May 22, 1946. Emphasis in original.

11.   *CIO News, Farm Equipment Edition*, March 25, 1940.

12.   *UE News*, February 20, 1950; "Contract between McCormick Works,
       International Harvester Company, and McCormick Local 108, FE-CIO,"
       June 30, 1948, in author's possession; US Congress Joint Committee on
       Labor-Management Relations, *Report Pursuant to Section 401 of Public Law
       101*, 1948, S. Rpt. No. 986, 80th Congress, 2nd Session (123), Washington,
       DC: Government Printing Office; IH labor relations letter No. 879, March
       24, 1948, IHA. Other left-wing unionists regarded a powerful steward system
       as integral to industrial democracy and workers' power. In the Allis-Chalmers
       farm equipment plant in Wisconsin, CP-influenced and anti-Reuther UAW
       Local 248 believed that "the steward structure and grievance procedure were
       much more than an institutional form of worker representation in the plant.
       The union leaders used them to register worker discontent with working
       conditions and to test the limits of worker authority and power in the shops.
       Most often, the union grievances turned on disputes over interpretation of the
       contract and touched on questions of wages, hours, and working conditions. In
       a sense, these grievances penetrated to the core of 'pure and simple unionism.'
       A careful examination of the more fundamental and basic questions revealed
       that worker disputes went far beyond the bounds of conservative trade
       unionism. Beneath the surface, the issues involved worker dignity, authority
       relations, and technical innovation. Gradually, Local 248 leaders used the

grievance procedure to rationalize workplace relations within the framework of what has been labeled a 'workplace rule of law.' Later, after the rationalization of Allis-Chalmers labor relations, they expanded the boundaries of union control and directly contested management's shop floor power." Stephen Meyer, *"Stalin Over Wisconsin:" The Making and Unmaking of Militant Unionism, 1900–1950* (New Brunswick: Rutgers University Press, 1992), 111.

13. US Congress Joint Committee on Labor-Management Relations, *Report Pursuant to Section 401 of Public Law 101*, March 15, 1948, S. Rpt. No. 986, 80th Congress, 2nd Session (119), Washington, DC: Government Printing Office; "Agreement between General Motors and the UAW-CIO," May 29, 1950, WSU.

14. *FE News*, May 22, 1946; "Agreement between Fort Wayne Works, International Harvester Company, and International Union UAW, Local 57," August 23, 1948, Contract collection, WSU; "Unions Should Be Responsible for the Things They *Can* Control," International Harvester letter sent to all employees, August 15, 1947, which also ran as an ad in the *Chicago Tribune* and in all plant city newspapers; both the ad and the letter are contained in the IHA.

15. Benjamin Selekman, Sylvia Selekman, and Stephen Fuller, *Problems in Industrial Relations* (New York: McGraw Hill, 1958), 613; "International Harvester Company Number of Work Stoppages Due to Labor Interruptions, Manhours Lost, and Estimated Pay Loss, by Works, October 1 1946 to October 1 1948", IHA; Jimmy Majors, interview with author, January 22, 1981.

16. *Courier-Journal*, June 26 and June 30, 1949.

20: Theory Meets Practice: The Louisville Shop Floor

1. Jim Mouser, interview with author, October 17, 1987.

2. US Congress, *Report of the Joint Committee on Labor-Management Relations*, March 15, 1948, 80th Congress, 2nd Session (123), Washington, DC: Government Printing Office; Jim Mouser, interview with author, October 17, 1987.

3. Jim Wright, interview with author, January 8, 1986.

4. H. C. Baker, (IH assistant manager of labor relations), address before the 14th training course in industrial relations, June 1953, IHA; *Courier-Journal*, October 14, and March 13, 1949; Jim Wright, interview with author, January 8, 1986.

5. Jim Wright, interview with author, January 8, 1986; Jim Mouser, interview with author, October 17, 1987.

6. *Courier-Journal*, March 13, 1949; FE, *The Louisville Story*, n.d. [1953] pamphlet, in author's possession; *Cub*, March 8, 1951 (emphasis in original), copy in author's possession.

7. *Cub*, June 1, 1947, copy in author's possession. Emphasis in original.

8. Sample 1949 headlines from the *Courier-Journal* include: "430 Idle in

Stoppages at Harvester Plant" on April 7; "Harvester Shuts Most of Its Plant After Walkouts" on June 17; "Punch-Press Men at IHC Walk Off Jobs in Time Row" on July 22; "3 Work Stoppages in One Day Stall IHC Production" on September 16; and "Welders' Walkout at IHC To Close Three Departments" on October 20.

9. *Courier-Journal,* June 30 and September 16, 1949; Letter to "Mr. and Mrs. FE" from Local 236 President Allen Coones, April 14, 1949, Carl and Anne Braden papers, WSHS.

10. FBI Louisville field reports, 100-213-799 (October 12, 1949); 100-213-810 (September 30, 1949); 100-71906-209 (March 13, 1950), in author's possession; *Courier-Journal,* September 20 and November 9, 1949.

11. FBI field report 100-213-799, October 12, 1949, in author's possession.

12. *Courier-Journal,* November 15, 16, 17, 28, 1949; *New York Times,* November 16, 1949; IH labor relations letter No. 1022, June 12, 1950, IHA; *Cub,* December 7, 1949, copy in author's possession.

13. *Courier-Journal,* February 12, 15, 1949; *Louisville Defender,* February 19, 1949 (the *Defender* front page is reprinted in the *FE News,* March 1949).

14. *The Louisville Story.*

15. Anne Braden, interview with author, March 9, 1991; FE, *The Crime of International Harvester,* n.d. [1953], UE Archives; John Hope II, *Negro Employment in Three Southern Plants of International Harvester Company* (Washington, DC: National Planning Association, 1953), 37, 41; "Unity Pays Off for Everybody in Fight on I-H Discrimination," *UE News,* June 25, 1951. As an indication of the recognition Fowler McCormick was accorded for his equal opportunity advocacy, he received the "Industrial Statesmanship Award" from the National Urban League in 1954; "Through the Color Barrier," *Time,* March 22, 1954, 104–5. Discussion of the complicated cafeteria situation can be found in *The Louisville Story;* in a letter from Vernon Bailey to Milt Burns, August 19, 1946, Carl and Anne Braden papers, WSHS; in Hope, *Negro Employment,* 53; and my interview with Jim Wright, January 8, 1986. Both Wright and *The Louisville Story* insist that it was the FE that called for the cafeteria to be integrated while the company resisted, but Bailey's early letter suggests a more nuanced story. The plant's first general manager, J. E. Harris, who had been brought in from Chicago before the plant opened, endeavored in 1946 to integrate the cafeteria and had some of his staff sit with Black employees during lunchtime to facilitate that process. Bailey gives Harris credit for his "progressive" efforts, which were evidently stymied when "local members of supervision" (i.e. foremen who were Kentucky natives) refused to sit with Black workers and insisted on maintaining segregated seating in the cafeteria. Harris then backed off and the cafeteria remained formally segregated until at least 1954. It may be that Harris, who didn't last long as plant manager in Louisville, was replaced by managers less committed to the integration ideal. It is clear, however, that Local 236 continued to challenge

segregated seating in the cafeteria, as an organizer's report filed by Jim Wright in 1954 indicated that "we finally maneuvered the company into the position of opening the cafeteria lines to both Negro and White"; in a follow-up a week later, Wright reported that "the cafeteria deal is going over pretty good. The Negro people are eating anyplace without any friction so far." Jim Wright, organizer's reports, April 26, May 10, 1954, UE Archives.

16.   For Ford in Louisville see John McTighe, *The Barefoot Boy on the Parkway: A History of UAW Local 862* (Louisville: UAW Local 862 publication, 1988); Vernon Bailey to Milt Burns, August 19 and September 14, 1946, Carl and Anne Braden papers, WSHS; Hope, *Negro Employment*, 126–27.

17.   Anne Braden, interview with author, March 9, 1991.

18.   *The Louisville Story; UE News,* June 25, 1951; *March of Labor,* September 1951.

19.   Anne Braden, *The Wall Between* (New York: Monthly Review Press, 1958), 47–48.

20.   Braden, *Wall Between,* 46; Jim Wright, interview with author, May 13, 1987.

21.   Jim Wright, interview with author, January 8, 1986.

22.   Charles Yates, interview, n.d. [1953?], Carl and Anne Braden papers, WSHS.

23.   Braden, *Wall Between,* 47.

24.   Anne Braden, interview with author, March 9, 1991.

25.   Anne Braden, interview with author, March 9, 1991.

21: Taking the Constant Campaign into the Community

1.   The recollections in this chapter from Jim Wright about desegregation efforts in Louisville come from my interviews with him in May, August, and October, 1987.

2.   Wade Hall, ed., *The Rest of the Dream: The Black Odyssey of Lyman Johnson* (Lexington: University Press of Kentucky, 1988), 130.

3.   Louisville's municipal government only began park desegregation in 1955, when police officers were quietly informed to stop enforcing segregation practices in the parks; *Courier-Journal,* September 13, 1956.

4.   *Louisville Defender,* January 27, 1951; Anne Braden, interview with author, March 9, 1991; Catherine Fosl, *Subversive Southerner: Anne Braden and the Struggle for Racial Justice in the Cold War South* (New York, Macmillan, 2002), 121–22; Luther Adams, *Way Up North in Louisville: African American Migration in the Urban South, 1930–1970* (Chapel Hill: University of North Carolina Press, 2010), 104.

5.   *Louisville Courier-Journal,* August 26, 1949; *Louisville Defender,* September 3, 1949; Millie Neal, interview, n.d. [1952?], Carl and Anne Braden papers, WSHS; *March of Labor,* June 1951.

6.   Anne Braden, *The Wall Between* (New York: Monthly Review Press, 1958), 49; *FE News,* June 1949; FBI Louisville field report 100-71906-222, January 30, 1951, in author's possession; Anne Braden, interview with author, March 9, 1991; Millie Neal, interview, n.d. [1952?], Carl and Anne Braden papers,

WSHS.

7.　Anne Braden, *Wall Between*, 49; Anne Braden, interview with author, March 9, 1991; interview with Millie Neal, Anne Braden papers, WSHS. Anne Braden, in *The Wall Between*, does not name the white woman who expressed reticence about the first auxiliary meeting, but in my interview with her she identified the woman as Jane Mahoney.

8.　Anne Braden, interview with author, March 9, 1991; Jim Wright, interview with author, August 8, 1986.

9.　Jim Wright, interview with author, October 20, 1987.

22: IH Prepares for a Showdown

1.　"Fowler McCormick: Self-Made Man," *Fortune*, September 1946, 111; William Haycraft, *Yellow Steel: The Story of the Earthmoving Equipment Industry* (Urbana: University of Illinois Press, 2000), 167; "Harvester's Sales, Profits Much Larger," *Chicago Tribune*, June 9, 1951.

2.　"Fowler McCormick: Self-Made Man," *Fortune*; *Chicago Tribune*, June 22, 1951, 218.

3.　Barbara Marsh, *A Corporate Tragedy: The Agony of International Harvester Company* (New York: Doubleday, 1985), 76–79; "Fowler McCormick: Self-Made Man," *Fortune*, 114.

4.　Randy Leffingwell, *Farmall: The Red Tractor that Revolutionized Farming* (Minneapolis: Voyageur Press, 2007), 208; Marsh, *Corporate Tragedy*, 78–79; *New York Times*, May 29, 1951; *Chicago Tribune*, May 29, 1951 and January 28, 1952; *Courier-Journal*, January 28, 1952.

5.　*March of Labor*, September 1952; Marsh, *Corporate Tragedy*, 80.

6.　Robert Ozanne, *A Century of Labor-Management Relations at McCormick and International Harvester* (University of Wisconsin Press, 1967), 180–81; *The Times* (Munster, Indiana), June 19, 1937; Alfred J. Smith, *Grievance Handling at International Harvester Company: The "New Look,"* (master's thesis, Loyola University Chicago, 1973), 20. For more on the tragic (for the workers, anyhow) story of the 1980 closure of Wisconsin Steel, see "Winners and Losers in Steel Firm Collapse," *Chicago Tribune*, June 8, 1980; David Ranney, "The Closing of Wisconsin Steel," in eds. David Craypo and Bruce Nissan, *Grand Designs: The Impact of Corporate Strategies on Workers, Unions and Communities* (Ithaca: ILR Press, 1993), 65–91.

7.　IH, *The Unstoppable*, pamphlet, 1953, IHA; *Daily Dispatch* (Moline, Illinois), September 22, 1952; H. C. Baker (IH assistant manager of labor relations), address before the fourteenth training course in industrial relations, June 1953, IHA.

8.　H. C. Baker, address before the fourteenth training course in industrial relations, June 1953, IHA; Remarks by W. F. Overman, public relations manager, IHC Richmond Works, December 15, 1952, IHA.

23: A Fight over Every Job

1   *Daily Dispatch* (Moline, Illinois), March 18, 1952; *UE News*, July 7, 1952.

2.   *Cub*, July 7, 1952, copy in author's possession; H. C. Baker, (IH assistant
       manager of labor relations), address before the fourteenth training course
       in industrial relations, June 1953, IHA; W. F. Overman, public relations
       manager, IHC Richmond Works, Remarks, December 15, 1952, IHA; FE
       Advertisement, "Why We Are On Strike at Harvester," *Palladium-Item*
       (Richmond, Indiana), August 28, 1952.

3.   Jim Wright, interview with author, January 8, 1986.

4.   *UE News*, July 23, 1951; Local 101 Resolution, January 20, 1952, UE
       Archives.

5.   *Courier-Journal*, February 7, February 19, February 25, March 3, 1952; *UE
       News*, March 3, 1952; *Chicago Tribune*, February 13 and February 20, 1952;
       Chicago Daily News, February 24, 1952, and *Worker*, February 24, 1952
       (both contained in FBI Chicago field report 100-7879-809, copy in author's
       possession).

6.   FE-UE pamphlet, n.d. [June? 1952], UE Archives; see also *UE News*, August
       18, 1952.

7.   Robert Ray to Julius Emspak, July 25, 1952, UE Archives.

8.   DeWitt Gilpin, "The Runaway Shop That Sat Down," *March of Labor*,
       September 1952.

9.   *Chicago Tribune*, July 31, 1952; *Chicago Herald-American*, July 31, 1952,
       contained in Ernie DeMaio scrapbook, CHMA; FE-UE Local 141 Press
       Release, July 30, 1952, UE Archives; *West Side Times*, August 7, 1952,
       contained in Ernest DeMaio scrapbook, CHMA; *Jet Magazine*, August 14,
       1952; Gilpin, "Runaway Shop."

10.   *Chicago Herald-American*, July 31, 1952, contained in Ernest DeMaio
       scrapbook, CHMA; *Chicago Daily News*, August 4, 1952, contained in Ernest
       DeMaio scrapbook, CHMA; Gilpin, "Runaway Shop." The Twine Mill sit-
       down received extensive coverage in publications ranging from *Jet* (August 14,
       1952) to *Business Week* (August 30, 1952) and in newspapers coast-to-coast,
       including front-page stories on August 1, 1952, in the Wilmington, Delaware,
       Morning News; the Rochester, New York, *Democrat and Chronicle*; the *Akron
       Beacon*; the *Kansas City Times*; and the *Arizona Republic* (Phoenix), among
       numerous others.

11.   *Chicago Tribune*, August 1, 1952; *Shreveport Times*, August 1, 1952; *Lancaster
       Eagle-Gazette* (Lancaster, Ohio), August 14, 1952.

12.   *Democrat and Chronicle* (Rochester, New York), August 1, 1952; *Chicago
       Tribune*, August 5, 1952; *Bakersfield Californian*, August 5, 1952; *Quad-City
       Times* (Davenport, Iowa), August 5, 1952; Gilpin, "Runaway Shop."

13.   *Chicago Tribune*, August 4, 1952; Gilpin, "Runaway Shop."

24: I Didn't See How We Could Lose

1. H. C. Baker, (IH assistant manager of labor relations), address before the fourteenth training course in industrial relations, June 1953, IHA.

2. Al Verri, interview with author, January 29, 1981; Joint statement, Ernest DeMaio, Grant Oakes, Gerald Fielde, and DeWitt Gilpin, September 2, 1952, UE Archives.

3. Jim Wright, interview with author, January 8, 1986.

4. Joint statement, Ernest DeMaio, Grant Oakes, Gerald Fielde, and DeWitt Gilpin, September 2, 1952, UE Archives.

5. "How to Win in 1955," FE position paper, n.d. [1954], in author's possession; "An Open Letter on the Harvester Strike," October 31, 1952, IHA.

6. *Wilmington News-Journal* (Wilmington, Ohio), June 6, 1952; *Daily Dispatch* (Moline, Illinois), August 19, 1952.

7. Jim Wright, interview with author, January 8, 1986; Jim Mouser, interview with author, October 17, 1987.

25: A Strong Picket Line Is the Best Negotiator

1. Jim Mouser, interview with author, October 17, 1987; *Courier-Journal,* August 21 and 22, 1952.

2. *Palladium-Item* (Richmond, Indiana), August 22, 1952; *The Daily Times* (Davenport, Iowa), August 21, 1952; *Daily Dispatch* (Moline, Illinois), August 21, 1952; *Chicago Tribune,* August 21, 1952; *Chicago Herald-American,* August 21, 1952.

3. FE Local 108 flyer, September 1952, included in Complaint for Injunction, International Harvester vs. UE Local 108, David Rothstein papers, CHMA; *Courier-Journal,* August 28 and September 3, 1952; *Daily Dispatch* (Moline, Illinois), August 28, 1952; *Des Moines Register,* September 12, 1952.

4. House Committee on Un-American Activities, "Communist Activities in the Chicago Area," 82nd Congress, 2nd Session, September 2–3, 1952, Washington, DC: Government Printing Office; *Palladium-Item* (Richmond, Indiana), March 21, 1941; House Committee on Un-American Activities, "Investigation of Un-American Propaganda Activities in the United States, Report on the CIO Political Action Committee," 78th Congress, 2nd Session, 1944, Washington, DC: Government Printing Office; Charlotte Pomerantz, ed., *A Quarter-Century of Un-Americana* (New York: Marzani and Munsell, 1963), 57–58; *Freeport Journal-Standard* (Freeport, Illinois), October 23, 1948; *Peoria Journal-Star,* August 28, 2015.

5. *Times* (Munster, Indiana), September 2, 1952; "Communist Activities in the Chicago Area," September 2, 1952; IH, *The Unstoppable,* pamphlet, 1953, IHA; *Shreveport Times* (Shreveport, Louisiana), June 15, 1952.

6. *Chicago Tribune,* September 3, 1952; "Communist Activities in the Chicago Area," September 2, 1952.

7.   "Communist Activities in the Chicago Area," September 3, 1952.
8.   *Chicago Tribune*, September 4, 1952; *Courier-Journal*, September 4, 1952; *The Daily Times* (Davenport, Iowa), September 4, 1952; *Daily Dispatch* (Moline, Illinois), September 4, 1952.
9.   *Daily Dispatch* (Moline, Illinois), September 3, 1952; *Chicago Tribune*, September 8, 1952.
10. UAW comments were contained in W. F. Overman, public relations manager, IHC Richmond Works, Remarks, December 15, 1952, IHA.
11. Jim Wright, interview with author, January 8, 1986; Hank Graber, interview with author, January 3, 1981.
12. *The Unstoppable.*
13. Al Verri, interview with author, January 29, 1981.

26: The Foremen's Crusade

1.   IH, *The Unstoppable*, pamphlet, 1953, IHA.
2.   *The Unstoppable*; *Daily Dispatch* (Moline, Illinois), September 19, 1952; *Des Moines Register*, September 23, 1952; *Courier Journal*, September 24, 1952; *Baltimore Sun*, October 8, 1952. "We are finished" is from Ivan Willis, International Harvester's vice-president for industrial relations, in 1950, quoted in Elizabeth Fones-Wolf, *Selling Free Enterprise: The Business Assault on Labor and Liberalism, 1945–60* (Urbana: University of Illinois Press, 1994), 80.
3.   Jimmy Majors, interview with author, January 22, 1981; *Baltimore Sun*, October 8, 1952; Jim Mouser, interview with author, October 17, 1981.
4.   Matt Halas quote from *UE News*, October 2, 1950; data on IH Black employment comes from Robert Ozanne, *A Century of Labor-Management Relations at McCormick and International Harvester* (Madison: University of Wisconsin Press, 1967), 192; information and identification of McCormick's Black leadership came through author's interviews with Chuck Hall, April 29, 1986, and April 4, 1986, and with Clarence Stoecker, July 20, 1986.
5.   FE, *Frame-up of Harold Ward*, pamphlet, October 1952, UE Archives.
6.   William Lyles, affidavit, October 4, 1952, contained in David Rothstein papers, CHMA; Jim Walter (McCormick Works public relations manager), memorandum regarding "employee courage," November 20, 1952, IHA.
7.   Jimmy Majors, interview with author, January 22, 1981; Al Verri, interview with author, January 29, 1981; FE National Harvester Conference Board, "An Open Letter on the Harvester Strike," October 31, 1952, copy in author's possession.
8.   Jimmy Majors, interview with author, January 22, 1981; Chuck Hall, interview with author, April 29, 1986.
9.   Hank Graber, interview with author, January 3, 1981.
10. Headlines in local papers underscore the volatile situation in Richmond and the Quad Cities: "Three Unionists Arrested as Clubs Fly During Harvester

Picket Line Clash," *Palladium-Item* (Richmond, Indiana), September 15, 1952; "Mayor Asks State Police Be Sent to Richmond; Union Official Arrested," *Palladium-Item*, September 29, 1952; "Fists Fly as Farmall Workers, Pickets Mix," *Daily Dispatch* (Moline, Illinois), September 29, 1952; "Worker Beaten, Window Broken," *Daily Dispatch*, October 1, 1952; "Moline IHC Worker Slugged on County Highway Near Orion," *Daily Dispatch*, October 4, 1952; "Police, Pickets Clash; Arrest Four," *Daily Dispatch*, October 27, 1952.

11.   *Courier Journal*, November 11, 1952; Jim Wright, interview with author, January 8, 1986.

12.   Jim Mouser, interview with author, October 17, 1987.

13.   *Courier-Journal*, October 15, 28, 1952; "Information on the Seven Discharged Workers," [1952], Irving Meyers papers, CHMA.

14.   "Democratic union" from the *Courier-Journal*, March 9, 1952. Some sample titles for *Courier-Journal* editorials during the '52 strike: "Picketing Doesn't Give License to Goons" (August 23); "The Police Chief Was Only Doing His Duty" (August 26); "The FE Union Hurts Itself More Than Any Witnesses Do" (September 4); "Union Rough Stuff Hurts Labor's Name" (October 17).

15.   *Chicago Tribune*, October 8, 1952; *Baltimore Sun*, October 8, 1952.

16.   FE, *Frame-up of Harold Ward*, pamphlet, October 1952, UE Archives; W. F. Overman, public relations manager, IH Richmond Works, Remarks, December 15, 1952, IHA.

27. We Were Gone

1.   FE, *Strike Call*, pamphlet, October 29, 1952, contained in Chicago FBI file 100-7879, in author's possession.

2.   *Chicago Tribune*, October 4, 5, 1952; *Palladium-Item* (Richmond, Indiana), October 3, 1952; "He Went To Work. . ." from *Bend Bulletin* (Bend, Oregon), October 3, 1952; "Strike Defier. . ." from *Miami News* (Florida), October 3, 1952.

3.   IH, *The Unstoppable*, pamphlet, 1953, IHA; *Chicago Tribune*, October 6, 1952; Memo to FBI director, October 9, 1952, FBI field report 100-71906-246, in author's possession.

4.   *Chicago Tribune*, October 4 and 7, 1952; *Chicago Herald-American*, October 6, 1952 (article quoted from in FE, *Frame-up of Harold Ward*, pamphlet, October 1952, UE archives).

5.   *Milwaukee Sentinel*, October 11, 1952; *Chicago Tribune*, September 23, October 11, 15, 1952.

6.   *Somerset Daily American* (Pennsylvania), October 11, 1952; *Frame-up of Harold Ward*, (emphasis in original); Chuck Hall, interview with author, April 4, 1989.

7.   *Frame-up of Harold Ward*.

8.   *Chicago Tribune*, October 11, 1952; *Honolulu Record*, January 11, 1952; *Militant*, December 15, 1952.

9. *Washington Post*, May 31, 2005 (Brown's obituary); *Chicago Tribune*, June 11, 2015; Oscar Brown, Jr., "They Want to KILL Harold Ward," *March of Labor*, December 1952; *Strike Call*, in FBI file 100-7879, in author's possession; *Jet*, July 17, 1952.

10. Cleveland FBI field report on the National Negro Labor Council convention, December 8, 1952, Ernie Lazar FOIA collection, https://archive.org/details /foia_Brown_Julia_C.-Cleveland-5a/page/n67.

11. *Chicago Tribune*, March 20, 1964 (Stewart's obituary). The character of Billy Flynn, played by Richard Gere in the movie version of *Chicago*, was a composite character based on both Stewart and O'Brien. See Douglas Perry, *The Girls of Murder City: Fame, Lust, and the Beautiful Killers Who Inspired Chicago* (New York: Penguin, 2011).

12. *Chicago Daily News*, November 3, 1952; *Chicago Herald-American*, October 15, 1952; *Chicago Tribune*, October 15 and November 3, 1952; letter, David Scribner to Elizabeth Moore, October 21, 1952, Irving Meyers papers, CHMA.

13. *Daily Dispatch* (Moline, Illinois), October 27, 1952; *Courier-Journal*, October 24, 1952; *Chicago Sun-Times*, November 3, 1952; *Chicago Tribune*, November 3, 1952; P. W. Johnson (works manager, Louisville), letter to Louisville Works employees, November 3, 1952, Irving Meyers papers, CHMA.

14. *Daily Dispatch* (Moline, Illinois), October 22, 1952; Don Harris to Charles Hobbie, et. al., November 13, 1952, UE Archives.

15. Don Harris to Robert Logsdon et. al., November 13, 1952, UE Archives.

16. "Screaming Chinese Reds" from *Daily Dispatch* (Moline, Illinois), October 20, 1952; "suspected Reds" from *Battle Creek Enquirer*, September 19, 1952.

17. *Courier-Journal*, November 7, 1952; *Daily Dispatch* (Moline, Illinois), November 1, 1952; Jim Wright, interview with author, January 8, 1986.

28: The Big Frame-Up, Revisited

1. Jim Mouser, interview with author, October 17, 1987; *Palladium-Item* (Richmond, Indiana), November 13, 1953; *Courier-Journal*, November 13, 1952.

2. IH, *The Unstoppable*, pamphlet, 1953, IHA; John McCaffrey to all IH employees represented by the FE, November 17, 1953, Irving Meyers papers, CHMA.

3. Barbara Marsh, *A Corporate Tragedy: The Agony of International Harvester Company* (New York: Doubleday, 1985), 87.

4. Milt Burns, "Should We Have Struck?" *March of Labor*, February, 1953; IH ad in *Daily Dispatch* (Moline, Illinois), November 19, 1952; *Militant*, December 1, 1952; the *Cub*, the Local 236 paper, said of the strike, "It is clear the FE suffered a defeat."

5. Milt Burns, "Should We Have Struck?"

6. Milt Burns, "Should We Have Struck?"; Milt Burns to all IH locals, September 11, 1953, David Rothstein papers, CHMA; James Foley, "Labor

Union Jurisdictional Disputes in the Quad Cities' Farm Equipment Industry, 1949–1955" (masters' thesis, University of Iowa, August 1965).

7. When African American businessman Lee Hansberry attempted, in 1937, to buy a home in Chicago's Woodlawn neighborhood, he and his family were greeted first by angry white mobs and then with a lawsuit, based on a neighborhood covenant that prevented the sale of homes there to Black people. The Hansberrys were forced to move when Illinois courts upheld the legitimacy of such restrictive covenants; Earl Dickerson then took the case to the Supreme Court. In 1940, Dickerson won his case, but only on a technicality based on the wording in the covenant (though because of this ruling five hundred homes in Woodlawn were opened up to African Americans). Two years later, the Supreme Court, in *Shelley v. Kraemer*, definitively struck down the use of restrictive covenants. Lorraine Hansberry, who was an eight-year-old child when her family first attempted to move into Woodlawn, would later base her famous play *A Raisin in the Sun* on this experience.

8. *Chicago Tribune*, August 24, 1959 (Green obituary); Hoyt Fuller, "Earl Dickerson: Warrior and Statesman," *Ebony*, December, 1961; *Chicago Tribune*, December 19, 1950; "Chicago, NYC Race Judges Win Acclaim," *Pittsburgh Courier*, February 9, 1952; *Chicago Tribune*, January 26, 1952.

9. *Chicago Tribune*, November 27, 1952; *Chicago Herald-American*, November 26, 1952; *Chicago Daily News*, November 26, 1952.

10. *Chicago Tribune*, November 25 and 26, 1952; *Beatrice Daily Sun* (Beatrice, Nebraska), November 26, 1952.

11. *Chicago Tribune*, November 29, December 1, December 2, 1952; *Pharos-Tribune* (Logansport, Indiana), December 2, 1952; Ernest DeMaio, "The Frame-up that Failed," *March of Labor*, January 1953; David Rothstein to David Scribner, December 9, 1952, David Rothstein papers, CHMA.

12. DeWitt Gilpin, "Comeback: This Union Got Up When It Was Being Counted Out," *March of Labor*, June 1953.

13. *Chicago Tribune*, December 3, 1952; *Courier-Gazette* (McKinney, Texas), December 3, 1952.

29: We Mean Business

1. Sonya Burns, interview with author, April 17, 1986.

2. *Palladium-Item* (Richmond, Indiana), May 24, 1953; Burns's affidavit is contained in the David Rothstein papers, CHMA.

3. Al Verri, interview with author, January 29, 1981.

4. "International Harvester's Attack on Radical Labor," *Factory Management and Maintenance*, December 1947, 73.

5. "Second-class citizens" is from Burton Foster, interview by Paul Kelso, June 2, 1978, Iowa Labor History Oral Project, http://digital.lib.uiowa.edu/cdm /compoundobject/collection/ilhop/id/1819/rec/1; FBI Springfield field reports

100-71906-239, August 11, 1952 and 100-71906-285, August 16, 1954, both in author's possession. A detailed examination of Watkins's post-1952 maneuvering is included in James Foley, "Labor Union Jurisdictional Disputes in the Quad Cities Farm Equipment Industry, 1949–1955," (master's thesis, University of Iowa, August 1965).

6.   FBI Chicago field report 100-71906-275, October 23, 1953, in author's possession; Grant Oakes to Ernest DeMaio, July 3, 1953, Ernest DeMaio papers, CHMA.

7.   *Cub*, December 3, 1952; "Information on the Seven Discharged Workers," n.d. [1952]; "Summary of Actions by Company on Firings," n.d. [1952]; "Statement Concerning Issues in the Matter of International Harvester Company, Louisville, Kentucky, Case No. 9-CA-648," n.d. [1953]; all from Irving Meyers papers, CHMA.

8.   IH labor relations letter No. 1271 (arbitrator's decision attached), July 23, 1953, IHA.

9.   DeWitt Gilpin, "Comeback: This Union Got Up When It Was Being Counted Out," *March of Labor*, June 1953.

10.   Gilpin, "Comeback"; "Harvester Suspends 55 in 'Slowdown,'" *Chicago Daily News*, February 24, 1953; "Harvester Company Suspends 293," *Chicago Tribune*, March 18, 1953; "2,200 Employees of Harvester Go on Strike," *Chicago Tribune*, March 20, 1953; "3,500 Chicago Harvester Men to End Strike," *Palladium-Item*, March 21, 1953.

11.   *Courier-Journal*, November 18, 1952, March 31 and April 1, 1953; IH labor relations letter No. 1271 (arbitrator's decision attached), July 23, 1953, IHA.

12.   IH labor relations letter No. 1271 (arbitrator's decision attached), July 23, 1953, IHA; *Courier-Journal*, April 2, April 10, April 12, 1953.

13.   IH labor relations letter No. 1271 (arbitrator's decision attached), July 23, 1953, IHA.

14.   IH labor relations letter No. 1264 (arbitrator's decision attached), July 23, 1953, IHA; *Cub*, May 12, 1953.

15.   "Statement Concerning Issues in the Matter of International Harvester Company, Louisville, Kentucky, Case No. 9-CA-648," n.d. [1953], Irving Meyers papers, CHMA.

16.   "Statement Concerning Issues in the Matter of International Harvester Company, Louisville, Kentucky, Case No. 9-CA-648," n.d. [1953], Irving Meyers papers, CHMA; *Courier-Journal*, February 24, February 27, March 21, 1953.

17.   *Cub*, May 12, 1953, emphasis in original.

18.   John McCaffrey to all employees represented by FE-UE, November 17, 1952, Irving Meyers papers, CHMA; *Cub*, January 30, 1953; FBI Louisville field reports 100-71906-274, 100-71906-281, March 24, 1954, in author's possession.

19.   Milt Burns to all Harvester locals, letter with attached report, September 11, 1953, David Rothstein papers, CHMA; "Harvester layoffs since May 1 . . ."

FE flyer, n.d. [1953], David Rothstein papers, CHMA; FE, *The Harvester Layoff and Your Community*, pamphlet [1954], UE archives.

20.   *Cub*, October 1, 1953; FBI Louisville field report 100-71906-281, March 24, 1954, in author's possession.

21.   Jim Wright, interview with author, October 20, 1987; Jim Wright, Organizer's Report, June 1–15, 1954, UE Archives.

22.   "Through the Color Barrier," *Time*, March 22, 1954; "Negroes Are Moving Up the Job Ladder," *Reader's Digest*, December, 1963.

23.   Jim Mouser, interview with author, October 17, 1987.

24.   Jim Wright, interview with author, January 8, 1986.

25.   *Palladium-Item*, January 21, 1953, April 8, 1953; *UE News*, January 9, April 13, May 4, 1953; *Daily Dispatch* (Moline, Illinois), April 9, April 17, 1953.

26.   H. C. Baker, (IH assistant manager of labor relations), address before the fourteenth training course in industrial relations, June 1953, IHA.

30: We Can't Survive

1.   *Daily Dispatch* (Moline, Illinois), August 29 and 31, 1953.

2.   *Daily Dispatch*, August 5, 1953; Milt Burns to all IH locals, September 11, 1953, David Rothstein papers, CHMA; James Matles to John Watkins, August 3, 1953 (reprinted in the *Cub*, August 28, 1953, copy in author's possession).

3.   *Daily Dispatch*, August 29, 1953.

4.   *Daily Dispatch*, August 5, 1953; *Daily Times* (Davenport, Iowa), May 27, 1954; *United Automobile Worker*, June 1954.

5.   Notes of IH staff meeting, June 23[?], 1954; Ernest DeMaio papers, CHMA. In some cases for the sake of readability I have added words to these notes; for instance where the notes say, under the name Gilpin, "labor unity very compelling" I added the word "was" in my text.

6.   Senator Paul Douglass to Milt Burns, telegram, October 21, 1953, Ernest DeMaio papers, CHMA.

7.   Ron Schatz, *The Electrical Workers: A History of Labor at General Electric and Westinghouse, 1923-1960* (Urbana: University of Illinois Press, 1983), 232.

8.   Al Verri, interview with author, January 29, 1981; Sonya Burns, interview with author, April 17, 1986.

9.   *United Automobile Worker*, January 1955; *UE News*, January 17, 1955.

10. Priscilla Murolo and Ben Chitty, *From the Folks Who Brought You the Weekend: A Short, Illustrated History of Labor in the United States* (New York: New Press, 2001), 124; "AFL-CIO Merger Agreement," *ILR Review* 9, no. 1 (October 1955): 122; Bert Cochran, *Labor and Communism: The Conflict that Shaped American Unions* (Princeton: Princeton University Press, 1977), 294–95.

11. "Statement of the Harvester Conference Board," FE press release, March 21, 1955, Ernest DeMaio papers, CHMA.

12.   *UE News*, March 28, 1955; Sonya Burns, interview with author, April 17, 1986.
13.   Jim Wright, interview with author, January 8, 1986.
14.   *United Automobile Worker*, May 1955.

31: The Descendants of the FE

1.   *Chicago Herald-American*, November 6, 1952, in scrapbook, Ernest DeMaio papers, CHMA.
2.   Jim Wright, interview with author, January 8, 1981.
3.   Al Verri, interview with author, January 29, 1981.
4.   Sonya Burns, interview with author, April 17, 1986.
5.   *Watkins v. United States*, 354 U.S. 178 (1957).
6.   *New York Times*, June 18 and 19, 1957; *Watkins v. United States*, 354 U.S. 178 (1957); *Paducah Sun* (Kentucky), June 28, 1957; *Opelousas Daily World* (Louisiana), June 27, 1957; *Hartford Courant* (Connecticut) June 30, 1957; *Ironwood Daily Globe* (Michigan), June 25, 1957.
7.   *Los Angeles Times*, June 18, 1957; *Jackson Clarion-Ledger* (Mississippi), June 29, 1957; *Waterloo Courier* (Iowa), July 4, 1957; US Senate Subcommittee to Investigate the Administration of the Internal Security Act, *Hearings on the Scope of Soviet Activity in the United States*, July 3, 1957, 85th Congress, 1st Session, (4068-4097), Washington, DC: Government Printing Office. Al Verri was also subpoenaed to testify before the Committee but was allowed to submit an affidavit—in which he essentially offered the same testimony as Burns and Gilpin—rather than appear in person.
8.   *Arizona Daily Star*, September 2, 1957; *Chicago Tribune*, December 27, 1957; *New York Times*, December 27, 1957; Decision of the Board, Public Review Board Cases 6–10, International Union UAW (copy in author's possession). For more on the UAW's Public Review Board see Nelson Lichtenstein, *Walter Reuther: The Most Dangerous Man in Detroit* (New York: Basic Books, 1995), 325–26.
9.   Al Verri, interview with author, January 29, 1981.
10.   *Chicago Tribune*, August 22, 1955; *Quad-City Times* (Davenport, Iowa), September 3, 1955; *Courier-Journal*, September 18, 1955.
11.   *Courier-Journal*, September 20, 1955; James Healy, ed., *Creative Collective Bargaining* (New York: Prentice-Hall, 1965), 110.
12.   These figures meant that during this period IH registered a grievance rate of nearly 30 grievances per 100 employees per year; labor relations experts consider a rate of 10–20 grievances per 100 employees per year excessive. Robert McKersie and William Shropshire, "Avoiding Written Grievances: A Successful Program," *Journal of Business* (April 1962), 135–45; see also Alfred J. Smith, "Grievance Handling at International Harvester Company: The 'New Look'" (master's thesis, Loyola University Chicago, 1973).

13. The UAW struck IH for nine weeks in 1958, for instance, and then for two weeks in 1971. In its 1971 settlement, Harvester workers won full dental coverage, entirely paid for by the company, thus becoming the first UAW members (and among the first workers anywhere) to secure this "precedent-setting" benefit. *Chicago Tribune*, January 24, 1971.

14. *Chicago Tribune*, April 28, 1959; "Wake Up! The Job You Save May Be Your Own," UAW leaflet, 1959 (in author's possession). For Reuther's opposition to the shorter hours push at the 1958 UAW convention, see Jonathan Cutler, *Labor's Time: Shorter Hours, the UAW, and the Struggle for American Unionism* (Philadelphia: Temple University Press, 2004), 137–57.

15. *Chicago Tribune*, May 16, 1969; "Stop the Plant Closings," UAW leaflet, 1969 (in author's possession).

16. In its nearly 140-year history, International Harvester demonstrated a peculiar affinity for company presidents whose names began with "McC" (or in one instance "McK"). There were all the various McCormicks, of course (five of them), but also Addis McKinstry and Sydney McCallister (both served briefly during the 1930s after Harold McCormick proved not up to the job), then John McCaffrey from 1946 through most of the 1950s, and Archie McCardell in the latter part of the 1970s. In all, of the thirteen company presidents, eight of them were either McCormicks or had names that began just like "McCormick" did.

17. Barbara Marsh and Sally Saville, "International Harvester's Story: How a Great Company Lost its Way," two-part series, *Crain's Chicago Business*, November 8 and November 15, 1982; Barbara Marsh, *A Corporate Tragedy: The Agony of International Harvester Company* (New York: Doubleday, 1985), 173–88; Carol Loomis, "The Strike that Rained on Archie McCardell's Parade," *Fortune*, May 19, 1981; *New York Times*, October 20, 1979.

18. Marsh and Saville, "A Great Company," November 15, 1982, 34; Marsh, *Tragedy*, 208, 219.

19. *Courier-Journal*, November 2, 1979; *Daily Dispatch* (Moline, Illinois), November 2, 1979; *Decatur Herald* (Illinois), March 7, 1980; "Big Lie Technique?" UAW flyer, 1980 (in author's possession).

20. *Chicago Tribune*, February 3, 1980; *Courier-Journal*, January 18 and March 24, 1980.

21. *Courier-Journal*, April 21, 1980; Loomis, "The Strike that Rained," 91; Marsh and Saville, "A Great Company," November 15, 36; *Decatur Herald* (Illinois), March 7, 1980.

22. For assessments of how Harvester's managerial blundering led to its decline, see Marsh and Saville, "A Great Company;" Marsh, *Tragedy*; Randy Leffingwell, *Farmall: The Red Tractor that Revolutionized Farming* (Minneapolis: Voyageur Press, 2007); "International Harvester: Can it Survive When the Banks Move In?" *Business Week*, June 22, 1981.

23. Marsh and Saville, "A Great Company," November 8, 25.

32: The Rank and File Loved that Union

1. *Chicago Tribune*, June 12, 1984.
2. Brody is quoted in Melvin Dubofsky, *Hard Work: The Making of Labor History* (Urbana: University of Illinois Press, 2004), 131.
3. Steve Rosswurm, *The CIO's Left-Led Unions* (New Brunswick: Rutgers University Press, 1992), 15; Nelson Lichtenstein, *Walter Reuther: The Most Dangerous Man in Detroit* (Urbana: University of Illinois Press, 1995), 290.
4. Karl Marx, *Capital*, Vol. 1 (New York: International Publishers, 1967), 299; Jonathan Cutler, *Labor's Time: Shorter Hours, the UAW, and the Struggle for American Unionism* (Philadelphia: Temple University Press, 2004), 181. For more about the bankruptcy of the Reuther ideology when it came to challenging deindustrialization, see Seth Widgerson, "The Wages of Communism: U.S. Labor and the Korean War," in ed. Shelton Stromquist, ed., *Labor's Cold War: Local Politics in a Global Context* (Urbana: University of Illinois Press, 2008).
5. Stephen Meyer, *"Stalin over Wisconsin": The Making and Unmaking of Militant Unionism, 1900–1950* (New Brunswick: Rutgers University Press, 1992), 222. The emphasis is mine.
6. The importance of what the CIO's unions did achieve, despite their many shortcomings, is stressed in Jack Metzgar's eloquent history/memoir *Striking Steel: Solidarity Remembered* (Philadelphia: Temple University Press, 2000).
7. Rosswurm, *Left-Led Unions*, 15; DeWitt Gilpin's eulogy for Pete Neputy, UAW flyer, n.d. [1969], in author's possession.

Index

About Haymarket Books

Haymarket Books is a radical, independent, nonprofit book publisher based in Chicago.

Our mission is to publish books that contribute to struggles for social and economic justice. We strive to make our books a vibrant and organic part of social movements and the education and development of a critical, engaged, international left.

We take inspiration and courage from our namesakes, the Haymarket martyrs, who gave their lives fighting for a better world. Their 1886 struggle for the eight-hour day—which gave us May Day, the international workers' holiday—reminds workers around the world that ordinary people can organize and struggle for their own liberation. These struggles continue today across the globe—struggles against oppression, exploitation, poverty, and war.

Since our founding in 2001, Haymarket Books has published more than five hundred titles. Radically independent, we seek to drive a wedge into the risk-averse world of corporate book publishing. Our authors include Noam Chomsky, Arundhati Roy, Rebecca Solnit, Angela Y. Davis, Howard Zinn, Amy Goodman, Wallace Shawn, Mike Davis, Winona LaDuke, Ilan Pappé, Richard Wolff, Dave Zirin, Keeanga-Yamahtta Taylor, Nick Turse, Dahr Jamail, David Barsamian, Elizabeth Laird, Amira Hass, Mark Steel, Avi Lewis, Naomi Klein, and Neil Davidson. We are also the trade publishers of the acclaimed Historical Materialism Book Series and of Dispatch Books.

Also Available from Haymarket Books

Autoworkers Under the Gun: A Shop-Floor View of the End of the American Dream
Gregg Shotwell, introduction by Lee Sustar, foreword by Jerry Tucker

Class Struggle and the Color Line
American Socialism and the Race Question, 1900–1930
Paul Heideman

The Lean Years and *The Turbulent Years*
Irving Bernstein, introduction by Frances Fox Piven

Lucy Parsons: An American Revolutionary
Carolyn Ashbaugh

On New Terrain: How Capital is Reshaping the Battleground of Class War
Kim Moody

Organized Labor and the Black Worker, 1619-1981
Philip S. Foner, foreword by Robin D. G. Kelley

Poor Workers' Unions: Rebuilding Labor from Below (Completely Revised and Updated Edition)
Vanessa Tait, foreword by Bill Fletcher, afterword by Cristina Tzintzún

Radicals in the Barrio: Magonistas, Socialists, Wobblies, and Communists in the Mexican-American Working Class
Justin Akers Chacón

Rank and File: Personal Histories by Working-Class Organizers
Alice and Staughton Lynd

Song of the Stubborn One Thousand: The Watsonville Canning Strike, 1985–87
Peter Shapiro

Women and the American Labor Movement
Philip S. Foner, introduction by Annelise Orleck

About the Author

Toni Gilpin is a labor historian, activist, and writer. She is coauthor of *On Strike for Respect: The Clerical and Technical Workers' Strike at Yale University*, and is the recipient of the 2018 Debra Bernhardt Award for Labor Journalism.